The Chandler Automobile

Also by James H. Lackey

The Jordan Automobile: A History
(McFarland, 2005; softcover 2015)

The Chandler Automobile

A History Including the Cleveland and Chandler-Cleveland Marques

JAMES H. LACKEY

McFarland & Company, Inc., Publishers
Jefferson, North Carolina

The present work is a reprint of the illustrated case bound edition of The Chandler Automobile: A History Including the Cleveland and Chandler-Cleveland Marques, *first published in 2018 by McFarland.*

LIBRARY OF CONGRESS CATALOGUING-IN-PUBLICATION DATA

Names: Lackey, James H., 1936– author.
Title: The Chandler automobile : a history including the Cleveland and Chandler-Cleveland marques / James H. Lackey.
Description: Jefferson, North Carolina : McFarland & Company, Inc., 2023 | Includes bibliographical references and index.
Identifiers: LCCN 2017044134 | ISBN 9781476663937 softcover : acid free paper ♾
Subjects: LCSH: Chandler automobile—History. | Chandler Motor Car Company—History. | Chandler, Fredrick Charles, 1873– | Automobile engineers—United States—Biography.
Classification: LCC TL215.C443 L33 2018 | DDC 338.7/6292220973—dc23
LC record available at https://lccn.loc.gov/2017044134

BRITISH LIBRARY CATALOGUING DATA ARE AVAILABLE

ISBN (print) 978-1-4766-9341-5
ISBN (ebook) 978-1-4766-2554-6

Front cover: *top* 1922 Chandler Royal Dispatch (from brochure "The New Chandler Six Royal Dispatch," July 1922, courtesy Roger Anderson); *bottom, left to right* 1920 Cleveland Touring (owner Gary Smith); 1929 Chandler Model 65 Four Door Sedan (owned by John W. Chandler at time of photo)

Printed in the United States of America

McFarland & Company, Inc., Publishers
Box 611, Jefferson, North Carolina 28640
www.mcfarlandpub.com

This book is dedicated to

Roger Anderson
He shared his vast collection of Chandler-Cleveland literature and memorabilia, which contributed greatly to this effort. His knowledge of Chandler-Cleveland is unsurpassed and this, along with his advice, he freely gave.

John W. Chandler
His encouragement, assistance and generous sharing of his Chandler archives made much of this book possible.

Barbara Murdock
She gave of her time as a professional photographer, printer, and computer expert to this cause. Without her help this would not have been accomplished.

Rachel Lackey
She has endured this for more years than I care to remember. My typist, advisor and love of my life for 56 years.

And to the memory of Fred Hansen, 1946–2008
Founder and president of the Chandler-Cleveland Motor Club until his passing.

Acknowledgments

A Special Thank You

Tom Murdock, Chesapeake, Ohio—almost every Friday for many months, his print shop was dedicated to the Chandler-Cleveland book project.

Chris Summers, Barboursville, West Virginia—his help in accompanying me on many research trips to various libraries in several states has been invaluable.

Chris and Joanie Garratt, M.D., Brookfield, Massachusetts—Chris, a computer expert, and Joanie, a capable physician and just as good with a computer.

Thank You

Jerry and Kim Hill, Reseda, California.

Roger and Shelia Chandler, Greenville, South Carolina—president and editors of the Chandler-Cleveland Motor Club newsletter.

Jan Hansen, Irving, New York—she assisted her late husband, Fred, in keeping the Chandler-Cleveland Motor Club going for many years.

Gary Smith, Wilmington, Ohio.

Tom Baumann, Wausau, Wisconsin.

Donn Wirtz, Somerset, Kentucky.

Chris and Jill Gorman, Monrovia, California.

Ross Fisk, Toronto, Ontario, Canada.

James S. Hall, Sunnyvale, California.

Jeffrey Godshall, Royal Oak, Michigan.

Paul Vossler, Wellsville, New York.

Mac and Wendy Weir, Sacramento, California.

Harold Wintz, Clarion, Iowa.

Greg and Susan Pemberton, Stilwell, Kansas.

Walter E. Gosden, Floral Park, New York.

Kathy M. Collins, San Luis Obispo, California.

Joseph Chabal, Gibsonia, Pennsylvania.

William Cochran, San Luis Obispo, California.

Wendell McCrady, Copley, Ohio.

Scott Copley (C & B Blueprint), Huntington, West Virginia.

Paul Klein (The Jewish Genealogy Society), Cleveland, Ohio.

Adelle Gloger (The Jewish Genealogy Society), Cleveland, Ohio.

Jack and Kay Dickinson, Barboursville, West Virginia.

June Ashworth, Huntington, West Virginia.

Dorene Paul (Sandusky Public Library), Sandusky, Ohio.

Bill Chapin (Automotive Hall of Fame), Dearborn, Michigan.

Chris Ritter (AACA Library & Research Center), Hershey, Pennsylvania.

Matthew Hocker (AACA Library & Research Center), Hershey, Pennsylvania.

Terry Feick, Washington Court House, Ohio.

Janie Bentley, Washington Court House, Ohio.

Ann Sindilar (Western Reserve Historical Society Library), Cleveland, Ohio.

Gene Stray, Centralia, Washington.

Paige Plant, Detroit Public Library, National Automotive History Collection, Detroit, Michigan.

Lynn Duchez Bycko, Special Collections Manager, Michael Schwartz Library, Cleveland State University.

RM Sotheby's.

RM Auctions, Inc., Sadie Chapple and Martin Steele.

Robert Kayle, Lorain, Ohio.

Table of Contents

Preface

Antique automobiles have been a passion of mine for many years. In fact, I have dabbled in old cars, trucks, motorcycles and airplanes for over fifty years. Although I am now unable to pass the required medical exam to keep my pilot's license current, and wisdom has taught me that an 81-year-old man should refrain from riding motorcycles, my love for old cars and trucks has not diminished. I still maintain a few, and I continue to research the history of early marques.

Several friends have long urged me to write a history of Chandler-Cleveland, a company about which I already knew a bit, having maintained a friend's collection of Chandlers for many years. After considerable thought and research, I decided to take on the task. The following is the result of that effort.

The Chandler Motor Car Company, formed in January 1913 by former executives and employees of the Lozier Motor Company, seemed destined for enduring success in the fast-growing automotive industry of the time. Barely six months after the company's formation, a newly built factory in Cleveland was turning out Chandler automobiles—slowly at first, with many other companies furnishing parts and services, but always with the aim of one day fulfilling all facets of production entirely within the confines of the Chandler factory.

The well designed, moderately priced six cylinder car was a rapid success and Chandler was well established as a manufacturer before World War I began. After adapting to wartime production for the military and weathering a postwar recession, the company rolled out innovations in its excellent Pikes Peak engine and clash-free Traffic Transmission, both in 1923, and kept pace with industry trends and advancements.

Meanwhile the Cleveland Automobile Company was started in 1919 as a separate but closely connected enterprise, building a lower-priced line of lightweight six cylinder cars. Just when Cleveland had hit its stride with the popular Model 31, however, the company was merged with Chandler to form Chandler-Cleveland Motors, and the Cleveland nameplate came to an end in the summer of 1926.

Chandler-Cleveland soon found itself in trouble as a larger company saddled with a bloated model range, dealer difficulties and costly aftereffects of severing a relationship with Fisher Body and bringing body production in-house. Even as it was building the best looking, handling and performing automobiles of its existence, it faced daunting economic problems. When a would-be buyer came courting, Chandler-Cleveland agreed to the sale of the company, extinguishing one of the bright stars of the early automobile industry.

I wrote this book to provide an exhaustive history of the Chandler Motor Car Company, the Cleveland Automobile Company and the merged Chandler-Cleveland Motors. It explores the personalities at the center of the companies and details the automobiles in chronological fashion, including the full range of models and body styles and the changes they underwent, as well as the substantial success of Chandlers and Clevelands in motorsports. It also attempts to identify the management mistakes and other factors that combined to foreshorten Chandler's existence, plunging the company from 1920s prominence to relative obscurity today.

All photographs not credited have been taken from Chandler, Cleveland and Chandler-Cleveland advertisements, brochures, catalogs and other promotional materials. I also drew extensively on corporate booklets, brochures, pamphlets, owner's manuals, parts books and other printed materials in the preparation of this book.

Introduction

They came from everywhere, drawn together by the desire to succeed in the fast growing automobile business. There wasn't a college degree among the lot. No Ivy Leaguers, no old school ties, no fraternity brothers, no old money. In fact, most had started work early in life, mostly out of necessity. Family roots reached back to England, Ireland, Russia and a few other countries.

All but two had ties to the bicycle industry and all had labored several years at the automobile trade. All had worked together at the Lozier Motor Company for a few years until a July 1912 restructuring resulted in their departures. Fred C. Chandler and Samuel Regar were now looking for employment; John V. Whitbeck, a bright young engineer, decided he ought to leave also and strike out on his own.

Plans for forming an automobile company had been incubating with several Lozier employees, and Chandler and Regar were now in position to put their plans into action. The Chandler Motor Car Company was incorporated in January 1913, with six former employees from Lozier joining the new company. Fred C. Chandler was the leader but the first name chosen was the Emise Motor Car Company. However, Charles A. Emise was apparently under contract to Lozier and would not be released to use his name. Thus, the Chandler Motor Car Company was born. Success came quickly and by the end of 1913, 550 cars had been assembled and sold and orders for more were piling up.

Chandler built a "Light Weight" six, at least "light" by the standards of the day. The price was reasonable for a car built to a high standard, and the company began a steady growth.

World War I did not materially hurt Chandler and may have actually helped, as the company built military tractors for the U.S. Army. New buildings went up and equipment for production was acquired; when the Armistice was signed these became available for automobile production.

After the war, a group of Chandler executives founded the Cleveland Automobile Company to manufacture a smaller, less expensive automobile which would be sold by most Chandler dealers. An entirely separate company, it was nonetheless controlled by Chandler stockholders. Despite its launch at a terrible time, just as a postwar recession hit the automobile industry hard, both Cleveland and Chandler, being controlled by a group of financially conservative men, survived and later flourished.

Names like Marvelous Motor, Royal Dispatch, Traffic Transmission, Pikes Peak Motor, Comrade Roadster, One Shot Lubrication, Westinghouse Brakes and a few others endeared the Chandler name to its followers.

Chandler's styling was fairly nondescript at first, on a par with many other manufacturers. An element of real style came with the introduction of the Dispatch Touring, later renamed the Royal Dispatch. With greater emphasis on design came such body style names as Comrade Roadster, Metropolitan Sedan, Chummy Sedan and Sport Touring.

By 1925 Chandler was riding high and Cleveland was finally thriving in its own right. But the strain of managing two companies was taking its toll on the executives who had positions on both firms, and it was decided to merge the Cleveland Automobile Company into the Chandler Motor Car Company, thus creating the Chandler-Cleveland Motors Corporation.

The merger made Chandler a much larger corporation. Briefly marketing both the Chandler and Cleveland nameplates, until the 1927 models appeared, Chandler-Cleveland now had three different types of cars. A confusing shuffle of model names followed the enfolding of them all under the Chandler name. Then, within months, the line grew further with the debut of Chandler's first eight cylinder engine. The proliferation of chassis, engines and body styles outpaced demand. Too much expense coupled with too few buyers quickly put Chandler into financial trouble.

Chandler's 1929 models—the best looking, best riding and best performing automobiles they had ever built—would be their last. The automobile business was being saturated at the time and the big corporations were in a much more favorable position than the smaller independents. When the Hupp Motor Car Company, needing room for expansion and a ready-made dealer network, wanted to talk, Chandler was ready to listen. Some Chandler executives wanted no part of the deal, but a majority of the stockholders, seeing a way to get out on very favorable terms, agreed to the deal and it was done. On April 15, 1929, Chandler was gone. In just a few months Hupp would suffer much the same conditions which caused Chandler's demise.

• One •

1912–1913
Roots and Beginning

On July 29, 1912, a tumultuous meeting of the directors of the Lozier Motor Company of Detroit, Michigan, was held in that city. When it was over Henry Abram "Harry" Lozier, Jr., was out as president and Harry M. Jewett was in. There were other casualties as well. Stockholders were upset that Lozier was not turning a profit and were determined to right the ship even if veteran Lozier personnel had to be sacrificed.

Jewett was also president of the Paige-Detroit Motor Car Company and one of the group of Detroit investors who had persuaded Lozier to locate in that city. He was also a very successful coal operator and would continue in his position at Paige.

When the smoke cleared, Fred C. Chandler, vice president and general manager of Lozier, had resigned or been fired. His friend Samuel Regar had been replaced as treasurer, and so he too tendered his resignation. They were replaced on the board of directors by two New Yorkers, E.P. Earle and H.E. Kahler.

Raymond B. Fosdick, a former commissioner of accounts for New York City, was made a vice president and treasurer, replacing Chandler and Regar. Chandler and Regar had been planning to leave, they just got hurried along. J.V. Whitbeck, Lozier's assistant chief engineer, had been planning to leave with his co-workers and also tendered his resignation. Warren S.M. Mead, who had been with Lozier since 1903, opted out also but had to stay until being released from his contract.[1]

Others of the old guard were highly disgruntled but would remain in their positions and await an opportunity to make their exit. John G. Perrin, vice president in charge of engineering and manufacturing, would have joined the departing group but he had three years remaining on his contract and Harry Jewett insisted that he stay and help rebuild Lozier.

Harry A. Lozier, Jr., remained a member of the board of directors, but his influence in the affairs of the company was gone. He would soon become disgusted and sever all relations with the company which had so proudly carried his name. He would go on to establish the Motor Patents Company in 1913 and take office space in the Ford Building, Detroit. By midyear 1915 he announced that he would build the H.A.L. Twelve automobile with his new H.A. Lozier Company, which he would incorporate in December, as the manufacturer.

The Lozier Motor Company would struggle along even though they did build a Light Six (Model 77 "Montclair") in 1913. They would succumb to bankruptcy on February 4, 1915. Attempts at a revival of the company were not very successful and the final one, Lozier Motor Car Company, folded in 1918. Ironically, the H.A.L., minus Harry Lozier who had deserted in 1916 after a very brief tenure, folded in 1918 also.

Harry Lozier would again try to build cars but his Lozier Brothers Company of Philadelphia, Pennsylvania, also folded. He was commissioned a major in the U.S. Army in 1918 and became a Chandler distributor in Albany, New York, in 1919. He passed away in December 1925 at Clearwater, Florida, as a result of pneumonia.[2]

Harry Lozier had assumed control of the Lozier Motor Company upon the death of his father on May 3, 1903. The elder Lozier had three other children but other than Henry Jr., only Edwin took any interest in the company. The Loziers had made their fortune building bicycles and sewing machines. The Cleveland Bicycle and New Home Sewing Machines were well known, high quality products in their day. The H.A. Lozier & Company bicycle business had started at Toledo, Ohio, in 1880 and the sewing machine business was located in Westfield, Massachusetts. Lozier factories were located in Toronto, Ontario, Canada; Thompsonville, Connecticut; Westfield, Massachusetts; and Toledo, Ohio, with company headquarters in Cleveland. Lozier also had facilities at Hamburg, Germany; London, England and Paris, France. The overseas facilities were managed by Fred C. Chandler and John R. Hall was the service and repair manager. In addition to the foreign branches, Lozier also had facilities in New York City, Boston, Philadelphia, San Francisco, Buffalo, Detroit, Baltimore, and in addition to the Toronto factory, they maintained a branch for distribution there as well.

By 1897, seeing the bicycle business beginning to be influenced by conglomerates and the proliferation of cheaply made products, Henry Sr. began looking for a way to get out. He found it in the form of the American Bicycle Company, which in 1899, purchased the four Lozier bicycle factories for the sum of four million dollars cash. The American Bicycle Company was created by Albert G. Spalding, who had a large mail order company and was heavily into bicycles. Foreign and domestic competition caused Spalding and Col. Albert Pope, who also controlled a large percentage of the bicycle trade, to merge and stifle their competition. The cost to the trust, as it was then called, was severe with nine million dollars in debt, but they virtually controlled the bicycle industry thereafter. When the American Bicycle Company began to fail, Colonel Pope managed to keep control of the Westfield, Massachusetts, factory and consolidated all his manufacturing there. Pope was the builder of the popular Columbia bicycle.

Lozier retained rights to lease a portion of the Toledo factory in order to continue experimenting with gasoline engines and boats. These experiments were successful and launched the famous bicycle builders into the boat business.

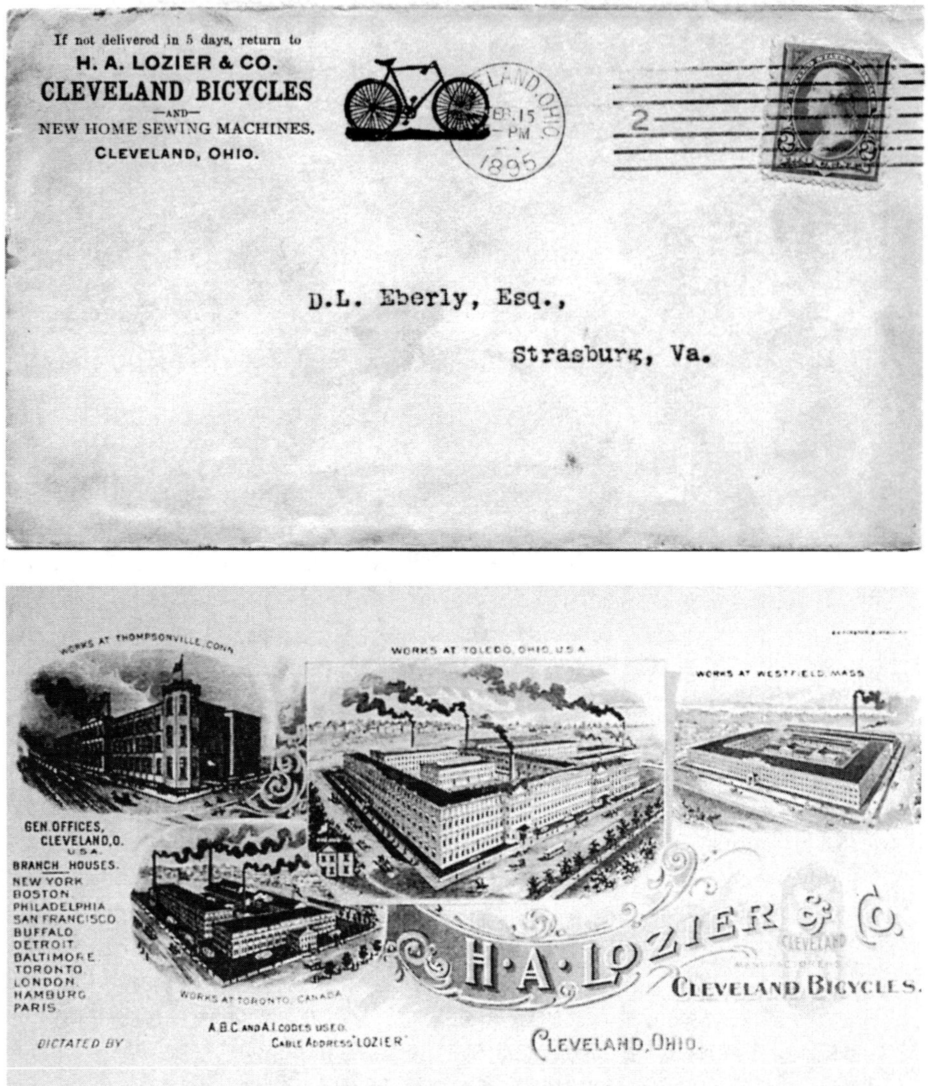

H.A. Lozier & Company envelope and letterhead (author's collection).

Henry Sr. retained in his employ his chief talents George R. Burwell and John G. Perrin as well as Charles A. Emise, who had proven his abilities over the years. Fred C. Chandler and John R. Hall, veteran Lozier employees, were working for Lozier in Hamburg when the bicycle works were sold to the American Bicycle Company and would stay on with the new owners. Chandler would stay until late 1905 when he, with his wife and three children, sailed for the U.S. on November 18 aboard the S.S. *Amerika*, arriving in New York on November 27. He would rejoin his friends and Lozier at their facility in New York City shorty after his return to the United States. Hall would stay in Hamburg until late 1906 when he would return to the U.S., accompanied by his wife and daughter, and also would rejoin his former employer.

Lozier had facilities in Plattsburg, New York; Stamford, Connecticut; and New York City at this time. The Stamford location had started as a machine shop owned by Charles P. Ball, who was the manager of the Lozier bicycle factory at Thompsonville, Connecticut, when it was sold to the American Bicycle Company. The Ball machine shop did work exclusively for Lozier. Not being satisfied with Ball's work, Lozier purchased the machine shop on July 6, 1906, and while going over the books found that George R. Burwell, their longtime superintendent, had been a silent partner in the business until October 1904. This resulted in a nasty lawsuit which Lozier won, contending that any profit made by Burwell belonged to Lozier. Ball appealed the decision to the New York Supreme Court, which in 1907 affirmed the lower court's decision. Burwell left Lozier on July 10, 1906, presumably by request. Burwell had insisted that the elder Lozier had known and approved of the arrangement and that his only interest in the machine shop had been to help Ball get started in business.

Lozier had begun experimentation with internal combustion

engines at Toledo and eventually turned to marine engines and motor launches. They had built a three-wheeled, gasoline engine propelled tricycle while in Toledo, but this went with the bicycle business when it was sold to the American Bicycle Company.

Samuel Regar would leave Lozier and go with the American Bicycle Company at their Westfield, Massachusetts, factory but would stay only until November 1901 when he returned to Lozier at Plattsburg.

The Lozier Motor Company was founded in 1900 and Plattsburg, New York, was chosen for a manufacturing site. While the boat business was steadily increasing, Lozier was also experimenting with automobiles. By 1905 the Lozier car was a reality and was shown in New York City in January of that year.

Lozier would build some of the finest automobiles ever made—big, stout, fast and expensive. They would go on to make a reputation in racing circles and with those who appreciated fine motor cars. In 1910 the Lozier Motor Company, with Harry Lozier at the helm, needed capital for expansion and was persuaded by a group of investors to relocate to Detroit. Many of Lozier's executives opposed the move but to no avail. Detroit was the logical place, since it was the hub of the automobile industry at this time. Harry Lozier was reportedly not eager to move the company but reluctantly agreed to do so because he had few options. Land was purchased and immediately construction began on a new factory, which Lozier moved into in 1911.[3]

By 1912 the major stockholders at Lozier were agitating to build a smaller, less expensive car, which they believed would generate profits that were then lacking. Disagreements over this strategy culminated in the shakeup and departures at the July 29 board meeting.

As noted previously, Chandler, Regar, and Whitbeck had been dissatisfied at Lozier for some time and had made plans for their own exit long before their actual departure. They immediately began to implement their plan for a new automobile company. Whitbeck, who had joined Lozier in 1908 as a designer, leased office space at 982 Woodward Avenue, Detroit, in September and hung out his shingle as a consulting engineer. He was soon employed by Chandler and Regar to design the new automobile.[4]

By early January 1913 those who had earlier departed Lozier were joined by several more coworkers from the old firm and promptly announced the formation of a new company to manufacture moderately priced, lightweight, six cylinder automobiles. This group consisted of Charles A. Emise, Warren S.M. Mead and J.R. Hall. Charles A. Carey would join the new company in February and Joseph I. Krall would leave Lozier and join Chandler a short time later.

Right: **Chandler brochure with temporary address (courtesy Roger Anderson).**

Charles A. Emise, formerly Lozier's sales and advertising manager, had been heavily involved in the very successful racing program which had made Lozier much of its reputation. Having worked with Lozier in some capacity since the bicycle days, he had been promoted from advertising manager to sales manager just a few months before the shakeup. He was expected to stay on, but conditions at Lozier were deteriorating rapidly and he decided to join his friends in the new venture.

Warren S.M. Mead had formerly held the position of Lozier Foreign and Eastern Sales Department manager. He had joined Lozier as a salesman while they were in the marine engine business, after the bicycle works were sold.

John Richard Hall, Lozier's service, supply and repair manager, had started with the Lozier family business 21 years earlier. When he resigned, the officers and employees threw a big party for him and Harry Lozier, Jr., presented him with a gold watch in recognition of his many years of service. Apparently he had been, at least technically, in the employ of Lozier while working with the American Bicycle Company in Germany. His passport application (1904) stated that he would stay in Germany until he was recalled by the Lozier Motor Company.

Charles A. Carey had formerly been Lozier's purchasing agent and had previously been employed by Ford as an assistant purchasing agent. Joseph I. Krall had been employed at Lozier as company auditor and assistant treasurer.[5]

Several trade publications had announced earlier that the new company would be the Emise Motor Car Company, but apparently Charles A. Emise was under contract to Lozier and would not be released to use that name. Regardless of reasons, the new venture was known as the Chandler Motor Car Company. This probably was the intention all along as Fred Chandler seemed to be the prime mover.[6]

The Chandler Motor Car Company was capitalized under the laws of Ohio on January 29, 1913. Capitalization was $425,000 with $200,000 being preferred and $225,000 common which would be given as a bonus to the holders of the preferred.[7]

The new company established temporary headquarters at 982 Woodward Avenue, Detroit, Whitbeck's office, and immediately began looking for a factory site. They would later establish temporary headquarters in the Swetland Building, Cleveland, Ohio.[8]

Founders of the Chandler Motor Car Company

Fredrick Charles Chandler

Fredrick Charles Chandler was born in Cleveland, Ohio, on July 12, 1873, the son of Fredrick C. and Ellen T. Butler Chandler. His parents were naturalized citizens with his father being born in England and his mother in Ireland.

Fredrick C. Chandler.

He supposedly left school at age sixteen after completing his second year of high school. He went to work for H.A. Lozier & Company, makers of the Cleveland Bicycle and New Home Sewing Machine at that time. Starting as an office boy, he worked himself steadily upward in the company.

Bicycling was a craze in the early 1890s, and Fred Chandler was one of the best amateur bicycle racers around. On August 26, 1892, he bested world champion Arthur A. Zimmerman of Freehold, New Jersey, in a one-mile race sponsored by the Cleveland Wheel Club and held at Athletic Park, which was owned by the Cleveland Bicycle Club. Chandler, being an amateur, was given a handicap which Zimmerman could not overcome. Zimmerman did win all other events he entered in the two-day event, except for the one in which he scratched. Since his employer's business was bicycles, this placed Chandler in good standing with his boss, Henry Abram Lozier.[9]

Chandler steadily advanced in the company and on September 30, 1896, at the age of 23, was sent to Hamburg in charge of Lozier's European business. After the bicycle business was purchased by the American Bicycle Company in 1899, he was employed by that firm. This is confirmed by his passport application of November 4, 1902, which stated that he probably would return to the United States sometime the next year and would reside wherever the American Bicycle Company saw fit.

He married Anna Nightingale on September 26, 1899. Three children were born while they resided in Hamburg. Fredrick Charles III was born on August 17, 1900, Sarah Evelyn on October 29, 1902, and William Howard on October 29, 1904. The couple stayed in Hamburg until 1905 when Fred was reunited with his friends in the employ of the Lozier Motor Company at their facility in New York City.

The boat and marine engine business at Plattsburg, New York, was fading and Lozier was now building the first of what would be one of the finest automobiles ever conceived.

An excellent employee, Chandler steadily advanced to the position of vice president and general manager. He moved with Lozier when they went to Detroit and resigned from that position on July 29, 1912, to engage in the manufacture of his own automobile.[10]

Samuel Regar

Samuel Regar.

Samuel Regar was born at Marblehead, Ohio, on August 30, 1875, the son of Mordeci David and Hannah Newman Regar. His parents were Austrian and had migrated to the United States in 1870. He was one of six children—four boys and two girls.

In 1890, at the age of fifteen, he was employed by the H.A. Lozier & Company as an office boy at the Cleveland headquarters. He steadily worked his way upward. When Lozier sold to the American Bicycle Company in 1899, he was employed by that firm until November 1901 when he was once again employed by Lozier at the Plattsburg, New York, factory, also spending time at the New York City facility. While in New York he was married to Amelia Alix at Queens on November 30, 1909. The marriage did not last and the couple separated a few years later.

He faithfully fulfilled every task undertaken at Lozier and worked his way up to board member and treasurer. When Lozier left Plattsburg in 1911, he went along and stayed with the company until August 1912 when he resigned his position and joined with Fred Chandler in forming the Chandler Motor Car Company. In addition to being treasurer at Chandler, he was also president of the Regar Realty Company which was totally owned by the Chandler Motor Car Company. He was also a board member of the Regar Brass Manufacturing Company which was owned by his family. His sister Esther was married to Dr. Michael Krall, a brother of Joseph I. Krall, another of the former Lozier people who formed the Chandler Company.[11]

John Verne Whitbeck

John V. Whitbeck.

John Verne Whitbeck was born on May 28, 1882, at Sodus, New York, the son of Elson Blackman and Emer DeEtta Pulver Whitback. He was educated in the public schools of Wayne County but decided he wanted more than the formal education he was getting and enrolled in an International Correspondence School course of mechanical drawing. Young John applied himself diligently while working at his father's meat market in Wolcott, New York, and upon graduating he secured a job with the H.H. Franklin Company of Syracuse, New York, a die casting manufacturer and parent company of the Franklin Automobile Company.

He started as a tracer in September 1904 and gradually learned his trade, remaining with Franklin until October 1906. In November 1906 he was employed by the Olds Motor Works at Lansing, Michigan, but only remained there until March 1907 when he moved to Buffalo, New York, as a designer for the E.R. Thomas Company. He left Thomas in October and went to work as a designer and checker for the United Spring Company of Buffalo. In 1908 he contacted the Lozier Motor Company of Plattsburg, New York, and secured a position as a designer and checker. He stayed with Lozier when they moved to Detroit in 1911. He was promoted to experimental engineer and remained in that position until 1912 when he resigned, along with his friends Fred Chandler and Samuel Regar, with the intention of going into business for himself. He would soon take on the task of designing the Chandler automobile. He was an experienced engineer by the time he left Lozier and proved himself capable of the job.

When Fred Chandler, Samuel Regar and others formed the Chandler Motor Car Company in early 1913, Whitbeck was named the chief engineer. He was married to Helen Melissa Reamer of Wolcott, New York, and they were the parents of one son, Paul Reamer Whitbeck, born February 26, 1918.[12]

Charles A. Emise

Charles A. Emise was born at Durant, Iowa, on April 17, 1871. His parents were of German descent. As a young man he became an excellent bicycle rider and racer which led him to Salt Lake City, Utah, in 1887, where he became manager of the Cleveland Bicycle dealership. While there, he became acquainted with William D. "Big Bill" Rishel, who was a bicycle enthusiast and became involved in starting clubs and racing. Rishel's exploits caught the attention of William Randolph Hearst, the newspaper magnate who owned the *New York Journal* and the *San Francisco Examiner*. Hearst formulated a plan to send a message from the *Examiner* in San Francisco to his office in New York by bicycle courier during 1896. Hearst chose

Charles A. Emise (*The Horseless Age*, September 18, 1912)

Rishel to scout the route from Truckee, California, to Kearney, Nebraska.

Rishel chose Charles A. Emise, who himself was an excellent rider and racer, to be his riding companion for the segment which began at Terrace and ended at Grantsville, Utah, sixty miles across the salt flats. For 22 hours they endured the hardships of scorching heat, sand dunes and mud so bad that they were compelled at times to carry their bicycles. Both survived the adventure—the first crossing of the salt flats by any vehicle other than a horse drawn wagon.

Rishel went on to promote bicycle racing and became sports editor of the *Salt Lake Herald* among many other activities while Emise's salesmanship and riding ability caught the eye of Henry A. Lozier, who wanted Emise at Toledo as assistant to his son Edwin R. Lozier, then in charge of the Toledo factory.

Emise married Gertrude Neisen, a native of Toledo, while working in that city and they were blessed with two daughters. Mary Dolores was born July 25, 1901, at Plattsburg, New York, and Gertrude C. was born on July 26, 1903, at Brooklyn, New York.

Emise stayed with Lozier in a selling capacity as they went from bicycles to marine engines and launches and finally to automobiles. He was in charge of Lozier's very successful racing program from beginning to end. An excellent salesman, he was promoted to advertising manager when the company moved to Detroit then to sales manager, in December 1912. He had been expected to stay with Lozier, having been promoted after Fred Chandler, Samuel Regar and J.V. Whitbeck departed. But he could see that Lozier had no future and the opportunity to be in at the beginning of a new automobile company was too alluring to pass up.[13] In January 1913 he joined his former coworkers to form the Chandler Motor Car Company.

John Richard Hall

John Richard Hall.

John Richard Hall was born in Dublin, Ireland, on November 21, 1866, the son of John Richard and Elizabeth Robinson Hall. He migrated to the United States, sailing from Liverpool, England, on April 12, 1882, and resided in Cleveland where he found work at H.A Lozier & Company. He became a U.S. citizen on September 22, 1890, having been granted his citizenship by the Common Pleas Court of Cuyahoga County, Ohio, on that date.

Hall worked for Lozier at Cleveland and Toledo until January 8, 1896, when he was sent to Hamburg, Germany, to be in charge of service and repair in Lozier's facility. He was skilled in production, manufacturing & repair. He remained in Lozier's employ until sometime in 1899 when Lozier sold to the American Bicycle Company. About this time, he married Marie Louise Laas and a daughter, Gretchen, was born in Hamburg on August 25, 1902.

He stayed on with American until late 1906 when he, his wife and daughter returned to the U.S. and he rejoined his friends at Lozier Motor Company at their facility in New York City. A son, John Richard Hall, Jr., was born on November 6, 1908, in New York City.

John Hall remained with Lozier in New York City in charge of their service department until July 1911 when he was transferred to San Francisco, California, where he assumed the same duties. He rejoined his friends in November 1911 after Lozier moved to Detroit, where he remained until he resigned to join the Chandler Motor Car Company in early 1913. He started at Chandler as superintendent of production and was eventually promoted to vice president of production.[14]

Warren Studley Morton Mead

Warren Studley Morton Mead was born December 8, 1868, at Brooklyn, Kings County, New York, the son of Benjamin F. and Sarah E. Studley Mead. He acquired his many names from his mother's side of the family. His grandmother was Elizabeth Morton (Studley) and his grandfather was James Warren Studley.

Warren Studley Morton Mead (U.S. Archives, Washington, D.C.).

He married Sara Florence Callan on July 2, 1895. He attended New York City schools and went to work for A.G. Spalding & Brother at an early age. The Spaldings were into mail order sporting goods and were in competition with Colonel Albert Pope for control of the bicycle business in the United States. Spalding formed the American Bicycle Company after acquiring 107 small bicycle companies. Colonel Pope decided to join Spalding in the venture and together they virtually dominated the bicycle business.

Warren Mead was promoted to assistant eastern sales manager for American and held that position until he joined Lozier at New York City in 1903. He eventually worked his way up to manager of the foreign and eastern sales department. He remained in New York until he joined Chandler in 1913 and stayed there as head of Chandler's eastern sales department and foreign sales. There is no record of the Meads' having children.[15]

Charles A. Carey

Charles A. Carey was born at Grand Rapids, Michigan, in September 1882, the son of Charles A. and Bridget Carey. He was one of eight children—three boys and five girls—and attended Kent County schools. Leaving Grand Rapids in 1908, he found employment at the Ford Motor Company in Detroit as an assistant purchasing agent. He left Ford for a job with Lozier when they moved to Detroit.

Carey married Clara C. Conlish and they were the parents of four children. Margaret was born in 1908, Josephine in 1909, Robert in 1912 and Phyllis Anne in 1917.

Carey left Lozier to help build the Chandler in February 1913. However, his tenure with Chandler only lasted until about 1917 when he left to build refrigerators at Jackson, Michigan.[16]

Joseph Irving Krall

Joseph Irving Krall was born in Minsk, Russia, on March 17, 1883, the son of Hyman and Anna Krall. The family immigrated to the United States in 1886. He was one of eight children—five boys and three girls. Four of the children were born in Russia while the other four were born at New Haven, Connecticut, where the family settled.

Joseph Irving Krall (courtesy the late Ellis Krall).

Young Krall was studious and ambitious and learned bookkeeping by self-study. He landed a job with Lozier in New York City and stayed with them when they moved to Detroit. He remained there until the Chandler Motor Car Company was formed, he being the last of the gang to leave Lozier.

He married Rae Elisberg and they were the parents of Ellis and Edith. Ellis was born at Detroit on January 27, 1911, and Edith at Cleveland in 1916.[17]

Building the New Company

On February 17, 1913, the big announcement came and Cleveland, Ohio, was chosen to be the permanent home of the Chandler Motor Car Company. This was not much of a surprise as Cleveland had been Fred Chandler's boyhood home and Samuel Regar had been raised just a few miles away at Marblehead, Ohio.[18]

The city was highly industrialized and had all the qualities necessary for any manufacturing need, especially good roads, water and rail transportation. Manpower was abundant and educational, entertainment, and artistic opportunities were numerous. Hoping to displace Detroit as the capital of automobile manufacturing, Cleveland was working hard to entice new manufacturers to locate there. More than eighty automobile manufacturers would locate in Cleveland over a period of several years.

On March 24 a six acre site was chosen at St. Clair and 131st Street. The Schaufler Realty Company handled the transaction. The Belt & Terminal Realty Company owned the property. Ernest McGeorge designed the building and the W. S. Ferguson Company, Consulting Engineers, would handle the letting of bids for the general construction. They had previously awarded contracts for the substructure and steel erection. The factory would be located on a Belt Line track which would expedite receiving materials for manufacturing and shipping the finished product as well.[19]

A small section of the site was owned by the Chandler Company and the rest by the Regar Realty Company (capital $60,000) whose stock was solely owned by the Chandler Motor Car Company. Then, as now, tax considerations came into play. The company also owned 315 out of 320 shares of the Taft-Avenue Construction Company, which owned 2.11 acres of land that would later be leased to the H.J. Walker Company. Walker, although based in Detroit, would do much, if not all, of Chandler's parts manufacturing and machining during the early years and Chandler may have had an interest in the company. They employed 500 highly skilled machinists and workmen and did nothing but Chandler work.[20]

The Chandler Company knew it needed room to grow and made provisions for that early on. They purchased land in an area where they could expand when the need arose. Those early plans would come to fruition much sooner than the most optimistic of the Chandler gang could have dreamed.

The construction of the factory, a 400 × 120 foot building, by the Bolton and Pratt Company began in April and was scheduled to be completed by June. The prototype car had been

***Top:* Chandler factory under construction (*The Automobile,* May 8, 1913). *Bottom:* Chandler's first factory building.**

under construction in a shop on East 65th Street in Cleveland for several months. Although the prototype was not finished in time for the New York International Auto Show, blueprints and drawings of the new car were on display in a hotel room and interested parties attending the show were invited to view the concept car drawings. The workmen beat the deadline for the Chicago show and the car was hauled to the Windy City for display. Being a new company, with its vehicle in the prototype stage, Chandler was not allowed to display in the show itself. But, not to be outdone, they rented a private garage nearby and held their own exhibition.[21]

The Chandler was well received, which was very encouraging to the new manufacturer. They left Chicago determined to begin production as soon as possible. The car was then shipped to New York, where Charles A. Emise and Warren S.M. Mead displayed the car at selected locations around the city.

Chandler announced that contracts amounting to $3,465,000 had been received from prospective dealers and orders were arriving faster than they could be processed. Chandler developed a unique plan to help dealers purchase their cars. Those dealers who had purchased Chandler stock could pledge that stock, dollar for dollar, toward the purchase of Chandler automobiles. If a dealer had not purchased stock, he could do so and would immediately be available for the plan. Radical, but it must have worked as they had no trouble obtaining dealers.[22]

The Cleveland Plain Dealer reported that the completed car had been shown in New York during the show but that was in error. After it was shown by Emise and Mead it was driven back to Cleveland by way of Pittsburgh, over seven Allegheny mountain ranges, in the middle of winter to test its durability. It passed the test admirably, completing the 600 mile trip in 23 hours and 10 minutes.

Factory construction, after an April 6 groundbreaking, was not completed by June as hoped but was virtually finished by July 30. Occupying the new facility the first week of August, Chandler found itself about two months off schedule but was finally beginning to build automobiles in a permanent factory.[23] Meanwhile the building of engines and machining of as many other parts as possible had been going on at the temporary facility, where the prototype had been assembled, for some time. As soon as bodies became available, those engines and parts were moved to the new factory; although it was not quite complete and not officially open, a few cars were assembled there.

***Opposite:* Cleveland city map showing Chandler factory location (courtesy Roger Anderson).**

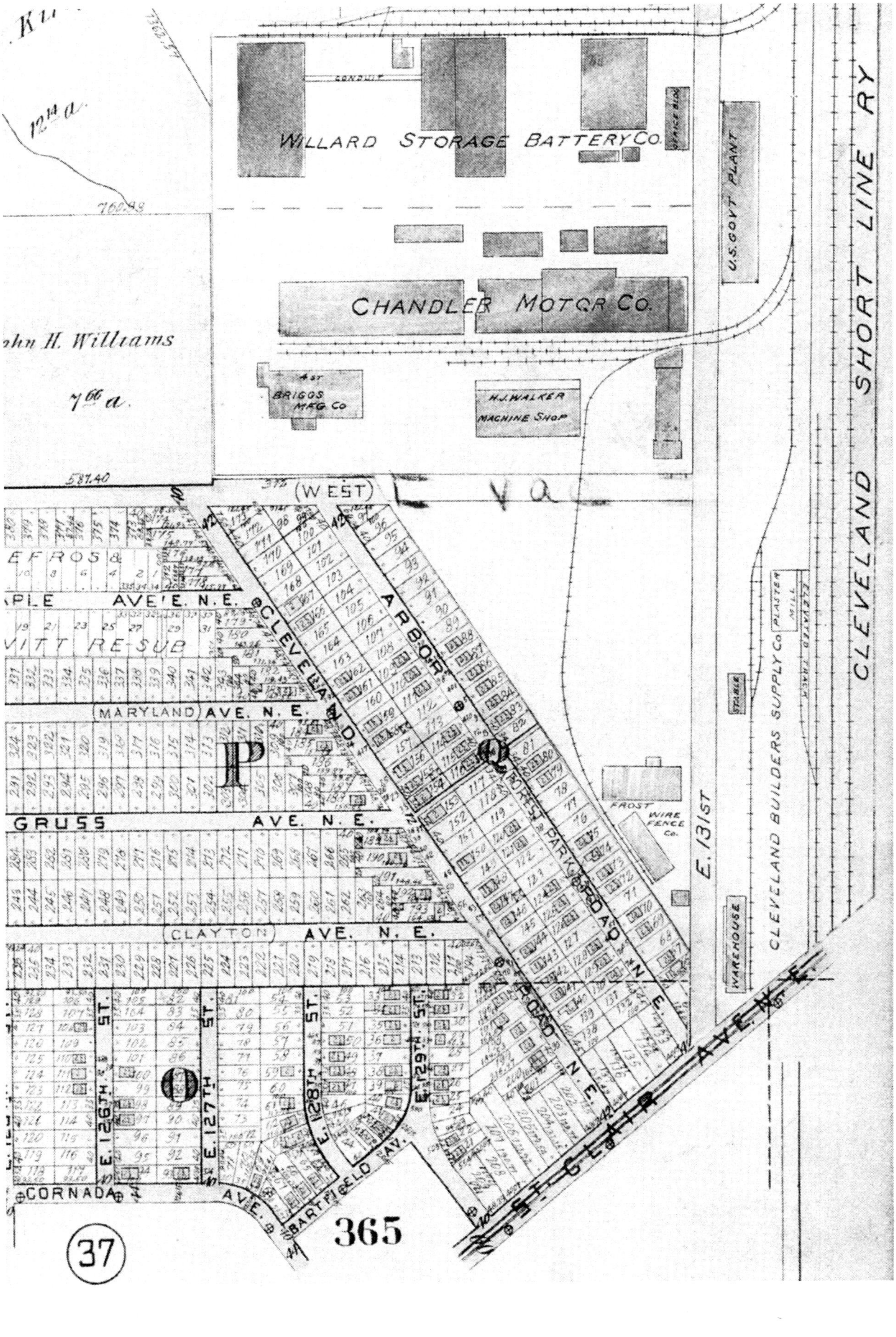
WILLARD STORAGE BATTERY CO.
U.S. GOV'T PLANT
CHANDLER MOTOR CO.
BRIGGS MFG. Co
H.J. WALKER MACHINE SHOP
CLEVELAND SHORT LINE RY
CLEVELAND BUILDERS SUPPLY Co.
PLASTER MILL
STABLE
WAREHOUSE
FROST WIRE FENCE Co.
E. 131ST
John H. Williams
(WEST)
CLEVELAND
ARBOR
FOREST PARK ROAD N.E.
MARYLAND AVE. N. E.
GRUSS AVE. N. E.
CLAYTON AVE. N. E.
E. 126TH ST.
E. 127TH ST.
E. 128TH ST.
E. 129TH ST.
CORNADA AVE.
BARTFIELD AV.
ST. CLAIR AVE. N. E.
365
37

***Top:* Chandler Light Six prototype. *Bottom:* Chandler Model 14.**

Car number one had been used for months by the time the others were ready to be shipped and had accumulated 20,000 miles on the odometer. It was used to chase stock for the purchasing department and driven between Ohio, Michigan and Pennsylvania at an average rate of 150 to 200 miles per day. In fact, the company did not have a car to show prospective dealers unless they just happened to catch number one between runs.

When word was received that Chandler would begin the assembly of cars before the factory was officially opened, Strong Motors, the Rochester, New York distributor, dispatched Barney Cane, a company employee, to Cleveland. His purpose was to observe Chandlers being built and to gain knowledge about the new car.

With a few cars completed by July 30, Chandler staged a publicity event to coincide with the opening of the factory. Drivers and executives from the distributors who would get the first cars were ready to drive them away. Promptly at 6 p.m. the first car to leave headed for Boston, driven by R.B. Nettleton of the New England Agency. Nettleton had been manager of the Boston branch of Lozier but had resigned to become a Chandler distributor. Three hours later the second car left the factory headed for Rochester with H.G. Strong at the wheel and Barney Cane as a backup driver. A short time later, car number four headed for New York City and the Brady-Murray Agency. All three cars were supposedly going to be driven straight through to their destinations without stopping except for fuel and necessities.

Before leaving the factory H.G. Strong made a bet with Charles A. Emise that they would catch the car headed for Boston before they reached Rochester. About 3 o'clock the next morning, with Barney Cane driving in a dense fog, they missed a curve just East of Westfield, New York, and destroyed a perfectly good utility pole. The car suffered a broken headlight, crumpled fender and a sheared radiator connection but there was no injury to either Barney Cane or H.G. Strong. Temporary repairs were made and they made it to Rochester without further delay. Mr. Strong lost his bet with Charles A. Emise but the car was repaired and remained in service with Strong Motors, rolling up well over 100,000 miles of service. The cars headed for Boston and New York completed their journey without incident.[24]

On August 11, a meeting of the directors of the new company was called for the purpose of electing new members of the board to fill the vacancies remaining.

W.R. Hopkins, president of the Belt & Terminal Realty Company, J.W. Deutsch of Cleveland, Albert Jarecki, president of the Jarecki Manufacturing Company, and W.P. Herbert of Philadelphia joined Fred Chandler, Charles A. Emise, Warren S.M. Mead and Samuel Regar on the board.

W.P. Herbert and his brother W.G. Herbert would be the distributors of Chandler automobiles in Philadelphia. By 1924 W.P. Herbert had established a dealership in Los Angeles, California.

The officers of the company were Fred C. Chandler, president; Charles A. Emise, vice president; Warren S.M. Mead, second vice president; Samuel Regar, treasurer; and Isidor Grossman, secretary. Grossman was an attorney and partner in one of Cleveland's leading law firms, having graduated from the

Harvard School of Law in 1904. He had already joined with a group of Cleveland businessmen to establish a distributorship for Chandler cars in that city. Early in January 1915, he would join another group of businessmen and incorporate the Chandler Oil and Gas Company. It is unclear what connections, if any, this had to the car company.[25]

The first Chandler ad for the public ran in the *Saturday Evening Post* on July 26, 1913. It featured only the Five Passenger Touring car built as the Chandler Light Weight Six and "Built by Men Who Know." The slogan could not have been more aptly stated because if any automobile manufacturer ever started with a lineup of men who knew the industry it was Chandler.

Actually, the first ads shown were of the prototype car, there being no hood louvers and the front wheel containing twelve spokes when regular production models featured a front wheel with ten spokes and hood louvers. A few could have been made with the prototype style but a photograph of Chandler number two shows hood louvers and ten spoke front wheels.[26]

The new Chandler rode on a 120 inch wheelbase frame with wheels 34 × 4 and fitted with Firestone demountable rims. It was powered by a six-cylinder L-head type engine of Chandler's own design with cylinders cast in two blocks of three. The bore and stroke were 3⅜ × 5 inches, giving it a horsepower rating of 35. The transmission was a three-speed selective shift type and the clutch was of a Raybestos multiple disc design. Coventry silent chains ran the camshaft, magneto and water pump. Oiling was by splash and pressure by an oil pump submerged in the base of the motor, and cooling was by Mayo radiator and water pump. The starter and generator were by Westinghouse and ignition by Bosch magneto. Fuel was fed from a twenty gallon tank mounted at the rear to a vacuum tank mounted on the firewall with pressure being maintained by a plunger pump operated by a valve lifter. An air pressure gauge was mounted on the toe board.

Steering was worm and sector with a turning radius of 37 feet. Brakes were 14" (rear only) and double expanding. F & S imported ball bearings were used throughout. Springs were three-quarter elliptic rear and one-half elliptic front. A large torque arm connected the rear axle to a frame crossmember just behind the transmission.

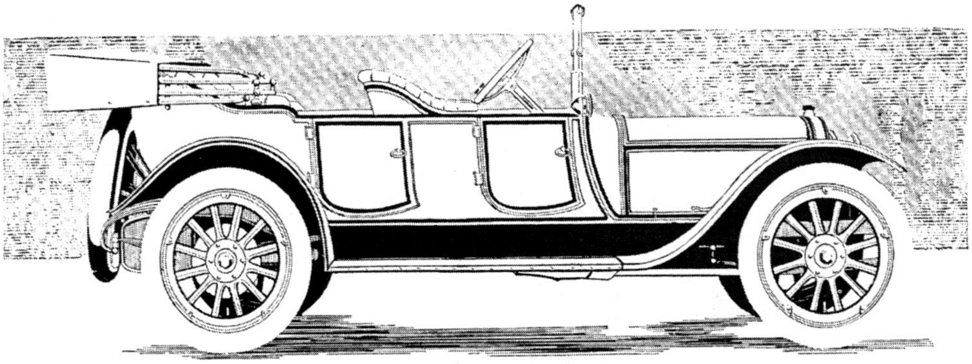

Not Only a Six You Can Afford to Buy —but a Six You Can Afford to Run

THE Chandler Light Weight Six is one of the highest class light weight sixes ever offered under $3000.

We believe no five-passenger car has ever had so many distinctive, high-class features in design or construction or employed such complete and high-grade equipment. These include left-side drive, center control, Westinghouse Electric Self-Starter and Generator and every similar feature demanded by experienced motorists.

How is it possible to produce such a remarkable car at the price?

The roster of men who make up the Chandler organization tells the whole story. They are all men who have had years of experience in building sixes of world-wide reputation. The Chandler organization starts out free of the enormous burden of expense which most other builders of sixes have incurred in experimenting.

There is not a single untried or experimental feature in the Chandler Light Weight Six. Every part and feature represents only time-tested and proved principles of design and construction.

Never before has so much of actual automobile value been sold at anywhere near the price of the Chandler Light Weight Six.

With full equipment the Chandler Light Weight Six weighs only 2979 pounds. This is actual scale weight. It is one of the lightest weight high-grade six cylinder cars ever built—yet it is roomy and sturdy, dignified and graceful.

Every car-owner should be interested in the weight of his car. He should not buy any car until he knows its actual weight. A heavy car means heavy upkeep expense.

Because of its light weight and the remarkably efficient motor the *Chandler Light Weight Six is most economical in tire wear, oil and gasoline consumption. The Chandler Light Weight Six is daily averaging 16 miles and more per gallon of gasoline.*

LIGHT WEIGHT SIX CHANDLER $1785 BUILT BY MEN WHO KNOW

THE Chandler motor is unique. It is designed exclusively for the Chandler Light Weight Six and will not be found in any other car.

With the Chandler motor you can make your way confidently through the most congested traffic. Your control is absolute from 3 miles per hour on high gear up to 55 miles an hour. And it will pick up in amazingly short distance.

The Chandler Light Weight Six and the Chandler motor have proved themselves. The first car ever built made a trial trip across seven ranges of the Allegheny mountains in the dead of winter, over roads considered impassable for any car.

Read the specifications. Study the design of the Chandler Light Weight Six. Note the long wheel-base, the handsome and roomy stream-line coach-type body with deep Turkish upholstering. Where will you find another car embodying so much grace and dignity, so much elegance and comfort, so many distinctive features, so much sturdiness and strength — so much value?

Over $4,000,000 worth of Chandler cars have been contracted for by leading distributors throughout the country. The allotment for your territory is necessarily small. We'll send you complete catalog—but to avoid disappointment make sure of a demonstration—at once.

THE CHANDLER MOTOR CAR CO. 507-527 E. 131st St., Cleveland

The Men Who Know

F. C. CHANDLER, former vice president, general manager and director, Lozier Motor Company.

C. A. EMISE, former sales manager and director, Lozier Motor Company.

W. S. M. MEAD, former foreign sales manager and director, Lozier Motor Company.

S. REGAR, former treasurer and director, Lozier Motor Company.

J. V. WHITBECK, former engineer, Lozier Motor Company.

C. A. CAREY, former purchasing agent, Lozier Motor Company; assistant purchasing agent, Ford Motor Company.

J. R. HALL, former manager supply, repair and service departments, Lozier Motor Company.

J. V. KRALL, former auditor, Lozier Motor Company.

The Car Itself

WEIGHT. 2979 pounds, fully equipped.

LEFT SIDE DRIVE—Center Control.

WHEEL BASE. 120 inches.

WHEELS. Artillery type—34 x 4 inches. Firestone Demountable Rims.

MOTOR. Six cylinders, 43 H. P. 3⅜ x 5 inches. "L" Head type. Cylinders cast in two blocks. Valves enclosed. Imported chains driving cam shaft, pump and magneto. Cam shaft and cams cut from solid drop forging. Heavy crank shaft.

OILING. Oiling by positive gear pump in oil base. Accessible filling tube for oil reservoir. Oil gauge on motor base. All exterior oil pipes eliminated.

IGNITION. Bosch High Tension Magneto.

CARBURETOR. Stromberg "Little Six." Hot air and dash priming attachments.

SELF STARTER. Westinghouse Electric Starter built into motor. All moving parts enclosed.

COOLING. Centrifugal pump. High-class square-tube radiator.

ELECTRIC LIGHTING. Westinghouse Electric Lighting Generator with large storage battery. Solar electric headlights. Solar electric side lamps built into wind-shield, and Solar tail lamp in combination with illuminated license bracket.

CLUTCH. Multiple disc, ball bearing. Discs of Raybestos and steel in oil tight case with motor.

TRANSMISSION. Three speeds and reverse.

REAR AXLE. Floating type. Annular ball bearings in wheels, shafts and differential. Drive shafts removable.

STEERING GEAR. Irreversible and adjustable for wear. Ebonized steering wheel.

GASOLINE SYSTEM. 20 gallon tank suspended in rear. Gasoline gauge.

STREAM LINE BODY. Five passenger coach type.

UPHOLSTERING. 16 inch cushions. High grade tufted leather. High grade springs. Rear seat 48 inches in width. High backs on front and rear seats.

WIND-SHIELD. Built in without rods or braces. Adjustable for rain, vision or ventilation.

TOP. Mohair top with "Jiffy" curtains. Bair patent locking top holders.

HORN. Genuine motor driven electric.

JONES SPEEDOMETER.

CLOCK. 8 day New Haven.

COLOR AND FINISH. Bodies, wheels, frame and running gear finished in handsome dark blue with silver stripe. Fenders, hood and cowl black. All hardware, lamps and fittings nickeled.

PRICE. $1,785.00. Chassis only, $1,585.00.

Chandler's first ad (*Saturday Evening Post*, July 26, 1913).

UNITED STATES PATENT OFFICE.

CHANDLER MOTOR CAR COMPANY, OF CLEVELAND, OHIO.

TRADE-MARK FOR AUTOMOBILES.

107,153. Registered Nov. 16, 1915.

Application filed July 12, 1915. Serial No. 87,886.

STATEMENT.

To all whom it may concern:

Be it known that Chandler Motor Car Company, a corporation duly organized under the laws of the State of Ohio, and located and doing business in the city of Cleveland, county of Cuyahoga, State of Ohio, has adopted and used the trade-mark shown in the accompanying drawing, for automobiles, in Class No. 19, Vehicles, not including engines.

The trade-mark has been continuously used in the business of said corporation since July 1913.

The trade-mark is applied or affixed to the goods by a name plate on the automobile itself, or by a reproduction thereof on the stationery and advertising matter of the said corporation.

CHANDLER MOTOR CAR COMPANY,
By WARREN S. M. MEAD,
Second Vice-President.

CHANDLER

DECLARATION.

State of New York county of New York ss:

Warren S. M. Mead, being duly sworn, deposes and says that he is the second vice-president of the corporation, the applicant named in the foregoing statement; that he believes the foregoing statement is true; that he believes said corporation is the owner of the trade-mark sought to be registered; that no other person, firm, corporation, or association, to the best of his knowledge and belief, has the right to use said trade-mark in the United States, either in the identical form or in any such near resemblance thereto as might be calculated to deceive; that said trade-mark is used by said corporation in commerce among the several States of the United States; that the description and drawing presented truly represent the trade-mark sought to be registered; and that the specimens show the trade-mark as actually used upon the goods.

WARREN S. M. MEAD.

Subscribed and sworn to before me, a notary public, this 8th day of July, A. D., 1915.

[L. S.] LEON MINTZ,
Notary Public.

Copies of this trade-mark may be obtained for five cents each, by addressing the "Commissioner of Patents, Washington, D. C."

Chandler Guarantee

We guarantee Chandler Motor Cars for ninety days from date of delivery to the original purchaser, this guarantee being limited to the replacement or repair at our factory of such parts of the car as shall, under normal use and service, be judged by us to have been defective in material or workmanship.

This guarantee is limited to the shipment to the purchaser or dealer, without charge, except for the transportation of part or parts repaired or intended to replace the part or parts claimed to have been defective, which parts, upon return to us at our factory for inspection, transportation prepaid, we shall have determined were defective.

This guarantee does not apply to repairs or replacement made necessary by accident, carelessness, negligence or abuse. It does not include adjustments, tuning up, general overhauling or replacement of parts worn out in service.

Our liability under this guarantee shall cease if the car to which it applies is altered or repaired outside of our factory or the shops of our authorized dealers.

We make no guarantee in respect to tires, rims, magnetos, lamps, starters, or other accessories not manufactured by us, other than the guarantees given by the manufacturers of these appliances. Claims as to these should be made to the manufacturers direct.

The purchaser understands and agrees that no other guarantee of the car is made or authorized to be made by the company, other than therein above set forth.

***Left:* Chandler logo design (U.S. Patent Office, Washington, D.C.). *Right:* Chandler's 90-day warranty.**

The body, frame and running gear were painted dark Victoria blue with silver striping while the wheels, fenders, cowl and hood were black. Upholstery was tufted leather with seats being 10 and 12 inches in depth. The top was mohair with "Jiffy" side curtains. Instruments were mounted under the dash with one on the toe board.

The car, weighing 2,979 pounds and priced at $1785,[27] was an almost identical copy of the Lozier Model 77 "Montclair" Light Six of 1913. In fact, John G. Perrin, who had designed the Lozier Model 77, said the Chandler was a virtual copy of his design. One writer, at a later date, suggested that if the laws of today had been in effect in 1913 someone would be in jail for patent infringement and the author would agree with that assessment. However, J.V. Whitbeck's application for a patent on the body was filed February 6, 1914, and granted on April 7, 1914, as patent number 45,579. This was a surprisingly short

The original Chandler six-cylinder engine.

Left: **Rear suspension of the Model 14.** ***Right:*** **Model 14 interior.**

time for a patent to be considered and approved. The patent drawings did show the hood with louvers.[28]

Although a number of small features distinguished the Chandler from the Lozier, they were hardly discernible. The spare tire of the Lozier, mounted at the rear, was tilted forward at the top while the Chandler's was mounted without any tilt. Hood louvers on the Lozier had a vertical tilt to the rear while the Chandler's were virtually the same. But next year's model would have the louvers absolutely vertical. There was a small tool compartment in the splash apron, just ahead of the left rear fender of the Lozier, and the apron itself had a bead pressed at the top and bottom which extended practically the length of the apron itself. Also, there was a slight difference in the rear compartment upholstery and the mounting of the top irons.

The Lozier Light Six Touring sold for $3,250 while the Chandler sold for $1,785, very reasonable for a six cylinder automobile built to a standard of excellence. The new car would be designated Model 14.[29]

The above information would lead one to believe that there were few, if any, body styles other than the Touring made in Model 14, although, the earliest parts manual lists four models. The Parts Books for Models 14, 15, 15B and 16 do list

The Chandler Model 14 (left) virtually copied the styling of the 1913 Lozier Model 77 "Montclair" as seen in these front views.

Above: **1913 Lozier Model 77.** ***Right:*** **Chandler Model 14 Limousine.**

Left: **Chandler Model 14 Coupe.** ***Right:*** **Chandler Model 14 Sedan.**

THE FOLLOWING is a list of the leading officials and department heads of the Chandler Motor Car Company:

F. C. CHANDLER. President. Formerly Vice-President, General Manager and Director of The Lozier Motor Company; twenty-one years business experience in manufacturing and selling; seven years of which as General European Manager for H. A. Lozier and Company and the American Bicycle Company, and eight years continuous experience in the manufacturing and selling of high grade four and six-cylinder motor cars.

C. A. EMISE. Vice-President and Sales Manager. Formerly Sales, and Advertising Manager and Director of The Lozier Motor Company; in charge of selling and advertising. Manager of all racing campaigns. Six years experience in manufacturing and selling marine gasoline motors; eight years of experience in advertising and selling high grade motor cars.

W. S. M. MEAD. Second Vice-President and Assistant Sales Manager. Formerly Director The Lozier Motor Company and General Manager Foreign Department and Eastern Sales; six years with A. G. Spalding & Brother; three years Assistant Sales Manager American Bicycle Company Eastern Department; eight years sales experience with high class motor cars.

SAMUEL REGAR. Treasurer. Formerly Treasurer and Director The Lozier Motor Company; twenty-one years of experience financing and accounting. H. A. Lozier & Company, American Bicycle Company, and Treasurer of Manufacturing Company building high class motor cars.

J. V. WHITBECK. Chief Engineer. Formerly Engineering Department The Lozier Motor Company, Olds Motor Car Company and Franklin Automobile Company; nine years continuous experience in engineering and designing motor cars.

J. R. HALL. Superintendent. Formerly Manager Service Supplies and Repairs The Lozier Motor Company; nine years as Superintendent of Service, Foreign Department American Bicycle Company, Hamburg, Germany; eight years continuous experience in Mechanical Department Motor Car industry.

C. A. CAREY. Purchasing Agent. Formerly Purchasing Agent The Lozier Motor Company and Assistant Purchasing Agent Ford Motor Car Company; seven years experience in purchase and supplies with motor car manufacturers.

J. I. KRALL. Auditor. Formerly Auditor The Lozier Motor Company; six years experience auditing and automobile factory accountant.

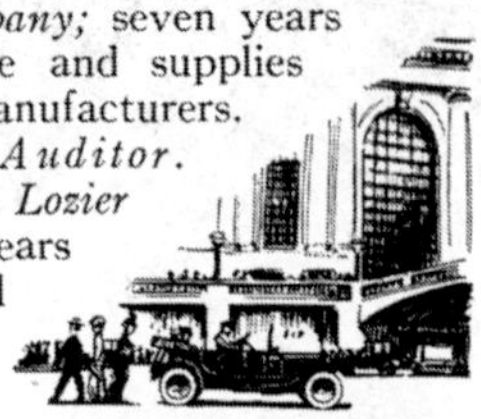

Chandler Model 14, car #3.

parts for body styles other than the Touring. The Briggs Manufacturing Company built the early Touring bodies at their factory in Detroit. They were then shipped to Cleveland where they were finished and painted in a small body factory adjacent to the Chandler plant. The Runabout (Roadster) was not manufactured as a Model 14 but would debut in February 1914 as a Model 15. All Model 14 Chandlers would be numbered between 1 and 550.[30]

Chandler entered a grueling 500 mile, three day reliability event on Wednesday, December 4, 1913. The run was performed in the New York–Connecticut area and was closely supervised by a technical committee. All cars had to pass a rigid inspection before the event started and at the end of each day. At the finish, two 1914 Buicks, one four cylinder and one six cylinder, had perfect scores. Chandler was second with only one demerit, a leaky hose connection at the water pump. Charles A. Emise always believed that the best way to prove a car's potential was in competition. He did a marvelous job of this at Lozier and this was Chandler's first in what would be a long line of trials.[31]

Opposite: **Chandler Motor Car Company founders.**

• Two •

1914–1916

Small Company, Big Success

Chandler began 1914 with the factory building as many touring cars as possible. Dealers were clamoring for more cars in any body style, but the Touring seemed to be the only one which was immediately available. An advertisement in a weekly family magazine stated that four body styles were available, those being the Runabout (Roadster), Four Passenger Coupe and Limousine in addition to the Touring. A leading trade magazine stated that the Five Passenger Sedan was available, but it is unlikely that anything but the Touring was being delivered in any substantial numbers.[1]

In fact, the first ad known for the Runabout never appeared until February. The Chandler closed cars had all aluminum bodies which were built by what was termed a leading manufacturer. Most likely they were built by Willoughby, which did build the Model 15 closed car bodies; an early Chandler brochure shows the Model 14 Coupe to be exactly the same as the Model 15.

Information on the Model 14 closed body Chandlers is almost nonexistent, but one beautiful brochure illustrates the Sedan, Limousine and Coupe. (It is the author's opinion that the Sedan and Limousine photo captions have been switched.) In this brochure, a line drawing of the Runabout (Roadster) is illustrated with the statement that deliveries would begin in January 1914. The new Model 15 Touring is also shown, which dates this information to late 1913 as this brochure was handed out at the New York show in early January.[2]

The new year saw few mechanical changes but several cosmetic body changes. The engine was unchanged from the Model 14 except in the carburetor connections and fittings. The Model 15, as it was now designated, came without cowl lights and outside door handles. The outside hinges on the front door had also disappeared.

The body had undergone a slight improvement with the elimination of the step-up just behind the rear doors, creating a straight line from cowl to rear where it gently flowed upward behind the seat. Fenders were no longer flat but had been crowned.[3] The rear fenders now had no upturn at the rear but continued to flow with the curve of the wheel. The rear seat had been redesigned where it joined the floorboard and the foot rest had also been changed.

The cowl had undergone a major change and was now one piece. The seams which flowed in a gentle curve from windshield to the bottom of the hood had been eliminated with the body lines flowing upward to the windshield, eliminating the sharp corner just ahead of the front door. The windshield had undergone a change where the posts joined the body at the cowl, the spare tire now tilted slightly forward at the top and the hood louvers were slightly angled to the rear.

But the change most welcomed by owners was the repositioning of the instruments from the firewall and toe board to a prominent place on the dash. All of these changes were slight but they were appreciated by owners as they contributed greatly to appearance, comfort and driver satisfaction. They also made manufacturing considerably easier.[4]

The Runabout was a snappy design and a very handsome automobile. It also had no cowl lights, outside door handles or exposed hinges. Price was the same as the Touring at $1,785.[5]

Prices for the other body styles were considerably higher with the Coupe going for $2,485, the Limousine for $2,985, and the Sedan for $2,885.[6] Information about the closed body styles could be had by writing the Chandler Company.[7]

Weight of both open cars was still under 3,000 pounds, but the enclosed body styles tipped the scales slightly above that figure: 3,025 for the Coupe and 3,100 for the Limousine. Sedan weight was not listed. This may have been by design because Chandler stopped advertising the Sedan for a while and ads listed only the other four body styles. The reason for this is unclear but Sedans were expensive and not very popular. Or Chandler may have needed time to get production of this body style up and going. By October the Sedan was being featured prominently in Chandler advertising. Colors were still dark blue with black fenders and hood.[8]

Chandler participated in the New York Auto Show for the first time in 1914, January 3–10, occupying spaces C 4–5. They exhibited five automobiles, an enameled chassis and a cutaway motor. One of the models exhibited, according to news accounts, was a five passenger Touring car with an English coach type body. In reality, this was just the Model 14 Five Passenger Touring embellished by a writer's colorful description. The Model 15 Touring was also shown along with the Limousine, Coupe and Roadster.[9]

The stockholders of the company met for the first time in early February. The treasurer reported that dividends had been earned on the company's preferred stock and a surplus equal to 32 percent per annum had been earned on the common as well. When issued the preferred had carried a 7 percent cumulative dividend, beginning January 1, 1914.

In view of the positive financial condition of the company, the board of directors voted to pay the dividend on the preferred from July 1, 1913, instead of January 1, 1914. Directors and stockholders also heard that a backlog of orders amounting to $2,500,000 had been placed and this was enough to ensure that the factory would be running at capacity through June 30.

The annual election of officers and directors, conducted at this meeting, brought no changes at the top. Fred C. Chandler was reelected as president, Charles A. Emise as vice-president, Samuel Regar as treasurer and Isidor Grossman as secretary. W.E. Hopkins, J.W. Deutsch, H.G. Strong, Albert Jarecki, W.P. Herbert, F. C. Chandler, C.A. Emise, W.S.M. Mead and Samuel Regar were elected as directors of the company.

Early in March, the company received the welcome news that it had been elected

Top: **Chandler Model 15 Touring.** ***Middle:*** **Model 15 Limousine (factory photograph, courtesy Roger Anderson).** ***Bottom:*** **Model 15 Roadster.**

Model 15 Sedan (Willoughby Company photograph, courtesy W.E. Gosden).

to membership in the National Automobile Chamber of Commerce. This was an honor given only to those who had been in business for more than one year and who had established a reputation for a quality automobile and sound financial foundation. The National Automobile Chamber of Commerce (NACC) had just recently been formed by combining the National Association of Automobile Manufacturers (NAAM) and the Association of Licensed Automobile Manufacturers (ALAM). These two organizations had previously vied for status as the spokesman for the automobile industry. The ALAM had consisted of manufacturers who sold automobiles registered under the Selden patent. There had been other organizations but the NACC finally represented most of the automobile industry.

Soon after production began, Chandler officials realized they needed more room. In March 1914, George Rutherford built a one-story 64 × 40 foot storage building north of the factory. Constructed of wood and corrugated tin, it was meant to be temporary only.[10]

Chandler received some notable publicity on May 2 when the Chicago Automobile Club and Findeisen & Kropf Manufacturing Company conducted an economy run over Chicago's boulevard park system. Thomas Hay, the local distributor, furnished the car which had been fitted with a Rayfield G-3 carburetor. W.C. Gruner piloted the car, accompanied by F.E. Edwards, chairman of the Chicago Auto Club Contest Committee, Darwin Hatch from the club's technical committee and one other official observer. Gruner was an experienced driver and had built a reputation by driving Fords on the Algonquin, Illinois, hillclimb. The car achieved a mileage of 24.4 on a measured gallon of gasoline. The top was lowered for the run and the windshield was down except for the first two miles. A test of hill climbing and acceleration, including slow speed performance in high gear, followed the economy test.[11]

Model 15 prototype body (Willoughby Company photograph, courtesy W.E. Gosden).

Just eleven days later the Automobile Club of America Technical Committee certified a test of another Chandler on the streets of Central Park, New York City, and the Long Island Motor Parkway. Over four total runs, two on each course, the car averaged 21.6 mpg. The car was furnished by the Brady-Murray Motors Corporation, New York distributors for Chandler. As in the Chicago test, the car was fitted with a Rayfield G-3 carburetor which was soon to be adopted as standard on all Chandler cars.[12]

In an earlier publicity event in February 1914, the Swedish Reliability Test, supervised by the Royal Swedish Automobile Club, a Chandler traversed more than 800 miles of storm wrecked roads which were deemed impassable. It was the only American made automobile to finish without a breakdown.

Meanwhile, in May, W.P. Herbert, the Chandler distributor for Philadelphia and one of the early backers of Chandler, was elected president of the Philadelphia Automobile Trade Association. He was also one of the early directors of the company.[13]

The Model 15 was manufactured in the 551 to 2500 serial number range before the Model 15 B was introduced in June with a few changes to the body and mechanicals. Most noticeably, the doors were now straight vertical openings with rounded corners at the bottom, the front radius being less than the rear. The beading on the top hood panels had now been removed, the cowling had been reworked to accommodate a lower windshield, the rear compartment upholstery had been redone and the fenders were slightly wider.

Mechanically, there were several changes. The new car was 100 pounds lighter, due mainly to a lighter flywheel and pistons. Several small reciprocating parts had also been pared down. Fitted with the Rayfield G-3 carburetor, the new car was advertised as having 10 percent more horsepower than the former Model 15. Wheelbase was still 120 inches and wheels and tires remained the same. The starter and generator were now furnished by Gray & Davis. Despite the claim of 10 percent more horsepower, the specifications remained the same with horsepower still listed as 35. The pistons now had only two rings but the physical appearance of the engine was the same as the Model 15.

The best news for potential owners was the price. Already something of a bargain at $1,785, the car now dropped to $1,595, seemingly too good to be true. Having established itself firmly in the automobile business, Chandler was now making enough money to be very competitive in their price range.

Sometime during 1914, George A. Crittenden, vice-president of Chandler Motors of New England in Boston, had a fancy speedster, based on a standard 15 B chassis, built for his pleasure. The body was supposedly designed by an unnamed French designer and constructed from one solid sheet of hand-hammered aluminum. The Pettingell Machine Company of

Top: **Model 15B Touring (factory photograph, courtesy John W. Chandler).** ***Bottom:*** **Model 15B Cabriolet.**

Amesbury, Massachusetts, constructed the body for Mr. Crittenden. A major manufacturer of high quality tools used by body builders, Pettingell had its own body building business for a short while. Amesbury was the home of several major body builders in the early part of the twentieth century.

The fancy body garnered much attention around Boston—so much so that several potential customers insisted that they too wanted to own one. Crittenden obliged and ordered several Chandlers, minus the bodies, for that purpose. Approximately three weeks were required to finish each car.[14]

Chandler entered two cars in the Chicago to Boston nonstop run to start in Chicago on June 20. Charles A. Emise, Chandler vice president and sales manager, commented that this was a very good way to prove the fuel economy and mechanical capabilities of the Chandler Six.[15]

With October's arrival came advertisements for the closed cars: "To meet the demands of the season and especially to fulfill the requests of many Chandler owners, we offer, for immediate delivery, four handsome closed body designs of the Chandler Light Weight Six." Those who wanted to know more could write for a new catalog and closed car booklet. Potential owners were delighted that they could now have something other than open cars. Although they had been listed for a year, closed Chandlers had been extremely difficult to obtain. One could now have a five passenger Sedan for $2,750, a Coupe for 2,200, a Cabriolet for $1,950, or a Limousine for $2,750. With a total of six body styles, Chandler now offered one to fit every need. There were no significant body changes between the Model 15 and 15B closed cars.[16]

November brought good news to stockholders as a special 10 percent dividend was declared on common stock. This was the second dividend within ninety days. Preferred stock also returned a quarterly dividend of 1¾ percent.

By December 1914 Chandler had announced that their full line was now available. Production of the Touring and Roadster had finally satisfied demand and they could now begin construction of the closed cars in earnest. As January approached, Chandler again was faced with the need for more space and added two buildings of a temporary nature, a 145 × 20 foot road testing garage and a 141 × 54 foot inspection building. They also added a 120 × 60 foot brick extension to the rear of building number one (the original factory) to house three Ingersoll-

***Top:* Model 15B Roadster. *Above:* Custom Model 15B Speedster built for George A. Crittenden. *Left:* Model 15B Sedan, Coupe and Limousine.**

Rand 300 psi compressors and three General Electric induction water pumps.[17]

January brought good news to those who had invested in Chandler. Business had been so good that the company was able to reduce the price of the Touring and Roadster by $300. Fred C. Chandler himself made the announcement and that was only the beginning. He also stated that Chandler stockholders had made a return of 117 percent on their original investment and that the company had placed in reserve an amount equal to that of the original cash capital of the company. Not bad for only two years in business.[18]

The Model 15B would be carried until the new year when the Model 16 would make its appearance. All Model 15 B Chandlers would fall in the 2501 to 3999 serial number range.

The announcement of the new Model 16 came January 23 at the New York Auto Show. Actually it had been around for a few weeks but had received little publicity. Fred C. Chandler brought good news to those who anticipated buying a new Chandler in 1915. The price of the Model 16 Touring car and Roadster was $1,295 compared to $1,595 for the previous Model 15B. And, to top it all, in April a Seven Passenger Touring would replace the five passenger version. The Model 16 featured a few cosmetic and mechanical changes. The cowling band was removed as well as the beading of the doors. However, the door opening remained identical to the 15B. The headlights were lowered, the top reworked at the rear, the spare tire mounted perfectly vertically and the rear fenders reshaped to follow the curvature of the wheel.[19]

Model 16 Chandlers would fall in the 4000 to 14,999 serial number range. The new Cabriolet which had been introduced in December 1914 was a welcome addition to the lineup. While Chandler closed cars seemed to suffer somewhat in styling, the Cabriolet did not. The body lines were virtually straight from radiator to rear with the top down and it was just as pleasing with the top up. With the spare tires mounted at the rear, it was one good looking automobile. The Cabriolet was expected to

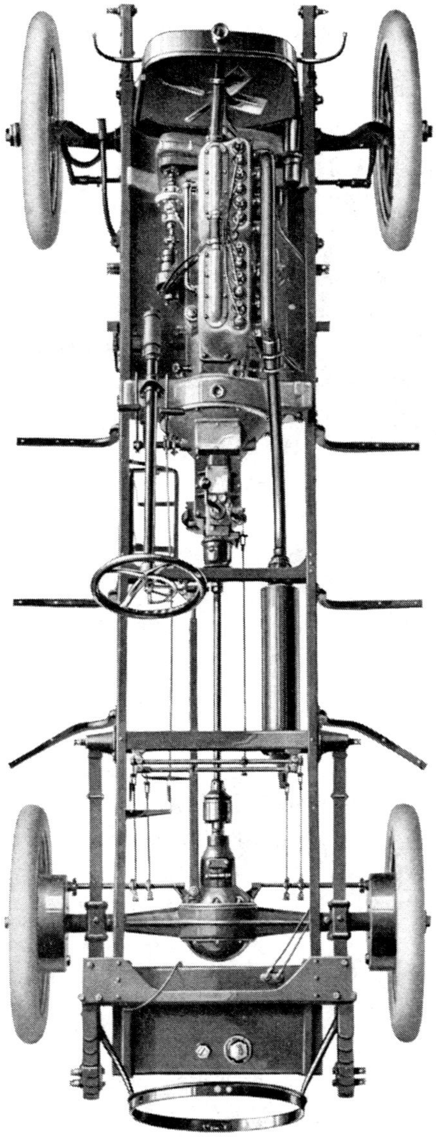

The Model 15B chassis.

Top: Model 16 Seven Passenger Touring. *Bottom:* Model 16 Roadster.

be Chandler's best seller according to Charles A. Emise, vice president and sales manager. The open cars were now fitted with the Golde patent one-man top and Jiffy side curtains.[20]

Mechanically, the rear drive was changed from bevel gear drive to worm bevel gear drive. Gray & Davis continued to supply the starter and generator. The oil pump, which had formerly used shaft driven gears and been mounted in the oil pan, was now plunger driven and mounted on the side of the crankcase. The starter was moved to the underside of the cast aluminum engine side pan. Apparently, the experiment with the two ring piston did not work out as the old three ring design returned.

The biggest change was a longer wheelbase, now 122 inches on all models. The additional two inches afforded slightly more room for passengers and enabled Chandler to build the Seven Passenger Touring.[21]

Chandler production had now hit its stride, and for April the shipping department reported that 233 percent more cars had been shipped than in April of 1914. May shipments were up by 433 percent and June shipments by 646 percent over 1914 figures. By April 1, Chandler was shipping 40 cars per day; by May 5, 50 cars per day; and by May 20, 60 cars per day. Two new factory buildings and a large addition to the main factory accounted for this accelerated rate of manufacturing. The two new buildings effectively doubled the manufacturing capability of the company, and a 1,000 foot shipping platform had recently been installed.[22]

All was not dull in the automobile manufacturing business at Chandler. To prove that point, 12 Model 16 Chandlers with 42 people aboard left Cleveland in a blinding rainstorm on Saturday, July 12, and headed for Cedar Point, Ohio, 72 miles away. They only became lost six times, which added about twenty miles to the trip. Cedar Point was then considered to be the Atlantic City of the Midwest with many and varied amusements. After a day of frivolity, which included the upending of a seaplane in Lake Erie with no one getting seriously injured, the Chandler group enjoyed a sumptuous dinner at the Hotel Breakers. The return trip to Cleveland was made after dark but all survived, with no one getting lost or injured. Samuel Regar, Chandler's treasurer, on hearing that a few employees who owned cars were planning the trip, financed the excursion with company funds and included everyone who wanted to go by using company cars for those who did not have transportation.[23]

An early November announcement stated that the H. J. Walker Company, which had been making many of Chandler's parts and doing most of their machining, was moving from Detroit, where they had been in business since 1910, to Cleveland. They would occupy a building which had been under construction since August. The building, 403 × 120 feet, was designed by Ernest McGeorge and constructed by the Bolton and Pratt Company. Another building for their use would be erected soon. At this time Walker was doing work exclusively for Chandler.[24]

November also brought good news of a financial nature as Chandler was recapitalized on November 16. Eastern financial interests wanted in, having noticed the excellent returns Chandler was generating. Company stock had ballooned to the point that speculators were offering as much as $350 per share. One individual was offering to sell at $450 per share. At the meeting where the board voted the change, all Chandler officers were reelected and control stayed firmly in the hands of the original founders. Chandler was now a $10 million company and its financial status was excellent. Hornblower & Weeks, bankers of Boston and New York, handled the stock transactions. When placed on the market the stock was 15 times oversubscribed. Rumors were circulating that the Maxwell Motor Company was pushing for a merger with Chandler, but President Fred C. Chandler would not confirm this.

In December, Bolton and Pratt finished the Ernest McGeorge designed Building A. The new two-story structure measured 120 × 40 feet and was attached to building number 1. It was to be used for office space and rear stairs connected it to the rest of the factory.[25]

Model 16 top with side curtains.

Late in the model year a new creation made its way into the lineup. The Seven Passenger Convertible Sedan debuted in September 1915. Although Chandler did not identify the body manufacturer it was apparently Springfield, as they advertised at this time that they were building Chandler bodies. The Convertible Sedan was a Springfield design, and an advertisement in a women's magazine for October (1916) referred to it as the Springfield Convertible Sedan. The first model would have loop style door handles but this would soon be changed to a straight, vertical style. This new body style was prominently advertised after appearing at the 1916 New York Auto Show as a Model 17 of the New Series. It was priced at $1,795.[26]

The Chandler Company was very generous with its employees, not only in wage increases and bonuses but in other ways also. As Christmas approached, they purchased three truckloads of turkeys and company employees, using company vehicles, delivered one to the family of each Chandler employee for their Christmas dinner.[27]

Chandler productivity was running at maximum, finances were in excellent shape and the future appeared unclouded as 1915 ended. The new year started with great fanfare—the "New and Greater" Chandler, the Model 17, had arrived. It was New because the body had been reworked and Greater because the wheelbase had been lengthened from 122 to 123 inches. With the start of the Model 17, Chandler would start identifying all models with a Service Series number. The 17 would start with serial number 15,001 and continue through the Model 18 to serial number 65,000.

Body lines had been reworked considerably from front to rear. A new cowling behind the front seat of the Touring, called the tonneau cowling, was covered with body metal and the area behind the front seat featured a beautiful walnut finish.

The body lines now flowed almost without interruption from radiator to rear, with only a slight elevation for the windshield and tonneau cowl visible. Seats did not project above the body as in previous models, and the hood louvers had the pressed outline bead removed, giving them a much smoother appearance.

Mechanically, one significant change did not receive much publicity. The rear springs were reduced from three-quarter elliptic to one-half elliptic, reducing body sway and enhancing control. One would have expected this to have been a selling point but little mention was made in Chandler ads or literature. The torque arm remained and the new car still rode on 34 × 4 tires.

The Mayo, Mercedes style radiator was dropped from all advertising as the radiator changed to a core and shell type, apparently manufactured by Harrison.

Chandler went to the 1916 New York Auto Show, held in the Grand Central Palace from December 31 to January 8, with a full lineup of the "New and Greater Chandler."

***Top:* Model 16 Seven Passenger Convertible Sedan (factory photograph, courtesy of Roger Anderson). *Bottom:* Model 17 Seven Passenger Convertible Sedan (factory photograph, author's collection).**

A new body style now made its appearance in grand fashion. With everything except the frame painted in gleaming white, the new four passenger Roadster was introduced. Not a traditional Roadster with a rumble seat, it allowed entrance to the rear section through the passenger door and between the driver and passenger seat. Being painted white (actually cream or ivory) broke a Chandler tradition as everything previous had been painted blue with black wheels, hood, and fenders. It is unknown if thereafter Chandler offered colors other than blue as everything seemed to carry on as usual.[28]

The Convertible Sedan was also at the show. It had entered the lineup in September 1915 as a Model 16 at a price of $1,795, but that was soon bumped up to $1,895 and then to $1,995. The door posts could be removed and the windows lowered to make a hardtop convertible. It was a very neat and good looking automobile with body by Springfield. The Two Passenger Roadster was dropped as the new four passenger version gained popularity.

Prices held steady for the open cars as the Seven Passenger Touring still went for $1,295 and the new Four Passenger Roadster the same. However, prices for all other body types were adjusted. The Three Passenger Cabriolet would now go for $1,650, the Four Passenger Coupe for $1,950, the Five Passenger Sedan for $2,250, the Seven Passenger Limousine for $2,950, and the new Seven Passenger Convertible Sedan for $1,795. Chandler was now ready to supply any body style the motoring public would desire.[29]

Many of the department heads at Chandler were present throughout the show, but Charles A. Emise was noticeably absent. He had left his position as sales manager due to a lingering illness. He moved to Redwood City, California, for a while and then took up residence at Englewood, New Jersey. Being a major stockholder, he would remain a vice president, attend all directors meetings and in general look after the sales department.

James Mack Dunlap, President of the Dunlap-Ward Advertising Company of Chicago and Detroit, spoke to the distributors and dealers about Chandler's 1916 sales and advertising plans. On February 1, he would be appointed sales manager at Chandler and take on the duties which had formerly been those of Charles A. Emise.[30]

Top: **Model 17 Seven Passenger Touring.** *Bottom:* **Model 17 Four Passenger Roadster.**

By now, 20,000 Chandler owners were touting the Chandler with the "Marvelous Motor," and marvelous it was as Chandler had designed a great engine.[31]

Cleveland would gain another automobile manufacturer in January 1916 as the Jordan Motor Car Company, headed by the flamboyant Edward S. "Ned" Jordan, would locate in the Forest City. They would also build six cylinder automobiles in the price range of Chandler.[32]

A significant event occurred in January when the National Automobile Chamber of Commerce announced that at their last meeting, they had voted to discontinue the manufacture of cars with 60 inch tread. This wider tread width (56 inches was then the norm) had been a concession to owners who lived in the South but had become a burden to manufacture as each one was practically a special unit. This tread width was popular in the Caribbean countries as well. The Ford Motor Company seemed to be the company most affected as they were building many more automobiles than most manufacturers. Ford announced that after July 31, there would be no more 60 inch tread and the other manufacturers agreed. Everyone did not always agree with Henry Ford but on this matter it was unanimous.[33]

By March, predictions were that Chandler would try to reach a manufacturing goal of 20,000 units for 1916. To accomplish this, they had added a new building of 25,000 square feet floor space adjoining the present factory. The new structure was constructed on a foundation sufficient to allow several floors to be added later should the need arise.

On April 24, 1916, John M. Howard of Chandler's Advertising department sent to Frank Connor of the Foreign Sales department, with headquarters in New York, a package of photographs and window transfer signs. Connor was preparing to travel to South America with the intent of establishing Chandler dealerships in several countries. The package contained two photographs of the Chandler factory for his use in dealing with potential dealers. One photograph was the new service building and one was of the Briggs Manufacturing Company factory. Chandler apparently wanted the foreign dealers to know who was making their bodies. Chandler would not continue this relationship for long.

Some confusion enters the picture here. An artist's conception published in the *Chandler Bulletin* shows a six-story building on the location of the Briggs Manufacturing Company plant, identified as the body department building. However, a Cleveland plat map of about this time shows the building to be four stories. An actual photo, circa 1923–24, clearly shows it as six stories and the Briggs name is still on the building. Willoughby, in all likelihood, built the first enclosed bodies and Springfield probably built the early Convertible Sedan and Coupe with Fisher eventually building most everything else until about 1926.[34]

On Sunday, May 14, Thomas J. Hay, Chandler distributor for Chicago, arrived in Cleveland with 40 people in his party to drive 30 new Touring cars and Four Passenger Roadsters back to Chicago. They arrived in two special Pullmans and were met by a host of Chandler officials and feted to breakfast at the Hotel Statler before beginning their journey home. They would make it to Toledo, Ohio, and spend the night there, resuming their journey to Chicago the next day.[35]

By September, Chandler had eased a new body style into production. The new Four Passenger Convertible Coupe would be available for delivery in October. It was on the style of the Convertible Sedan with a removable post and was a two door version. It apparently carried a body by Fisher, and the price was the same as its Seven Passenger companion at $1,895. The body featured a small bustle at the rear, the spare tire had a noticeable slant and the rear compartment would seat two people comfortably. The new design would become very popular and the price would soon be raised to $1,995.[36]

Also in September, Chandler announced that a new

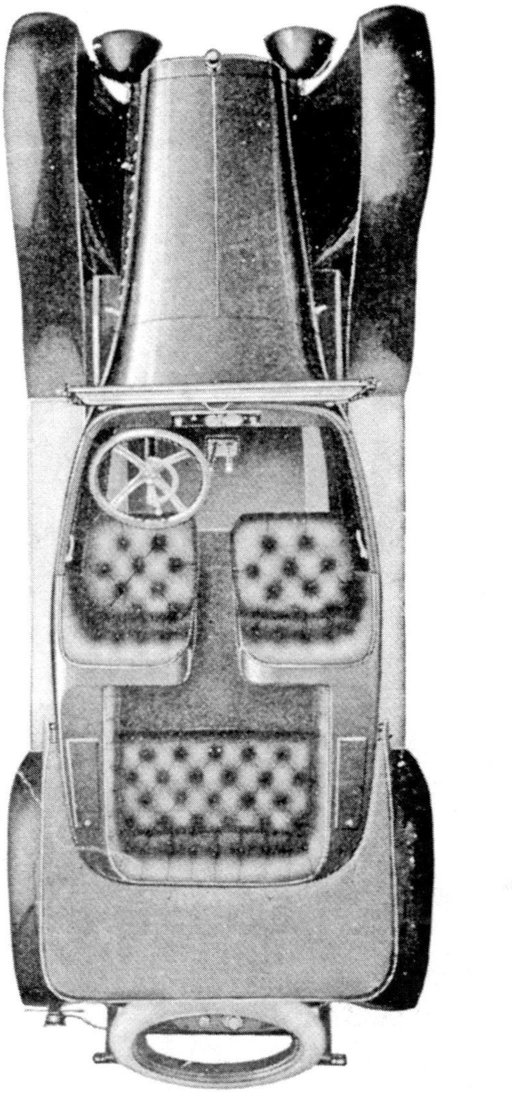

***Both photographs:* Interior of the Model 17 Four Passenger Roadster.**

Top, left: **Model 17 Cabriolet.** ***Top, right:*** **Four Passenger Convertible Coupe.** ***Bottom:*** **Chandler office employees' outing to Crystal Beach, July 22, 1916. The car in front center is a prototype fitted with a new style headlight mounting and a dealer license plate (factory photograph, courtesy of Roger Anderson).**

four-story building which would be known as Building #3, measuring 60 × 500 feet, would be built and ready for production in the spring of 1917. Ernest McGeorge designed the structure and the Crowell-Lundoff-Little Construction Company did the building. The structure was too innovative for Cleveland's building commissioner and he insisted that the construction company do a series of load tests before he would allow occupancy. At the same time the Gaylord Feaga Company finished construction of a one-story 60 × 160 foot special service building which had also been designed by Ernest

A group of Chandler employees on a picnic (factory photograph, unknown source).

McGeorge. The building stood in front of and was aligned with Building #3.[37]

By October the Limousine had been treated to a facelift and the models for 1917 were making their appearance. Actually, there was no change in the models as the Model 17 was carried into the new year unchanged and would continue until the 1918 models made their appearance. Prices of the Seven Passenger Touring and Four Passenger Roadster would remain at $1,295 for the rest of the year with the Convertible Sedan and Coupe priced at $1,995 and the Limousine at $2,595. Somewhere in the life of the Convertible Sedan and Coupe the door handles reverted to the loop style.

In November, Warren S.M. Mead, vice president of eastern sales and export sales manager, moved his office out of the Brady-Murray Company, Chandler distributors for New York, because of a lack of space. Both he and Brady-Murray needed more space because of increased volume of sales. The arrangement had been mutually beneficial to both parties but each now needed room to expand.[38]

Apparently, Fisher Body had replaced both Briggs and Springfield as body makers for Chandler. Briggs had supplied some of Chandler's early bodies and Springfield must have started out furnishing the Convertible Sedan and Coupe bodies as they were advertised as Springfield bodies. Later they were advertised as "Fisher Built."

On November 21, 1916, Fisher was sued by the Springfield Body Corporation of New York and the Springfield Body Company of Springfield, Massachusetts, charging infringement of their patents and unfair competition. Fisher responded by denying any infringement and stated they would defend their actions vigorously. It is not known whether Fisher was sued because of an infringement of the body patent or what the unfair competition entailed. On November 29, Fisher Body assured everyone who owned a car with this type body that they would protect their rights and Fisher's own interest as well. This announcement was made in a weekly automotive trade magazine. What effect the lawsuit would have on production of their bodies, as far as Chandler was concerned, was uncertain but they would continue to build both the Convertible Sedan and Convertible Coupe without interruption.

The Springfield Body Corporation of New York had been formed in February 1916 and claimed all patent rights to the Springfield type bodies patented by the Springfield Body Company of Springfield, Massachusetts.[39] The patent litigation would drag on for more than a year until it was settled on January 22, 1918, with no terms being disclosed. Springfield was being broken up because of bankruptcy and its assets were being sold to the Detroit Shell Company while the sale of its patents were negotiated with other body manufacturers.

The Model 17 used serial numbers in the 15,001 to 65,000 range but would now be listed as Service Series 25. The Model 18 would also fall in this serial number range and Service Series.[40]

• THREE •

1917–1918
The War Years

As 1916 came to a close so did Chandler's policy of holding the line on prices. Actually, most prices had been reduced regularly, especially on the open models. This would change as the New Series, which was introduced as the Model 17, would continue on as the Model 18. Prices were raised by $100 per vehicle across the board, starting December 1, 1916, in response to rising labor and material costs. World War I was now raging in Europe and the United States would enter the conflict in April 1917. Many sacrifices would be made before peace finally came on November 11, 1918.

The Seven Passenger Touring and Four Passenger Roadster would now sell at $1,395, the Four Passenger Convertible Coupe and Seven Passenger Convertible Sedan would go for $1,995 and the Limousine had been bumped up to $2,695, with the chassis going for $1,195.[1]

The Model 18 was introduced with little fanfare. Mechanically, the engine had its bore increased to 3½ inches from 3⅜ but the stroke remained the same at 5 inches. The few other mechanical changes were insignificant. Not so with the body. The windshield now took on a noticeable rearward slant on all open cars. The Four Passenger Roadster had a dramatic hump in the rear bustle and the spare tire's forward tilt was reduced considerably. The two personal effects compartments of the Roadster were removed from the rear seat area, giving the passengers extra room.

The Convertible Coupe had the same rear bustle treatment as the Roadster. Headlights on all models, except the Limousine, were mounted on a bar which extended from fender to fender and were much higher than the previous model's. The Convertible Sedan now had a driver's door, and passengers entered through a center door on the opposite side. Interiors of the Convertible Sedan and Coupe were finished in gray whipcord while the Limousine was finished in plush. Wheelbase remained at 123 inches and wheels remained at 34 × 4. Paint color was still blue with black fenders, splash aprons and hood.

The Four Passenger Convertible Coupe was becoming quite popular and the Four passenger Roadster still retained its charm. Five body styles for virtually any need at popular prices would keep the Chandler factory operating for the foreseeable future.[2]

Distributors had been invited to the factory to view the new Chandler and sign their contracts for 1917 in November of 1916. Apparently they liked what they saw, signing orders in the amount of $30 million, exclusive of foreign sales.

Aware that good employee morale tends to increase production, Chandler's officials always treated their workers with dignity and respect. On January 2, 1917, the company increased employees' wages by 10 percent. In addition, it was announced that on July 20, a 10 percent bonus would be paid to all employees who were working for the company as of July 1. For workers who had been employed the previous twelve months, this amounted to about five weeks' wages.[3]

The new 60 × 500 foot four-story building begun in September 1916 was completed in March and added much needed space for body work, painting, and assembly.[4]

The Chandler Board of Directors met on February 28 and elected officers and declared dividends. Fred C. Chandler was reelected president; Charles A. Emise, although not active in the company, was reelected vice president with Warren S.M. Mead also elected vice president; Samuel Regar was elected treasurer; and Isador Grossman was elected secretary. The directors reelected were Fred C. Chandler, Samuel Regar, J. V. Whitbeck, C.A. Otis and J.W. Sherwin, all of Cleveland. Warren S.M. Mead and J.W. Prentiss of New York completed the board. At this meeting the directors declared a regular dividend of 2 percent and an extra dividend of 1 percent, the latter being in favor of the Red Cross and amounting to $70,000. Chandler had also purchased $40,000 in Liberty Bonds and the Chandler employees had purchased $95,000 also. Patriotism was flourishing at Chandler.[5]

Chandler went to the Boston Automobile Show, March 3–10, 1917, with a good lineup of cars, but one in particular received the majority of attention. A Seven Passenger Touring car, painted solid white and with a tonneau top with fancy landau irons, was a very good looking vehicle but not very practical. Chandler Motors of New England furnished all cars for the display and manned the space, assisted by factory officials.[6]

First quarter sales of Chandlers showed an 83 percent increase over the previous year's first quarter, and on April 10 a record 144 cars were shipped, making this the biggest day in Chandler history. Many of the cars had to be shipped in open "gondola cars" as a shortage of boxcars was affecting the railroad due to the war effort. This did not discourage Chandler officials as they just devised an ingenious plan to get them loaded.[7]

Tuesday afternoon, March 20, saw a gathering of Chandler distributors from throughout the United States assembled at the Hollenden Hotel for a conference. Earlier that day they had visited the factory, toured many of the buildings where manufacturing was in progress and chatted with employees. At 2 p.m. they assembled at the Hollenden for business and were addressed by Thomas J. Hay, the Chandler distributor in Chicago. At 6 p.m. they retired to the hotel's dining area where business of a less serious nature was conducted.

A fire at the Palmer Garage, the Chandler dealer in New London, Connecticut, damaged 32 cars in early March. Only quick work by the local fire department saved them from total destruction and possibly the loss of 15 other cars on another floor of the building.[8]

The United States Congress declared

***Top:* Model 18 Four Passenger Roadster. *Middle:* Model 18 Four Passenger Roadster fitted with custom winter top (factory photograph, courtesy of Roger Anderson). *Bottom:* Production Manager Karlson (left) and Superintendent Hall confer about final assembly of the Model 18.**

war on Germany on April 6, and the scarcity of raw materials brought on by the war caused Chandler to announce a price increase of $200 across the board for all models beginning July 1. Chandler would hold the line until June 30 but after that date the motoring public would pay more to own a Chandler.[9]

Saturday, June 2, was a joyous occasion for the Chandler factory as "Flag Raising Day" was celebrated. Chandler officials and employees participated in an employee sponsored ceremony, showing their patriotism for their country. A two-mile parade in which all employees, officials, and military personnel participated preceded the flag raising ceremony. The idea for the celebration originated with the hourly employees of the company, headed by O.O. Gilbert who was a veteran of the Spanish-American War. Chandler had lost many of its workers to the armed forces.[10]

Early August saw another gathering of Chandler distributors assembled in Cleveland for a three-day conference. The first day was devoted intensely to business. After a morning session on the second day, the afternoon was spent at League Park watching the Chicago White Sox and Cleveland Indians play baseball. Dinner followed at Waldruhe, an attractive country restaurant. The evening session was devoted to business, as was the following day. Sales manager Dunlap was kept busy speaking and discussing business and felt the conference was very much a success. In early August, Duffield Miles was appointed purchasing agent for Chandler. He succeeded Charles A. Carey, who had resigned and relocated to Jackson, Michigan, and a new career building refrigerators.[11]

On August 4 Chandler executives and employees made another excursion to Cedar Point for a day of amusement. This was the second of what would become an annual affair.[12]

At the November meeting of stockholders, a 2 percent dividend was declared payable on January 2, 1918, to stockholders of record on December 14. A special dividend of 1 percent was

Top: **Model 18 Seven Passenger Touring (factory photograph, author's collection).** ***Middle:*** **1918 Chandler with body attributed to Harley Earl (factory photograph, courtesy Roger Anderson).** ***Bottom:*** **Model 18 Seven Passenger Convertible Sedan.**

Top: **Model 18 Four Passenger Convertible Coupe.** ***Bottom:*** **A chassis being lowered to the final assembly floor where a body will be mounted.**

again voted in favor of the American Red Cross. Chandler's people were very patriotic and wanted to show their support for an organization which was giving aid and comfort to American soldiers serving their country during wartime.

Sometime during 1917, the Van Dorn Iron Works supplied material for another bridge 9 × 114 feet long between Building #1 and the H. J. Walker Company building. The Crowell-Lundoff-Little Company also built an elevated steel-framed bridge, which contained a monorail, between buildings #2 and #3. Both structures were designed by Ernest McGeorge. Other buildings constructed were a 60 × 16 foot tool shed and a 40 × 20 foot saw storage shed. During 1917 Chandler also purchased two tracts of land close to the factory: a semi-circular tract across 131st Street from the current factory and a triangular tract located on Coit Road at the end of 131st Street. The property across 131st Street was utilized almost immediately with the construction of a 290 foot loading dock along the site's rail siding. In addition to a shipping point the property would be utilized for vehicle storage.

The year ended with all bills paid and sufficient manufacturing material stockpiled to last for several months. Chandler officials had foreseen shortages and price increases and had stockpiled the necessary materials for manufacturing in advance. This put them in a much more favorable position to deal with shortages when they did come about. They also had $900,000 deposited in Cleveland area banks. For 1917 Chandler had manufactured 15,000 cars with gross income of $3,277,715, up $843,945 over 1916. Their net earnings of $2,328,403 for the year, before taxes—a gain of $666,235 over 1916—amounted to 34 percent of the $7 million of outstanding stock. Stockholder earnings amounted to $34 a share on outstanding stock compared to $25.50 for 1916.[13]

Chandler executives were beginning to be a factor in the automotive industry by 1918. At the annual meeting of the Society of Automotive Engineers in early January,

John V. Whitbeck, Chandler's chief engineer, was elected as one of three councilors.

With the new season came a new car. As 1918 dawned the Sport Model Touring was introduced. Actually, it had been introduced in the fall of 1917 but received little publicity except for inclusion in a late 1917 brochure. It was formally introduced at the New York Show, held on January 5–12 at the Grand Central Palace.

The hood was three inches higher with more and longer louvers. Body lines were generally straight with a noticeable drop in the body where the windshield joined the cowl, then flowing straight to the rear with the rear cowling hardly noticeable. The headlights sat high on a bar on all models, the Sport Touring having set the trend. This would be the forerunner of the new design, but the others would not follow until January of 1920 and the line would not fully change over until the 1921 models were introduced in October.

The Sport Model Touring was painted Electric Blue (body, hood and radiator shell) with black fenders and chassis. Trade publications and later Chandler literature reported the color as Copenhagen Blue. The price was $1,675 and for $110 more one could have five wire wheels, painted cream and riding on 32-inch tires with gear ratio of 3.78 to 1.

The windshield had a noticeable rake rearward and was higher. Mechanically, there were few changes other than the wheels. With this model, Chandler styling had finally come of age. The new model was introduced as the Sport Model, but factory literature also referred to it as the Despatch and Dispatch, finally settling for Dispatch, although the parts book would refer to it as the Despatch. Deliveries would begin immediately.[14]

At the show, the new model got plenty of attention but the Four Passenger Roadster, now being referred to as the "chummy type," received its share

***Top:* Model 18 Touring bodies being lowered onto chassis in the final assembly line. *Bottom:* Loading Chandlers into open rail cars due to shortage of boxcars.**

also. This model had accounted for one-third of Chandler sales in 1917 and its popularity was expected to continue unabated. Chandler again departed from its policy of blue only and showed the Roadster painted solid black and featuring wheels painted cream. Spectator acceptance was so good that Chandler decided to go to the Chicago Show with the same display.[15]

All enclosed bodies were now built by Fisher except the limousine, which was probably made by Willoughby.[16]

Prices held at the previous levels as the war in Europe continued to cause supply and delivery problems. In fact, freight cars were so scarce that Chandler started employing young women, as were many other manufacturers, to drive cars to their dealer destinations. All available men were either working or were in the armed forces, but there were women available and they were employed to do many jobs formerly done by their male counterparts. Although automobile manufacturing was not curtailed during the war it was affected by a shortage of material and railroads were using all available equipment to keep war materials flowing.[17]

During the war many manufacturers were being called upon to produce automobiles, trucks, planes, tanks and other equipment necessary to conduct a war. Chandler was no exception. Early in 1918 Chandler received an estimated $10 million contract for the production of 10-ton military tractors for the U.S. Army. These were the "crawler type" which were necessary to haul military equipment through the mud of the bat-

***Left:* Chandler ad announcing a price increase (*The Literary Digest*, June 9, 1917). *Below:* The Chandler factory in 1917.**

tlefields. The army designed these vehicles in consultation with manufacturers of similar equipment used in civilian life, one of which was the Holt Manufacturing Company of Stockton, California. They would be built under the license of the Holt patent with supervision by Holt. Later Holt would merge with the Best Tractor Company, another California concern, and form the Caterpillar Company, a name recognized by construction companies and road builders worldwide.[18]

The contract with the Army would take a few years to fulfill. The automobile factory was used to make as many parts as possible while buildings were being built on the site previously purchased across 131st Street from the factory and where a railroad siding and loading dock had just been built.

Ernest McGeorge, engineer, with offices in the Leader-News building, designed the new factory and the Sam W. Emerson Company began construction of the 400 × 80 foot building in March. Although only of one floor it was designed to have three more added. Chandler was thinking ahead to the time when the war would be over and more space to manufacture automobiles would be necessary.

Meanwhile the property at the end of 131st Street and Coit Road was being prepared as a test area for the military tractor that would soon be built. Joe Krall supervised construction of the test area and was cited by the U.S. Army Quartermaster Corps for his work.[19]

The first tractor building (#6) was completed in early July and tractor production began immediately. With a stockpile of

Top: 1918 Chandler Sport Model. _Bottom:_ Brothers August, Albert and Eugene Koch of Los Angeles with their Model 17 Touring cars.

parts on hand the work would proceed rapidly. As soon as Building #6 was completed the construction of two more buildings began. A 240 × 30 foot tractor paint shop and a 220 × 44 foot tractor test shop were completed in record time. They were constructed on the same side of the street as the first tractor building but closer to Coit Road. The A.A. Lane Construction Company of 1836 Euclid Avenue erected the buildings, which had been designed by Ernest McGeorge.

At the same time as the tractor buildings were being built, two office buildings in the automobile factory complex were being enlarged by installing a mezzanine floor in one and removing existing walls to double usable space in the other. This work was also performed by A.A. Lane on an accelerated schedule. Extra personnel needed to complete the Army contract necessitated more office space.

***Top:* Model 18 Dispatch (late version). *Bottom:* Model 17 Limousine (1917–1918).**

As coal for manufacturing grew scarce, the U.S. Government Fuel Administrator, Dr. H.A. Garfield, ordered all nonessential industries and businesses to shut down for one week. Chandler was shut up tight for the week of January 20–26. The street car company was put on a Sunday schedule, which caused essential industry workers problems and made schoolchildren late for school. Chandler, not to be deterred, moved part of its offices to the lobby of the Hollenden Hotel for the week.[20]

Many automobile manufacturers were engaged in the manufacture of equipment necessary for the war, and domestic production was drastically scaled back. In September 1918 Ford, Studebaker and Packard announced they would build no more cars until the conflict was over. Fortunately, the hostilities ended before the buying public was materially affected.

Chandler did get their tractor operation going and delivered 100 to the government in October, just weeks before the Armistice was signed. They expected to turn over 1,000 by January 1, 1919. But with the war over it was not certain that the full order could be completed. By March 1, it was clear that many contracts would be cancelled but others were allowed in order to resupply equipment which would be needed during peacetime.[21]

Very little is known of Chandler's wartime work and that was the way they wanted it. With a war in progress the U.S. government did not want its enemies or anyone not directly concerned with wartime production to know its business. For that reason Chandler never said anything about military tractor production until the conflict was over. The Ohio War Industries Board rode hard on all manufacturing during the conflict as all plans for building, buying and related activities would be done as locally as possible to save transportation costs. It did have one positive effect as all receipts and payments went through one government representative in Cleveland.

Prices of raw material, due to shortages brought on by the war, had increased to the point that Chandler was forced to raise the prices of all models by $200 on May 25, 1918. The Touring and Roadster, which had been selling for $1,295 in 1916, had undergone two price hikes in 1917, first to $1,395 and then to $1,595, and were now selling for $1,795—a 40 percent increase in slightly over two years.[22]

Above: Women's National Army Drivers (factory photograph, author's collection).
***Right:* Ten ton military tractor as received by U.S. Army.**

The war was affecting the prices of many other products, including food. Potatoes had become so expensive as to be almost out of reach for anyone of modest means. Although it did not compare to the great potato famine in Irish history, it nonetheless was causing a great hardship for Chandler's employees. The company, always mindful of the welfare of its workers, purchased a large supply from Michigan at a reduced price and distributed them to their employees at cost, which was considerably less than market value. Company service trucks delivered the potatoes to each individual worker's home. Chandler employee H.E. Price, who had received considerable recognition for his work with

Top: Charles Hopfensack's stolen roadster as it was found. _Bottom:_ New factory building where military tractors were built.

***Above:* Model 18 engine. *Right:* Model 18 Tourings in Nisqually Canyon with Mount Rainier in the background.**

the Red Cross and Liberty Loan campaign, was put in control of the potato distribution and did a most satisfactory job of it.[23]

Car thieves were very active around New York during the war years as a market for used parts flourished. Mr. Charles A. Hopfensack, sales manager for Brady-Murray, Chandler distributor in New York, had his new Four Passenger Roadster stolen from his residence at Broadway and 147th Street. This car had many extras added which must have been an inducement for the thieves. After several days he feared his car was gone forever, but a tip from a man who had rented a barn to someone who wanted a place for a repair shop caused police to investigate, and they caught the thieves red-handed. Hopfensack's car was completely dismantled but he carted it back to Brady-Murray and it was made into a window display, urging motorists to keep their automobiles out of the street and in garages if possible.[24]

Chandler had been able to offer a car at reasonable prices through the war but once again raised prices on November 4, 1918, to offset higher costs of raw materials. A substantial increase it was, with prices rising by $300.[25] Nineteen eighteen was the first year in the history of the automobile industry that yearly production had declined. Much of this was due to domestic manufacturing being scaled back for war production. The Chandler Company and its employees were very patriotic and along with other U.S. manufacturers, contributed greatly to the war effort.[26]

• FOUR •

1919–1922

Postwar Recession and Recovery

The automobile business was in the doldrums as 1919 opened. The war, with its price increases and many potential owners serving in the armed forces, had depressed the automobile industry. However, the doughboys would be coming home soon and the market would rebound somewhat.

There was no International Auto Show in New York for 1919. The NACC had decided to forgo automobile shows for the duration of the war, and although the ban was lifted when the war ended on November 11, NACC officials decided that sufficient time was not available for proper preparation to be made. And the Grand Central Palace, home to previous shows, was being used as an Army hospital.

Nevertheless, the Automobile Dealers Association of New York announced on November 30, 1918, that it would have its own show at Madison Square Garden in February or March. They finally settled on February 1–8 for cars and February 10–15 for trucks. Realizing that there would not be enough room to handle even the reduced demand for spaces, they announced on December 14 that the adjacent 69th Regiment Armory had been rented also. Patrons could attend either show or both on the same ticket, even on different days.

Chandler was there, in the armory, with the Dispatch, Touring, Coupe and Sedan. In addition to the automobiles displayed, New York State had a display of fake license plates which had been confiscated during the previous years and also a display of current plates from every state in the union and the territory of Hawaii.

There was also a Chicago show of some sort, at the Coliseum. Little information is available about this event, at which Thomas J. Hay, the Chandler distributor in Chicago, had an exhibit of cars on the main floor. A Dispatch, Touring and Four Door Convertible Sedan were shown.

The Seven Passenger Convertible Sedan was the only body style reworked for 1919. The hood now had taller louvers than the previous model and the body now had four doors. The Four Passenger Roadster and the Seven Passenger Touring would be restyled after the design of the Dispatch and released for sale on April 10. About this time, a Sedan and Coupe of conventional design were offered, replacing the old style Convertible Sedan and Coupe.

The complete line, with the exception of the Limousine, had now shed the Lozier look and vastly improved in appearance. The hood was three inches higher and featured considerably more louvers of the new taller type. When the 1920 models were released in September 1919, the Limousine would adopt the new styling also. All body designs still rode on the 123 inch wheelbase frame and were still powered by the "Marvelous Motor" which had been reworked in 1918.[1]

From January 11 through 18 the Motor Car Dealers Association of Los Angeles, California, held their eighth annual display of new automobiles. The lack of a building large enough to hold the event was overcome by renting and erecting three large tents with 150,000 square feet of floor space. These tents were decorated with oriental furnishings valued at $150,000 and cost the dealers $50,000 to rent. This was said to be the most beautiful setting for an automobile show that the Los Angeles area had ever seen. The automobile business on the West Coast had been stale for some time and the dealers were making a Herculean effort to revive it.

Pacific Coast body builders were invited to display their art at the show and some beautiful examples of craftsmanship were exhibited. One was a stunning Town Car built on a Chandler chassis. Low and long with motorcycle style fenders and individual step plates for running boards, it was a magnificent sight. The step plate running board design would influence Chandler's 1922 Royal Dispatch Model.[2] This magnificent specimen of automotive genius had been brought to the show by Earl Automobile Works of Los Angeles, a builder of custom bodies for mostly the Hollywood set, having gained popularity by doing work for the movie industry. J.W. Earl's son, Harley, was responsible for the creation which was described by the *Los Angeles Times* as the grandest design ever exhibited on the West Coast or anywhere else for that matter.[3]

King Vidor, a well-established movie director who would go on to become world famous, is reported to have paid $9,100 for the Chandler on the show floor. It was a gift for his movie star wife Florence Vidor, who also would become famous for her beauty and acting ability. She later sent the Chandler company a photo of the car with a note which read, "For dignified elegance and comfortable riding qualities I find that my Chandler town car meets every requirement."[4]

Harley Earl would go on to work for the famous custom body building firm of Don Lee, a prominent Cadillac dealer in Los Angeles, who purchased the Earl Automobile Works from Harley's father and made Harley the chief designer. In 1927 he would join General Motors as chief of the Art and Color Section. He would have a long and storied career at General Motors, his design ideas influencing automobile styling for decades.[5]

Not everyone who visited the Los Angeles Show could afford such luxury as King Vidor, but when the affair was over the dealers came away with the feeling that the automobile business was beginning its revival.

February 22, 1919, marked a major turning point in Chandler history. On that date the *Cleveland Plain Dealer* reported the formation of the Cleveland Automobile Company. Established as a separate company but headed largely by Chandler officers, Cleveland was to build a smaller, cheaper car in a new $400,000 factory. The news had been leaked to the automotive press on February 17. The second part of this book details the history of Cleveland.

Top: **1919–20 Seven Passenger Touring fitted with windwings, visor and front bumper (factory photograph, courtesy John W. Chandler).** ***Bottom:*** **1919–20 Seven Passenger Touring with custom California top (courtesy Roger Anderson).**

In March 1919, it was reported that orders for 3,823 of the 10 ton military tractors had been cancelled but that 628 were still needed. By that time 2,800 had been delivered, but it is not known with certainty how many of these were manufactured by Chandler. Supposedly, they did build and deliver 700. Chandler's military production, as noted earlier, occurred quietly, leaving little information for historians. With a war in progress, the less anyone knew about their work, the better it was for the U.S. government and all parties concerned.[6]

Early in 1919, Ernest Wooler resigned his position as engineer at Chandler to assume the duties of chief engineer at the new Cleveland Automobile Company.[7]

Chandler production took a hit in July when a strike at the Interstate Foundry Company of Cleveland left them without transmission cases and cylinder blocks. They had also been having problems with delivery of parts that were being made in Detroit, for more than a month. Alternate sources of supply would enable the company to resume full production within a week.

Being caught up in another manufacturer's labor problems was not good for business. Chandler fully realized that more room was needed for making their own parts and made plans accordingly, thereby reducing the need for outside suppliers.[8]

The war having caused Chandler to curtail some car production, they were unable to supply their dealers with all the cars they wanted. But by July 1919 they had fulfilled their obligation to the army and the buildings which had been used for artillery tractor production were available for automobile production. However, they were not suitable for that purpose in their present form. Chandler undertook a large expansion program immediately. Building #6, which was a single floor design, was now being renovated and enlarged to four floors, with the first floor fireproofed and two elevators added. John Gill and Son did the renovation and construction. The two elevator shafts connected to a tunnel which ran under 131st Street and joined the existing plant. These elevators and tunnel would prove vital when Chandler decided to build their own bodies. At the same time as the work on Building #6 was being done, John Gill and Son were constructing a 420 × 60 foot enlargement of Building #3. Ernest McGeorge had designed both projects, which were well under way in October.

Top: **1919–20 Four Passenger Roadster.** ***Middle:*** **1920 Chandler Dispatch fitted with side curtains, aftermarket disc wheels, spotlight and taillight (photograph courtesy of Roger Anderson).** ***Bottom:*** **1919 Chandler Touring car built on a late 1918 Sport Model chassis with a body design by Harley Earl (*Motor World*, January 23, 1919).**

This increased Chandler's production capacity by 80 to 100 percent.

With more production capacity also came a need for additional office space. A new five-story building, 90 × 42 feet, constructed by John Gill and Son adjoined Building #3, now under renovation, and contained a restaurant and dining rooms for employees and executives. Suitable waiting rooms for visiting distributors, dealers and salesmen were also included. The old two-story office building was renovated and became a part of the plant. A total of $1,000,000 was expended for all projects completed. Chandler also purchased additional land for stocking parts and storage about this same time.[9]

In August, Chandler earnings for the first seven months of 1919 amounted to $2,800,000 or about $40 per share of stock, before taxes. Also in August came numerous personnel changes at Chandler. Frank Connor, a veteran employee of the foreign sales department, was promoted to manager of that department, succeeding vice president W.S.M. Mead, who had held dual roles as manager of the Eastern sales department and foreign sales. Mead would now handle Eastern sales only and act as an advisor to Connor. Also in August, K.R. Spencer assumed the work of former assistant sales manager Sid Black, who had been appointed vice president in charge of sales at the Cleveland Automobile Company. R.C. Quincy was promoted to auditor, replacing Joseph I. Krall, who had taken the position of treasurer at the Cleveland Automobile Company. George F. McGinnis was promoted to assistant purchasing agent, succeeding R.C. Hodge, who had moved to the Cleveland Automobile Company as purchasing agent. Charles E. Lohr took over the production department duties of Edward Karlson, who had joined the Cleveland Automobile Company as factory superintendent. O.T. Hillshafer was promoted to service manager and R.M. Fraser assumed Mr. Hillshafer's former duties of assistant sales manager.[10]

The 1920 Chandler models made their appearance in September. By now all body styles had received a welcome infusion of good looks, featuring the high hood, straight line design.

The Coupe and Sedan were no longer the convertible type with the removable posts and hardtop look. Why did Chandler drop the Convertible Coupe and Sedan? The lawsuit which

Top: **Movie star Florence Vidor owned this 1919 Chandler Town Car built on a late 1918 Sport chassis (photograph courtesy Roger Anderson).** ***Bottom:*** **1920–21 Four Passenger Coupe (factory photograph, author's collection).**

Springfield had started against Fisher in November of 1916 had been settled. Perhaps the popularity of the design had simply played out. Both models were now a truly conventional design. The Coupe had a unique seating arrangement with the driver's seat to the left extending rearward slightly past the passenger seat. The seat for the fourth passenger was located to the right of the driver and could be folded away when not needed. The limousine was well appointed with mahogany paneling, an autophone, mahogany smoking and toilet cases, a dome light, reading light and automatic step lights.

Chandler ended 1919 with six body styles in production, finances in excellent condition and the future of the company looking bright. Prices increased by $100 on all models at the beginning of 1920.[11]

Chandler took a hit early in January when it was revealed that one Manuel de Silva Carmo of Oporto had obtained control of the automobile markets of Europe and South America by simply registering the copyright trademarks in his name for several countries. Under the Berne Trademark Convention he was entitled to register 43 trademarks in Portugal, thereby giving him rights to these trademarks in Switzerland, Holland, Mexico, Italy, Hungary, Austria, Belgium, Brazil, Spain, France and Tunisia as well as Portugal. Chandler's Cleveland neighbor Jordan was another company affected by this chicanery. The ruse was discovered when Albert E. Parker, an attorney, attempted to register Jordan and Mercer trademarks in Europe. Under existing laws nothing could be done; Carmo was the only person authorized to sell those brands registered in his name and had the right to confiscate any vehicle sold by anyone but himself. This ploy had been worked on several tire manufacturers in 1918 and the automobile makers should have been aware of such schemes.[12]

On March 15, 1920, Duffield Miles resigned as Chandler's purchasing agent, a position he had held for three years, to take over the general manager's job at the Automobile Machine Company, a jointly owned subsidiary of both Chandler and the Cleveland Automobile Company. He apparently had been appointed purchasing agent in 1917, about the time Charles A. Carey left that position at Chandler. Mr. Miles was succeeded as purchasing agent by George E. McGinnis, who had previously been appointed as assistant purchasing agent.[13]

Although Chandler introduced no new body styles during 1920, prices fluctuated wildly. The $100 hike which went into effect in January was followed by another $100 increase in May, and in August the Four Passenger Coupe and Seven Passenger Sedan had their prices bumped up another $100. Somewhere between August 1 and September, prices rose another $100, but a Chandler brochure dated September 30, 1920, showed the prices reduced by $200. However, Chandler's brochure prices did not always match those quoted in magazine ads.[14]

During 1920 the Fisher Body Company constructed a new factory on Coit Road in Cleveland. Fisher Body Ohio was incorporated at $10 million with $350,000 going toward the construction of a five story building. Fisher had started with

Top: **1921 Chandler Coupe (courtesy Roger Anderson).** ***Bottom:*** **1921 Chandler Limousine.**

Chandler building the Convertible Sedan and Coupe and would now build practically all Chandler bodies. The exception to this would be the Seven Passenger Limousine which was built by both Milburn and Willoughby. Briggs had started out furnishing most Chandler bodies, but by 1918 Fisher seemed to have captured the business. The new factory was only two blocks from the Chandler location. The first body delivery occurred on October 30, 1921, and went to Chandler. Fisher also supplied bodies for the Cleveland Automobile Company.[15]

Homes for automobile workers were scarce in Cleveland, which prompted the manufacturing companies to organize the Capital Housing Company. In April, the Chamber of Commerce joined with the automotive companies, some of which were already involved in this effort to provide affordable housing. Chandler also was considering joining the effort.

October saw the Seven Passenger Touring, Four Passenger Roadster and Four Passenger Dispatch having their prices reduced by $100, back to the price at which they were selling in January. Coal and material shortages were still plaguing the automobile industry even though the war had been over for a year.[16]

Chandler began 1921 with seven "Splendid Body Types." Six were carryovers from the previous year, but a new two passenger Roadster joined the line. Created by demand, the new version was a snappy looking job and would be popular with businessmen who needed storage space for their wares. In addition to the trunk, the car offered ample space behind the seat. Chandler again departed from tradition by painting the new body style a pleasing shade of gray which was later listed as Battleship Gray.

By March 1921, prices once again rose. The Seven Passenger Touring was now $1,930, the Four Passenger Dispatch $2,010 and the Four Passenger Roadster $1,930. The new Two Passenger Roadster sold for $1,930, the Four Passenger Coupe for $2,930 and the Five Passenger Limousine for $3,530.[17] The automobile industry had had a slow year in 1920, and 1921 would be harder as a recession brought on by the end of the war was now gripping the nation.

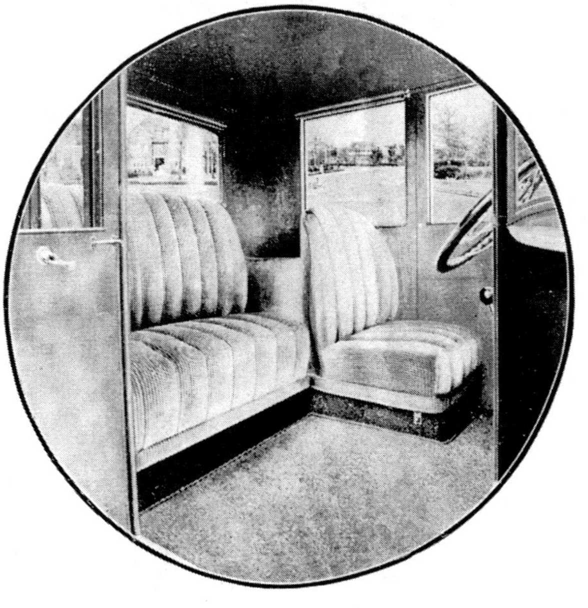

***Top:* 1921 Two Passenger Roadster. *Middle:* 1921 Dispatch. *Bottom:* 1921 Four Passenger Coupe interior.**

The new year began with the economy in a terrible state. Things were so bad that Chandler began looking for someone who could help right the ship. One of the moves they made was to lure George M. Graham away from Pierce-Arrow. He had been vice president there and would hold the same title at Chandler, taking charge of sales, advertising and service. Chandler had diluted their executive staff with the formation of the Cleveland Automobile Company and the need for new talent was evident.

In January Hiram Walker was advanced from assistant engineer to chief engineer at Chandler. J.V. Whitbeck, finding that being president of the Cleveland Automobile Company and chief engineer at Chandler was more work than one man could do, resigned his position at Chandler.

Chandler advertising continued at its pre–1921 pace until about June when it virtually dried up and did not resume its former level until the new body designs were released in early 1922.[18] On June 13, Chandler reduced the price of its Touring car to $1,785, the same as it sold for at the beginning in 1913. Prices of all other body styles were slashed accordingly.[19]

On August 20, the Chandler Company was saddened to learn of the death of Charles A. Emise. Still a vice president of the company, he was living in Edgewater, New Jersey, at the time of his death. Emise had been ill for several years but maintained his interests in the company. Fred C. Chandler, Samuel Regar and W.S.M. Mead attended the funeral.[20]

When things were going well Chandler produced enough automobiles to satisfy the demand. When the economy turned sour, they continued to make more than the dealers could handle. They also had a large supply of parts needed for manufacturing, well in excess of demand. The decision to redesign for the 1922 models left Chandler with an inventory which they did not need. Nonetheless the

***Top:* 1921 Four Passenger Roadster. *Middle:* 1921 Seven Passenger Touring. *Bottom, left:* George Graham, Chandler vice president for advertising, sales and service. *Bottom, right:* Hiram Walker, Chandler chief engineer, January 1921.**

company opted to scrap tons of material and go with the new design rather than risk continuing with the same line of cars. Another year like 1921 and a lot of automobile makers would be out of business.

At their meeting on December 14, Chandler's directors voted a $1.50 dividend to stockholders of record by December 24. Speculators had been predicting that the stock would fall and were selling it short. Although this dividend had not been earned it was paid out of the surplus, and it seemed to achieve a desired effect. Chandler stock rose by 6.5 points, from 45½ to 52. Although 1921 had been a very bad business year, stockholders were still ahead of the game as they had received $8,677,750 in dividends since the inception of the company. In fact, economic conditions were so poor, Chandler discontinued the *Chandler Bulletin* (company newsletter) for several months.

As 1922 began, Fred C. Chandler welcomed dealers and distributors from across the country to a big conference at the Hollenden Hotel in Cleveland on Friday, January 6. They were there to see what was available for the new year and to get assurance that Chandler was doing everything possible to help them market automobiles.

After a short welcoming address, Mr. Chandler turned the meeting over to George M. Graham, the new vice president in charge of sales, advertising and service. Mr. Graham had been associated with Chandler for only a short while, leaving a vice president's job at Pierce-Arrow to assume like duties at his new employer. He was a veteran executive in the automobile industry, and Chandler expectations were that his expertise would help to turn things around. Mr. Graham outlined many ideas for selling. Chandler would have eighteen district managers and each one would be responsible to see that his territory was fully represented by a Chandler dealer in every town of 5,000 or more—and this was to be accomplished in three months. A high powered advertising campaign was to begin immediately, not only by the parent company but by distributors and dealers, with Chandler communicating with them on a fixed schedule every week. Graham gave a lengthy talk, touching on what was wrong with the industry and what could be done about it before relinquishing the podium to Hiram Walker, Chandler's chief engineer. Walker then proceeded with an equally lengthy address touching upon 24 major points where the Chandler had been improved. And improved it was—top to bottom and front to rear! In truth, only the Marvelous Motor was spared with everything else being of new design.[21]

The body received the majority of change. Gone were the beveled edges, replaced with flowing corners. The fenders were now motorcycle-style, running boards were replaced by individual aluminum step plates and the radiator shell was now nickel plated. Running boards were available if desired, but no cars so equipped were displayed. Black and nickeled drum type headlights graced the front and miniature versions were mounted on the cowl. The top had been lowered and reworked, the tail light bracket was now attached to the frame and the windshield stanchions were nickel plated. Chandler was not alone in using step plates as H.C.S. and Cleveland, among others, did likewise.

Substantial mechanical changes came for 1922, too. The frame was beefed up with more crossmembers and was now 37 percent stronger. Springs were increased ¼ inch in width and 2½ inches in length, with the rear being underslung, and the emergency brake was moved from the rear wheels to the rear of the transmission. Universal joints were now flexible discs, the rear axles and housing were 27 percent stronger, the transmission had been made smoother and the differential was now of the Hotchkiss design. The torque arm, which had been a feature of every Chandler, was eliminated. Many other small changes combined with these to make the new car practically a total redesign.

An array of new colors arrived, but the fenders remained black as did the wheels, which received a delicate white stripe.[22]

Probably the most welcome news was a lower price on some body styles, with the Two Passenger Roadster and Seven Passenger being reduced by $185. The Coupe was reduced by $500 and the Limousine by $490. All other prices remained steady.

The new Five Passenger Touring car was priced at $1,595, as were the Two Passenger and Four Passenger Roadster. The Seven Passenger Touring now went for $1,695, as did the Four Passenger Dispatch. The Four Passenger Coupe sold at $2,295, the Seven Passenger Sedan at $2,395 and the Seven Passenger Limousine at $2,995.[23]

1922 Four Passenger Coupe.

A new design, a new body style and reduced prices were promising steps to bring Chandler back to profitability. The dealers liked what they were seeing and hearing. That afternoon they saw the new cars and received demonstrations as well. Communication was not one of Chandler's shortcomings as proven by the events of the convention. A copy of the *Chandler Bulletin* was handed to each dealer as they boarded the trolley for a tour of the factory that afternoon, and a second edition was passed out when they reached the factory.

On arriving at the factory the convention attendees were ushered into a "Little Theater" built especially for the first showing of the new Chandler line. A 12 foot revolving stage allowed the dealers and distributors to view the entire car from their seats. As one body style was driven from the stage another would be driven on until all had been displayed.

On viewing the new creations the dealers were astonished to see the Touring car and Four Passenger Roadster painted in Chandler Green; Dispatch and Two Passenger Roadster in Chandler Maroon and the Sedans, Coupe and Limousine in Chandler Blue. Optional colors were Chandler Blue for the Touring car; Chandler Maroon for the Four Passenger Roadster; Chandler Twilight Grey for the Dispatch and Two Passenger Roadster; and Chandler Green for the Sedan, Coupe and Limousine.

Top: **Original 100,000 mile club member's plaque (courtesy Chris & Jill Gorman).** ***Bottom:*** **1922 Five Passenger Touring.**

On Saturday morning, the dealers and distributors were treated to a tour of the Fisher Body facility on Coit Road. Saturday night saw all attending a gala banquet where entertainment was grand, food delicious and liquid refreshment plentiful. In fact, the attendees were so enthusiastic that at midnight Tom Cahill, who was in charge of transportation, had a difficult time getting them all aboard two special trains that were to take them to New York for more entertainment at Chandler's expense. This included viewing the big auto show then in progress at the Grand Central Palace. A third copy of the *Chandler Bulletin* was handed out as the train departed and a fourth copy would be awaiting them when they returned home.[24]

The new models sold well, and it was not long before the recession was history. Soon Chandler's new body styles gained a couple of siblings.

Looking to attract new owners and be of aid to those who already owned a Chandler, the company opened a touring service in March. Housed at the factory, it allowed owners to avail themselves of information concerning any trip they were planning. Maps, road conditions, types of pavement and known hazards could be had for the asking if you owned a Chandler.[25] Previous to this, Chandler had formed a club for owners who had driven their Chandlers 100,000 miles or more. In April they announced that all club members would receive a beautiful nickeled plaque with a blue background for display on their automobile.

On May 2, Pierre S. du Pont, president and chairman of the board of directors of General Motors, visited Cleveland to inspect the new Fisher Body of Ohio plant which had recently been completed. Others in attendance included a number of high ranking General Motors officials, several Cleveland businessmen who helped finance the new factory, six of the Fisher brothers and several officials from Cleveland industries and automobile companies. Fred C. Chandler and Samuel Regar from Chandler along with J.V. Whitbeck from the Cleveland Automobile Company were also in the group. With both Chandler and Cleveland purchasing bodies from Fisher, it was in their interest to be there. Du Pont made the trip because General Motors owned 60 percent of Fisher common stock, having purchased it in 1919, and would have it all by June 1926. The Fisher Ohio plant, largest of all Fisher plants, was producing 300 bodies per day with the output expected to increase dramatically in the near future.[26]

When the Cleveland Chamber of Commerce held its annual business meeting in June for the election of officers, Fred C. Chandler, who had been a member of the Board of Directors for some time, was reelected for another term. Another Cleveland automaker, Edward S. "Ned" Jordan, was elected to his first term as a member of the Board.[27]

Without fanfare Chandler had introduced a new Five Passenger Sedan into the lineup in June. The Metropolitan was a four door family sedan with an interior finished in silken mohair and with wide seats, just the right depth for comfort. Glass in all doors lowered and there were small package compartments on both sides of the rear seats. The two side and rear windows were equipped with silk roll curtains. There was a trunk space at the rear and aluminum step plates were standard.

In July the stunning Royal Dispatch was introduced. The Dispatch had always been a beautiful car, but now it had been refined to a state of perfection. New steel disc wheels (or wire for an extra cost) replaced the wooden wheels. Twin sidemounts now left space at the rear for a trunk rack set off by five vertical protection rails which added much to the appearance. The introductory price was $1795.

August brought price cuts on all body styles, ranging from $20 to $300. The Five Passenger Touring, Four Passenger (Chummy) Roadster and Two Passenger Roadster dropped from $1595 to $1495, the Seven Passenger Touring and Dispatch from $1695 to $1645 and the new Royal Dispatch from $1795 to $1745. Closed cars received the greatest reductions as the Five and Seven Passenger Sedans fell from $2595 to $2295, the Limousine from $2,995 to $2,895 and the Coupe from $2,295 to $1,995.

On September 2, the H.J. Walker Company announced that 75,000 shares of no par common stock would be offered for sale at five dollars per share. Walker had moved to Cleveland in order to do work exclusively for Chandler and had a machine shop in the Chandler complex. Apparently Walker was no longer doing Chandler's work but had started building engines on its own. By 1920 they were supplying engines for the entire line of the Grant Brothers Automobile Company of Cleveland, but by 1921 their engines were used in one body style only. The Walker factory was not working due to a lack of capital and this was an effort by company directors to satisfy their creditors and bondholders and get the company working again. Apparently, Chandler had severed relations with Walker and was doing its own machine work.

In an experiment conducted by automobile manufacturers, the engineers of the various companies would exchange cars. Chandler would loan its car to the Peerless engineer and

Top: 1922 Limousine. *Middle:* 1922 Royal Dispatch (factory photograph, author's collection). *Bottom:* 1922 Seven Passenger Sedan.

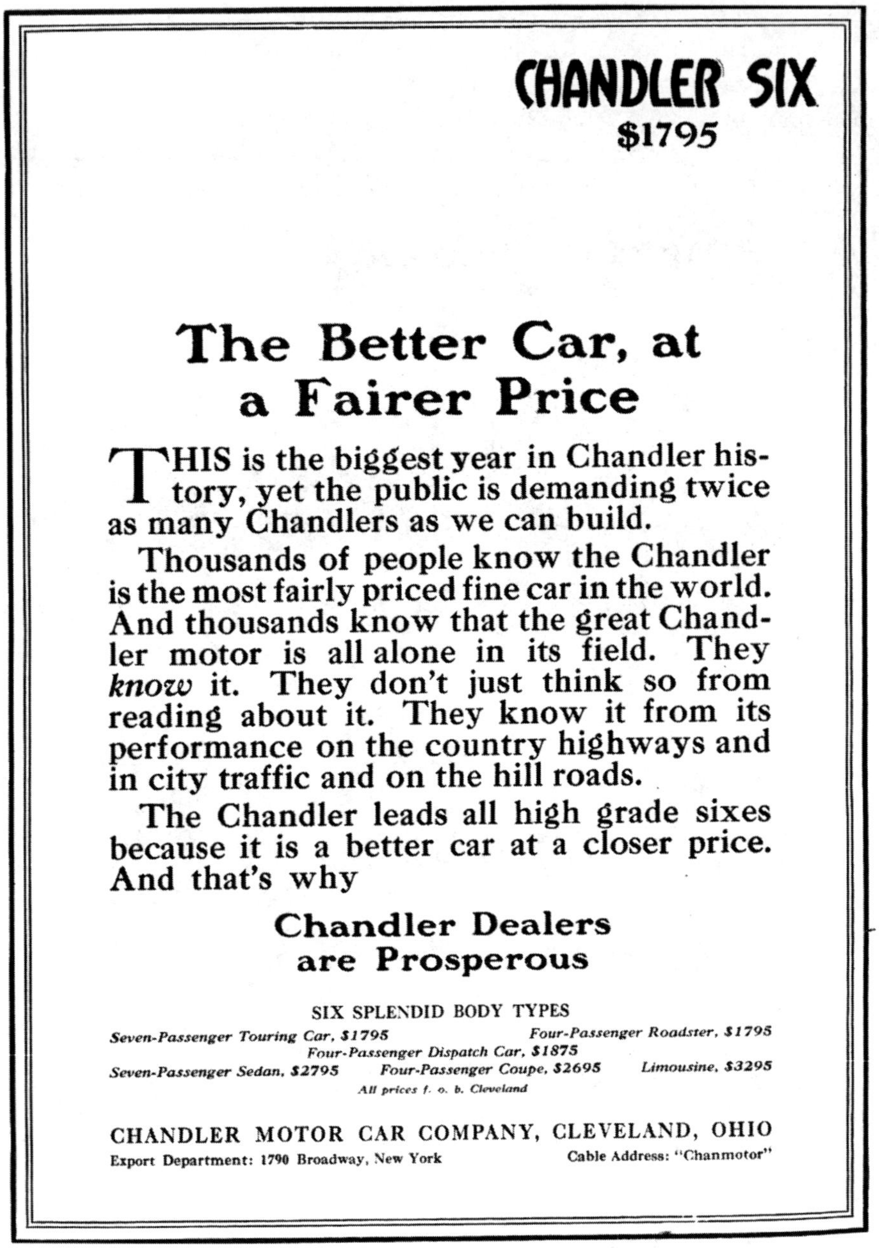

Chandler ad from the back cover of *Motor Age*, September 25, 1919.

in turn the Chandler engineer would drive a Peerless. This was all conjured up by George Graham, Chandler vice-president at a meeting of the Cleveland section of the Society of Automotive Engineers.[28]

By November 1922 the war had been over for four years and the postwar recession was a thing of the past. With the economy back to normal and budget constraints now relaxed, Chandler decided to exhibit at the London Motor Car Show, an international event, beginning on November 3. Chandler was one of 18 U.S. entries in the exhibit of 159 makers.[29]

• Five •

1923–1924

The Pikes Peak Motor and Traffic Transmission

Chandler began 1923 in a big way by hosting a three-day convention of distributors and dealers from across the nation. The company had been guarded as to what the new year would bring, but the secret would be revealed on Wednesday, January 3, at the Hollenden Hotel. Hundreds of distributors and dealers poured into Cleveland for two days and one special train brought 70 representatives from the Herbert Brothers, Chandler distributors for the Philadelphia area.

At 10 o'clock sharp on Wednesday, Fred C. Chandler welcomed the group and spoke for a short while before relinquishing the podium to George Graham, vice president, who spoke until 12 noon when the group broke for lunch. At 1 o'clock the throng took special streetcars to the factory for a tour.

During demonstration rides that afternoon, Gates Mills, a small community outside Cleveland, was a popular destination. Cleveland car manufacturers often chose to demonstrate their vehicles there because the hills in that area seemed to challenge a car's performance. The rides continued all day, ceasing only when it was time for the evening banquet at the Hollenden.

Thursday brought more of the same, ending with a party at Keith's new Palace Theater where Sophie Tucker was performing, making her entrance in a new Royal Dispatch.

Friday featured an afternoon program designed for distributors, dealers, salesmen and service personnel. Chandler demonstrated a variety of advertising aids for the dealers and distributors, enabling them to return home ready for the new selling season.[1]

What the dealers and distributors saw when they arrived in Cleveland was a line of automobiles that were much improved in appearance. The chassis was lower, the radiator shell taller and deeper, the lines of the hood and cowl more graceful; in addition the tops of the open cars adopted a new design.

Amid a number of other refinements, the greatest improvement was the new "Pikes Peak" engine, so named because Chandler engineers had spent many months testing the new design on the tortuous roads of that mountain. It had also been tested on the famous hill at Uniontown, Pennsylvania, and various other locations throughout the country. Having been in development since July 1919, it was now ready to be tested by the public. All 1923 Chandlers would be powered by this engine. Billed as "The Engine Built to Master a Mountain," it lived up to the slogan. Chandler was so proud of the new power plant that they patented the name. And proud they should have been because it was a vast improvement over the engine that had served so well for the past ten years. In a radical departure from the previous "Marvelous Motor," the new L-head engine adopted a monobloc cylinder block casting with a detachable head and bore and stroke of 3½ × 5 inches. A redesigned intake manifold gave a more even flow of gasoline to all cylinders. The pistons were engineered to give higher compression and utilized heavier piston pins. A much heavier crankshaft rode in four main bearings, and the camshaft was also made heavier with larger bearings.

The fan was now a high efficiency six blade affair and a V-type belt replaced the previous flat one. The water pump was improved and a gear-driven oil pump mounted on the side of the crankcase allowed for easy servicing. Driving chains were reduced from three to two, with the timing chain being externally adjustable. All 1923 models came with a distributor as standard equipment or a magneto at extra cost.[2]

During the long development process, a contingent of Chandler executives and engineers, including Ralph Mulford, driver and engineer, took four cars to the famous Colorado mountain and tested for weeks before they came up with the combination they wanted in the new engine. Some of the higher echelon Chandler executives, including Fred C. Chandler himself, paid occasional visits to watch the work in progress. Finally, having satisfied themselves that the new creation was worthy, they released it for production.

Left and above: 1923 Royal Dispatch (factory photographs, courtesy Donn Wirtz).

Above: The Pikes Peak engine. *Right:* Trademark registration (U.S. Patent Office, Washington, D.C.). *Below:* Fred C. Chandler at Pikes Peak.

Registered Jan. 8, 1924. **Trade-Mark 178,203**

UNITED STATES PATENT OFFICE.

THE CHANDLER MOTOR CAR COMPANY, OF CLEVELAND, OHIO.

ACT OF FEBRUARY 20, 1905.

Application filed November 17, 1922. Serial No. 172,145.

PIKES PEAK

STATEMENT.

To all whom it may concern:

Be it known that The Chandler Motor Car Company, a corporation duly organized under the laws of the State of Ohio, and located in the city of Cleveland, county of Cuyahoga, and State of Ohio, and doing business at East 131st St. and St. Clair Ave., Cleveland, Ohio, has adopted and used the trade-mark shown in the accompanying drawing, for INTERNAL-COMBUSTION ENGINES, in Class 23, Cutlery, machinery, and tools, and parts thereof.

The trade mark has been continuously used in the business of said corporation since about October 1, 1922.

The trade mark is applied to the goods by placing thereon a label or a plate on which the trade mark is shown, or it may be stamped or stenciled thereon.

THE CHANDLER MOTOR CAR COMPANY,
By ISADOR GROSSMAN,
Secretary.

PRESIDENT F.C. CHANDLER, AT WHEEL OF ONE OF THE TEST CARS, FINISHING CLIMB TO TOP OF PEAK.

Ralph Mulford, a mechanical wizard as well as one of the best race car drivers in the world, had come to the attention of Charles A. Emise in 1901. When Mulford repaired a boat motor for a Mr. Hedenburg of Fairhaven, New Jersey, Emise was so impressed with the young man's work that he recommended that Lozier, then building launches and motors at Plattsburg, New York, hire the lad of 16 as an engine mechanic. They did and he spent the next several years as a mechanic/engineer, finally graduating to automobile engines and then becoming a race driver. He piloted a Lozier in the inaugural Indianapolis 500. Most everyone thought he won the race—everyone, that is, except the official scorer, who, after considerable deliberation and delay, awarded him second. A Marmon "Wasp," a hometown manufactured car, was awarded first. There was considerable debate among the racing fraternity over this incident but Mulford, being the gentleman he was, shrugged it off and never became bitter at losing what he thought was surely a win.[3]

All closed models and the Royal Dispatch were fitted with 33 × 4½ inch tires. All other body styles received 32 × 4 tires, and on cars with wood wheels the number of front spokes increased from ten to twelve. Wheelbase remained at 123 inches.[4]

Chandler went to the New York and Chicago shows with a lineup of eight cars, the Two Passenger Roadster, Coupe and Dispatch having been dropped. With the Royal Dispatch being so popular, there was no need to build the less expensive version. The Chummy Five Passenger had just been added to the line. The Chummy would be called a Sedan when in reality it was a two door coach. However, both front seats folded forward, allowing passengers to enter from either side.

Prices had been adjusted somewhat with the Five Passenger Touring car now selling for $1,395, the Four Passenger Roadster and Seven Passenger Touring for $1,595 and $1,545, the Royal Dispatch and Chummy Sedan for $1,695 and the new Metropolitan Sedan for $2,195. The Seven Passenger Sedan and Limousine were now the most expensive at $2,295 and $2,995 respectively.

Step plates were standard on all models except the Five Passenger Touring and Chummy Sedan, which were fitted with running boards and a black radiator shell. All other body styles were equipped with the nickel plated radiator shell.[5]

From all available data, Fisher Body appears to have built all Chandler bodies at this point, in its new factory on Coit Road.

All closed models were painted blue as were the Five and Seven Passenger Touring cars. The Four Passenger Roadster and Royal Dispatch both came in a special green and had Disteel wheels fitted as standard equipment. All body styles were one-half inch lower thanks to a new dropped front axle along with underslung rear springs.

In 1923 Chandler's hill-climbing and racing ability would

Top: **1923 Chummy Sedan.** ***Middle:*** **1923 Metropolitan Sedan (both factory photographs, courtesy Donn Wirtz). Bottom: A 1923 Five Passenger Touring on an outing (courtesy Roger Anderson).**

be put to the test. It seems everyone who purchased the new model with the Pikes Peak engine wanted to go test it on a hill or in a race. Competition will be covered in some detail in Chapter Eleven.

A fire at the United States Malleable Casting Company of Toledo, destroyed the factory on April 6. This caused a disruption at Chandler as the company was one of their suppliers. Also in April, Fred C. Chandler and some company executives were extended an invitation to the International Automobile Exposition to be held in Gothenburg, Sweden, on May 9. On April 26, George M. Graham, Chandler vice-president, was the toastmaster for the Society of Automotive Engineers meeting held in Cleveland.[6]

Chandler was not only doing well in racing and hill climbing but was again prospering financially. Employees received a handsome bonus on July 30, as $200,000 was distributed among all employees. Each employee received from 10 to 13 percent of their yearly wages, the higher percentage going to those with the longest time at the company. This was profit sharing at its best and Chandler wanted to keep their employees happy. As a consequence, labor problems never were a bother to Chandler. In fact, Chandler was doing exceptionally well. The company estimated a profit of $1,250,000 for the first quarter of 1923. This amounted to $4.50 per share of Chandler stock.[7]

On July 29 company employees learned that James M. Dunlap, Chandler's former director of sales and advertising, had died at Rockford, Illinois. Dunlap had succeeded Charles A. Emise in that position in 1916 when Emise left active participation in the affairs of the company. The very next day, on July 30, Chandler employees were saddened to learn that Roger M. Fraser, purchasing agent, had also expired. He was a longtime employee, having joined the company in 1916. E. J. Filiatrault, a veteran Chandler employee who had worked his way up through the purchasing department ranks, succeeded Fraser as chief purchasing agent.[8]

***Top:* 1923 Five Passenger Touring (factory photograph, author's collection). *Bottom:* 1923–24 Chandler Limousine (factory photograph, courtesy Donn Wirtz).**

Chandler treated a large party of super salesmen from across the United States to a short, thrilling vacation in August. Ten Chandler cars were shipped from the factory to Colorado Springs, where they were prepared by the engineering staff under the direction of Ralph Mulford and Fred C. Chandler, Jr., for an assault on Pikes Peak and the surrounding area. Forty-seven visitors climbed the mountain, where they encountered a severe snowstorm in the middle of August. They also visited various other tourist attractions in the nearby vicinity. The frivolity became subdued and entertainment was cancelled when news of the death of U.S. President Warren G. Harding was announced.[9]

On September 16, a caravan of 50 cars left New York City headed for California. Dubbed the "California Caravan," it was just a collection of automobile enthusiasts having fun. The route had been scouted by Syl McDowell and Warren K. Fryer of California under sponsorship by the Santa Monica Chamber of Commerce. The car

1924 Automobile Show, San Francisco (factory photograph, courtesy Roger Anderson).

used as a pathfinder was a 1923 Chandler Five Passenger Touring powered by the new Pikes Peak engine. Cities visited along the way were Columbus, Indianapolis, St. Louis, Kansas City, Denver, Colorado Springs, Santa Fe, and Albuquerque with the end point being Santa Monica.[10]

Chandler announced the lineup of 1924 models on September 23. They had abandoned the model designations with the introduction of the New Series after the Model 17. Some still called the first New Series the Model 18, but that is where the model numbers ended. The 1924 body styles were basically clones of the 1923 models with a few changes and additions. An aluminum cowl band had been added to all models. This served to protect the paint as the hood was being raised and lowered as well as giving a touch of class to the new models. Aluminum kick plates were added to all models with running boards, lending another touch of elegance to the already good looking bodies. Running boards were optional on all models equipped with step plates and step plates were optional at an extra cost on the Seven Passenger Touring. All body styles except the Chummy Sedan and Five Passenger Touring came with nickeled radiator shells.[11]

The one new body style introduced was the gorgeous Two Passenger Comrade Roadster, which made its debut on November 5, 1923. With the spare tire mounted on a rakish angle at the rear, windwings, pin striping, and disc wheels, it was a beautiful car—more so if it was equipped with wire wheels. The price was attractive at $1,695. Aluminum bars were placed between the trunk space and the top to protect the paint when the top was down. For now the car provided a single seat for 2–3 passengers, but a rumble seat was in the future. Paint was light brown or light blue as an option.

Chandler's reason for introducing a new one-seat roadster

is not clear because they had just recently dropped a roadster of practically the same design. Breaking from the tradition of using Fisher bodies, the Comrade Roadster wore a body by the Ohio Body & Blower Company.

Two new sedans also joined the lineup, although they were not shown until the New York Auto Show opened on Saturday, January 5, 1924. A four door Five Passenger Sedan joined the Metropolitan Sedan as an economy version of its fancy counterpart, priced at $1,895 and lacking the nickel plated radiator shell, aluminum protective bars at the rear and a few other frills. The rear side window was rounded at the bottom rear corner and running boards replaced step plates.

A new Seven Passenger Sedan also joined the economy line, similarly devoid of nickeled radiator shell and bearing running boards and an interior less fancy than the other Seven Passenger Sedan. At an economical price of $2,095, it was a good choice for those needing a large closed car. The more expensive version sold at $2,385 and came equipped with step plates.

The Chummy Sedan and Four Door Sedan were also offered in a special version. Their nickeled front bumper and radiator shell, rear view mirror, deluxe trunk rack

1924 Chandler Prices

Model	Pass.	Price
Touring	5	$1485
Touring	7	1635
Comrade Roadster	2-3	1695
Roadster	4	1685
Royal Dispatch	4	1785
Chummy Sedan	5	1745
Chummy Special	5	*1845
Four-Door Sedan	5	1895
Four-Door Special	5	*1995
Metropolitan Sedan	5	2270
New Seven Sedan	7	2095
Sedan	7	2385
Limousine	7	2995

*Special models include front bumper, nickel radiator shell, rear view mirror, de luxe trunk rack, and light blue color.

Top: **1924 Comrade Roadster (factory photograph, courtesy John W. Chandler).** ***Middle:*** **1924 Four Door Sedan for Five Passengers (factory photograph, courtesy Donn Wirtz).** ***Bottom, left:*** **1924 Chandler price list.** ***Bottom, right:*** **1924 Chummy Special (factory photograph, courtesy Roger Anderson).**

and bars and light blue paint made these slightly more appealing than their plain counterparts. The Chummy Special at $1,845 and Four Door Special at $1,995 were each priced just $100 above their standard counterparts. One wonders why the sedan was offered in a special version which moved it closer to the Metropolitan Sedan priced at $2,270.

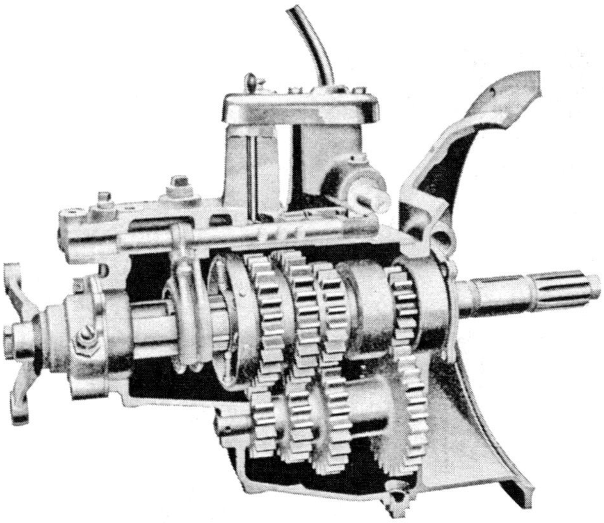

What the Traffic Transmission Means to the Woman Motorist

The following comment on the 1924 Chandler won a prize in the Traffic Transmission Week contest held at San Francisco. It is particularly interesting as an expression of the typical point of view of the woman motorist.

By Mrs. John E. Carr
168 Kellogg Ave., Palo Alto, California

BEING a woman, I do not know anything about a car's insides. What is more, I do not want to have to learn.

I do know this: I was not the least bit fussed when driving the Chandler with the Traffic Transmission. I just drove it, that's all.

There is really nothing to it. The first thing I noticed was how easily it operated. Only a slight pressure was needed to move the lever. The simplicity of it was positively fascinating. Then the salesman told me to shift from high back to second. I did that and then from second to low. It was just as easy as going up.

Then we went down a long steep hill and I found that I could completely control the speed of the car by shifting gears and was not obliged to tire myself holding down a foot brake.

I suppose that the men find the principle of this Traffic Transmission very interesting. My husband and his father discussed it for an hour. What they said was all Greek to me.

The thing that impressed me was this: That operating the new Chandler with the Traffic Transmission is so simple and easy and requires so little effort, either mental or physical, that a woman finds herself free to devote all her attention to the problems of the traffic. She is relieved of that feeling of suspense.

With my present car I often go out of the way avoiding hills and traffic to escape the annoyance of shifting gears. Gear-shifting makes me so nervous. Sometimes I do it all right and then for no apparent reason they grind and clash and make me feel that I am doing something terrible.

But when I drove the Chandler, "up" hill and "down" looked the same to me and I was not the least bothered in the thick traffic, though it was the first time I ever tried the Traffic Transmission. Somehow it gave me a new feeling of confidence.

My husband is always threatening to buy me a car with a set of rubber gears in the transmission. I think I will ask for the Chandler instead.

Prices of the other models were $1,635 for the Seven Passenger Touring, $1,485 for the Five Passenger Touring and $1,685 for the Four Passenger Roadster, which had now lost its striping. The Royal Dispatch was priced at $1,785 while the Limousine was the most expensive of the Chandler line at $2,995.

The Chummy Sedan's standard color was dark blue, but it could be had in red or light blue as an option at $16 extra. The Chummy's rear side windows were reworked, now being rounded at the bottom rear. This conformed to the other closed cars' treatment. The double striping was gone, replaced by a single stripe. The Metropolitan Sedan was available in dark blue with light blue as an option, and the Limousine came in dark blue with green as an option. This rainbow of colors was a contrast to the sole offering of blue just a few years previous. The automobile business was growing up with the public demanding more of everything. If you expected to survive, you listened to what they had to say.[12]

Mechanically, the big news was the introduction of the Traffic Transmission, a revolutionary new design built entirely by Chandler under license of the Campbell patent. Gear clashing was supposed to be eliminated by the gears running in mesh while shifting was taking place. The shafts turned inside the gears and were engaged by pawls, eliminating the clash which was a common complaint of most motorists. One could theoretically shift up or down at any speed. Chandler stressed this point in their advertising, particularly in ads and photographs of the period depicting women at the wheel.[13]

Chandler promoted the new gear box heavily. During Traffic Transmission Week, December 2–9, 1923, demonstrations were given at all Chandler dealers. In Allentown, Pennsylvania, the local dealer mounted a cutaway transmission on the front bumper of a Chandler and cruised the street giving demonstrations. This created so much attention that the streets were blocked and the police ordered him off the main thoroughfares because he was creating a traffic hazard. In San Francisco, the

Left, top: **Chandler Traffic Transmission.** ***Left, bottom:*** **Traffic Transmission plaudit from a satisfied owner.** ***Above:*** **1924 Metropolitan Sedan (factory photograph, courtesy Donn Wirtz).**

Chandler distributor offered $500 in prizes for the person who rode in a Chandler and wrote the best essay about the merits of the new transmission. The top prize of $250 was won by G. Bordman Edmonds, director of vocational education at Berkeley.[14]

Although Chandler had now been in business for ten years, they were still advertising for dealers, proclaiming that open territory existed and prospective dealers should inquire.[15]

With the Pikes Peak engine, Traffic Transmission and the rear axle which went into production in 1922 and had not had a failure since, the 1925 models became available in June 1924.[16]

***Top:* 1924 Seven Passenger Touring (factory photograph, author's collection). *Bottom:* 1924 Royal Dispatch (factory photograph, courtesy Roger Anderson).**

• Six •

1925–1926

Racing Success, Internal Struggles and Merger

The 1925 model year began June 7, 1924, with the announcement appearing in several trade magazines and followed the next day with the news appearing in Chandler's own publication. Chandler was ahead of the competition by starting early but was quoted as saying they had been ahead of their competitors, mechanically, for the last two years anyway.

The 1925 models offered balloon tires as standard equipment and four wheel brakes as a new option. The Traffic Transmission was now the rage among women motorists and the Pikes Peak engine had proven its worth over the past two years. Add a long list of other improvements, led by the Zerk pressure system of chassis lubrication, new headlights, carburetor, instrument panel and a host of engine improvements, and you have one fine automobile. However, with all these improvements came a price hike of $100 across the board.

There were no new body styles announced for the model year, and other than headlights the bodies were the same as the previous year. But changes would come later and some were dramatic. Strangely, the Metropolitan Sedan was not listed as an available body style when the new models were announced.[1]

The status quo held until September 4 when two new sedans made their appearance. They really were not new—just improvements over the existing Chummy and Metropolitan sedans. The Chummy retained its name and had a nickel radiator shell added, but the Metropolitan had De Luxe added to its title. The bodies were updated by the addition of a leather visor and a new ventilating windshield. Referred to as the V.V. (Vision and Ventilation), it was a great improvement over the former two-piece hinged windshield. The driver could now raise and lower the windshield a few inches by a small crank located at the top center. No more thumb screws, braces or rubber weather-strip to worry with in a rainstorm; just the crank of a small handle and the windshield was tightly closed.

The ventilation system was unique in that by raising the windshield slightly, one could allow air to circulate throughout the whole car, and raising it more let the air come directly into the interior. An automatic windshield wiper and rear view mirror were also added. The window moldings and dash were of Circassian walnut, and the interior hardware was a combination of dull and bright silver finish. Carpets and seats were gray.

The two new bodies had a double belt of molding, with the lower bead running the full length of the car from the nickel radiator shell to the rear and around, with the upper belt running from the windshield to the rear and around. The bodies were lower and the rear corners were rounded considerably more than the previous models. An automatic windshield wiper and Motometer came as standard equipment. Front bumpers were added to both models, and the door handles were changed from the loop style to conventional and raised to fit in the space between the moldings. As on the other 1925 Chandlers, balloon tires were standard (33 × 6) and front wheel brakes were optional. The Metropolitan Sedan De Luxe sold for $2,195 and the Chummy for $2,045. Both cars had luggage racks, and colors were Black and Luxor Blue.[2]

Since developing the Pikes Peak engine, Chandler had been involved in racing on the famous hill, and on September 1, they were there for the annual event. It was a miserable day with one inch of snow and a temperature of 24 degrees at the summit, and only the first two cars escaped the rain and fog which plagued all the competitors. A Chandler driven by Ott Davis finished well back in the pack.[3]

Chandler was doing well as 1924 came to a close and again chose to share the wealth with the employees. On September 1, bonuses were distributed to 1,000 factory and office workers. In a total payout of $200,000, each employee received at least 10 percent of their annual wages with long term employees receiving up to a maximum of 13 percent. This was the ninth consecutive year in which Chandler had paid a bonus to employees. Executives shared in a different bonus.[4]

Models and Prices 1925 Chandlers

Model	Pass.	Price
Touring	5	$1585
Touring	7	1735
Comrade Roadster	2-3	1795
Roadster	4	1785
Royal Dispatch	4	1885
Chummy Sedan	5	1845
Four-Door Sedan	5	1995
New Seven Sedan	7	2195
Limousine	7	3095

Prices include balloon tires as standard equipment.

Four-wheel brakes optional at an extra cost of $60.

Special light-blue paint on Chummy Sedan and Four-Door Sedan $60 extra.

As calendar year 1925 began, new body designs arrived. The Coach Imperial was an economy version of the Chummy Sedan. It seated five, had a leather cadet visor added, carried a trunk rack and was equipped with the V.V. windshield. The finish was Luxor Blue Duco with are no other color options, and gray woolen upholstery adorned the interior. Balloon tires and wooden wheels were standard but four wheel brakes were still an option. The body was rather plain with no raised belting running from radiator to rear as on the other closed cars. However, the door handles were changed from loop to conventional. There were cowl lights and the radiator shell was nickeled as were those of all Chandlers now. The Coach Imperial, priced at $1,585, was an attempt to capture some of the market share for closed cars in the price range of less expensive open cars.

The Sport Touring was a good looking, nicely designed Five Passenger Phaeton which had a one piece windshield and wind wings as standard equipment. Paint choices of two-tone gray-green Duco or Luxor Blue Duco were paired with long grain leather interior upholstery.

A front bumper and Motometer atop the nickeled radiator

***Left:* Chandler models and prices, June 1924. *Below:* 1925 San Francisco Auto Show (factory photograph, courtesy John W. Chandler).**

shell set this beauty off admirably at a price of $1,585. With the introduction of the sport model, the standard Five Passenger Touring was discontinued.

The Comrade Roadster was reworked to accommodate four passengers. Without dramatically changing the body lines, designers added a rumble seat with a unique way of opening. A front bumper was optional but there was none at the rear. To assist in entering, however, a large step plate was added at the upper front of the rear fender on the passenger side. By using the running board, step plate and considerable dexterity you could be seated in a rumble seat which had more room and was more comfortable than most. A small door added just ahead of the left rear fender, commonly called the golf club door, actually was for umbrellas, small packages or golf clubs. A one piece windshield with nickeled posts, wind wings and a green glass sun visor set this beauty off quiet well. The spare tire at the rear was set at a rakish angle and mounted on a simulated wheel, a copy of the natural finish wood wheels that came as standard equipment. The simulated wheel could be used in an emergency but was not recommended for extended service. The standard body color was two-tone gray-green Duco, and upholstery was olive tinted Spanish leather. The new Roadster, priced at $1,795, replaced the Two Passenger Comrade in the lineup. The Comrade bodies were now being built by Baker of Cleveland, Union City of Union City, Indiana, and Griswold of Detroit, Michigan. Fisher still dominated the building of Chandler bodies, but their grasp was beginning to slip.

The Metropolitan Sedan Deluxe was reworked once again, with the body stretched five inches and the roof at the rear revised slightly. In the new version the rear of the roof, above the belting, was covered in leather which extended to the rear windows and across the top where the roof fabric ended. The rear windows were shortened and given rounded corners at the rear, and landau irons were mounted in the space between window and rear of the car. Although slight, the cosmetic changes added a very elegant touch. Chandler would not use the Deluxe name after this except on price lists.

Although front bumpers were rarely illustrated in company literature, they were standard equipment on some Chandlers, the Metropolitan being among that group.

Colors were standard two-tone Brown Duco or optional Sagebrush Green Duco with the area between the belting, top of hood and cowling finished in a contrasting color, which did a lot to improve the car's already good looks. The interior was gray mohair with a smoking set and innovative spring loaded

Top: **1925 Chandler front styling.** ***Middle:*** **1925 Five Passenger Touring.** ***Bottom:*** **1925 Royal Dispatch.**

armrests for the passengers' comfort. The $2,195 Metropolitan was probably Chandler's best looking closed car if not the best of all. The Chandler parts book for 1925 lists the Metropolitan body as being made by Murray, but all other advertising touts the body as having the V.V. windshield, a Fisher trademark. Any automobile body advertised as having the V.V. windshield would have been built by Fisher. Murray did build some bodies for the early Metropolitan and Twentieth Century Sedans, as they are the same; this information is listed in the flat rate section of the Chandler parts manual. Chandler advertising in most trade publications and Chandler literature touted the Fisher Body with V.V. windshield. The January 1925 Chandler sales brochure still listed the body as being made by Fisher.

The Chummy Sedan shared the Metropolitan's rear roof treatment, minus the leather covering and landau irons. It also received the improved door handles, which were raised to the space between the belting. A raised bead beltline extended from the radiator to around the rear, and a second one ran from windshield around the rear. A front bumper was standard and the interior was equal to the Metropolitan. The paint color was Sagebrush Green Duco or Luxor Blue varnish as an option. Add a leather covered visor to the above and the Chummy was otherwise unchanged from its introduction in September 1924.

Joining the Chummy would be a new two door coach known as the Coach Imperial, an economy version of the Chummy Sedan priced at $1,585. Although the Chummy (Coach), now priced at $2,045, was never as popular as some other body styles it did command its share of the trade. The Four Passenger Comrade Roadster, Royal Dispatch, Seven Passenger Sedan and Four Door Sedan would remain unchanged until the 1926 models were announced.

Three views of the 1925 Comrade Roadster (factory photographs, top and middle courtesy John W. Chandler, bottom courtesy Roger Anderson).

However, this would be the last hurrah for the Royal Dispatch. As the popularity of the Sport Touring had increased, the Dispatch had faded and would be dropped.[5]

Chandler went to the New York, Chicago, Detroit and Boston auto shows with a full line of cars and a cutaway engine painted in a bright hue of red-orange and mounted in a black chassis. The engine also had several of its working parts painted other colors for a great contrast and attracted many show attendees as it was not just a static display but rotated continuously, allowing show visitors to see how an internal combustion engine really worked.

The forgotten body style of the whole line was the Limousine, of which little if any mention was made in advertising and factory brochures. Virtually the only place to find anything about it is in the price list, where it was still carried as a 1925 model at $3,095.[6]

With everything at Chandler going well, Fred Chandler decided to take a two week vacation and headed for Bermuda in March.[7]

July 9 brought the 1926 models and some design changes. All enclosed bodies would be on the style of the previously introduced Chummy and the Metropolitan Sedan. The one new body style introduced, a Seven Passenger Sedan, was just a remake of the 1925 version which it replaced. The rear was rounded off at the top and a cadet visor now graced the windshield, which had an automatic windshield wiper. The Metropolitan Sedan underwent some design changes also.

Upholstery was rich gray mohair and paint was Dark Blue Duco with an option of two-tone Brown Duco or Sagebrush Green. The body, by Fisher, had heavy beading accentuating the double belt effect with the two-tone paint being used to good advantage.

The major change for all models was the adoption of three vertical bars in the radiator. The headlights and cowl lights were the same design as the 1925 with the exception of the Metropolitan Sedan, Seven Passenger Sedan and Comrade Roadster. These three body styles would have a new, fully nickel plated headlight design. A new radiator badge retained the shape of the previous one but was made

***Top:* 1925 Metropolitan Sedan (factory photograph, courtesy Roger Anderson). *Bottom:* 1927 Seven Passenger Sedan (factory photograph, author's collection).**

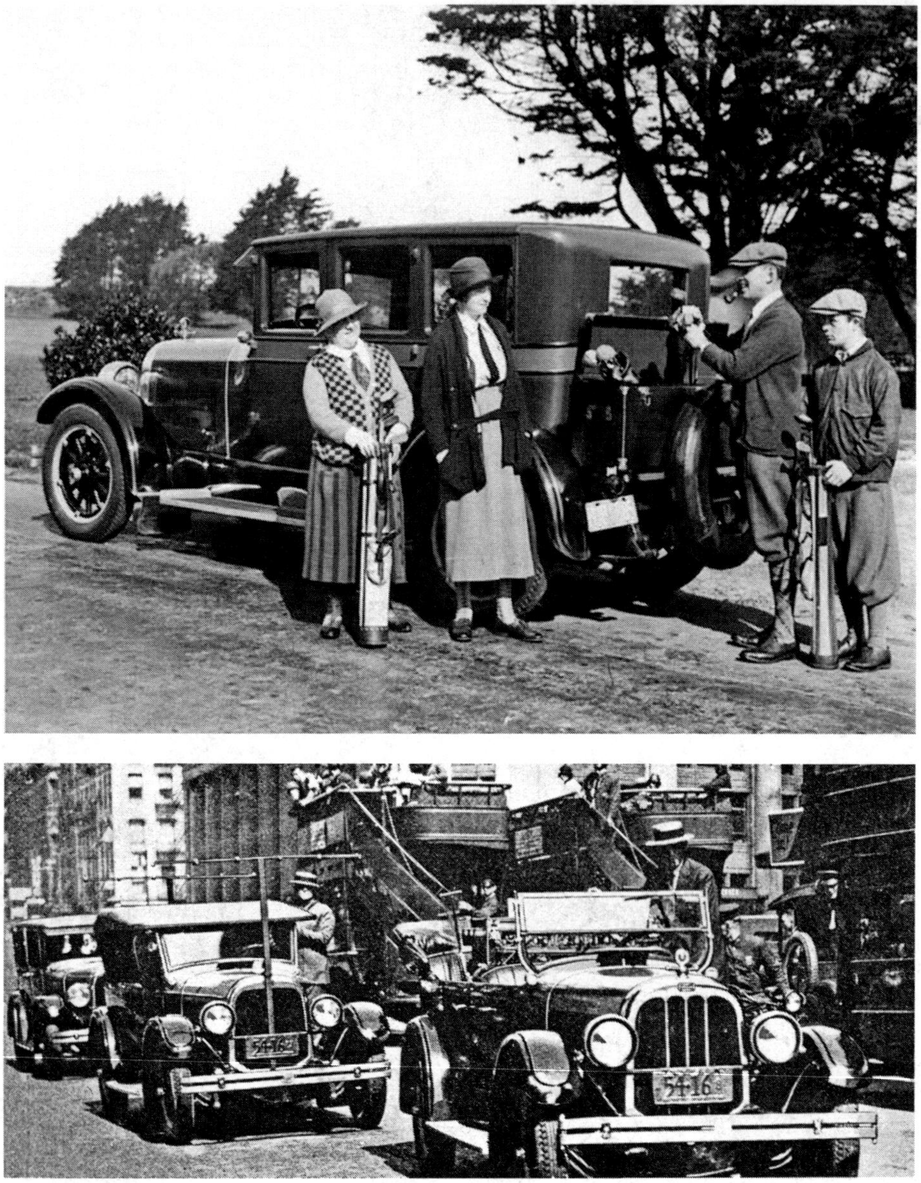

***Top:* 1926 Metropolitan Sedan (factory photograph, author's collection). *Bottom:* (front) 1926 Chandler Touring radio-controlled on the streets of New York (*Motor Age*, September 10, 1925).**

of gunmetal with white enamel letters on a black background with the border in white and gold.

These were very simple changes, but they enhanced the beauty of all Chandlers. The door handles of all enclosed Chandlers now rode higher and were of the conventional type. Gone forever is the old loop style. The Metropolitan Sedan also underwent some changes, losing the leather at the rear just six months after its inception, as well as the landau irons, enabling the rear windows to be increased in size. "Deluxe" was restored to the name, which leads to speculation that it was a mistake by the advertising department which caused the name to be dropped in the first place. This makes three different bodies the Metropolitan had had within the past twelve months.

Mechanical changes were few but noteworthy. The distributor by Bosch was now mounted on the generator, thereby eliminating another shaft and coupling. A small flywheel was mounted at the front of the engine for balance and the manifold was redesigned with the exhaust port now at the front of the engine. Modifications in the clutch reduced the length of the transmission by two inches.[8]

Shortly after the introduction of the 1926 Chandler, one of the new touring cars traveled the streets of New York without a driver. It was controlled by radio signals from another Chandler following closely behind. It was also preceded by a Chandler touring car. The inventor of the radio system, Francis A. Houdina, stood on the running board but did not touch the steering wheel, clutch or brake and maintained a speed of 5 to 10 miles per hour.[9]

Early September saw the annual gathering of Chandler dealers and distributors in Cleveland. Setting entertainment aside, they got down to the business at hand which was automobiles. The new body styles were introduced with great fanfare. George Graham, vice president of sales and advertising, welcomed the attendees and proceeded to expand on the changes incorporated in the new model year. He reminded the guests that there would not be a straight eight Chandler despite rumors that had been circulating to that effect. The chassis, Traffic Transmission and rear axle had received little change as they were considered to be near perfection. Four wheel brakes received a lot of attention, although they remained optional on the 1926 models according to all references. The clutch had been improved with a new throw-out mechanism and the transmission mounting had been changed to shift the weight from the flywheel housing to the crankcase. The intake manifold was reworked to improve starting and better fuel economy. An upgrade to the exhaust manifold eliminated back pressure and reduced noise. Steering and springs were improved. Exteriors had not changed dramatically, but a new dash with gas gauge now adorned all Chandlers.

Graham went on to explain changes that would affect dealers and distributors, including a new advertising campaign for which they would be expected to share one-third of the expense.

He gently broke the news that there would be shortages of the Comrade Roadsters, Seven Passenger Sedans and 20th Century Sedans. Why this news when everything seemed to be going so well? Chandler had broken ties with the Fisher Body Company and was scrambling to find body builders that could supply its needs. The break with Fisher apparently occurred late in the 1925 model year.[10]

The Murray Body Corporation would be making the Seven Passenger, 20th Century and early Metropolitan Sedan bodies while the Comrade Roadster bodies were being made by Baker, Union City and Griswold. Budd would soon be building the Metropolitan Sedan bodies, which would be all steel. Fisher was still building bodies for the early Five and Seven Passenger Tourings, but this would change with Chandler soon building their own. Other reliable sources list Murray as building all Chandler closed bodies and Chandler building the open ones. That would be the case late in the 1926 model year, but soon Chandler would build all bodies in their own factory.[11]

Why the break with Fisher was made is not known, but president Fred Chandler referred to it as an unfortunate decision on Chandler's part in an address to stockholders in March 1927. General Motors owned the majority of stock in Fisher Body Corporation and would take over completely in June 1926. It could have been their need for Fisher to supply more bodies for GM or a desire to rid themselves of outside business or a decision to adjust prices. However, president Chandler's remarks seem to confirm that it was Chandler's decision. Regardless, the break was made and Chandler would lose considerable business during the 1926 model year as a result.[12]

The convention, like all Chandler conventions, was held at the Hollenden Hotel where good food, good entertainment and goodwill abounded. In addition to car business the dealers and distributors enjoyed some business of a less serious nature at B. F. Keith's Palace Theater during the week. On Thursday night they were treated to an appearance by Annette Kellerman, world renowned diving Venus. She made her appearance in a new Comrade Roadster, gleaming under the lights, and struck her famous pose standing on the cowling of the car. Another great act was performed by Corrine Sales and her rotund partner, J. Francis Dooley, with a story concerning a new fur coat and a new Chandler Comrade Roadster. She finally got the car but had to wait until Christmas before she could have the coat.

Saturday night at the Hollenden Hotel saw a magnificent array of stars from the B.F. Keith circuit. They performed a total of 52 acts, 45 of them by beautiful ladies. A full orchestra and plenty of singers, in addition to other acts, kept the entertainment going for four hours. The attendees went home feeling enthusiastic about the future of Chandler business.[13]

Chandler's commitment to racing on Pikes Peak finally paid off as Charlie Meyers drove a Chandler to a new record on September 7 and won the event, adding to the list of Chandler achievements. His feat will be described more fully in Chapter Eleven.[14]

Although the new line had been introduced on July 9, it was not until the September convention of distributors and dealers that the complete line was fully shown. The former Coach Imperial had been dolled up and renamed the Brougham. A beaded belting ran from radiator to rear, new aluminum strips at the rear protected the body from trunk damage and the finish was Sage Brush Green Duco. Following the trends started with some late 1925 models, the rear top corners were rounded off as were those of all other closed cars. A front bumper, rear view mirror, automatic windshield wipers, Motometer and trunk rack were standard. The new three bar radiator shell was a big hit and the Brougham, at a price of $1,695, was a nice improvement over the Coach Imperial and Chummy Sedan which it replaced.

The 20th Century Sedan was another new entry—not exactly a new body style but a revision of the former Five Passenger, Four Door Sedan. Touting it as the greatest single accomplishment in Chandler's thirteen year history in an ad was probably overstating their case, but it was a nice looking sedan. The rear roof received the same treatment as all of Chandler's 1926 closed cars, but the 20th Century Sedan went without a trunk rack or front bumper as this was an attempt to capture the market for a four door sedan at a moderate price. Finished in Buckingham Gray Duco with black upper body, fender and splash shields, it was a very handsome car. Most handsome of all was the price at $1,490. In fact all Chandlers received a substantial reduction in price ranging from $400 to $505. Chandler ads no longer carried the "Body by Fisher" logo as the long standing relationship had ended.

In October, George C. Graham, Chandler vice president, represented the National Automobile Chamber of Commerce before the tax hearings of the Congressional Ways and Means Committee in Washington, D.C.[15]

In November the Murray Body Corporation announced it had taken on Chandler Motor Car Company as a new account, although in fact they had been building Chandler bodies for some time.[16]

In December, Chandler declared a quarterly dividend of 75 cents per share of stock payable to stockholders of record as of December 21.[17]

Big news followed on December 31, 1925, as Chandler announced that it would be merging with the Cleveland Automobile Company. An application had been filed with the state of Delaware to that effect. Stockholders of the two companies would have until January 15, 1926, to approve the merger—a foregone conclusion as most Cleveland stockholders were

Chandler executives, distributors and dealers.[18] Why the merger? It could have been because they needed space to build bodies for Chandler and the Cleveland models which would become Chandler, now that Fisher was no longer making all Cleveland bodies. Or it could have been that it was an impossible task for executives to run two car manufacturing facilities simultaneously. The Cleveland line would be continued until the 1927 model year began.

The beginning of 1926 brought higher prices and the introduction of the Bowen "One Shot" automatic chassis oiler. Prices increased from $50 to $100 on all models except the Brougham and Comrade Roadster. The addition of the chassis oiler was hailed as a great advancement for car owners, especially women. All the labor of crawling over and under a car to lubricate it supposedly had ended. Just step on a plunger at the driver's left heel and your car is lubed. It sounded great—and it was, when it worked, but unfortunately it did not always perform to expectations. Many Chandlers so equipped were later found to have the system removed. Chandler and the Bowen Products Corporation of Auburn, New York, were jointly advertising the system, which had been standard equipment on Cleveland automobiles for nearly two years.[19]

Chandler had adopted the Zerk pressure system just one year earlier and had now abandoned it. The 1925 and early 1926 models would be the only ones ever to have this type of lubrication with the exception of the 1929 Model 65.

On February 1, in a letter to stockholders, Fred C. Chandler announced that the merger of Chandler and Cleveland had been declared effective. Henceforth the new name would be Chandler-Cleveland Motors Corporation, but it would take a few months before all advertising carried the logo. By April most advertising did carry the new logo but some still continued the old into August.[20]

On April 29, Chandler added a Seven Passenger Berline Sedan to its lineup at a price of $2,095. This car was designed specifically for the undertaker trade and was advertised and marketed as such. The front seats were separated from the rear by a sliding glass partition which would give the bereaved family privacy, but they could communicate with the driver if necessary. It was finished in two-tone tan or blue. Standard features were a front bumper, automatic windshield wipers, trunk rack, sun visor,

***Both photographs,* 1926 Comrade Roadster, Model 35 (factory photograph, courtesy John W. Chandler).**

cowl ventilator, rear view mirror, engine heat gauge, gasoline gauge, cowl lights, smoking set, door and gearshift lock. This model probably represented a remake of the former Seven Passenger Sedan and Murray was supposedly building the body. Everything would be renamed when the 1927 models were introduced anyway.[21]

Sometime after the introduction of the 1926 models the Traffic Transmission was dropped. Why this would be done is open to speculation. Was it a dispute between Chandler and Campbell? Was it too expensive to manufacture? Were maintenance problems making owners wary? For whatever reason, it was dropped without explanation and the new transmission was merely listed as a sliding gear, selective shift, four-speed transmission. The only public hint of a change came in a trade magazine article that referred to the clutch being modified which necessitated a change in the emergency brake mechanism because the transmission was 1½ inches shorter. Otherwise no mention of these changes appeared anywhere except in Chandler's Service Parts Price List, in an addendum to the Service Series 35. A different transmission, transmission lock, propeller shaft (driveshaft) and transmission brake assembly (emergency brake) are listed as beginning on cars numbered 165,001 and after. Chandler's 1926 advertising brochure only lists the transmission as selective sliding. The Traffic Transmission is not mentioned in any form of advertising after the 1926 models were shown.

***Top:* 1926 Seven Passenger Berline. *Bottom:* 1926 Seven Passenger Berline interior. The Berline replaced the Limousine.**

In an address before 600 distributors and dealers on September 11, 1925, vice president George Graham discussed the new clutch and revision of the transmission but not one word was said concerning the Traffic Transmission.

The merger of Chandler and Cleveland, which was being discussed at the time, may have been a factor since Mechanics Machine was already building the Cleveland transmissions. Chandler probably did not want two different transmissions and in all likelihood they decided to go with their own design and pay no more licensing fees. Mechanics Machine of Rockford, Illinois, completed a new factory in April 1926 and was expected to be in full production by June 1. They probably could have handled Chandler's business without difficulty.

What can be said with confidence is that after 5,345 series 35 1926 Chandlers were manufactured, car #165,000 was the last to be fitted with the Traffic Transmission.[22]

As the new model year approached, Chandler would be a much larger corporation.

• SEVEN •

1927 Model Year

Too Many Models, Too Little Profit

The merger of Cleveland into the Chandler organization brought many changes. The former Chandler Motor Car Company and the Cleveland Automobile Company were now the Chandler-Cleveland Motors Corporation, a company with an investment of $10,000,000 in land, buildings and equipment with two factories occupying 31,000 feet of floor space and located on 31 acres of prime industrial real estate.

Those Chandler officials who had served dual roles were affected little by the merger; they just kept their former titles, assumed new ones, or were promoted to better positions. Fred C. Chandler had never relinquished his title of president at Chandler and would continue in the same position. J.V. Whitbeck, who left Chandler as their chief engineer, became vice president of engineering. Joe Krall was eased back into the Chandler fold. Sid Black, who had been vice president in charge of advertising at Cleveland, became a vice president and general manager at Chandler. John R. Hall was vice president of production at Chandler and production manager at Cleveland. He would keep his position at Chandler while Samuel Regar, who also had dual roles, did the same.[1]

As the 1927 model year began the new company found itself building 19 different automobiles on three different chassis, and by January that number increased to 26 on four different chassis.

The former Chandler Six, now the Chandler Big Six, came in seven body styles and retained its previous specifications. The Brougham was replaced by a Four Passenger Coupe selling at $1,675. The Metropolitan Sedan led the parade at $1,595, a cut of $360 from its former price—and was the only Big Six closed car to keep the cadet visor. All others had a visor built in as part of the roof (top). The Five Passenger Touring was reduced by $60 to $1,495 with the Seven Passenger Touring going for $1,645, also $60 less. The Comrade Roadster sold for $1,695, $60 below its former price. The 20th Century Sedan now sold for $1,495, a reduction of $155, and the Seven Passenger Sedan was the most expensive body style made at $1,795, a $260 reduction. The Limousine was no longer in the lineup.

The Big Six models were furnished in an array of colors, both standard and optional. Lacquer paint was now used on all models. Interiors were richly appointed and upholstery came in an array of fabrics and two leathers.

Four wheel brakes were now standard on all Chandler vehicles as was the "One Shot" lubricating system, which had been moved to the motor side of the firewall with a plunger extending through the firewall above the driver's feet. Air cleaners and oil filters were also standard equipment. The radiator shell had undergone a slight modification and was topped with a dog-bone cap sporting an eagle with wings spread. The bowtie radiator badge which was redone on the 1926 models was standard on all models but had had another remake with white lettering on a black background, bordered completely in bronze. This was the last of the bowties as both the 1928 and 1929 models would have new emblems.

Tires were 33 × 6 balloon. High pressure motor lubrication, self-adjusting spring shackles and reworked steering were a few of the refinements. Bumpers, bumperetts, combination tail and stop light and shock absorbers were an option package at $46.[2]

Bodies were now being furnished by several companies, and Chandler was building some of its own. The 20th Century Sedan body was built by Murray with Budd supplying the Metropolitan Sedan as well as the Big Six Sedan. Chandler built both the Five and Seven Passenger Touring bodies and Union City supplied the bodies for the Comrade Roadster and the new Coupe, which came with the visor built as part of the top.[3]

The Chandler Special Six, formerly the Cleveland Model 43, rode on a 115 inch wheelbase chassis. Manufactured in five body styles, it was powered by a scaled down version of the Pikes Peak engine with bore and stroke of 3⅛ × 4¾. The engine, transmission and rear end were entirely manufactured by Chandler.

Four wheel brakes and "One Shot" lubrication were standard also. The carburetor was by Schebler with Delco-Remy supplying the electrics and Borg & Beck furnishing the clutch. As with the Big Six, bumpers, bumperetts and combination tail and stop light were available at an extra cost. Tires were 31 × 5.25.[4]

The five body styles were the Touring, which sold for $1,145, the Sport Touring and Sedan for $1,295, the Coupe for $1,195 and the De Luxe Coupe for $1,285. All five were virtual copies of the larger Big Six. All Chandler bodies were lower, and the use of double belting on most models made them appear longer. All Special enclosed cars were equipped with a cadet visor and carried the nickeled radiator shell topped with the dog bone and eagle radiator cap.

If you did not care for the eagle, you could have a goddess type ornament called Aquilla. Both the eagle and Aquilla were made by the Irving Florman Company of New York and available from Chandler dealers at a cost of three dollars.

After Chandler severed relations with the Fisher Body Company, the Cleveland was also affected. Cleveland had been building their own touring bodies for some time but many of the sedan bodies were built by the Gotfredson Brothers Company of Detroit. When Chandler and Cleveland merged the Gotfredson Brothers would continue to supply bodies until Chandler could build their own.[5] All Special bodies, with the exception of the Sedan, were built by Chandler. Murray built the Sedan for the present, but by the time the 1928 models appeared it would be Chandler that built all Special bodies. Interiors came in a variety of fabrics and leather and body colors varied with many selections for some models.[6]

***Top:* 1927 Chandler radiator treatment (factory photograph, courtesy Roger Anderson). *Middle:* 1927 Big Six Coupe (factory photograph, courtesy Roger Anderson). *Bottom:* 1927 Big Six Comrade Roadster (factory photograph, courtesy John W, Chandler).**

Chandler did not do the two smaller lines of cars justice, as the Big Six got the majority of advertising coverage and the Standard and Special models got precious little. The Standard Six, formerly the Cleveland 31, rode on a 108½ inch wheelbase chassis and was powered by a still smaller version of the Pikes Peak engine: bore and stroke of 3 × 4¼ as compared to the former Cleveland Standard Model 31's 2⅞ × 4 ¼. Horsepower was reduced by 25 percent compared to the Big Six. It was equipped with a Tillotson carburetor, Delco Remy electrics and Borg & Beck clutch. Four wheel brakes and "One Shot" lubrication were standard and steering was by Gemmer. As on all Chandlers, bumpers, bumperetts and combination tail and stop light came at extra cost. Tires were 30 × 5.

Chandler Records Prove Performance Superiority

Has More Achievements to Its Credit Than Any Other Car

Pikes Peak

In an open contest with many other cars, Chandler smashed all records scaling the heights of Pikes Peak, 14,109 feet above the sea—world's highest automobile climb. Time: 17 minutes, 48-⅗ seconds.

1000 Miles in 689 Minutes

Great power is responsible for Chandler's amazing speed and durability record at Culver City, Calif.—1000 miles in 689 minutes, at an average speed of 86.9 miles per hour.

Mt. Diablo

At Mt. Diablo, Chandler won the Tribune Cup and Alexander Trophy by ascending further in high gear than any other car has yet been able to go.

Continental Divide

At Continental Divide (altitude 5984 feet) Chandler sped to the top in 13½ minutes—to a new world record.

Mt. Washington

On Mt. Washington, the highest accessible peak east of the Rockies, Chandler established a new record of 17 minutes flat.

Records Abroad

In India, at the Bombay-Poona reliability run, Chandler won the trophy cup and was the only car to compile a perfect score of 200 points.

At the annual flexibility contest in Sydney, Australia, Chandler triumphed over twenty-two other cars in all-around performance, compiling a grand total of 2247.73 points.

Mt. Wilson

Chandler Six holds the Los Angeles Express challenge trophy for breaking all records climbing Mt. Wilson, California. Time: 24 minutes, 47.04 seconds.

San Francisco to Portland

Chandler Six made the fastest time from San Francisco to Portland, and return, ever made by a closed motor car.

Salt Lake City to Los Angeles

20 hours, 2 minutes—that is the record time established by Chandler Six between Salt Lake City and Los Angeles—just 3 hours and 48 minutes faster than the scheduled running time of the fastest Union Pacific train.

Speed Record on Mt. Diablo

Chandler Six holds the speed record up the towering slopes of Mt. Diablo. Time: 22 minutes, 36-⅗ seconds.

Optional Color Schemes With Different Models Present Strong Sales Appeal

Big Six Metropolitan Sedan: Lotus blue below the belt; upper structure black. Window edges in lotus blue. Raised bead with special striping. Wheels, lotus blue striped with bronze. Optional two-tone color: below the bead light silver gray; between bead and belt Sheridan gray; windows edged in Sheridan gray; upper structure black; special striping parallel with bead and belt. Wheels, silver gray, black hubs.

Big Six Coupe: Upper structure Sheridan gray; between bead and belt moulding to full length of deck silver gray; below bead Sheridan gray; bead and moulding black with special striping. Wheels Sheridan gray with gold stripes.

Big Six 20th Century Sedan: Upper structure dark brown; below the bead, dark brown; between bead and belt moulding, light brown; mouldings and bead light brown with special striping. Wheels black. Optional two-tone color: Upper structure black; below the bead, Buckingham gray; between the bead and belt steel gray; moulding black with special striping.

Big Six 7 Passenger Sedan: Upper structure black; rest of body dark blue with black bead and special striping. Optional color: Upper structure dark brown, between bead and belt moulding, light brown; below the bead dark brown with black moulding specially striped.

Big Six Roadster: From the bead down, pearl gray; above the bead, deep olive green; black bead with special striping. Wheels natural wood finish. Optional color: from bead down navy gray; above the bead, dark blue; bead in black with striping. Natural wood finished wheels.

Big Six 5 Passenger Touring: Above the bead, light gray green; below the bead dark gray green; bead black with stripes. Optional color: body Luxor blue; bead black with stripes.

Big Six 7 Passenger Touring: Above the bead, light gray green; dark gray green below bead; black bead with stripes. Second optional color: entire body Luxor blue with black bead and stripes. Third optional color: body light brown with black bead and stripes. Fourth optional color: entire body dark blue; black bead with stripes.

Special Sedan: Body in two-tone sage-brush green with black bead and special striping. Wheels light sage-brush green.

Special and Standard Coupes: Upper structure black; body blue and buff. Optional color: Upper structure Brewster green; below bead, sage-brush green.

Special and Standard De Luxe Coupes: Two-tone green with raised bead.

Special Sport Touring: Two-tone sage-brush green, with dark green raised bead. Disc wheels match body.

Special Touring: Two-tone brown with raised black bead.

Standard Sedan: Lotus blue; upper structure black with black bead and stripes. Optional color, Cleveland blue with raised bead.

Standard De Luxe Sedan: Black upper structure. Sage-brush green lower. Brewster green between beads. Wheels Brewster green. Optional color: beaver brown with black upper structure.

Standard Touring: Two-tone beige brown with raised black bead.

Standard Touring De Luxe: Two-tone sage-brush green with raised bead. Natural wood wheels.

Standard Roadster: Beige brown above upper bead and Nevada gray below upper bead.

PASS

CHANDLER

GUESTS

ARE KINDLY REQUESTED
NOT TO TALK TO WORKMEN

(OVER)

Date Nov 23 1926

Name D. R. Wessling

Address Lytton Iowa

YOU ENTER THIS PLANT
AT YOUR OWN RISK IN
CASE OF ACCIDENT

Signed D. R. Wessling

DISPLAY THIS PASS WHEN IN PLANT
AND PLEASE RETURN WHEN
LEAVING.

FORM 1079 1M 10-26 IDEAL 2132

(OVER)

***Above:* Chandler plant visitor's pass from November 1926 (courtesy Roger Anderson). *Below:* Aquilla 1927–1928 Chandler optional radiator ornament (photograph courtesy Roger Anderson).**

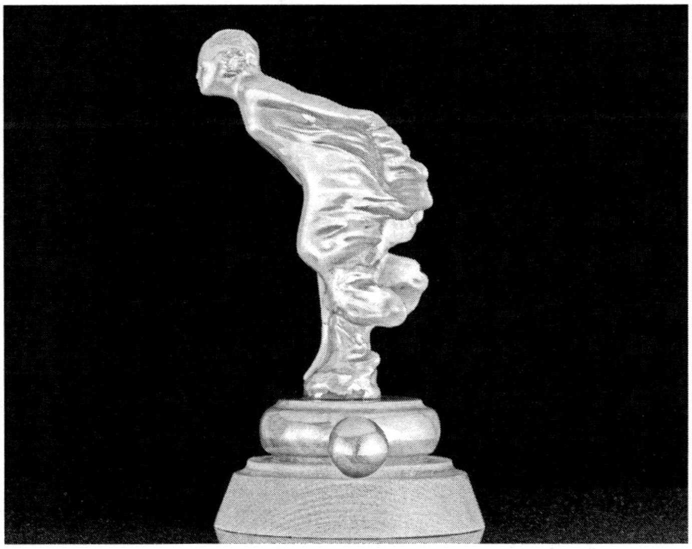

The Standard was offered in seven body styles, but three of these were De Luxe versions of the originals. The Touring sold for $945 and the De Luxe Touring for $1,005; the Sedan sold for $995 and the De Luxe for $1095; the Coupe sold for $1035 and the De Luxe Coupe for $1,125. The Roadster finished off the Standard lineup at $1,135. All Standard bodies except the Roadster, which was built by Union City, were built by Chandler.

Some models offered a wide variety of interior finishes and body colors. As with the Special models, all Standard enclosed bodies had the Cadet visor, and extra equipment was the same.[7]

For those dealers who had previously sold only Chandlers or the Chandler-Cleveland duo, there was little change. If they sold only Clevelands and were in a territory where there was a Chandler dealer they probably would be out of business. Chandler tried to alleviate these problems by adding more dealers, but not all Cleveland dealers ended up with a Chandler franchise.

Chandler's volume of business picked up considerably with the new model year, but how much of this was due to the merger was not stated. The quarterly dividend on preferred stock was only $1.00.

Chandler owners were loyal to the company with 93 to 98 percent of business being repeat customers. The closed cars were accounting for 88 percent of all sales. New dealer appointments dramatically increased after the merger of the two companies.[8]

With Chandler now building as many of its bodies as possible, some changes were made at the factory. At the original Chandler factory (Plant #1) a complete installation was made of the most modern conveyer system, spraying and drying equipment to accommodate the need for increased production. Many more workers would now be employed and more would

***Opposite, left:* Chandler performance records, August 1926. *Right:* 1927 Chandler optional colors, August 1926.**

Top: **1927 Metropolitan Sedan (factory photograph, courtesy Roger Anderson).** ***Middle:*** **1927 Big Six Seven Passenger Sedan (factory photograph, courtesy Roger Anderson).** ***Bottom:*** **1927 Special Sedan (factory photograph, courtesy John W. Chandler).**

be added when Chandler began building all their bodies.

At the former Cleveland factory (Plant #2) a similar operation took place. A new four-story building, 80 feet × 100 feet, was added for body building purposes, and improvements and new equipment in the assembly and machining departments enabled the company to employ 550 additional workers.[9]

Chandler's net profit for the September quarter amounted to $381,512, and sales gains had increased dramatically compared to the previous year.

A new car entered Chandler's line in November as the Metropolitan Sedan De Luxe was unveiled. In reality it was a spruced up version of the old Metropolitan, which had had the De Luxe name off and on for years.[10]

Back at the beginning of 1927 Chandler had delivered a big surprise for those who felt they would never build an eight cylinder automobile. As late as September 1925, George M. Graham, Chandler vice president, had stated that Chandler would not build an eight cylinder car. Chandler's neighbor, Jordan, had gone to the eight cylinder engine for their 1925 models and there was some agitation for Chandler to do the same. They apparently were developing the eight at that time and were not ready to make a public announcement.

At the New York Show (January 8–15, 1927) the new Royal Eight was unveiled, boasting an inline eight which produced 80 horsepower at 3,000 RPM and was reported to do 75 miles per hour with ease. The engine was an L head design with bore and stoke of 3³⁄₁₆ × 4¾, based on the Pikes Peak version which had been so successful. Continuing with what had been successful, the Royal Eight employed a Schebler carburetor, Delco-Remy electrical system and Borg & Beck clutch. Four wheel brakes and "One Shot" lubrication were standard. With an advanced design manifold, air cleaner and oil filter, the new engine was state of the art. Tires were 33 × 6 balloon six ply and the frame had a total length of 171 inches.

Only four body styles were shown at the show, those being the Five Passenger Sedan, Seven Passenger De Luxe Sedan, Coupe and Roadster. Only the Five Passenger Sedan was immediately available, but in March the other three would join the lineup and be accompanied by a Seven Passenger Touring. All Royal Eight bodies were supplied by the Sedan Body Company of Union City, Indiana.

A wide variety of Duotone colors and interiors finished in a wide variety of fabrics and leathers graced the Royal Eights. The Seven Passenger De Luxe Sedan sold for $2,295 while the Five Passenger Sedan, Four Passenger Coupe, Roadster and the Seven Passenger Touring fetched $2,195. After 200 of the Royal Eight were made, presumably all Sedans, someone realized that it needed to be pepped up a bit. Consequently, changes were made starting with the engine. The bore grew from $3\frac{3}{16}$ to $3\frac{1}{4}$ with stroke remaining at $4\frac{3}{4}$. The rear end ratio was changed from 4.9 to 4.5 and tire size was changed from 33×6.00 ($21 \times 4\frac{1}{2}$) to 32×6.00 ($20 \times 4\frac{1}{2}$).

All Royal Eight closed cars had the visor built in as part of the roof and the hood now had three rows of horizontal hood louvers. Bumpers, bumperetts, combination tail and stop light and shock absorbers came in a package at $38 extra.

A unique feature of the new car was that the headlight dimmer switch was foot controlled. Practically all closed cars of all four models had the visor built in as part of the top, but there are exceptions, notably the Special Six Sedan and the Big Six Metropolitan Sedan.[11]

Chandler dealers now had a broad range of styles and prices to cover most of the trade: five Royal Eights, eight Big Sixes, five Special Sixes and seven Standard Sixes. A couple of coupes joined this already crowded lineup in April 1927. Called the

Top and middle: **1927 Standard Roadster (both factory photographs, courtesy John W. Chandler).** ***Bottom:*** **1927 Standard Coupe (factory photograph, courtesy Roger Anderson).**

Country Club Coupe, they entered the Big Six and Royal Eight lines. The Big Six Coupe sold for $1,695 and the Royal Eight Coupe for $2,195. Each had two color options and both interiors were blue-gray, deep tufted mohair, though the Eight had an optional interior of champagne-toned broadcloth. Shortly after the two coupes were announced, another addition was made to the Special Six line: a Sedan De Luxe finished in optional two tone lacquer with blue-gray mohair interior.

Chandler's business for March, April and May 1927 saw them earning $576,919 net, and production had improved substantially over the previous year. However, this is the total for what had been two companies. When Chandler's balance sheet for 1925–26 was released in March, included among the assets was a $100,000 entry listed as a "settlement with vendor." Could this have been with Fisher Body or could this have been related to Chandler dropping the Traffic Transmission?[12]

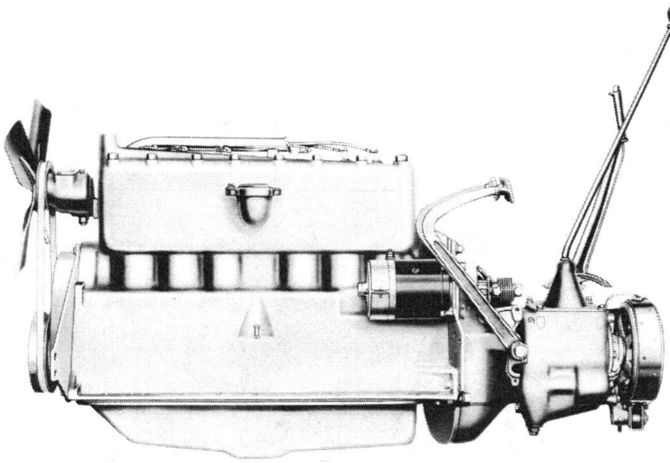

***Top:* 1927 Standard Six Touring with Cleveland top (factory photograph, courtesy Roger Anderson). *Middle, left and right:* 1927 Chandler Standard six engine. *Bottom:* 1927 Royal Eight Five Passenger Sedan (factory photograph, courtesy Cleveland State University Archives).**

On June 12 the Chandler management and employees were saddened to learn that John Richard Hall had passed away at his home located at 2885 Scarborough Road, Cleveland, at the age of 60. He was buried in Knollwood Cemetery, Mayfield Heights, on June 15. He had started with Lozier in 1892 and had maintained some connection with Fred Chandler and many other employees since that time. He helped create both the Chandler Motor Car

CHANDLER-CLEVELAND MOTORS

Balance Sheet

Assets	Dec. 31, '26	Nov. 30, '25
Fixed assets, less depr.	$7,289,617	$7,505,896
Goodwill	5,000,000	5,000,000
Cash	432,837	3,036,917
Notes and accts. rec.	252,739	792,158
Cars for exports	99,678	272,169
Settlement with vendor	100,000	....
Debit balance	....	7,939
Inventories	4,821,430	4,531,090
Invest affil companies	116,888	129,287
Other assets	162,440	98,460
Deferred charges	169,459	87,952
Total	$18,445,088	$21,461,868
Liabilities		
*Cap stock and surplus	$15,570,187	$16,599,045
Notes payable	703,897	194,686
Accounts payable	1,252,326	3,420,650
Accrued taxes	265,675	363,260
Reserve for taxes	....	396,849
Minority interests	1,681	....
Dealers' deposits	133,896	187,378
Dividends payable	217,426	......
Cont. res.	300,000	300,000
Total	$18,445,088	$21,461,868

* Represented by 350,000 shares of no-par preferred and 280,000 no-par shares of common stock.

Top, left: **1927 Royal Eight Roadster, Model 37 (factory photograph, courtesy John W. Chandler).** ***Top, right:*** **1927 Royal Eight Coupe (author's collection).** ***Middle, left:*** **1927 Big Six Country Club Coupe (factory photograph, courtesy Roger Anderson).** ***Bottom, left:*** **Chandler upholstery department in 1927 (photograph courtesy National Park Service, U.S. Department of the Interior).** ***Above:*** **Chandler-Cleveland Motors balance sheet as of December 31, 1926 (*Automotive Topics*, March 5, 1927).**

1927 New York Auto Show (factory photograph, courtesy John W. Chandler).

Company and the Cleveland Automobile Company. The ranks of the original founders were being thinned as Charles A. Carey had left in 1917 and Charles A. Emise had died in 1921.

With more Chandler dealers being added almost daily there became an acute need for more factory representatives to look after the trade. Consequently, in February, Chandler employed four additional people to serve those territories where a special need existed.

Philip Simmons, who had formerly been employed by the Florida Chandler Motor Company Incorporated of Sanford, Florida, was assigned to Alabama. E.H. Hyland was assigned to Nebraska and South Dakota. He had formerly worked for Frank C. Phillips, the Studebaker distributor at Omaha, Nebraska. J. Ford Kelly would cover West Virginia and Kentucky. Kelly had formerly been associated with the Federal Motor Truck Company, the Paige-Ohio Company of Cleveland and the Rickenbacker and Rollin Company. G.F. Horn was assigned to cover Utah and Idaho. He had formerly been employed by Roy C. Bothwell, Chandler distributor at Salt Lake City, Utah.[13]

A Special Six Sedan joined the proliferating Chandler line late in the spring. Not really a new body style but just a fancied up version of the Sedan, it was called the Sedan De Luxe. Featuring blue-gray mohair upholstery and two-tone lacquer paint, it was priced at $1,345. Horizontal hood louvers were introduced with the Royal Eight and others would follow. The Five Passenger Stavndard Six De Luxe Sedan was similarly equipped as was the Special Six De Luxe Sedan, but they had only two rows of louvers.[14]

As the 1927 model year ended Chandler was making many cars but no money.

Dealer tag found on a 1927 Chandler Model 31 (courtesy Greg Pemberton, owner).

• Eight •

1928 Model Year

Big Sixes, Big Eights, Big Trouble

As the 1928 model year began in August 1927, Chandler offered an array of fine automobiles designed to please any discriminating buyer. The lineup initially consisted of twenty-three body styles in three series: the Royal Eight, Big Six and new Royal Six. (Some confusion surrounds the number of chassis as two of the three—the Royal Eight and Big Six—shared the same 124 inch wheelbase, the Big Six chassis having been modified to accept the eight cylinder engine.) The Standard Six was not among the 1928 offerings as it lasted only one short year and had now been relegated to history. Actually, 23 was the number of body styles but De Luxe editions of some would inflate the count to 28 before the model year ended.[1]

The Royal Eight topped the lineup, appearing in six body styles and a wide range of colors and interior appointments. Prices were reduced by $200 on most models and by $100 on the rest. The wheelbase and bore and stroke stood unchanged at 124 inches and 3¼ × 4¾. All Royal Eight closed cars had the large visor built into the roof. The front end featured a new radiator shell, cap and emblem, and the fenders retained a graceful sweep to the rear. The three vertical radiator bars were still present but the shell had become more square at the corners and the sweeping curved indentation which had gracefully arched over the radiator emblem was gone. The Chandler bowtie radiator badge was replaced with a loving cup surrounded by a crest and topped with a crown. The loving cup represented the trophy which Chandler-Cleveland Motors Corporation won for climbing Mt. Wilson, California, in record-breaking time and the crown was an emblem of royalty from which the Royal Six and Royal Eight names came. The eagle radiator cap was replaced by one with no ornamentation.

Body styles were the Five and Seven Passenger Sedan, Coupe and Country Club Coupe, Seven Passenger Touring and Roadster. The Sedan Body Company still supplied all Royal Eight bodies. All enclosed body styles came with mohair interiors but could be purchased with broadcloth for an extra $100. The most expensive of the lot was the Seven Passenger Sedan with mohair interior at $2095. Add broadcloth at $100 and the Chandler price range from the least expensive Special to the most expensive Royal Eight was $995 to $2,195. (Some magazine advertisements listed the least expensive at $945.) The Five Passenger Sedan, Coupe, Country Club Coupe, Seven Passenger Touring and Roadster all sold at $1,995. The Royal Eight was a magnificent automobile priced in the upper middle range, and those who could afford it were not disappointed.[2]

The Big Six was available in eight body styles and a wide array of colors, but with less elaborate interior appointments than the Royal Eight. Body styles were the Metropolitan Sedan, Metropolitan Sedan De Luxe, Coupe, Country Club Coupe, Seven Passenger Touring, Seven Passenger Sedan, Roadster and Royal Six Sedan. The Royal Six, a new Five Passenger Sedan, was a virtual copy of the Royal Eight Sedan, combining the chassis and wheelbase of the Big Six and the body of the Royal Eight. The Royal Six Sedan bore the former radiator shell but with the same emblem as the Eight. However, it was displayed with wooden wheels and the eagle radiator cap from 1927. In fact, the 1928 Big Sixes were introduced with the eagle radiator cap and the old style radiator shell, but somewhat later only the Metropolitan Sedan and Coupe would be so equipped. Engine displacement remained the same as in the former Six.

The Royal Six Five Passenger Sedan and Big Six Seven Passenger Sedan were the most expensive of the Big Six series, selling at $1,795. The Seven Passenger Touring and Roadster were priced at $1,695 with the Coupe and Country Club Coupe bringing $1,675. The Metropolitan Sedan De Luxe brought $1,595 and its plain sister, the Metropolitan Sedan, brought up the rear at $1,495, a $100 reduction. Unlike the Royal Eight, the Big Six had only one interior type.

The Big Six fit well between the Royal Eight and the new Special series. With the Standard series having been dropped there was more room for both the Big Six and Special Series to

New Emblem Adorns 1928 Models

A BEAUTIFUL new Chandler emblem, enameled in maroon, blue and gold appears on the tri-bar radiator of all the 1928 series of Chandlers.

This new emblem is in the shape of a shield outlined in gold. On a field of blue is a crown over a small shield embellished with a loving cup. The crown is gold and maroon. The small shield provides a maroon background for the gold loving cup.

This emblem is not merely a beautiful design. Its creation was fathered by the wish to secure a device which would be truly expressive of the spirit and individuality of the magnificent line of Chandler motor cars.

Emblems of Royalty

The crown and shield, emblems of royalty, reminiscent of courts and kings, are symbolic of the majesty and magnificence of the Chandler series. No other adornment would be more appropriately significant of the luxurious charm of the new models, "fit for a King."

The gold cup in the design represents the trophy the Chandler-Cleveland Motors Corporation holds for breaking all records in climbing Mt. Wilson in California. This permanent record was made over a treacherous nine-mile-and-a-half stretch in 24 minutes, 47.04 seconds, and won the Los Angeles Express Challenge trophy which will remain Chandler property for all time.

This cup, symbolic of power, dependability and endurance, and the crown, emblematic of resplendent magnificence have been incorporated in a unique design, which Chandler officials believe admirably expresses the beauty and quality of Chandler motor cars.

New Prices of Various Chandler Models

SPECIAL SIX

	List Price
Touring	$ 945
Sedan	995
De Luxe Touring	1005
Coupe	1035
De Luxe Coupe	1125
De Luxe Sedan	1135
Roadster	1135
Coupe (Rumble Seat)	1135
Sportster	1145
De Luxe Coupe (Rumble Seat)	1235
Chassis only	845

BIG SIX

Metropolitan Sedan	$1495
Metropolitan Sedan De Luxe	1595
Coupe	1675
Country Club Coupe	1675
7-Pass. Touring	1695
Roadster	1695
Royal Six Sedan	1795
7-Pass. Sedan	1795
Chassis only	1345

ROYAL EIGHT

7-Pass. Touring	$1995
Roadster	1995
5-Pass. Sedan	1995
Coupe	1995
Country Club Coupe	1995
7-Pass. Sedan	2095

Left: **Chandler news release, August 1927.** ***Above:*** **Chandler prices, August 1927.**

expand. The Sedan Body Company of Union City, Indiana, furnished the Touring, Coupes and Royal Six bodies and Edward G. Budd Manufacturing Company of Philadelphia, Pennsylvania, supplied the Metropolitan Sedan De Luxe and Sedan bodies.[3]

Prices were reduced by $100 on both the Metropolitan Sedan and Metropolitan Sedan De Luxe as well as the Seven Passenger Sedan.

With the introduction of the Special for 1928, Chandler caused a great deal of confusion. Last year's Standard, formerly the Cleveland 31, had now become the Special. Last year's Special, formerly the Cleveland 43, was discontinued. In order to keep the confusion at a minimum. Chandler issued two explanatory memoranda to all dealers and distributors on July 14, 1927, and the news appeared in one of the company newsletters also.

Apparently the shorter wheelbase, lighter car had caught the fancy of buyers and Chandler, burdened with too many selections to produce, dropped the 115 inch wheelbase in favor of the 108½ inch version. Everything remained practically the same as on the former Standard, including the engine bore and stroke of 3 × 4¼, but the height of the hood was raised slightly.

The Special was offered in ten body styles and a variety of colors, with several fancy options for the interior as well. All Special bodies were now built by Chandler. Body styles consisted of Sedan and Sedan De Luxe, Coupe and Coupe De Luxe, Coupe with rumble seat and De Luxe Coupe with rumble seat, Touring, De Luxe Touring, Sportster and Two Passenger Roadster with rumble seat.

The new Sportster, though part of the 1928 lineup at the beginning, was not given much publicity until September 1927. It was a dual cowl phaeton with windwings on the front windshield, cowl lights, wood spoke wheels and a rear mounted spare. Front and rear bumpers were standard from the beginning. Although trade publications reported that it was equipped with windwings they were not available when it was first introduced. However, it was illustrated with windwings in the first known advertising for the Special. The paint scheme for the Sportster varied from Chandler tradition by having a panel on the rear door painted the color of the fenders and splash aprons.

Prices for the Special body styles ranged from $1,235 for the Four Passenger De Luxe Coupe to $995 for the Five Passenger Sedan and Five Passenger Touring. In between you could have the Four Passenger Coupe, Sportster and Two Passenger Roadster with rumble seat at $1,135, the Three Passenger Coupe at $1,035 or the Five Passenger De Luxe Touring for $1,005.

Chandler prices in general were reduced $100–$200 from the previous year. The Five Passenger De Luxe Touring would be dropped from the Special line shortly after the 1928 models were announced. There was little demand for that body style because the Touring and Sportster had that market covered.[4]

Although all Chandlers were displayed with bumpers, they still remained an option; four wheel brakes, however, were now standard. Drum type headlights,

***Top:* 1928 Royal Eight DeLuxe Sedan (early) (factory photograph, courtesy John W. Chandler). *Middle:* 1928 Royal Eight Coupe (early) (factory photograph, courtesy Roger Anderson). *Bottom:* A 1928 Chandler Royal Eight Sedan fitted with aftermarket mirrors and additional light (courtesy Roger Anderson).**

Chandler-Cleveland Motors Corporation

CABLE ADDRESS:
"CHANMOTOR" NEW YORK
CODES:
A.B.C. 5th EDITION AND PRIVATE
BENTLEYS LIEBERS
WESTERN UNION

GENERAL OFFICES AND FACTORY,

CLEVELAND, OHIO, U.S.A.

July 14, 1927.

TO ALL DISTRIBUTORS AND DEALERS:

Gentlemen:

For your information, all models on the 31 chassis, heretofore, known as Standard will in the future carry the designation of SPECIAL MODELS.

Please do not confuse the title SPECIAL on the 31 series in the future with the 43 series just discontinued.

Yours very truly,

CHANDLER CLEVELAND MOTORS CORPORATION

Vice President

SB:MC

***Top:* 1928 Big Six Metropolitan Sedan (early) (factory portfolio, courtesy Roger Anderson). *Above:* Chandler memo to dealers, July 1927. *Right:* 1928 color options.**

STANDARD AND OPTIONAL COLORS OF NEW CHANDLER ROYAL EIGHT, BIG SIX AND SPECIAL SIX SERIES

ROYAL EIGHT SERIES

Five-Passenger Sedan: Holyoke Blue. Optional color: Solid Hemlock Grey with Mountain Ridge Green mouldings and Light Green stripe.

Coupe: Hemlock Grey, with Mountain Ridge Green stripe. Grey wheels. Optional color: Two-tone Green with Green wheels.

Country Club Coupe: Hemlock Grey. Grey wheels. Optional color: Two-tone Green with Green wheels.

Roadster: Two-tone Fawn. Modena Lake between mouldings on doors. Gold stripe on moulding.

Seven-Passenger Sedan: Holyoke Blue. Optional color. Dark Blue.

Seven-Passenger Touring: Holyoke Blue. Optional color: Two-tone Fawn.

BIG SIX SERIES

Coupe: Hemlock Grey, with Mountain Ridge Green stripe. Grey wheels. Optional color: Two-tone Green. Green wheels.

Country Club Coupe: Hemlock Grey. Grey wheels. Optional color: Two-tone Green. Green wheels.

Metropolitan Sedan: Finished in Two-tone Fawn the same as our former model 35 Met. De Luxe Sedan with an optional color of Ardsley Green with Mountain Ridge Green moulding and Gold stripe.

De Luxe Metropolitan Sedan: Finished in solid Cumberland Beige with Mountain Ridge Green moulding (no striping), to be equipped with trunk same color as body. Optional color of solid Lotus Blue with Gold striping; also equipped with trunk.

Seven-Passenger De Luxe Sedan: Two tone Fawn. Optional color: Dark Blue.

Roadster: Two-tone effect, Pearl Grey and Olive Green. Optional color: Above the bead, Dark Blue. Below the bead, Navy Grey. Bead, Black with special striping.

Seven-Passenger Touring: Holyoke Blue. Optional color: Two-tone Fawn.

Royal Six Five-Passenger Sedan: Holyoke Blue the same as the 1927 Royal Eight Five-Passenger Sedan with optional color solid Hemlock Grey with Mountain Ridge Green mouldings.

SPECIAL SIX SERIES

Coupe: Blue Devil Blue. Black superstructure. Wheels Black. Optional color: Two-tone Grey. Upper and lower body, Silver Grey. Belt, Sheridan Grey. Wheels Black.

De Luxe Coupe: Blue Devil Blue. Black superstructure. Wheels Blue. Optional color: Two-tone Grey. Upper and lower body, Silver Grey. Belt, Sheridan Grey. Wheels Silver Grey.

Coupe (with Rumble Seat): Body—below the bead, Tuscan Tan. Above the bead, Beverly Brown. Top, Tuscan Tan. Mouldings, Beverly Brown with Gold stripe. Wheels Beverly Brown with Gold stripe.

Standard Sedan: Buckingham Grey all over—Tonopah Grey reveals and mouldings. Black wheels, Gold stripe. Single Apple Green stripe on mouldings, 1/16" wide. Optional color: Cabriolet Grey all over, Apple Green reveals. Paradise Grey mouldings, single Ivory stripe 1/16" wide on mouldings. Black wheels, Ivory stripe.

Standard De Luxe Sedan: Two-tone Fawn as at present. Apple Green reveals and mouldings. Apple Green wheels, mouldings to carry a single Ivory stripe 1/16" wide. Wheels to have Ivory stripe. Optional color: Blue Devil Blue all over, Grenada Blue reveals and mouldings, single Gold stripe on mouldings. Blue Devil Blue wheels, Gold stripe.

Roadster: Beige Brown and Nevada Grey.

Touring: Two-tone Beige Brown.

Touring De Luxe: Two-tone Sage-brush Green.

Sportster: Cumberland Beige with Mountain Ridge Green mouldings and Mountain Ridge Green stripe on hood louvers. Wheels, Mountain Ridge Green with Cumberland Beige stripe. Top panel rear doors, Mountain Ridge Green. Optional color: Andrews Grey with Blue Devil Blue mouldings. White stripe center of moulding. Blue Devil Blue stripe on hood louvers. Blue Devil Blue on top panels rear doors. Wheels, Blue Devil Blue.

with those of De Luxe models and the Sportster being nickeled, still adorned the front but the eagle radiator cap was gone. The De Luxe models and Sportster had two rows of horizontal hood louvers but all others retained vertical ones. The new radiator badge adorned all Specials. However, the radiator shell was still the old style, with new emblem.

The "One Shot" lubrication was shown with the plunger still

CHANDLER-CLEVELAND MOTORS CORPORATION

CABLE ADDRESS:
"CHANMOTOR" NEW YORK
CODES:
A.B.C. 5TH EDITION AND PRIVATE
BENTLEYS LIEBERS
WESTERN UNION

GENERAL OFFICES AND FACTORY,
CLEVELAND, OHIO, U.S.A.

July 14, 1927.

TO ALL DISTRIBUTORS AND DEALERS:

Gentlemen:-

We want to particularly call your attention to the fact that the Special Series which you have been familiar with on the 43 chassis will no longer be built.

These models have been entirely discontinued, due to the fact that the reduction in price of the Metropolitan Sedans on the Big Six chassis is so close to the Special Sedan on the 43 chassis that the volume production which would justify the continuance on the latter car is impossible.

Yours very truly,

CHANDLER-CLEVELAND MOTORS CORPORATION

Vice President

SB:MC

Former Special Six Series Discontinued

Right now it might be well to advise that from now on the 43 series or former Special Six has been discontinued, owing to the fact that the lowered price of the Big Six Metropolitan Sedan brought this model in such a close price range with the price of the former Special Six sedan that it would be impossible to maintain sales volume on the latter. Nevertheless, due to close price range of the former Standard Six series to the former Special Six series, it has been deemed advisable by the company to carry the thirty-one series from now on under the name of Special Six series.

passing through the firewall. All Chandlers were now equipped with self-oiling, self-compensating spring shackles that acted much like shock absorbers.

Chandler-Cleveland had doubled the number of its dealerships during 1927 and was expecting to add even more in the coming year. However, most of the additions were former Cleveland dealers who took on the Chandler as a way of survival. Chandler-Cleveland Motors suffered a very bad year in 1927, accruing a net loss of $473,109.75 by December 31.[5] Almost all of this was due to setting aside $500,000 in a special reserve fund. Fred C. Chandler, in his address to stockholders, stated that efforts to increase the dealer network accounted for the loss. Nothing was said about the fact that Chandler was incurring a huge expense by tooling up for their body building. Although they had shipped more cars in 1927 than 1926 they were still losing money.

Nonetheless 1928 began in a big way for Chandler. Company officials went to the New York show in January sporting a lineup of 28 body styles (20 plus eight De Luxe versions). New body styles, colors (a total of 33 hues on bodies and fenders) and features were abundant but the big news was the new Westinghouse brake system. Chandler was the first American automobile company to introduce the vacuum assisted brake system developed by the Westinghouse Air

Top, left: **Chandler memo to dealers, July 1927.** ***Top, right:*** **Chandler memo to public, July 1927.** ***Bottom:*** **Special Six Sportster, Model 31A (early) with no windwings (factory photograph, courtesy John W. Chandler).**

***Top:* 1928 Special Six Rumble Seat Coupe. *Middle:* 1928 Special Six Rumble Seat Roadster (early) (both, factory photographs, courtesy Roger Anderson). *Bottom:* 1928 Big Six Cabriolet with wire wheels, sidemount spare and trunk rack (photograph courtesy Roger Anderson).**

Brake Company—not a hydraulic brake but one which used vacuum to assist the driver. The brakes were so sensitive that a touch of the toe now had as much effect as a great deal of foot pressure formerly had. It was warmly welcomed, especially by women.[6]

In addition to the new brake system, Chandler greeted the new calendar year with new body styles and appearance and performance revisions. In the Royal Eight line, horsepower was raised by increasing the engine bore to 3⅜ inches with the stroke remaining the same as the previous model.

A Cabriolet with rumble seat joined the Royal Eight line, priced at $1,895. All enclosed models except the Coupe now featured a cadet type visor. Bullet type headlights were now standard on all body styles except the Seven Passenger Touring, and all were nickel plated. Cowl lights, matching the style of the headlights, were relocated to a lower position and moved forward somewhat. A later Chandler brochure stated that all Royal Eights were equipped with nickel plated, bullet type headlights, but the same brochure showed the Touring with the old style drum headlights. Front fenders took on a much more sweeping design, and on cars with sidemounts the tire now rested in a well. All these changes made for a better looking automobile.

The De Luxe Five Passenger Sedan came equipped with wire wheels, which were optional on all other models, with a side mounted spare and rear mounted trunk. The Seven Passenger Sedan had landau irons added at the rear. There is some confusion concerning the total number of body styles offered in the Royal Eight Series; some references list six and others list seven. None lists a Roadster after January 1, 1928. The availability of regular and De Luxe versions of some body styles likely accounts for the confusion.

Prices now ranged from a high of $2,195 for the Five Passenger De Luxe Sedan and Seven Passenger Sedan to a low of $1,995 for the Seven Passenger Touring,

Four Passenger Coupe, Country Club Coupe and Five Passenger Sedan. The Cabriolet was in the middle at $2,095.[7]

The Big Six lineup underwent many changes and additions to match their Royal Eight companions. To add horsepower the engine bore was increased to 3¾ inches with the stroke remaining at 5 inches. A new Seven Passenger Sedan carried virtually the same body as on the Royal Eight. Both the Big Six and Royal Eight Series had three rows of horizontal hood louvers. The total lineup included the Metropolitan Sedan, Royal Six Sedan, Royal Six Sedan with special equipment, Seven Passenger Sedan, Coupe, Country Club Coupe, Cabriolet and Seven Passenger Touring. No mention was made of a Roadster. The Big Six Coupe was shown with vertical hood louvers, eagle radiator cap, old style radiator shell and the visor built into the top. A later brochure illustrated the radiator cap as being flat. The Metropolitan Sedan also had the old style radiator shell with eagle cap.

All enclosed bodies, with the exception of the Coupe, had cadet visors. Headlights were bullet type and nickel plated. (The Metropolitan Sedan and Coupe would later be shown with bullet type headlights painted black with nickel bezels, however.) The Seven Passenger Sedan had black and nickel landau irons at the rear and the Cabriolet had fully nickeled irons. Cowl lights were miniatures of the headlights.

The Royal Six Sedan with special equipment boasted wire wheels, two side mounted spares and rear mounted trunk, all of which were available on all body styles at an additional cost. The Big Six and Royal Six Sedans also came with a heater.

Prices now ranged from $1,925 for the Seven Passenger Sedan down to $1,525 for the Metropolitan Sedan; the Seven Passenger Touring, Four Passenger Coupe, Coun-

***Top:* 1928 Royal Eight Five Passenger Sedan. *Middle:* 1928 Royal Eight DeLuxe Sedan. *Bottom:* 1928 Royal Eight DeLuxe Sedan, late version (all factory photographs, courtesy Roger Anderson).**

try Club Coupe and the Royal Six Sedan all went for $1,725. The Cabriolet, newly added to the line, went for $1,825. Prices had changed in the last few months and some did not reflect the difference between De Luxe and regular models.[8]

The Special Six Series underwent basically the same transformations as the others, and two new body styles were introduced with some offering as many as three levels of trim and equipment. A gasoline gauge was added to the instrument panel. However, the Specials did not receive the fender treatment of the other models in the Chandler lineup and retained the old style radiator shell until the new Model 65 was introduced for the 1929 model year.

"Invincible" was a new name to enter Chandler nomenclature, with the Special Series as the beneficiary. In the beginning, Chandler referred to only two of the seven body styles now offered as the "Invincible": the Special Six Invincible De Luxe Sedan with special equipment and the Special Six Invincible De Luxe Sedan for five passengers.

The other five Special body styles were the Special Six Coupe for three passengers, Special Six Rumble Seat Coupe for four passengers, Special Six Cabriolet for four passengers, Special Six Touring for five passengers and Special Six Sportster for five passengers. The Sportster had already received a facelift and now sported six wire wheels, wind wings on the front windshield, and a trunk mounted on a rack at the rear. A good looking car to begin with, it was now a beautiful creation. A Roadster with rumble seat would be added to the line within a few weeks.

Top: **1928 Royal Eight Seven Passenger Sedan (late).** ***Middle:*** **1928 Big Six Cabriolet for four passengers (late).** ***Bottom:*** **1928 Special Six Coupe for three passengers (late).**

The 1928 Special Parts Book lists five body styles in addition to the Sedans. You could have the Rumble Seat Coupe, Cabriolet, Sportster and Roadster. The Sedans were apparently grouped together as they shared the same body and only paint, upholstery, wire wheels and side mounted spare distinguished them.

The Invincible had its engine bore increased from 3 inches to 3⅛ but the stroke remained the same at 4¼. Two of the previous Specials lingered on as the Five Passenger Touring and Five Passenger Sedan. With drum type headlights and vertical hood louvers, they sold for $995. If you were looking for economy, these were the ones to own. They would continue until the Model 65 was introduced in August. All body styles were Invincible even though the Five Passenger Touring and Five Passenger Sedan retained their former bodies. All were designated the Series 131 as of January 1928; however, they would only be made until July 1928 when the Model 65 was introduced as the Series 132. Their production was so brief that the Invincible name never had time to catch on. All Invincibles fall in the serial number range of C 40,001–C 45,000.

AUTOMOBILE NEWS FROM CHANDLER-CLEVELAND MOTORS CORPORATION

June 5, 1928.

Chandler Has Unique Club

Mileage of Owners' Cars Determines Eligibility.

"Everywhere throughout the world, there are automobile clubs, most of which any motorist can join, but we can't say as much about Chandler's exclusive club, known as the 100,000 Mile Club," states ________________ local Chandler distributor.

"As its name signifies, this club is composed of Chandler owners who have driven one or more Chandlers in excess of 100,000 miles.

"The headquarters of the club is at the Chandler factory in Cleveland. Chandler officials are naturally proud of this organization, because it offers exclusive evidence that Chandler is a car of long life, a quality that is as highly important as the various performance attributes for which Chandler is already notable.

"The club now numbers among its membership, thousands of Chandler owners from every state in the Union, and practically every country throughout the world.

"Each member of this exclusive club carries on the radiator of his or her Chandler, an emblem in blue enamel on white background, which is furnished by Chandler to all 100,000 Mile club members gratis.

"If you see a Chandler adorned with this plate," further states Mr. ______________, "you can be assured that the owner has driven his or her car over 100,000 miles, and in all probability has owned two or more Chandler cars. It seems to be prevalent with 100,000 Mile Club members to have owned more than one Chandler - even to the extent of ten. Therefore, from the foregoing, one can appreciate that this club is really made up of enthusiastic, as well as veteran Chandler owners.

Are You in Chandler's Club?

Your Mileage Determines Your Eligibility

EVERYWHERE throughout the world, there are automobile clubs, most of which any motorist can join, but we can't say as much about Chandler's exclusive club, known as the 100,000 Mile Club.

As its name signifies, this club is composed of Chandler owners who have driven one or more Chandlers in excess of 100,000 miles.

The headquarters of the club is at the Chandler factory in Cleveland. Chandler officials are naturally proud of this organization, because it offers exclusive evidence that Chandler is a car of long life, a quality that is as highly important as the various performance attributes for which Chandler is already notable.

The club now numbers among its membership thousands of Chandler owners from practically every state in the union, and many countries throughout the world.

Each member of this exclusive club, carries on the radiator of his or her Chandler, an emblem in blue enamel on white background, which is furnished by Chandler to all 100,000 Mile Club members gratis.

If you see a Chandler adorned with this plate, step up to the owner and engage him in conversation. You will find the owner a Chandler enthusiast, as the mileage on the car alone will testify, and that he or she has interesting stories of experiences as a driver.

Incidently, we might add that any Chandler owner who has driven 100,000 miles and is not in this club, should be, and can be by writing for membership to the Chandler factory.

Radiator Emblem supplied gratis to all Chandler owners who have driven Chandler cars over 100,000 miles. Communicate with your dealer for particulars.

***Top, left:* 1928 Special Six Invincible DeLuxe Sedan with special equipment. *Top, right:* 1928 Special Six Cabriolet for four passengers (late). *Bottom, left:* Chandler-Cleveland Motors Corporation memo, June 5, 1928. *Above:* Chandler-Cleveland Motors Corporation memo, circa 1928.**

The Invincible series was distinguished by bullet type, nickel plated headlights and two rows of horizontal hood louvers. Wire wheels, sidemounts and rear mounted trunk were standard on the Sportster and De Luxe Sedan with special equipment but six wire wheels could be supplied at an extra cost on other models. In fact, bumpers, combination tail and stop light and shock absorbers could be furnished at extra cost also. The two Sedans came with cadet visors but the Coupes had their visors built in as part of the top. Finishes were an array of Duotone colors, and any special color could be furnished for a fee. Upholstery included blue-gray mohair or rich figured wool plush for the enclosed cars, black leather for the Touring and Coupe, and smart Spanish leather for the Roadster, Sportster, Touring De Luxe and the rumble seat of the Coupe.

The Cabriolet was the most expensive Invincible at $1,215 with the Sportster next at $1,165. The Rumble Seat Coupe, Roadster and Five Passenger De Luxe Sedan sold for $1,155, the Five Passenger Sedan and the Five Passenger Touring for $1,085 and the Coupe for $1,055. One Chandler brochure lists

Condensed Consolidated Balance Sheet
Chandler-Cleveland Motors Corporation, Cleveland and Subsidiaries
as of the close of business, December 31st, 1927

ASSETS			
CURRENT			
Cash on Hand and on Deposit		$ 189,158.23	
Customers' Notes Receivable	$ 89,848.41		
Less: Allowance for Doubtful	2,000.00	87,848.41	
Customers' Accounts Receivable	$ 114,096.38		
Cars and Parts sold for Export	83,245.65		
	$ 197,342.03		
Less: Allowance for Doubtful	11,853.05	185,488.98	
Merchandise Inventories, based upon the lower of cost or market values		3,231,786.25	
Creditors' Debit Balances		15,438.60	$ 3,709,720.47
OTHER ASSETS			
Investments and Sundry Securities Owned		$ 81,888.00	
Miscellaneous Notes Receivable		36,996.75	
Employees' and Miscellaneous Accts. Rec., Advances and Claims		104,285.51	
Capital Stock of Chandler-Cleveland Motors Corporation 18,007⅜ Preference and 3,600 Common Shares	$ 294,085.64		
Less: Balance due on purchase thereof	193,740.64	100,345.00	323,515.26
PERMANENT			
Land and Buildings	$4,250,597.35		
Machinery, Equipment, etc.	6,360,853.90	$10,611,451.25	
Less: Allowance for Depreciation		3,427,801.52	7,183,649.73
GOOD WILL			5,000,000.00
DEFERRED			
Prepaid Expenses, including Unamortized Organization Expense			156,937.59
			$16,373,823.05
LIABILITIES			
CURRENT			
Notes Payable of Subsidiary		$ 28,633.59	
Accounts Payable		747,122.50	
Customers' Credit Balances		63,995.67	
Accrued Real, Personal and Corporate Taxes		187,654.60	
Dealers' Deposits		79,471.94	$ 1,106,878.30
RESERVES			
For General Contingencies		$ 300,000.00	
For Contingencies in Connection with Dies, Jigs and Tools, Commitments and Inventories		500,000.00	800,000.00
NOMINAL			
CAPITAL STOCK—NO PAR VALUE			
Capital Stock of Chandler-Cleveland Motors Corp., outstanding, including 8,537⅜ Preference Shares and 3,289 Common Shares to be exchanged for certain shares of The Chandler Motor Car Co. and Cleveland Automobile Co. not yet transferred: Declared Capital Value.			
350,000 Preference Shares at $25.00	$8,750,000.00		
280,000 Common Shares at $1.10	308,000.00	$ 9,058,000.00	
CONSOLIDATED SURPLUS			
Balance December 31st, 1927		5,408,944.75	14,466,944.75
			$16,373,823.05

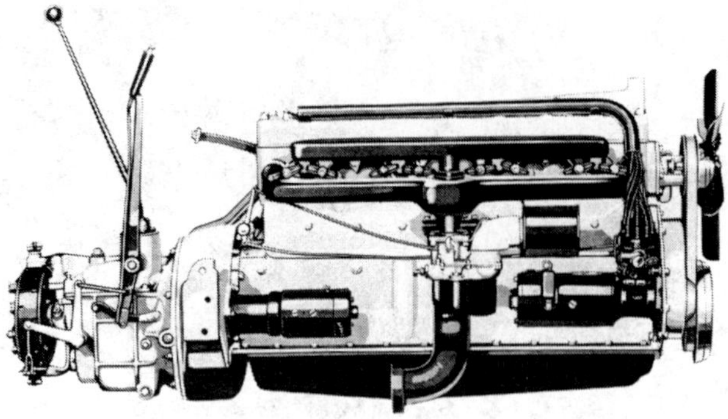

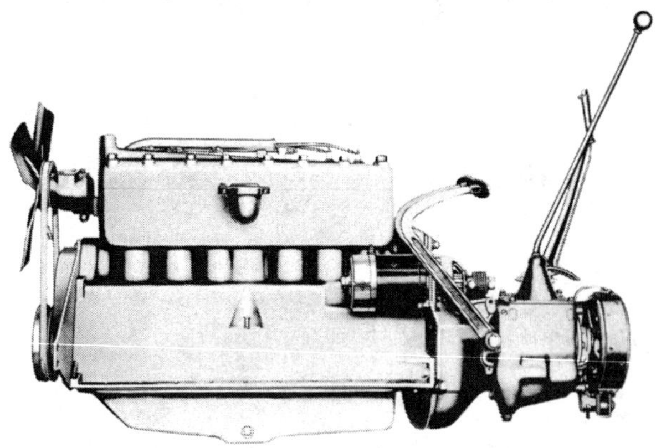

Above: **Chandler-Cleveland balance sheet as of December 31, 1928.** ***Right, from top:*** **1928 Royal Eight engine; 1928 Big Six engine; 1928 Special Six engine; 1928 Royal Eight and Royal Six Sedan interior.**

ten body styles, but many are De Luxe and special equipment models. This makes prices nearly impossible to ascertain without error. Illustrations and descriptions did not always agree in brochures, trade publications and Chandler bulletins. They were prone to using some earlier illustrations and information which introduces confusion in describing certain models.

By 1928 Chandler was shipping 15 percent of all cars manufactured to foreign countries. Their export business had increased dramatically and was as good as any American car company. Cars were being shipped to 103 countries and, remarkably, the Canadian business had increased by 128 percent over the 1927 total.[9]

In early June, Chandler-Cleveland sent dealers and owners a couple of memos, reminding them of the 100,000 mile club plaque which they could have by driving their Chandler the required mileage. This award could be secured by driving one or more Chandler vehicles. Some owners had previously accumulated the required mileage by driving only one vehicle while others had driven as many as ten different Chandlers.

Chandler was building a lot of cars and offering a variety of makes and models to please everyone but they were not making money. As the end of the 1928 model year came to a close they were barely breaking even. After the nearly half million dollar loss in 1927, Chandler-Cleveland was doing everything possible to retain their dealers and increase their sales. Company officers were scurrying around the country trying to stimulate business. Sidney Black, vice president and general manager, met with a group of dealers at Buffalo on February 24, for example, assuring them that everything was fine. But it was not so. The financial report for April, May and June revealed that a profit of only $3,796 had been earned and only $52,266 was the total earnings for the preceding quarter.[10]

Chandler was in serious trouble as the 1929 model year approached.

• Nine •

The End of Chandler

As the 1929 model year began in August, Chandler was scrambling to stay solvent, showing a net profit of less than $4,000 for the quarter ending June 30. This amounted to less than two cents per share of their common stock when people were making millions in the stock market. This was totally unacceptable to stockholders and officials of the company alike.

Advertising in magazines, trade journals and newspapers had virtually ceased by early 1928. Chandler did, however, continue to produce a steady stream of factory brochures and pamphlets. These were available at the dealers, and if prospective customers wanted the latest information, a trip to the nearest dealer was necessary. It was not an ideal way to attract potential owners, but something had to be done to alleviate the money crunch, and advertising was the department which suffered. When advertising money dries up, so does free publicity and thus it was with Chandler.

In order to stimulate sales, Chandler added a new eight cylinder series to the line and changed the names of two others.[1] The Royal Eight became the Royal 85 and a smaller new eight was designated the Royal 75. The Big Six Series survived but the Special Series was replaced by the Model 65. All models came with the Westinghouse vacuum brake system with the exception of the Model 65, on which it was available as an option.[2]

Supposedly customers were standing in line to see the new creations, but were they interested enough to buy? According to Chandler, they could not build cars fast enough to keep up with the demand—but why were they losing money?[3]

These were the days of excess and everyone supposedly had money. However, the competition was fierce and customers had the choice of many makes and models. The days of the small independent companies were coming to an end as the large corporations began to apply the squeeze. Regardless of the circumstances, Chandler had a lineup that should have been pleasing to everyone. And the factory had finally gotten its body building facilities operating at a rate which would enable them to build all Chandler bodies with no further need for outside suppliers.

All Chandlers once more sported a new radiator badge, and it was a beauty. Apparently the design of the 1928 badge had not been well received by Chandler loyalists, the chief complaints being that it was generic and the Chandler name was not mentioned. In the new multicolor cloisonné shield, Chandler was lettered across at a downward angle with a numeral 6 or 8 in the bottom section. The new badge adorned a slightly redesigned radiator shell which was taller with the corners slightly more squared, while keeping the three vertical bars. It was the best looking treatment the Chandler had received in a long time.[4]

The Royal 85 maintained the previous Royal Eight body styles and most mechanical specifications but a Berline Sedan was added to the line. The Berline became the most expensive Chandler, selling at $2,295, followed by the Seven Passenger Sedan at $2,195 and the Cabriolet at $2,095. The De Luxe Sedan and Seven Passenger Touring sold for $1,995, the Coupe and Country Club Coupe for $1,925 and the Sedan for $1,795. The Royal 85 Seven Passenger Sedan was equipped with chrome plated landau irons and the De Luxe Sedan came with six wire wheels and a trunk at the rear.[5] The basic body was the same as the late 1928 models, but the interior and various details were redesigned along with the radiator, hood and bumpers. A new design stamped into the front fenders mimicked the design on the headlights and cowl lights. New plush interiors, hardware by Butler and numerous paint schemes made this one of the best Chandlers ever offered. Brightwork was now chrome finished on all four series.

The Royal 75 was a smaller version of the Royal 85, riding on a wheelbase of 118 inches and powered by an eight cylinder L head engine based on the Pikes Peak Six, with a bore and stroke of 3 × 4½ inches. Like all Chandlers, with the exception of the Model 65, it had the "One Shot" lubrication system. It was initially offered in four body styles: the Brougham (two door), Sedan, De Luxe Sedan and Coupe. A Rumble Seat Coupe soon joined the line—just a fancied up version of the regular Coupe with a rumble seat and black and chrome landau irons added.

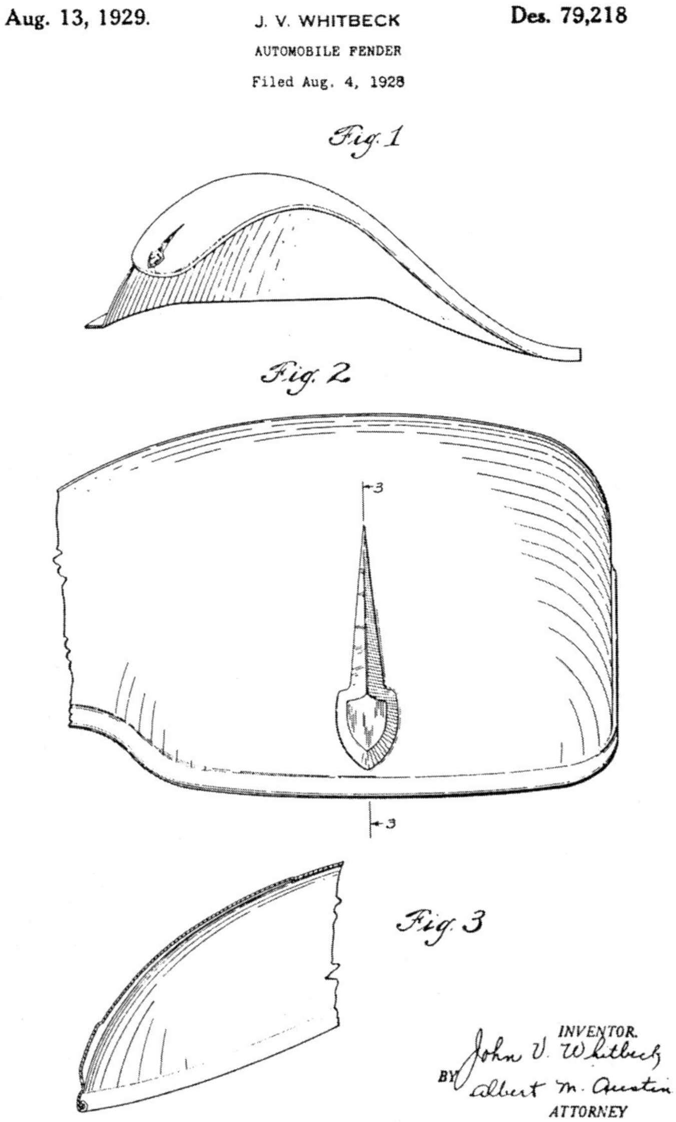

***Above:* 1929 Chandler fender design (factory photograph, author's collection). *Right:* Patent drawing of 1929 Chandler fender design.**

Prices ranged from $1,495 for the De Luxe Sedan to $1,295 for the Coupe, Rumble Seat Coupe and Brougham, with the Sedan going for $1,395. The De Luxe Sedan was a better equipped version of the Sedan with wire wheels, side mounted spares and a trunk at the rear. Bumpers were shown on all Chandlers, but they would remain an option until the end. Lovejoy shock absorbers and a combination tail and stop light were also optional. Six wire wheels, sidemounts and trunk could be had on any Royal 75 at an extra cost. Mohair was the upholstery in Royal 75 cars with broadcloth being an extra on the De Luxe Sedan. The Coupe could have a leather interior for an extra cost.[6]

The Big Six was available in eight body styles with the Berline Sedan having been added for the new model year. The seven other body styles were the Seven Passenger Touring, Metropolitan Sedan, Coupe, Country Club Coupe, Royal Six Sedan, Cabriolet and Seven Passenger Sedan. Prices ranged from $1,525 for the Five Passenger Metropolitan Sedan to $2,025 for the Berline. In between were the Seven Passenger Touring, Four Passenger Coupe, Three Passenger Country Club Coupe and Five Passenger Royal Six Sedan at $1,725, the Cabriolet at $1,825 and the Seven Passenger Sedan at $1,925. Exterior finishes included a wide range of Duotone colors and the interior was done in plush fabrics, mohair for the closed cars and Spanish leather in the open cars. The Cabriolet was equipped with chrome plated landau irons and champagne colored pigskin upholstery.[7]

The 65 combined elements of previous models. The 108½ inch wheelbase originated with the Cleveland Model 31, continued with the Chandler Standard Series, reappeared as the 1928 Special for that model year only and now been continued as the Chandler 65. The six cylinder engine had been proven in the previous Special and would move the smallest Chandler very efficiently. Seven body styles made up the line with the Three Passenger Cabriolet being the most expensive at $1,075 and the Three Passenger Coupe lowest at $875. In between were the Five Passenger De Luxe Sedan and Five Passenger Sportster at $995, the Five Passenger Sedan and Five Passenger

Prices of the Various Chandler Models

"65" Series

Model	Price
Sedan	$895
De Luxe Sedan	995
Cabriolet	1075
Rumble Seat Coupe	955
Coupe	875
Sportster	995
Touring	895

Royal "75" Series

Model	Price
Sedan	$1395
De Luxe Sedan	1495
Brougham	1295
Coupe	1295

Big Six Series

Model	Price
Metropolitan Sedan	$1525
Seven Passenger Sedan	1925
Berline	2025
Cabriolet	1825
Country Club Coupe	1725
Coupe	1725
Seven Passenger Touring	1725

Royal "85" Series

Model	Price
Sedan	$1795
De Luxe Sedan	1995
Seven Passenger Sedan	2195
Berline	2295
Cabriolet	2095
Country Club Coupe	1925
Coupe	1925
Seven Passenger Touring	1995

Left: **Chandler price list, August 1928.** ***Above, from top:*** **1929 Royal 85 Seven Passenger Sedan (factory photograph, courtesy Roger Anderson); 1929 Royal 85 DeLuxe Sedan (factory photograph, author's collection); 1929 Royal 75 DeLuxe Sedan (factory photograph, courtesy Roger Anderson).**

Touring at $895 and the Four Passenger Rumble Seat Coupe at $955. Like the larger Chandlers, the 65 offered a multitude of Duotone paint colors and rich figured plush or mohair interiors available in the closed cars while the open cars sported Spanish leather.

"One Shot" lubrication was available at a cost of $60. Otherwise, you got the Alemite Zerk system. Westinghouse brakes were an extra at $75. All brightwork was chromium including headlights, cowl lights, radiator shell and bumpers if ordered. The Rumble Seat Coupe and Cabriolet also sported chromium landau irons. The De Luxe Sedan and Sportster looked their best when wire wheels were provided. Both were available with twin mounted spares also and the Sportster had a trunk rack at the rear. The Model 65 was Chandler's economy car but there was nothing economical about its looks. It looked like a million dollars.[8]

With all this opulence on four distinctive lines with every body style imaginable, it would seem logical that success was inevitable. Not so! Chandler was going broke while building the best automobiles they ever produced. For the quarter ending July 30, 1928, they made a profit of only $3,796. Even while reporting that shipments were up substantially, they continued the downhill slide, suffering a loss of $61,569 by October 31.[9]

Although business was terrible in late 1928, Chandler-Cleveland decided to build a four-story 100 × 80 foot extension to the former Cleveland factory (# 2). Ernest McGeorge designed the structure and the William Dunbar Company did the construction. In October they also began the construction of a one-story addition to the former Cleveland machine shop which was completed in December.

Fred C. Chandler, being the astute businessman he was, knew something had to be done in a hurry. When DuBois Young, president of the Hupp Motor Car Corporation, made overtures of a purchase, he was ready to listen and so were a majority of the board of directors. Hupp had just completed a year of unprecedented success and needed a new factory and dealers in place to continue this progress. Chandler had both and wanted out. Fred C. Chandler was conspicuously absent while the negotiations were conducted. He supposedly was in Europe making the rounds of the auto shows for new ideas in the automobile industry, but in all likelihood he simply didn't want to answer the hundreds of questions being asked about the deal, and if he really was in Europe it was to avoid doing so.

Samuel Regar, Fred C. Chandler and A.B. Rinehart, a director from Akron who controlled a large block of Chandler-Cleveland stock, put a price on their holdings and that, apparently, was enough to insure that the deal would be made. John R. Hall and Charles A. Emise, two others who had controlled large amounts of stock, were deceased and their estates had been settled by this time. The remaining stockholders were in a minority and the deal was closed over the objections of some, reportedly Joe Krall and John Whitbeck.[10]

An offer of $18 million was made for what supposedly was only about $10 million in total assets (some sources say as much as $16 million), including not only the two Chandler factories in Cleveland but two subsidiaries as well. The Automobile

Top: **1929 Royal 75 DeLuxe Sedan (factory photograph, courtesy Roger Anderson).** ***Above:*** **George Graham points out the virtues of the engine on a 1929 Royal 75 Sedan (photograph courtesy Greg Pemberton).**

Top: **1929 Royal 75 Brougham. *Middle:* 1929 Royal 75 DeLuxe Sedan (both factory photographs, courtesy Roger Anderson). *Bottom:* 1929 Big Six Sedan (factory photograph, author's collection).**

Machine Company, located at Euclid Avenue and London Road, which machined all gears for Chandler, was included. The Automobile Machine Company was run by Duffield Miles, who had come to work for Chandler as purchasing agent in 1917 and resigned at Chandler on March 15, 1920, to be named as the plant manager at Automobile Machine. The Atlas Manufacturing Company of Fostoria, Ohio, makers of Chandler's crankshafts, was another part of the deal. Chandler also had its own facilities for nickeling but it is not clear whether it was a subsidiary or a part of the manufacturing complex. With company president Chandler in Europe, Samuel Regar handled the negotiations with Hupp.

On Friday, November 22, it was confirmed that Hupp had purchased Chandler-Cleveland. On December 11, all Chandler officers and directors resigned at a Chandler-Cleveland stockholders meeting and a slate of officers associated with Hupp were elected. DuBois Young was elected president of Chandler-Cleveland and new directors were C.D. Hastings, J. Walter Drake, H.J. Halle, Moritz Rosenthal, Arthur von Schlagel, Robert C. Schaffner, John Sherwin, Jr., and Charles L. Bradley. The two board members who had not previously been on the Hupp board were Charles Bradley and John Sherwin, Jr. These two were chosen to represent Cleveland businessmen who had an interest in the deal. Bradley was formerly associated with the Union Trust Company of Cleveland and had been instrumental in bringing the Jordan Motor Car Company to that city in 1916. He was now president of the Union Terminal Company and had been a former director and vice president at the Jordan Motor Car Company. John Sherwin, Jr., was a vice president of the Union Trust Company and son of its president.

Young was backed by Dillon, Read and Company (who were principal players in the Chrysler-Dodge merger) and the deal was sealed. Joe Krall and J.V. Whitbeck wanted to stick it out but they were in a minority and could not convince the other directors to go along. Clarence Dillon and his company had supposedly taken a financial bath with Dodge, and one wonders why they would want anything to do with another automobile company.

The deal would be final when 95 percent of Chandler stock had been deposited. Stockholders would receive one share of Hupp for every two shares of Chandler-Cleveland preferred and one share of Hupp common for each 3½ of Chandler-Cleveland common. The Chandler-Hupp combination would start 1929 with total assets of $40,000,000 and securities worth $100,000,000.[11]

There were rumors that W.C. Durant and the railroad baron Van Sweringen Brothers had been interested in Chandler, but most people in the know dismissed them as having little merit. However, the Van Sweringen Brothers did own considerable stock in Hupp. There were reportedly promises made that the Chandler nameplate would continue, but promises are easily broken.

DuBois Young did state that the Chandler name would continue and that the two lines of automobiles complemented each other instead of competing. However, on January 19, 1929, R.S. Cole, Hupp's vice president in charge of sales, stated that all four lines of the Chandler would be dropped. Hupp did not acquire Chandler-Cleveland for the purpose of continuing the name. They wanted their factories in order to build more automobiles and their ready-made dealer network to sell Hupmobiles. If there were Hupmobile and Chandler dealers in the same town, you could be sure who had to go.

What caused Chandler's downfall? Was it mismanagement? Or just a combination of small things which added up to one big problem? The cars they were building were surely the best they had ever produced, so it would seem not to be a fault of the product.

Competition was fierce at this time with the large companies building cars to compete in every price range. They also had finance systems available to buyers who could not afford a car without a payment plan. Mismanagement probably did cause the debacle in late 1925 when Chandler stopped buying their bodies from Fisher. This resulted in lost business which could not be recovered and it may have led to the Chandler-Cleveland merger. Executives with too many positions caused talent to be diluted and they found that managing two large companies was becoming an impossible task. Meanwhile Cleveland was affected by the Fisher decision and they too were scrambling for a supplier.

Top: **1929 Model 65 showing fender design.** ***Above:*** **1929 Model 65 Sedan (both factory photographs, courtesy Roger Anderson).**

Top: **1929 Model 65 DeLuxe Sedan (photograph courtesy Roger Anderson).** ***Middle:*** **1929 Model 65 Three Passenger Coupe (factory photograph, courtesy Roger Anderson).** ***Bottom:*** **1929 Royal 75 Sedan and 1930 Hupmobile Sedan at Price Motor Sales, Rupert, WV (photograph courtesy John W. Chandler).**

Chandler was producing four lines of cars with too many body styles and was unable to find a market where they would all fit. In reality, they were competing against themselves.

A persistent rumor has held that some Chandler officials were paying too much attention to the stock market and not enough attention to their jobs. The stock market was wild at that time and a lot of people were making more money than they had ever dreamed of. Perhaps things other than producing automobiles were beginning to be more appealing. Direct evidence is lacking, but the rumor may have some merit.

Whatever the reasons were, a great company which built some fine automobiles became a casualty of the times. For those who loved the Chandler it was and is a tragedy. Chandler lived on until April 15, 1929, when the last car came off the assembly line. Six weeks later a Hupmobile Model S six cylinder automobile rolled out of the former Chandler factory.[12]

The Hupp Motor Company was founded by Robert C. Hupp on November 8, 1908. He had a background of various industrial jobs and along with Emil Nelson as designer-engineer and Charles D. Hastings' management skills had made a success of the company. Robert Hupp's other interests caused him to neglect his duties at the Hupp Motor Company and on September 1, 1911, he departed the firm. He was barred by contract from using his name in another automobile venture, but undeterred, he just changed the name of his other holdings to the R.C. H. Corporation and proceeded to build the R.C. H. automobile which survived until 1914. While Robert Hupp went on to many other ventures, the original Hupp Motor Company

Opposite, top: **Chandler Factory, Building 6 (the former army tractor plant), seen at left after sale to Hupp (photograph courtesy Cleveland State University Archives).** ***Bottom:*** **Chandler Building 1, the original assembly plant, seen after it was occupied by Weatherhead (courtesy U.S. Department of the Interior, National Park Service).**

DLER

Top: **Chandler factory after Hupp ceased production—first building and office (photograph courtesy U.S. Department of Interior, National Park Service).** ***Bottom:*** **Chandler Factory Building #6 where military tractors were built, later expanded to four floors (photograph courtesy U.S. Department of Interior, National Park Service).**

became a successful automobile company and by 1928 had a desperate need for expansion. The acquisition of Chandler satisfied the need to expand manufacturing and gave them a much larger dealer network.

Hupp totally stripped the original factory (Plant #1) and refitted it for production within 45 days. The Cleveland factory (Plant #2) was reworked about the same time and used as a body building facility.[13]

In hindsight, the Chandler-Cleveland board of directors got it right. Hupp, on the other hand, could not predict the future and just eleven months later they paid the price as the economy went bust. The Great Depression would take down every car maker in Cleveland before it was over. Hupp would linger in Cleveland until the mid-thirties but eventually abandoned all manufacturing there. The factory buildings would be used for other purposes with some falling into disrepair. Some remain to this day and are occupied by tenants of various interests.

Fred Chandler went on to help his sons start another manufacturing company[14]; Samuel Regar retired and lived out his life at the Statler Hotel. John Whitbeck, who picked up the title of Colonel, went on to invest in real estate and became president of the Elco Grease Company.[15] W.S.M. Mead retired but lived only until October 31, 1931, and Joe Krall went on to another endeavor.

Charles A. Emise and John Richard Hall were both deceased before Chandler sold. Charles A. Carey had left the company about 1917 and moved to Jackson, Michigan, where he had a career making refrigerators but only lived until the mid-twenties.

• Ten •

Advertising, Personalities, Distributors and Dealers

Sales and Advertising

Chandler advertising, although not as impressive as that of some major manufacturers and independents, was plenty adequate. They kept their dealers supplied with an abundance of sales literature and the trade magazines gave the company liberal coverage of newsworthy events throughout the life of the company.

Charles A. Emise, Chandler's original vice president of advertising and sales, had a wealth of knowledge in that field. He had sold bicycles, motor launches, marine engines and automobiles while employed at Lozier. Having attracted press coverage while in charge of Lozier's successful racing program, he knew how to use this to Chandler's advantage.

When Emise left active participation in the affairs of the company in 1916 his advertising duties were assumed by James Mack Dunlap. Co-owner of Dunlap-Ward Advertising Company of Chicago and Detroit, Dunlap was persuaded to leave his business by Chandler officials who wanted someone knowledgeable in the field. His firm had previously handled many of Chandler's advertising needs.[1] On July 1, 1920, Dunlap was promoted to director of sales and advertising.[2]

By November 1921, George Graham had been lured away from Pierce-Arrow, where he was a vice president, and appointed vice president in charge of sales, service and advertising at Chandler. Chandler felt the need for new leadership in their sales and advertising department because sales had plummeted drastically. They felt Graham was the person who could help the company regain its former position in the automotive industry.

Frank Connor, formerly in charge of foreign sales, was advanced to the position of domestic sales manager. John M. Howard was now heading up advertising and R. M. Fraser had taken charge of service. Apparently, James M. Dunlap left Chandler about this time.[3]

In addition to the trade magazines, Chandler made good use of newspapers and household magazines to get their product before the eyes of the public. The *Saturday Evening Post* and *The Literary Digest* were the major beneficiaries of Chandler's early advertising efforts. Later *The Literary Digest* and *The National Geographic* were favored, but the *Post* regained Chandler's favor in the last few years of production.

In between, there was an abundance of ads in *Collier's, Harper's, Review of Reviews, Life* and the *American Magazine. Leslie's Weekly, The Companion, Cosmopolitan, The Worlds Work Advertiser, Vogue, House and Garden, The National Geographic* and *Country Gentleman* also got their share of the business. Chandler also advertised heavily in the leading trade magazines of the day. Occasionally an ad could be found in some other magazine. Customers could also write the company requesting information on certain models and the location of the nearest dealer. By 1927 Chandler had representatives in 61 countries. Their boast was the "Sun Never Sets on Chandler."[4]

Advertising virtually ceased in 1928. When Hupp purchased the company in December of that year, they knew the Chandler name would be dropped and they did almost no advertising while they closed out the marque.

Personalities Who Endorsed Chandler

During the years of Chandler's production, as today, manufacturers were always looking for a way to keep their product before the eyes of the public. Endorsements by sports figures, movie and stage stars and other prominent people are probably the best advertising there is. Chandler used this method of advertising extensively—in fact, they were probably the best of all the early manufacturers at employing celebrity endorsements.

The following is a short list of prominent people who endorsed Chandler or at least were associated with them in some way.

Annette Kellerman

Annette Marie Sarah Kellerman, born on July 6, 1888, was a record holding swimmer who went on to star in motion pictures starting in 1909 and finishing in 1924. She was a women's rights activist and was one of the first women to wear a one-piece bathing suit, for which she was arrested. Her championship form in swimming led to roles in vaudeville and the movies. She was also a writer of note. She was the first major actress to do a nude scene which she performed in *A Daughter of the Gods* in 1916.

She was born in Darlinghurst, New South Wales, Australia. At an early age she was diagnosed with a weakness in her legs which required the wearing of painful steel braces. Her parents enrolled her in swim classes in order to strengthen her body and she enjoyed the water to the extent that it led to her career. She drove a 1926 Comrade Roadster.[5]

Jane Novak

Johana B. Novak was born on January 12, 1896, in St. Louis, Missouri. Her parents were from Bohemia and her father died when she was a child. She ran away from home as a teenager and formed a vaudeville act, later being invited to California by an aunt who had some influence in the motion picture industry. This was an opportunity to help her niece and Jane appeared in a film on her 17th birthday.

She had a long acting career which spanned several years and 115 movies. She was the first actress to be paid a four figure salary for a single role and was an accomplished writer of cookbooks. She drove a 1925 Chandler Comrade Roadster.[6]

Early Chandler ad (showing the prototype) (*Life*, September 18, 1913).

Priscilla Dean

Priscilla Dean was born in New York City on November 25, 1896. Raised in a theatrical family, she appeared in her first movie at age four and made her credited film debut at age fourteen, signing her first contract with Universal in 1911.

Her claim to fame came in the movie *The Gray Ghost* in 1917. She did not have a great voice and when sound took over the movies in the late 1920s her career declined. Miss Dean drove a 1925 Comrade Roadster.[7]

Leatrice Joy

Leatrice Joy Zeidler was born in New Orleans on November 7, 1893. She made her film debut in New Orleans in 1915. Two years later she moved to Hollywood and began appearing in comedy films.

Her film career saw her work for several of the major studios and appear opposite many well-known actors and actresses. She was one of the few whose voice allowed her to go from silent to talking films with moderate success and her career spread over forty years. She drove a 1925 Comrade Roadster.[8]

"Lefty" Flynn

Maurice Bennett Flynn was born at Greenwich, Connecticut, on May 26, 1892. He attended Yale University where he starred in football but was expelled after he married a chorus girl in January 1913. They separated after eleven days and were divorced in 1914.

He got his nickname "Lefty" because he kicked with his left foot. Flynn was a handsome young man whose good looks took him to the movie industry where he appeared in 40 feature films between 1914 and 1927. He drove a 1925 Comrade Roadster.[9]

Hal Chase

Harold Homer Chase was born at Los Gatos, California, on February 13, 1883. A baseball player supreme, he broke into the sport at the turn of the century and was considered by many to be the best first baseman to ever play the game, starring with the New York Highlanders (1905–13), Chicago White Sox (1913–14), Buffalo Blues (1914–15), Cincinnati Reds (1916–18), and New York Giants (1919).

He was an excellent hitter and considered without peer for his defense. However, his career was tainted by allegations that he gambled on baseball. Chase was eventually banned from the sport and was not voted into the Hall of Fame. He later admitted that he had bet on baseball. He drove a Chandler Roadster.[10]

Alfonso XIII of Spain

Alfonso León Fernando María Jaime Isidro Pascual Antonio de Borbón y Austria-Lorena was born in Madrid, Spain, on May 17, 1886. He became King of Spain at birth, since his father Alfonso XII had died before he was born. His mother, Maria Christina of Austria, was his regent until he became King in 1902 at the age of sixteen.

He ruled Spain until 1931 when he fled the country and lived in exile until his death. He was a great promoter of tourism and was said to be the happiest and best loved king that Spain had ever known. He drove a Chandler Royal Dispatch.[11]

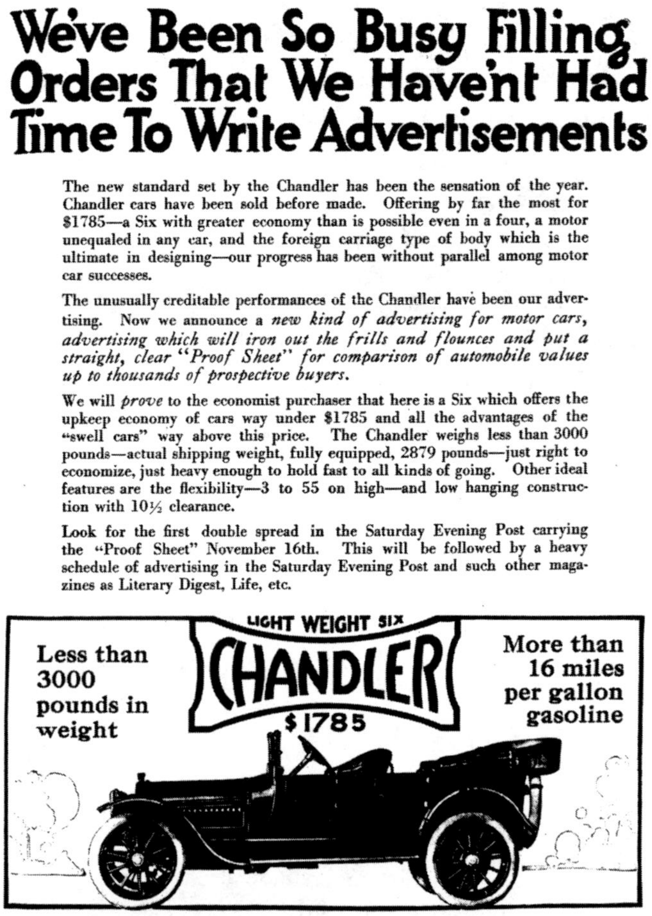

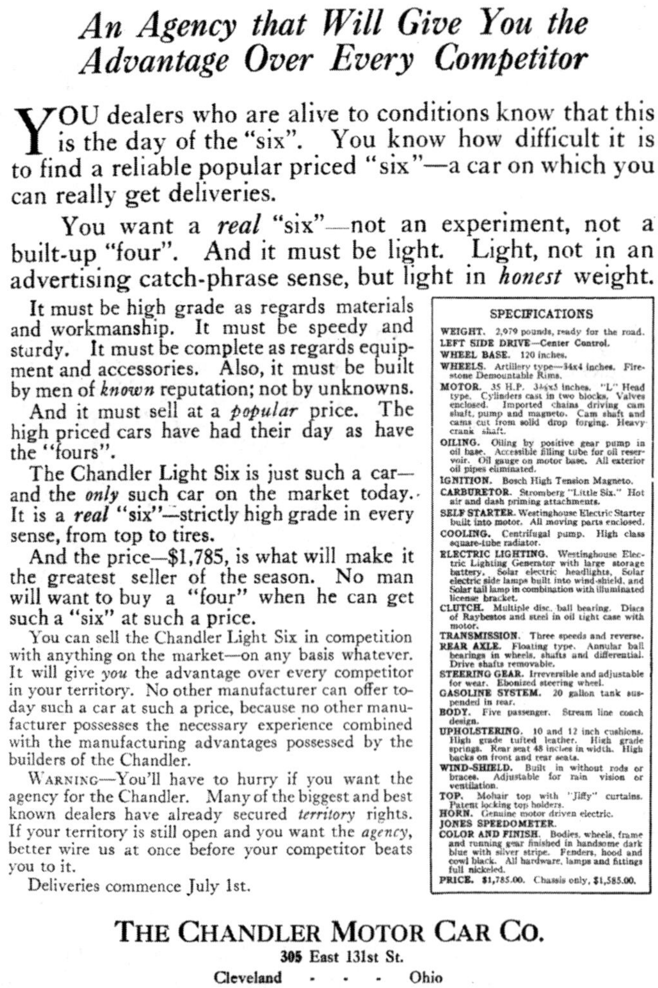

***Left:* Early Chandler ad showing the Model 14 as manufactured (*Saturday Evening Post*, November 15, 1913). *Right:* Chandler ad seeking dealers (circa early 1913, unknown source).**

***Left:* Chandler ad showing price reduction (*Cosmopolitan*, October 1916). *Right:* Chandler ad, ca. 1917–1918, listing San Francisco dealer Peacock Motor Sales Co.**

Pat Moran

Patrick Joseph Moran was born at Fitchburg, Massachusetts, on February 7, 1876. A catcher for the Boston Beaneaters, Chicago Cubs and Philadelphia Phillies, he became a student of the game and was promoted to manager of the Philadelphia Phillies in 1915. The Phillies were the National League champions that year but lost the World Series to the Boston Red Sox. Moran was fired in 1918 and hired by Cincinnati in 1919. The Reds won the National League Pennant and World Series that year.

While at Philadelphia he was given a Chandler Touring car by the Phillies fans as an appreciation for leading the team to greatness.[12]

Katherine Stinson

Katherine Stinson was born at Fort Payne, Alabama, on February 14, 1891. Katherine was the fourth woman in the United States to obtain a pilot's license, which she received on July 24, 1912, at the age of 21. She initially wanted to have a career in music and took up exhibition flying to earn money for piano lessons, but she liked flying so much that she gave up her musical ambition and concentrated on aviation.

She was the first woman to do a loop and went on to perform the maneuver more than 500 times without an accident. She was one of the first women to carry airmail for the United States during World War I, flying a Curtiss JN-4D. Her influence in aviation was so great that her brothers formed the Stinson Aircraft Company, which became a major aircraft manufacturer. She drove a 1916 Chandler Touring car.[13]

Adele Rowland

Adele Rowland was born at Washington, D.C, on July 10, 1883. She was a film actress during the silent era and performed on Broadway. Her career lasted until 1950. She drove a Chandler Four Passenger Convertible Coupe.[14]

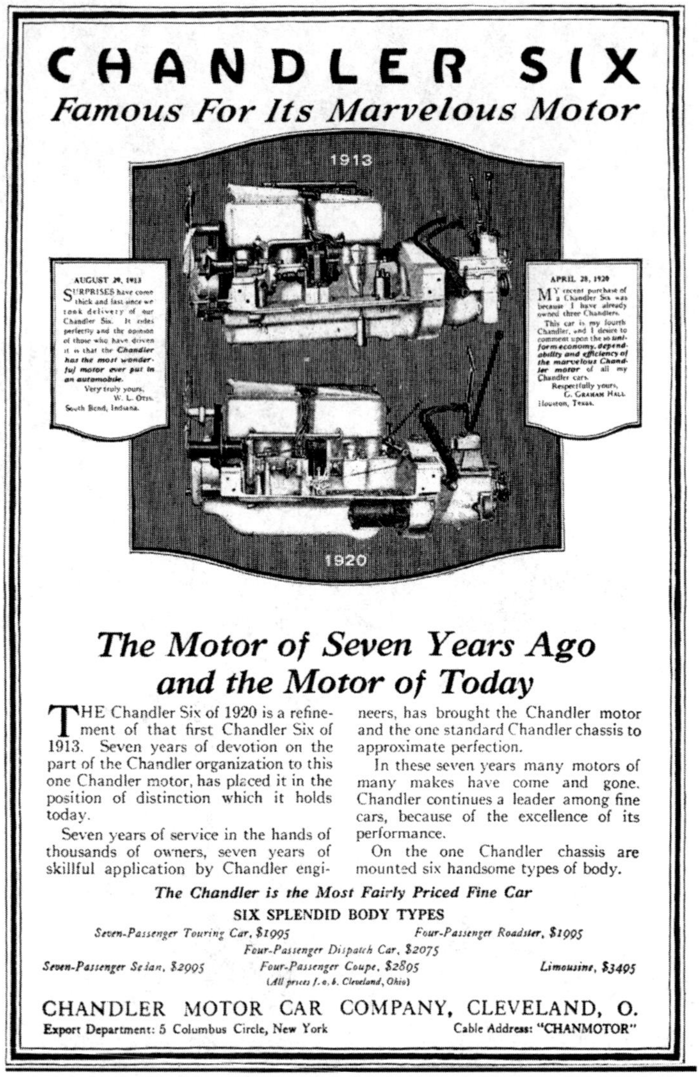

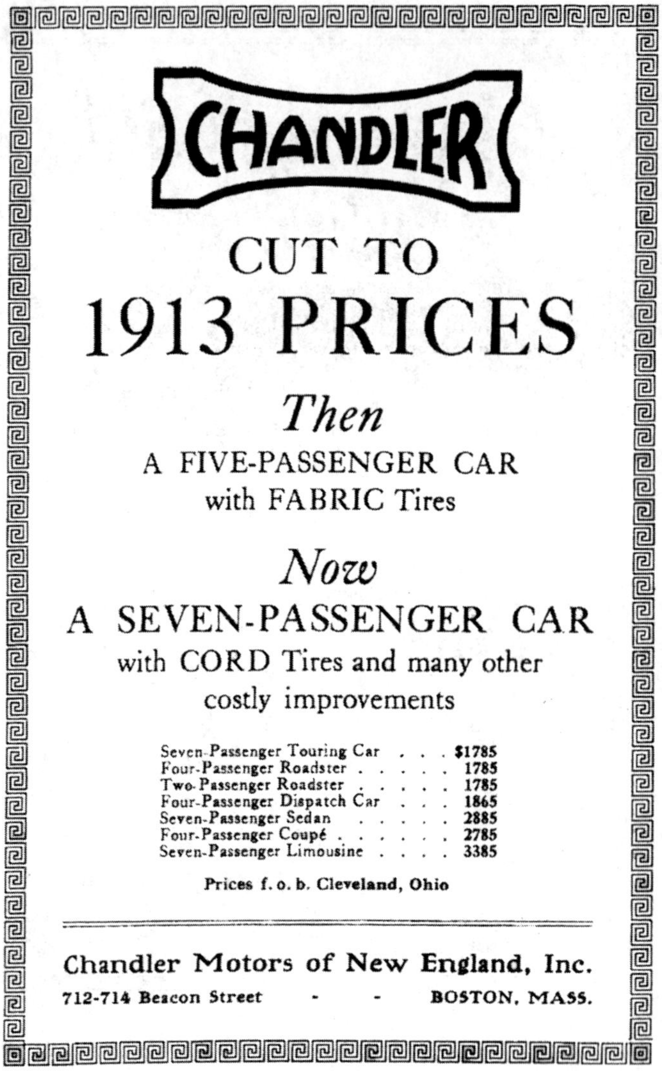

***Left:* Ad from *The Literary Digest*, July 10, 1920. *Right:* Chandler distributor ad (*Chan-Cleve Hub*, July 1921).**

Kathleen Kirkham

Kathleen Kirkham was born at Menominee, Michigan, on April 15, 1895. A film and stage actress, she was regarded as the best dressed woman in Hollywood.

One of her favorite things was picking up schoolchildren in her neighborhood and driving them to school in her Chandler Touring car as she left for work at the studio. By 1934 she was working as a bank teller.[15]

Nat Butler

Nat Butler was born at Cambridge, Massachusetts, on June 1, 1870. He was an early cycling champion whose career spanned from 1893 to 1910. He turned professional in 1901 and was friends with several of the Chandler crowd who also were into bicycling. He drove a Chummy Roadster.[16]

Jean Tynes

Miss Jean Tynes was born in Galveston, Texas, and grew up in New York. She was a star of stage screen and enjoyed driving her Chandler. *The Pretty Baby* was one of her best roles.[17]

Fritzi Scheff

Fredrike Scheff was born in Vienna, Austria, on August 30, 1879. A stage, film, and television actress, she gained her greatest success as a singer and vaudeville performer. She was married three times, her second husband being John Fox, author of *The Trail of the Lonesome Pine*. She owned and drove a Chandler.[18]

Walter Hagen

Walter Charles Hagen was born at Rochester, New York, on December 21, 1892. A champion U.S. golfer, Hagen won

Left: **Chandler ad after merger with Cleveland (*The Literary Digest*, August 28, 1926). *Above:* Mr. and Mrs. A.C. Sharkey of Los Angeles showing off their Chandler Camper at Redwood Park, California (photograph courtesy Roger Anderson). *Below:* Actress Jane Novak sporting her 1925 Comrade Roadster around Hollywood.**

eleven professional major tournaments during his career. His accomplishments included winning the U.S. Open twice, the British Open four times, the PGA Championship five times and the Western Open five times. He also captained and played on many Ryder Cup teams. He won a total 45 PGA tournaments during his career.

Walter Hagen drove a Chandler special built sports car with a body by A.H. Gable of Rochester, New York.[19]

Charlotte Greenwood

Frances Charlotte Greenwood, star of vaudeville, Broadway, screen and radio, was born at Philadelphia, Pennsylvania, on June 25, 1890. Known for her long legs, she was quoted as saying that she was the only woman in the world who was able to kick a giraffe in the eye.

Star of *So Long Letty* and many other films, she played with many of the leading

stars of the day and retired after a role in *Oklahoma* in 1955.

Greenwood drove a Chandler Convertible Sedan.[20]

Helen Keller

Helen Adams Keller was born in Tuscumbia, Alabama, on June 27, 1880. Blinded by a disease at age 18 months, Miss Keller went on to be the first deaf-blind person to earn a Bachelor of Arts degree, which she did at Radcliffe College in 1904.

Author, lecturer and political activist, Keller never let the loss of her sight or her inability to speak impair her work. She learned to read Braille and taught herself to speak.

She espoused many causes—some controversial. She was a member of the Socialist Party of America and the Industrial Workers of the World, and campaigned for women's suffrage, socialism, workers' rights and other radical causes including birth control. She also helped organize the American Civil Liberties Union. Miss Keller's personal transportation was a Chandler Coach.[21]

Suzanne Lenglen

Suzanne Rachel Floce Lenglen was born at Compiegne, north of Paris, France, on May 24, 1899. In her youth she suffered many health problems and took up tennis to strengthen her body. Within four years she won her first tournament. Flamboyant and passionate about her game, she went on to win many titles including the French Women's Singles six times, Wimbledon six times, French Women's Doubles five times, Wimbledon Doubles six times, French Mixed Doubles five times, and Wimbledon Mixed Doubles three times.

One of the greatest women's tennis champions ever to play the game, Lenglen

***Top:* Actress Leatrice Joy and her 1925 Comrade Roadster. *Middle:* Film star Adele Rowland drives her Convertible Coupe. *Bottom:* Early bicycle champion Nat Butler drove a Chummy Roadster.**

was chauffeured about the U.S. in a Chandler Metropolitan Sedan.[22]

Irvin S. Cobb

Irvin Shrewsbury Cobb was born at Paducah, Kentucky, on June 23, 1876. Cobb started a journalistic career at age 17 by working for *The Paducah Daily News* and worked his way up to editor by age 19. He later worked for the *Louisville Evening Post.*

He moved to New York in 1904 and went to work for the *Evening Sun*, later working for Joseph Pulitzer's *New York World.* He also covered World War I for The *Saturday Evening Post.*

He became a writer and several of his books, which numbered more than 60, were made into films. He took up acting, appearing in 10 films between 1932 and 1938. He had starring roles in two films and was host of the 6th Academy Awards in 1935. Cobb drove a Chandler Metropolitan Sedan.[23]

Prince Harald of Denmark

Harald Christian Frederik was born on October 8, 1876, at Charlottenlund Palace, Gentofte, Denmark. The son of Frederik VIII of Denmark, Prince Harald was the brother of King Christian X who succeeded his father. He served in the military most of his adult life and rose to the rank of Lieutenant General. He followed the lead of his brother the King and purchased a Chandler Sedan.[24]

Top: **Actress Jean Tynes loved her Chandler.** ***Bottom:*** **Golfing great Walter Hagen drove his special bodied Chandler speedster.**

Major Hessian

John W. Hessian was undoubtedly one of the best rifle shooters ever to compete. His skill did not come naturally but from a long period of tedious practice. In 1907 he won three firsts in American competition. In 1908 he went to London as a member of the United States Olympic rifle team. In 1909 he won six first place matches and thrilled the world by shooting 57 consecutive Bulls Eyes at 800 yards in the Camp Perry, Ohio National Matches. In 1912 he was a member of the Pan American Championship team and the United States long range military rifle team which won the world championship at Ottawa.

Achieving the rank of major before World War I, Hessian was a central figure in helping the allies with large war contracts. Major Hessian drove a Chandler Model 16 Touring Car.[25]

Other Notables

Miss Edna Earle and Miss M.E.M. Gibsone were actresses who drove Chandlers. Miss Earle was born September 26, 1886, at McPherson, Kansas. Her best film was *The Eagle* in 1918. She also was featured in the *Bluebird* production and her personal transportation was a Chandler Coupe. Miss Gibsone played bit parts and piloted a Chandler Dispatch.[26]

Vaudeville personality Camille Personi, known as the "Butterfly Girl," drove a Chandler.[27]

Ralph Wagner, noted psychic who predicted some significant events, drove a Chandler Eight Roadster.[28]

***Top:* Film stars Edna Earle (right) and M.E.M. Gibsone drove their Chandlers. *Bottom:* Doris Eaton with her 1926 Comrade Roadster (factory photograph, courtesy Roger Anderson).**

"Little Peggy" Ames of the "Our Gang" comedies owned a Chandler Royal Eight Sedan which her mother used to drive the young star to her studio sessions.[29]

Doris Eaton Travis was born March 4, 1904, at Norfolk, Virginia. She was an actress, vaudeville player, dancer, Arthur Murray dance instructor, the last Ziegfeld Follies girl, writer and rancher. She drove a 1927 Comrade Roadster. She returned to school late in life and earned several degrees at the University of Oklahoma. She lived to the age of 106.[30]

Distributors and Dealers

Dealers are a crucial part of any automobile manufacturing business. The sale of an automobile depends greatly upon ready availability and upon what customers have learned from the owner of a similar vehicle. Service, in most instances, determines whether the owner becomes a repeat customer and recommends the product to someone else.

Chandler established a network of distributors and dealers throughout the United States and 61 foreign countries. All large towns and most small ones had a dealer who was ready, willing and able to sell and service any model made by Chandler. Chandler attended all major shows and had officials ready to answer any questions the public might have. Their network was probably as strong as most major manufacturers of the day.[31]

The following is a partial list of those responsible for merchandising the Chandler automobile.

Abbott Automobile Company, Ltd. (New Orleans)
A.B.D. Motor Company (Kansas City)
Achen Motor Company (Milwaukee)
Guy H. Ackerman (Chandler Motor Sales) (Beloit, Wisconsin)
Aimilia Automobile Company (Bombay, India)
W.W. Albee (Augusta, Maine)
Karl Otto Anderson (Kristineham, Sweden)
E.C. Andrews (New Haven, Connecticut)
Arcade Motor Company (Little Rock, Arkansas)
Earl V. Armstrong, Inc. (Los Angeles)
E.S. Austen (Darien, Connecticut)
Ed Austin (Hobart, Tasmania)
Automotive Sales Company (Grand Forks, North Dakota)
Averman-Lynn Inc. (Pittsburgh)

Babbitt-Polson Company (Phoenix)
A.W. Baird Motor Company (Shreveport, Louisiana)
The Banting Machine Company (Toledo)
R.V. Barnes (Panama, Canal Zone)
Barton Auto Exchange (Barton, Vermont)
F.A. Batterly (Brattleboro, Vermont)
Batts-Elder Motor Sales Company (Marion, Illinois)
Becker Motor Company (Fort Wayne, Indiana)
C.T. Beckman (Jersey City, New Jersey)
Bennet Motor Car Company (Fort Wayne, Indiana)
Bennet Motor Car Company (Jamaica, New York)
W.H. Berkhemer Sr. (Batavia, Java & Sumatra)

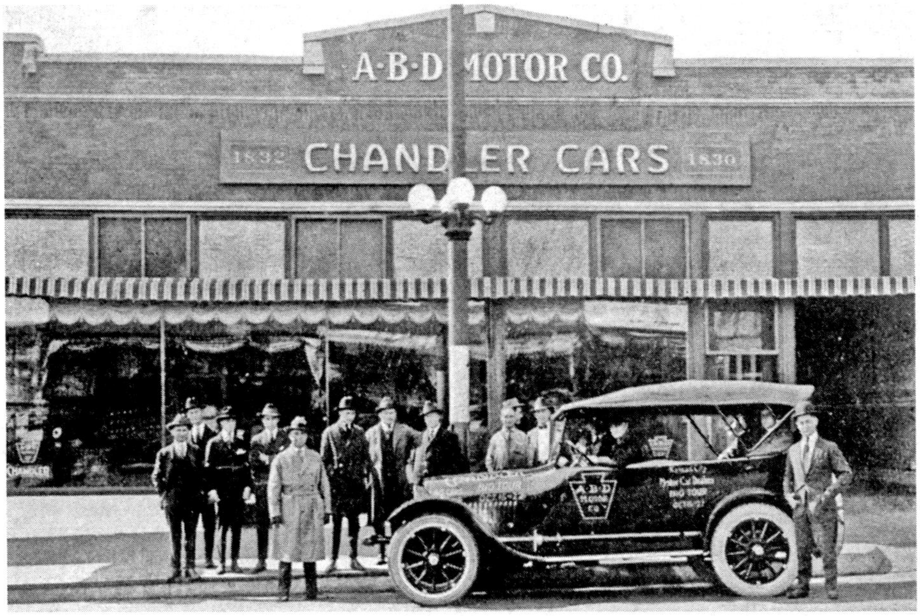

A.B.D. Motor Company, Kansas City, Kansas.

Berkshire Motor Auto Company (Pittsfield, Massachusetts)
J. F. Bieber Garage (Erie, Pennsylvania)
Bixby-Long Motor Car Company (Santa Barbara, California)
Blackburn & Turner (Ellwood City, Pennsylvania)
B.A. Blenner (Richmond, Virginia)
Hugo S. Block (Baltimore)
Borderland Motor Car Company (Phoenix)
Roy C. Bothwell (Salt Lake City)
Boulevard Company (Waterbury, Connecticut)
Hite D. Bowman Company (Louisville, Kentucky)
Bradley & Holland (Brisbane, Australia)
Brady-Murray Company (New York)
Bratton Motor Company (Luverne, Minnesota)
H.H. Brinker, Agent (Huntington, West Virginia)
Broadway Garage Company (Butte, Montana)
H.G. Buford & Company (London, England)
Burns Brothers (Birmingham, Alabama)
Burton-Lary Motors Company (San Antonio)
Buton-Roundtree Company (Houston)
Cadillac Sales Company (Knoxville)
Callahan Motors Company (Louisville, Kentucky)
Callahan-Whiteside, Motor Company (Louisville, Kentucky)
Campbell-Simpson Motor Company (Birmingham, Alabama)
Gordon Campbell's Garage (Toronto)
Card Adams Motor Company (Lincoln, Nebraska)
Central Gas & Engine Works (Singapore)
Central Motor Sales Co. (Fall River and New Bedford, Massachusetts)
D.J. Chandler (Fitzroy, Australia)
Chandler & Company (Auckland, New Zealand)
Chandler-Bianchi (Soerabaga, Java)
Chandler-Cleveland Automobile Sales Co. (Kansas City)
Chandler-Cleveland Motor Car Company (San Francisco)
Chandler-Cleveland Sales Company (Worcester, Massachusetts)
Chandler-Cornelian Company (Indianapolis)
Chandler Motor Company of Colorado (Denver)
Chandler Motor Company of Maine (Portland, Maine)
Chandler Motor Company of N.E. (Boston)
Chandler Motor Company of R.I. (Providence, Rhode Island)
Chandler Motor Company of Texas (San Antonio)
Chandler Motor Sales (Guelph, Ontario)
Chandler Motor Sales Company (Grand Rapids, Michigan)
Chandler Motors of Springfield, Inc. (Springfield, Massachusetts)
Chandler Sales & Service Company (Nashville)
Chandler Sales & Service Company (Montreal)
Chandler Sales Co. of Keene, N.H. (Keene, New Hampshire)
Chandler Six Company (Kansas City)
Charley Cars Limited (Melbourne, Australia)
Charter Oak Motor Sales Company (Hartford, Connecticut)
Cheney Motors, Ltd. (Adelaide, South Australia)
F.M. Chinoy Company (Bombay, India)
E.T. Clark (Seattle)
Marcus Clark & Company, Ltd. (Sydney, Australia)
Clevenger-Smith Company (Yakima, Washington)
Clive Engineering Company Ltd. (Delhi, India)

Central Motor Sales Co. operated in Fall River (top) and New Bedford (middle), Massachusetts. *Bottom:* Chandler Motors of New England, Boston, Massachusetts.

Cobb-Evans Automobile Company (Fresno, California)
W.A. Colt & Son (Las Animas, Colorado)
Columbus Motor Sales Company (Columbus, Ohio)
F.C. Colwell Company (Cincinnati)
J. Ward Conde (Ottawa, Illinois)
Concourse Motor Car Company (Bronx, New York)
George A. Cox (Temple, Texas)
S. Ashton Cox (Wollaston, Massachusetts)
Paul Crawford (Birmingham, Alabama)
Cruikshank & Son (Columbus, Ohio)
Cushman Motor Car Company (Greenville, South Carolina, and Charlotte)
Cuyahoga Sales Company (Cleveland, Ohio)
C.E. Daily & Company (Sioux City, Iowa)
C.E. Daily & Company (Sioux Falls, South Dakota)
Dansk Motor Company (Copenhagen, Denmark)
H.L. Dietrich (Waterloo, Ontario)
Don Sales Company (Rock Island, Illinois)
Duluth Implement Manufacturing Co. (Duluth, Minnesota)
Dunn Motors, Inc. (Seattle)
Dury & Goette, Inc. (Corona, Long Island, New York)
Dykes & Company (Bengal District, India)
H.H. Edgely (Altoona, Pennsylvania)
Edwards Auto Company (Watertown, New York)
Elder-Myers Motor Company (Wichita, Kansas)
Electric City Auto Exchange (Schenectady, New York)
Elm Street Garage (Rutland, Vermont)
Empire Garage Company (Port Chester, New York)
Erie-Penn Auto Company (Erie, Pennsylvania)
Bert Farnsworth (Santa Rosa, California)
Farrell Auto Company (Brooklyn)
Federal Motor Company (Tulsa, Oklahoma)
Federal Motor Company (Wichita, Kansas)
Ferros & Oliveira (Lisbon, Portugal)

Florida-Chandler Motor Company Inc. (Sanford, Florida)
James R. Fones (Ocean Park, California)
E.D. Foote (Concordia, Kansas)
Forsyth & Davis (Kingston, New York)
Bert J. Fralick (Barrie, Ontario)
Fraser & Chalmers, Ltd. (Johannesburg, South Africa)
Freitas Irmaos & Company (Funchal, Madeira Islands)
Frigon & Baker (Montreal)
Fudge Motor Sales (Toronto)
Fulton Chandler Company (Fulton, Illinois)
Fulton-Colwell Company (Cincinnati)
Gardner & Mosher Motor Sales Company (Poughkeepsie, New York)
R.C. Gerhart Motor Company (Little Rock, Arkansas)
Gerlinger Motor Car Company (Portland, Oregon)
Gibson Motor Company (Des Moines, Iowa)
Gilbertson Brothers (Whitehall, Wisconsin)
Good Hope Garage (Milwaukee)
Gordon Auto Sales Company (Detroit)
Grand Garage duClair (Cairo, Egypt)
Graves Auto Company (Waterloo, Iowa)
S.E. Green (Birmingham, Alabama)
Green Auto Company (Danbury, Connecticut)

Top: **Marcus Clark & Company, Ltd., Sydney, Australia.** ***Bottom:*** **A trainload of Chandlers headed for Sioux Falls, South Dakota, and C.E. Daily & Company.**

Green Auto Company (Ogden, Utah)
Greene & Fleming (San Diego)
Gregory & Johnson (Middlebury, Vermont)
M.G. Grief (Somerville, New Jersey)
Guarantee Auto Company (Laredo, Texas)
Hanson-Tyler Company (Webster City, Iowa)
Hardin Motor Car Company (Chester, South Carolina)
Hastrich's Garage (Milwaukee)
Mason B. Hatch, Inc. (Buffalo)
Thomas J. Hay, Inc. (Chicago)
Henderson's Garage (Shreveport, Louisiana)
Henning Garage (Milwaukee)
J.M. Henry (New Haven, Connecticut)
Henshaw Motor Company (Boston)
W.P. Herbert (Los Angeles)
Herbert & Cook (Philadelphia)
Herbert Brothers (Philadelphia)
Herrick Hardware Company (Waco, Texas)
Hess-Thompson Motor Company (Minneapolis)
Hodge-Long Motor Company (Hamilton, Ohio)
P.A. Hoffman (Siam)
Hogan & White Motor Company (Yonkers, New York)
J.R. Holland Automobile Company (Jacksonville, Florida)
Holland Garage (Springfield, Ohio)
G.T. Honeyman (Bound Brook, New Jersey)
Howitzer Battery Company (Melbourne, and Hobart, Tasmania, Australia)
Hudson Boulevard Garage (Jersey City, New Jersey)
Hughes Motor Company (Cleveland)
Hulett Motor Car Company (New York)
Hullett & Law (Atlanta)
Hullett & Law (Indianapolis)
Industrial Garage (Los Angeles)
Jackson Motor (Jackson, Mississippi)
Jacobs & Jacobs (Bradford, Vermont)
H.H. Johnson (Norfolk, Virginia)
J.W. Johnson (Cedar Rapids, Iowa)
Jolly-Baker Motor Car Company (Willmar, Minnesota)
F.H. Jones (Muncie, Indiana)
Jones & Edwards (Long Branch, New Jersey)
Jones Chandler & Cleveland (Huntington, West Virginia)
Keil Motor Company (Wilmington, Delaware)
W.J. Kennerly (San Juan, Puerto Rico)
Keystone Garage (Ancon, Panama Canal Zone)
Kinsey Motor Car Company (Dayton, Ohio)
Koontz & Bachman (St. Joseph, Michigan)
Kwee, Kim, Toen (Java)
Lake Shore Motors Company (Cleveland)
C.W. Landers (Mineola, New York)

Don Sales Company, Rock Island, Illinois.

C. Lauritsen (Hong Kong, China)
J.J. Laverty (New Haven, Connecticut)
T. C. Leach (St. Albans, Vermont)
Perry Lewis Automobile Company (St. Louis, Missouri)
Lichtie Auto Company (Toledo)
T.L. Little (San Antonio)
Lohigorry Brothers (Montevideo, Uruguay)
Lone Star Motor Company (El Paso, Texas)
Lowa's Garage (Yonkers, New York)
Harry A. Lozier (Albany, New York)
F.W. Lute (Hammond, Indiana)
George P. Lutz (Toledo)
Mack Brothers (Reno, Nevada)
Charles A. Maino (San Luis Obispo, California)
Mammen & Drescher (Copenhagen, Denmark)
J.H. Marguetta (Chicago)
H.A. Mark (Philipsburg, Pennsylvania)
Markham Motor Company (Oklahoma City, Oklahoma)
T.J. Marlier Company (Milwaukee)
Massaline Motor Car Company (Jersey City, New Jersey)
McArthur Brothers (Phoenix)
Joseph McCarren (Charlesville, Ohio)
Martin D. McCarthy (Lowell, Massachusetts)
McCarty-Greene Motor Company (Birmingham, Alabama)
McCord-Harris Company (Columbus, Ohio)
Mecum, Flynn & Hunter Company (San Francisco)
Merrill & Freeman (Napa, California)
Miami Chandler Company (Miami)
Mileage Motor Sales Corp. (Buffalo)
Miller Motor Car Company (Mobile, Alabama)
L.D. Mills & Son (Burlington, Vermont)
Millwood Motor Company (Camden, New Jersey)
Minnesota Chandler-Cleveland Co. (Minneapolis)
A.P. Mitchell Auto Company (Ft. Worth, Texas)
Moncrieff Engineering Company (Melbourne, Australia)
Morris Garage (Gloversville, New York)
Jacob Mossoff Company, Inc. (Fall River, Massachusetts)
Motor Sales Company (Wichita, Kansas)
Mott-Frazier Corporation (Glen Falls, New York)
Motta & Rezende (Rio De Janeiro, Brazil)
Mountain Motor Company (Montpelier, Vermont)
Julius Moyer Motor Sales Company (Sharon, Pennsylvania)
A & M Multedo (Argentina)
Mustin Motor Car Company (Tuscaloosa, Alabama)
N.S. Naquin (El Paso, Texas)
Neal-Simmons Motor Company (San Antonio)
A.S. Nelson & Son (Champaign & Peoria, Illinois)
New Motor Inn (Sioux Falls, South Dakota)
Newcomer Brothers Company (Wheeling, West Virginia)
Newmont Motors Inc. (Newmont, New York)
Noble-Davies Motors, Inc. (Bronx, New York)
North Ohio Motor Company (Cleveland)
Northern Motor Car Company (Seattle)
Northwestern Automobile Company (Minneapolis)
Novack's Garage (Cleveland)
J.J. Omerberg (Duluth, Minnesota)
Leonard B. Orloff Company (Detroit)
Pacific Motors Limited (Auckland, New Zealand)
The Palmer Motor Sales Co. (New London, Connecticut)
G.Y. Parish (Tulsa, Oklahoma)

Left and right: **A trainload of Chandlers for Charles A. Maino, San Luis Obispo, California (courtesy Kathy Collins, Maino granddaughter).**

Chandler

Length Over All—38½ inches.
Finish—Light chrome green, with forest green panel, white striping.
Wheels—10x½ inch rubber tired disc, finished green to match body, black stripe.
Equipment—Cast steering wheel. Gas control. Nickeled motor meter. One piece steel seat. Steel front radiator. Rubber pedals. Gear shift. Trunk. Signal horn. Metal head-lights. License tag. Adjustable windshield. Spring equipment. Bumper. Oil can.
No. 7516—One in extra heavy container; weight 40 pounds.......
....................Each $....

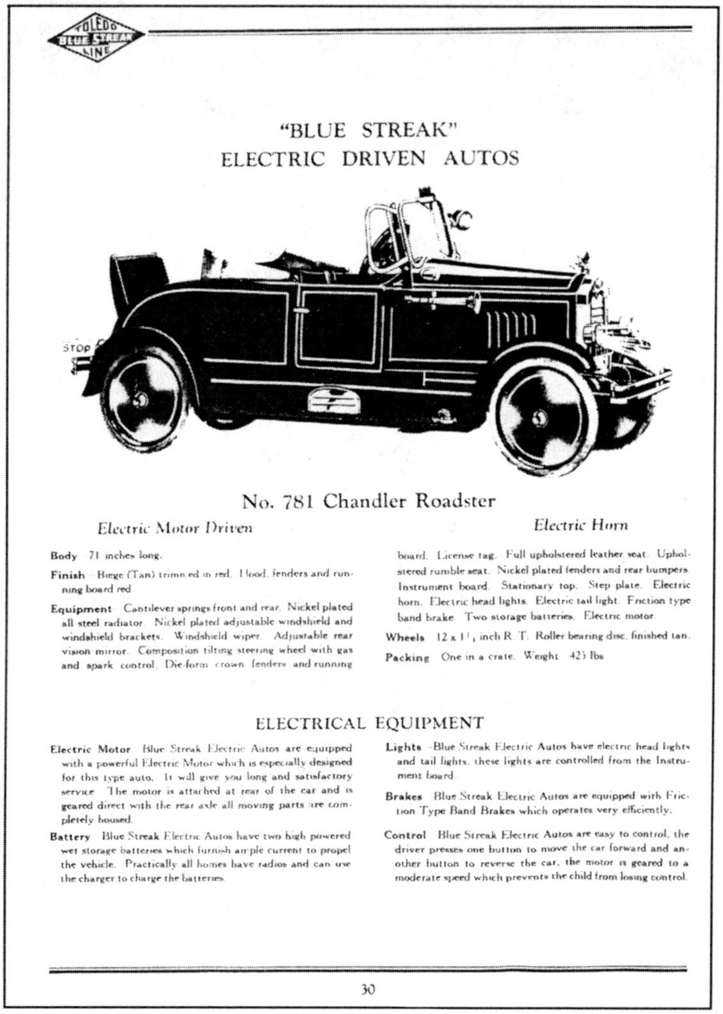

"BLUE STREAK"
ELECTRIC DRIVEN AUTOS

No. 781 Chandler Roadster

Electric Motor Driven *Electric Horn*

Body 71 inches long.

Finish Biege (Tan) trimmed in red. Hood, fenders and running board red.

Equipment Cantilever springs front and rear. Nickel plated all steel radiator. Nickel plated adjustable windshield and windshield brackets. Windshield wiper. Adjustable rear vision mirror. Composition tilting steering wheel with gas and spark control. Die-form crown fenders and running board. License tag. Full upholstered leather seat. Upholstered rumble seat. Nickel plated fenders and rear bumpers. Instrument board. Stationary top. Step plate. Electric horn. Electric head lights. Electric tail light. Friction type band brake. Two storage batteries. Electric motor.

Wheels 12 x 1¼ inch R. T. Roller bearing disc, finished tan.

Packing One in a crate. Weight 425 lbs.

ELECTRICAL EQUIPMENT

Electric Motor Blue Streak Electric Autos are equipped with a powerful Electric Motor which is especially designed for this type auto. It will give you long and satisfactory service. The motor is attached at rear of the car and is geared direct with the rear axle all moving parts are completely housed.

Battery Blue Streak Electric Autos have two high powered wet storage batteries which furnish ample current to propel the vehicle. Practically all homes have radios and can use the charger to charge the batteries.

Lights Blue Streak Electric Autos have electric head lights and tail lights, these lights are controlled from the Instrument board.

Brakes Blue Streak Electric Autos are equipped with Friction Type Band Brakes which operates very efficiently.

Control Blue Streak Electric Autos are easy to control, the driver presses one button to move the car forward and another button to reverse the car, the motor is geared to a moderate speed which prevents the child from losing control.

30

84

Above and right: **Kiddy car advertisements (unknown source and date)**

Park Garage (Redlands, California)
William Parkinson (Newark, New Jersey)
G. W. Patterson (Red Bank, New Jersey)
Peabody Garage (Peabody, Massachusetts)
E.L. Peacock Motor Sales Company (San Francisco)
Peoples Garage (Bath, Maine)
Perth Amboy Garage Company (Perth Amboy, New Jersey)
Peterson-Keyes Auto Co. (Indianapolis)
Pierson Motor Company (Indianapolis)
Pittsburgh Motor Corp. (Pittsburgh)
Place and Nobile (Paris, France)
Paul Polk (St. Joseph, Missouri)
T.O. Poole & Son Motor Company (Atlanta)
Portsmouth Chandler Company (Portsmouth, Ohio)
Price Motor Sales (Rupert, West Virginia)
B. E. Proctor Jr. (Charleston, West Virginia)
Putnam House Garage (Bennington, Vermont)
C.A. Quigley (Salt Lake City)
Randal-Adams Company (Dallas)
Rauch & Lang Electric Car Company (Minneapolis)
Andrew Redman (Harrisburg, Pennsylvania)
Reitz Auto Company (Evansville, Indiana)
Renshaw Motor Company (Wilkes-Barre, Pennsylvania)
R. E. Restrepo & Company (Medellin, Colombia & Rio De Janeiro, Brazil)
A.A. Richardson (Tacoma, Washington)
A. Robitaille (Putnam, Connecticut)
Rohde Auto Company (Milwaukee, Wisconsin)
Rose Motor Company (Dallas)
W. A. Rutz-Rosco Trading Co. (New Haven, Connecticut)
San Joaquin Auto Company (Stockton, California)
Sebastian Motors Company (Joplin, Missouri)
Scheveningsche Automobile Company (Scheveningsche, Holland)
Schreiber-Boorse Motor Car Company (Milwaukee)
John P. Schiffman (Chicago)
P.H.T. Schmidt (Bergen & Kristiania, Norway)
Seattle Automobile Company Inc. (Seattle)
Sehorn & Hipp (Charlotte)
J.R. Seidner (Youngstown, Ohio)

Service Motors, Ltd. (Winnipeg, Manitoba, Canada)
Sharkey's Chandler Services (Los Angeles)
Harry Shaw (New Kensington, Pennsylvania)
W.R. Shaw (Syracuse, New York)
Shockley Service Sales Corp. (Casper, Wyoming)
Siegel-Zeckendorf Company (Detroit)
Simmons Motor Car Company (Cleveland)
Simpson & Leftwich Motor Co. (Fort Smith, Arkansas)
C. A. Smith (Manchester, New Hampshire)
Smith-Bush Motors, Inc. (Binghamton, New York)
John W. Snyder Jr. (Amsterdam, New York)
South Bend Chandler Motor Co. (South Bend, Indiana)
Southern-Saxon Company (Atlanta)
Southwell-Hunter Auto Company (Stockton, California)
Spokane Chandler Company (Spokane, Washington)
Spring Motor Car Company (Houston)
Stahl Chandler Motor Car Co. (Hagerstown, Maryland)
Standard Motor Car Company (Norfolk, Virginia)
Star Garage Company (Shanghai, China)
Strong Motors, Inc. (Rochester, New York)
Stuyvesant Motor Company (Cleveland)
James R. Sullivan (Manchester, New Hampshire)
Sutter–Golden Motor Company (Scranton, Pennsylvania)
Wm. C. Swope, Inc. (Brooklyn)
Tasche & Company (Amsterdam, Holland)
A.G. Templeton, Inc. (Minneapolis)
William C. Theleman (Colorado Springs, Colorado)
William Thomas (Wilkes-Barre, Pennsylvania)
Toe Laer & Company (Sumatra)
Tokyo Gas, Electric, & Industrial Company (Tokyo, Japan)
Tolksdorf & Ulloa (Havana, Cuba)
Toskey Auto Company (Berlin, New Hampshire)
Tri City Motor Company (Albany, New York)

Top: **A & M Multedo, Buenos Aires, Argentina.** ***Bottom:*** **Peacock Motor Sales Company, San Francisco, California (photograph courtesy Roger Anderson).**

Twin States Motor Car Company (Portland, Oregon)
Valley Motor Car Company (Memphis)
Vesper Automobile Company (Oklahoma City, Oklahoma)
Walker Motor Company (Worcester, Massachusetts)
W. H. Warinner (Denver)
Warrington Motor Car Company (Washington, D.C.)
WCD Motor Car Company (Newark, New Jersey)
Welbon Motor Car Company (Cincinnati)
Welbon Motor Car Company (Indianapolis)

West End Auto & Carriage Company (Bridgeport, Connecticut)
Wheeler Motor Sales Company (San Antonio)
White Auto Company (St. Paul, Minnesota)
F.M. White Motor Company (Memphis)
White Plains Garage (White Plains, New York)
Whitefish Bay Garage (Whitefish Bay, Wisconsin)
Whiting-Arnold Motor Company (Baltimore)
Windsor Garage (W.H. Johnson) (Cedar Rapids, Iowa)
Withers Brothers (Grafton, West Virginia)
Wright Brothers (Long Beach, California)
Yangco Rosenstock & Company (Shanghai, China)
Yon Hamm Young Company (Honolulu)

CHANDLER

Arctic, R. I., P. V. Auto Co.
Attleboro, Mass., Chas. L. Rogers
Augusta, Me., W. W. Albee
Ayer, Mass., E. O. Proctor
Bangor, Me., Frank S. Sawyer
Barton, Vt., Barton Auto Exchange
Bath, Me., People's Garage
Bennington, Vt., Putnam House Garage
Berlin, N. H., Toohey Auto Co.
Bradford, Vt., Jacobs & Jacobs
Brattleboro, Vt., F. A. Betterley
Brockton, Mass., Bell-Gregory, Inc.
Calais, Me., Border Motor Co.
Cambridge, Mass., Church & Keith, 1280 Cambridge Street
Claremont, N. H., J. H. Carroll
Concord, N. H., A. J. Boutwell & Son
Corinna, Me., J. H. Winchester
Damariscotta, Me., Motor Service Station
Danforth, Me., Silas White
Fall River, Mass., Brainin Motor Co.
Fort Fairfield, Me., Reed Motor Co.
Franklin, Mass., Geb-Chapman Co.
Gardner, Mass., L. H. Parcher Co.
Gloucester, Mass., Gloucester Auto Sales Co.
Gt. Barrington, Mass., Berkshire Garage
Haverhill, Mass., Geo. H. Smith
Henniker, N. H., Carl Rowe
Holyoke, Mass., Peltier's Garage
Keene, N. H., Burnell-Faulkner Co.
Laconia, N. H., J. S. Smith
Lawrence, Mass., Lawrence & Caswell, Inc.
Lebanon, N. H., E. A. French
Lewiston, Me., Park St. Motor Corp.
Lowell, Mass., Pentucket Motors Co.
Lynn, Mass., Central Motors Co.
Malden, Mass., W. H. Pembrook
Manchester, N. H., Chandler & Cleveland Sales Co.
Mansfield, Mass., Clarence C. Fuller
Mars Hill, Me., Hovey & Co.
Milo, Me., West & Tye
Nashua, N. H., Central Garage
Newburyport, Mass., Shattuck Motor Co.
Newport, R. I., L. E. Brown
Northampton, Mass., A. L. Gloyd
Norwood, Mass., O'Brien Bros.
Palmer, Mass., C. A. Smith
Pittsfield, Mass., Berkshire Auto Co.
Plymouth, Mass., Old Colony Auto Sales Co.
Portland, Me., D. C. McCann's Sons
Portsmouth, N. H., The Neal Motor Co.
Providence, R. I., Chandler Motors of R. I.
Rumford, Me., Rumford Drug Co.
Salem, Mass., Almy Bigelow & Washburn
Smyrna, Me., J. E. Tarbell & Son
Springfield, Mass., Chandler Motors of Springfield, Inc.
Springfield, Vt., Adnabrown Garage
Taunton, Mass., Central Garage
Turner Falls, Mass., Turner Falls Garage
Waltham, Mass., MacGregory Garage, Inc.
Waterville, Me., Louis K. Saliem
Webster, Mass., City Garage
Westerly, R. I., N. F. Tuckerman
Westfield, Mass., Park Sq. Garage
Woonsocket, R. I., Joseph E. Grenon
Worcester, Mass., Standard Motors, Inc.

Chandler Motors of New England list of dealers, a typical group of dealers supplied by one distributor (*Can-Clev Hub*, January 1921).

Clockwise from left: **1924 Chandler catalog; Billboard poster stamp, circa 1916, actual size 2 × 2⅝ inches (courtesy Roger Anderson); two 1929 Chandler brochures.**

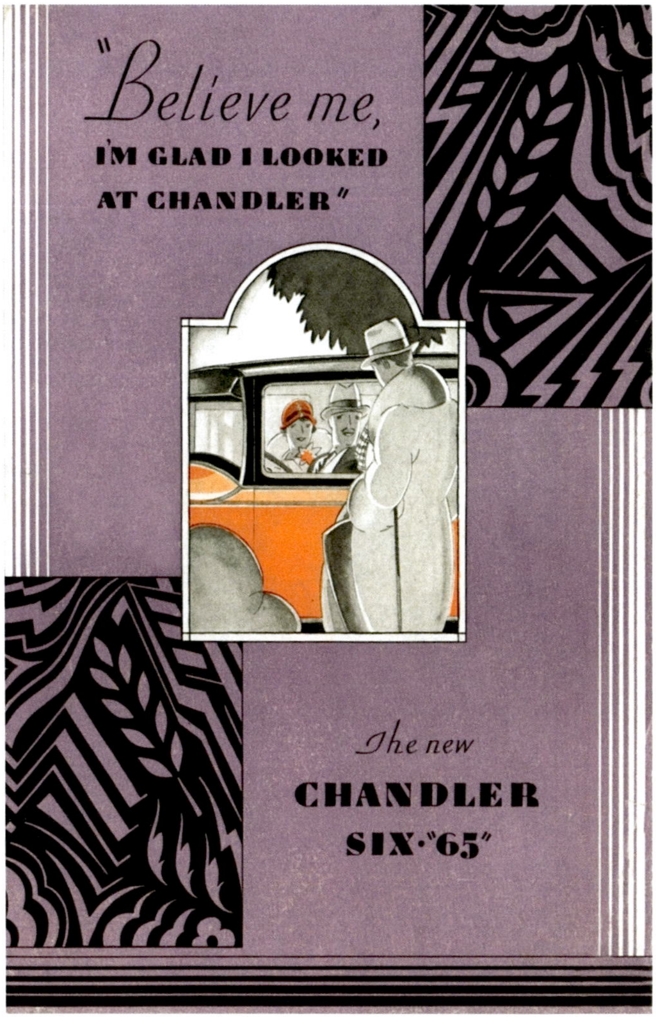

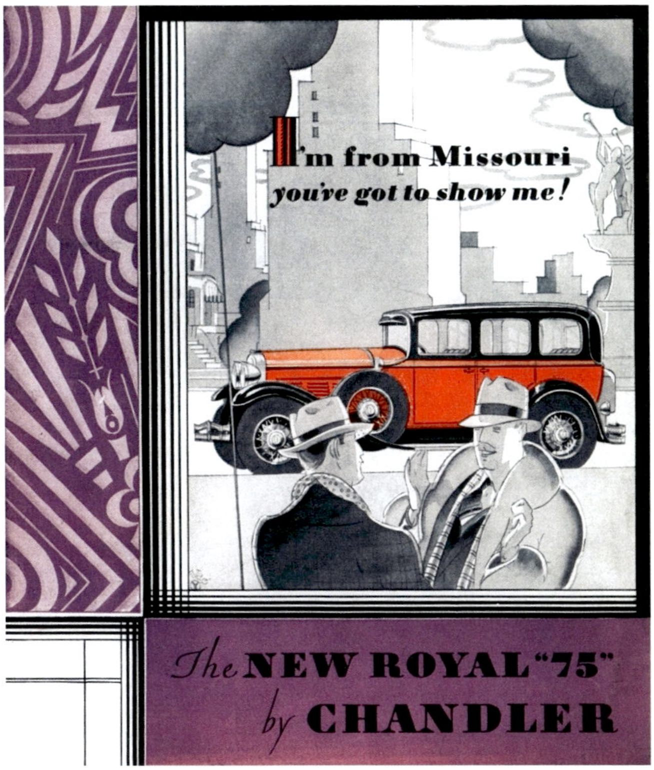

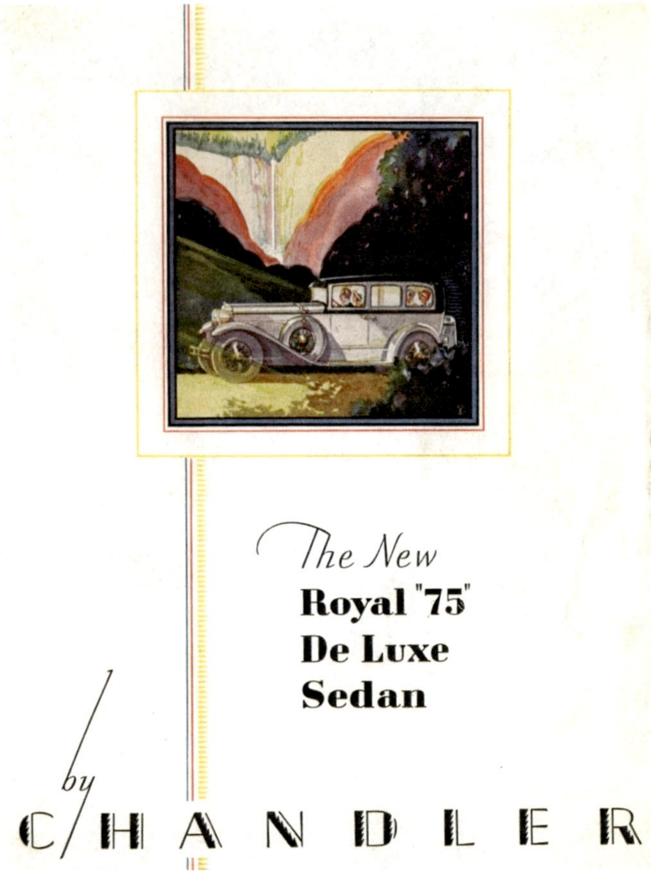

Above: Chandler brochure, ca. 1929. *Right:* Postcard, November 12, 1914.

Image from a 1917 Chandler brochure.

THE SATURDAY EVENING POST 53

C3

Inwardly and Outwardly Magnificent

—and how these new Chandlers do perform!

FAR and wide, by word and manner, America is registering unfeigned admiration for the new Royal Eights and new Sixes by Chandler.

In numbers swiftly multiplying, these new Eights and Sixes are brightening and enlivening the nation's highways and byways from ocean to ocean. Cars beautifully distinctive in body design. Magnificent in all the little fine points of luxury and comfort. Fairly bubbling over with energy and stamina; and very smooth, very quiet.

On the road you'll notice how very few cars ever try to pass a Chandler on the hills—or attempt to outstep its quick getaway in traffic. That very fact reveals the prestige and respect that Chandler has earned by the surpassing results of its Pikes Peak power principle.

Chandler goes the limit, too, in offering a wide variety of models: Cars in four chassis sizes, in a total of twenty-eight beautiful body designs—all models possessing the "One Shot" centralized lubrication system, and dozens of other important advantages. And with the Sixes priced at $945 to $1895, and the Royal Eights at $2195 to $2295 (f. o. b. Factory), *price* is still another reason why Chandler is making such galloping gains in sales. Look around. Compare!

CHANDLER-CLEVELAND MOTORS CORPORATION · CLEVELAND

CHANDLER

ROYAL EIGHTS BIG SIXES SPECIAL SIXES STANDARD SIXES

Ad for the Royal Eight Five Passenger Sedan (*The Saturday Evening Post*, July 25, 1927).

Above: **Chandler ad for the Royal Dispatch (unknown trade magazine).**

Chandler Model 18 Seven Passenger Touring (courtesy RM Auctions Inc., Sadie Chapple & Martin Steele).

Ad from *House & Garden*, June 1927.

Left: **Chandler advertising novelty, circa 1926 (courtesy Roger Anderson).** ***Right:*** **Souvenir button from relay race in which Charles A. Emise participated (actual size ⅞ inch).**

Above and right: **Chandler badges (courtesy John W. Chandler).**

Above, left and right: **1927 Chandler Model 35 Big Six (owner Joseph Chabal).**

Top: **1925 Chandler Model 33 Comrade Roadster (courtesy John W. Chandler, owner).** ***Bottom, left:*** **1926 Chandler Model 33A Comrade Roadster.** ***Bottom, right:*** **Stoplight on the same car (courtesy John W. Chandler, owner).**

1929 Chandler Royal 75 Rumble Seat Coupe (courtesy Roger Anderson, owner).

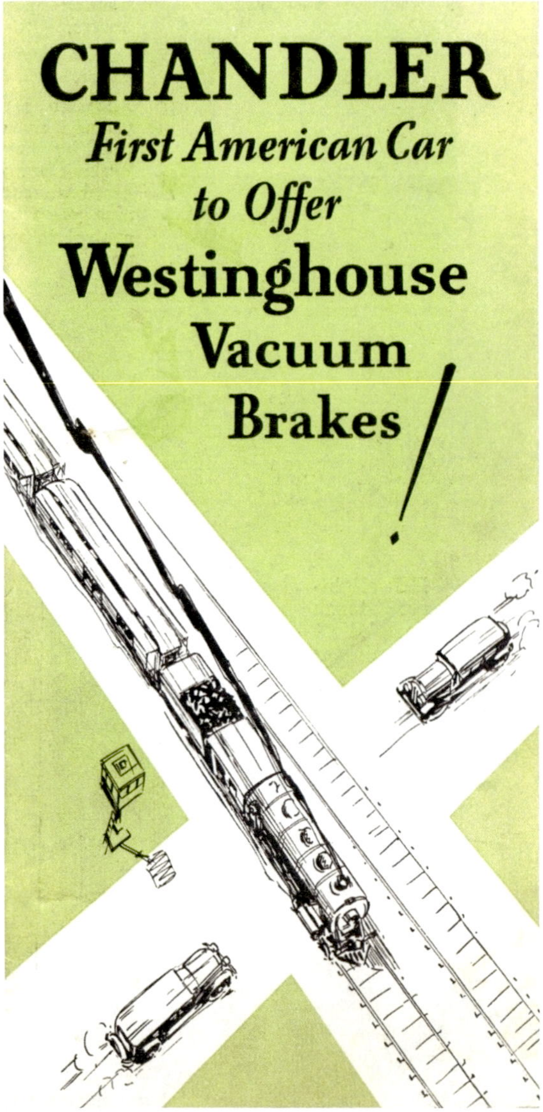

Above: Chandler Model 18 Chummy Roadster (courtesy Roger Anderson, owner). *Right:* Chandler brochure, circa 1928 (courtesy Roger Anderson).

1929 Chandler Model 65 Sportster (Dual Cowl Phaeton) (courtesy John W. Chandler, owner).

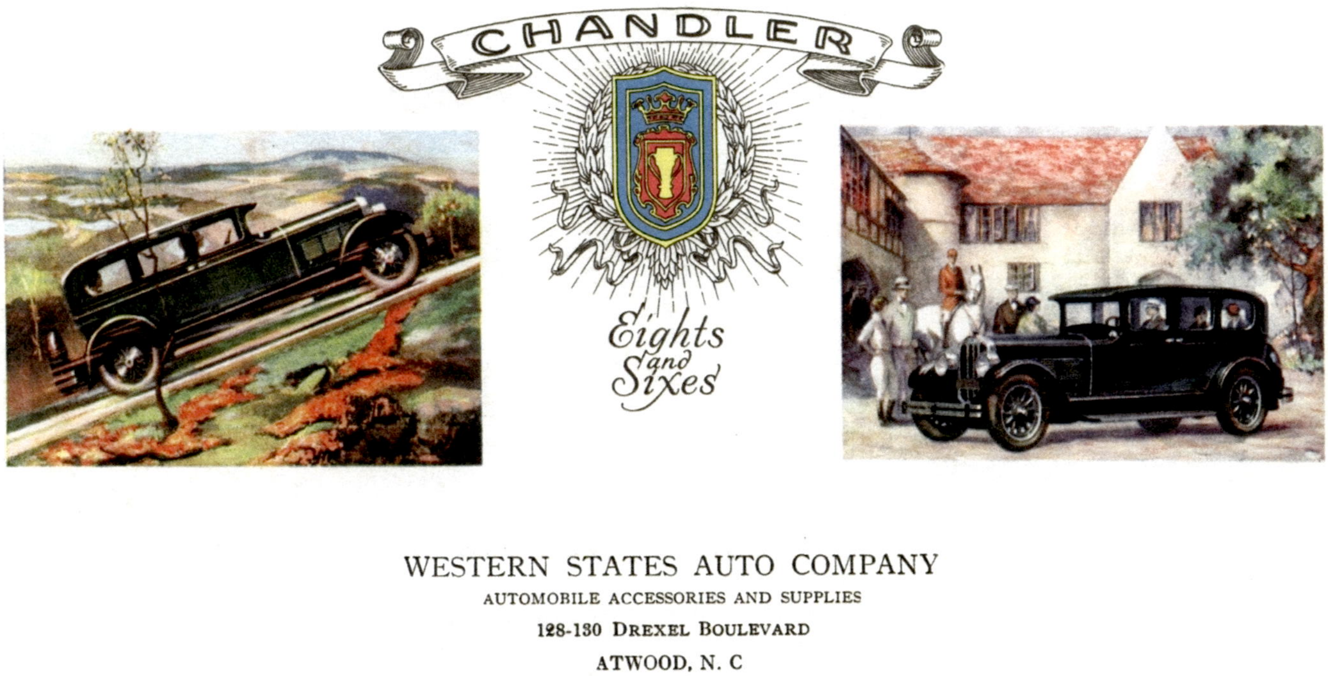

Middle: Letterhead, circa 1927-28. *Above:* Letterhead, February 16, 1917 (courtesy Roger Anderson).

Top: **1929 Chandler Model 65 Four Door Sedan (courtesy Paul Vossler, owner).** *Bottom:* **1920 Cleveland Touring (courtesy Gary Smith, owner).**

Top: **1927 Chandler Royal Eight catalog (courtesy Roger Anderson).** ***Bottom:*** **1927 Chandler Model 31 Touring, right hand drive (courtesy Jan Hansen, owner).**

Top and bottom: **1920 Cleveland Roadster (courtesy Terry Feick, owner at the time of photographs, and John and Anita Fildes, current owners).**

Above: Chandler watch fob (courtesy John W. Chandler).

Right, from top: 1923 Chandler Royal Dispatch (courtesy Roger Anderson, owner); Señor Blanchiardi's Curtiss-powered Chandler race car as it appears today (courtesy RM Sotheby's); 1923 Chandler Royal Dispatch (courtesy RM Auctions Inc., Sadie Chapple & Martin Steele).

Left: **A four-inch badge worn by the employees of the North Ohio Motor Company at the Chandler Convention, September 12, 1925 (courtesy Donn Wirtz).**

Right: **Cleveland Model 43 brochure, circa 1925 (courtesy Roger Anderson).**

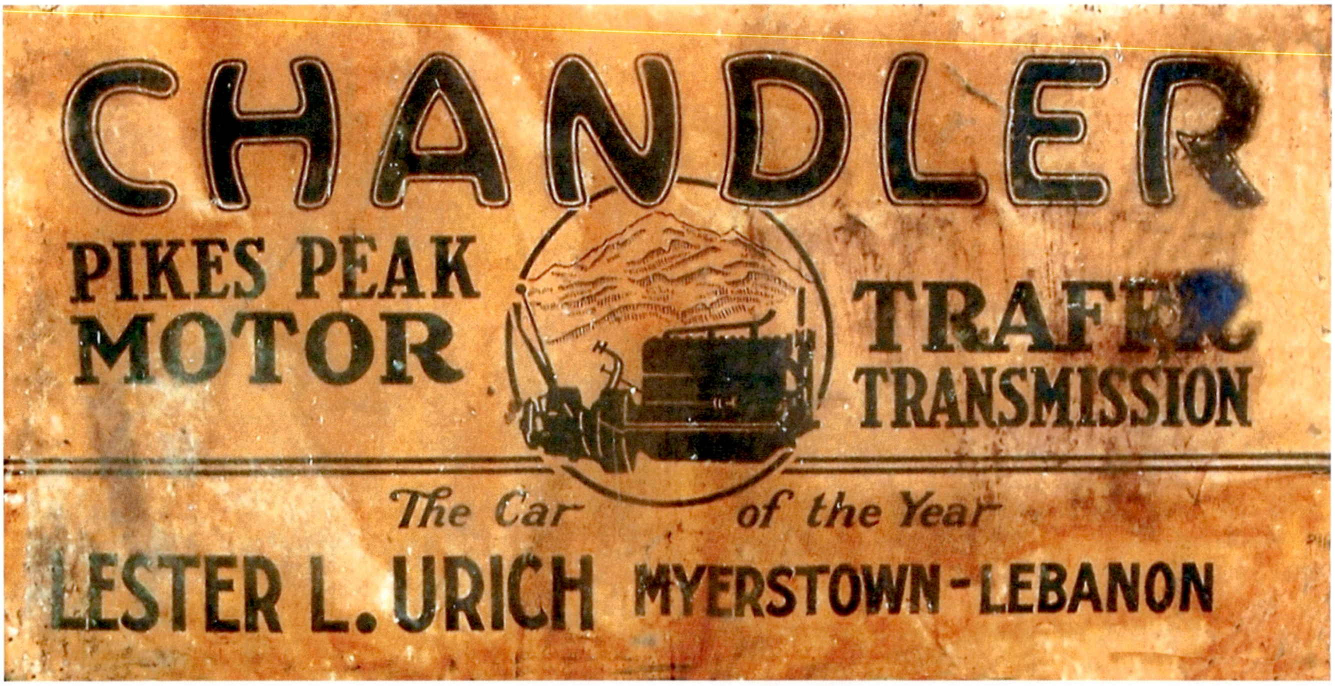

A 4 by 8 foot dealer's sign (courtesy Donn Wirtz).

Clockwise from above: **Cleveland Standard-Special advertising brochure, circa 1926; 1926 Cleveland catalog (courtesy Roger Anderson); Back cover of 1919 New York Auto Show booklet (courtesy Roger Anderson); 1929 Chandler Royal 75 Four Door Sedan (courtesy Roger & Sheila Chandler, owners).**

Top: **1925 Chandler board track racer (owned by Lindley Bothwell as of 1965).** ***Bottom:*** **1923 Chandler Royal Dispatch (owner Gene Stray).**

• ELEVEN •

Racing, Hill Climbing, Endurance and Other Competition

Other than well-known hill climbs, Pikes Peak and the board track event at Culver City, Chandler racing was confined mostly to distributor, dealer and individual sponsored events. That is not to say that Chandler did not participate in racing, but factory sponsorship was fairly limited in those days.

Numerous demonstrations of Chandler's hill climbing ability were carried out during the lifetime of the company, mainly small local events which Chandler used for advertising purposes. Chandler was, without question, one of the world's best at climbing steep grades and the company took great pride in advertising these accomplishments at every opportunity. This chapter will look at some of those events and other competitions and demonstrations involving Chandlers.

As early as 1915, a Chandler distinguished itself in a remarkable endurance stunt (detailed more fully in Appendix A). Al Waddell, a publicity seeker from Los Angeles, persuaded Don Smith, manager of the Chandler Motor Car Company of Los Angeles, and in turn Earl V. Armstrong, the Chandler distributor for Southern California, that a nonstop automobile run from Mexico to Canada would generate publicity for their product. And nonstop in this case meant literally nonstop: The wheels were never to stop rolling and the engine was never to be shut off. Armstrong provided a Chandler Touring car with about 2,000 miles on the clock for the torturous journey.[1]

The Automobile Club of Southern California, managed by Frank Jordan, assisted in mapping the route and securing sites for gasoline and provisions. A pilot car would be used at times but the drivers would be left to their own devices most of the time. In only three days of preparation, a crew installed new Goodyear Cord tires and two swiveling searchlights and taped the springs, and the car was about ready to go. A special funnel was fabricated to aid in refueling while the car was in motion and a few other necessities were added before the journey began. No mention was made as to how the drivers attended to the call of nature.

Claude H. Hunter, the primary driver, was assisted by Don Smith, Ben Knoth and Andrew Kooler. Al Waddell and Jack Griffin were the official observers and Joe Waddell of Universal Motion Picture Corporation was in charge of the camera. (This being a publicity stunt, pictures were a necessity.)

Lew Falk of the Panama-California Exposition placed seals on the starter pedal and tires, ensuring that the engine could not be stopped nor the tires replaced during the trip without detection.

Earl V. Armstrong of the Chandler Motor Car Company of California wishes the travelers good luck at the start.

At 8 a.m. on Sunday, September 26, the flag was dropped at the Tijuana, Mexico, international border marker and the event was under way. Don Smith took the wheel for the first leg to Los Angeles where they took on fuel and food and continued the journey. Heavy traffic, not only of automobiles but horse-drawn vehicles as well, gave driver Claude Hunter a challenge around Los Angeles. Earl and Lionel Armstrong were driving another Chandler as a pathfinder and managed to clear the way, enabling Hunter to get through without stopping.

Clearing Los Angeles and the canyons beyond, the pathfinder car turned back leaving the four men on their own. Andrew Kooler took the wheel for the run across the desert to Mojave, where they refueled at a slow roll. Across Tehachapi they journeyed, down White Wolf grade into Bakersfield on time where more gasoline was taken. A wrong turn between Visalia and Fresno was nearly disastrous; while searching for the right path they entered a farmyard with no way to turn around. Driver Claude Hunter did the only thing he could and drove through a grove of small orange trees to return to the road.

Fifteen miles past a warm reception in Fresno, they established a new record of 505 miles without stopping. Later, after passing through Sacramento, they left the good roads behind, not to see them again until they were well into Oregon.

In order to avoid taking a ferry across the Pitt River, thus stopping the wheels, they had to hire a pilot to guide them through canyons, over hills and mountains past Ingot to Fall River Mills and on to McCloud where roads improved.

Leaving California, with Hunter driving and Joe Waddell observing, they took the wrong road, forcing their guide to open and close several gates in order to set them on the right course. The guide became exhausted and had to be helped by Ben Knoth and Al Waddell while the Chandler drove slowly to a place where he was able to re-enter the car.

Undaunted by more wrong turns, road blockages, another detour to avoid a ferry, and a close call with running out of gas, the men pushed on. Missing a big reception in Portland as a result of taking another wrong road, they were now coming to the apex of the journey. The Chandler was going to be allowed to take the railroad bridge across the mighty Columbia River.

The only ways from Portland to Vancouver on the Washington side were by ferry or the railroad bridge. To suggest that a lone automobile be allowed to tie up five transcontinental railroads while crossing a five million dollar bridge was laughable. But the Chandler agents at Portland (Dulmage-Manley) were very persuasive and had the backing of some influential people. Superintendent A.H. Davidson and his assistant Mr. Wegener, at first scornful of the idea, finally warmed to the idea.

***Top:* The team en route, seen up close. *Bottom:* On the railroad bridge across the Columbia River, near Portland, Oregon.**

Arranging the crossing was no mean feat. Trains were stopped, switches jumped, "frogs" bypassed and three miles of ties had to have boards laid down to accommodate the car. Boats on the river had to be stopped because the drawbridge could not be raised until the Chandler crossed. All this being accomplished, the people of Portland fed the hungry crew and a convoy of cars led them out of town headed north.

At one point farther north, rain compelled the men to install chains on the tires. This is not an easy feat with an automobile stopped but with one rolling it is almost impossible. After several tries, with two men to a side, they finally succeeded but with much disgust and colorful language.

By the time the men approached the Canadian border on Friday, October 1, they looked as if they had never slept, shaved or taken a bath, but they were elated that it was nearly over. The Chandler looked considerably better than the crew and its engine purred like a kitten after more than eighteen hundred miles and more than five days of continuous running, its wheels never stopping.

At the border Customs officials gave the crew their papers and took serial numbers while the car slowly circled. After being welcomed to Canada they journeyed on into Vancouver where they were given a royal welcome. They and their faithful Chandler had completed a remarkable feat.[2]

Top: **Chicago Automobile Club's pathfinder car, summer 1915.** ***Bottom:*** **Driver H.J. Wilkinson and owner J.M. Marrone after winning three of four events at Deerfield, New York, on October 16, 1915 (*Chandler Bulletin*, November 1915).**

Also during the summer of 1915, a Chandler Touring car, piloted by J.C. (Ted) Henderson, was chosen as the pathfinder car for the Master Drivers Contest sponsored by the Chicago Automobile Club. The Chandler completed the 470 mile run from Chicago to Peoria, Illinois, to Davenport, Iowa, and back to Chicago with a perfect score.[3]

One of the earliest Chandler racing events recorded was at the Deerfield half-mile track in Utica, New York. On October 16, 1915, a car owned by J.M. Marrone and driven by H.J. Wilkinson won three of the four events held that day. Wilkinson was driving a 1915 Roadster, serial number 6365, which had been delivered to Mr. Marrone on June 22. The car had been stripped of its fenders, running boards and top but otherwise was stock. With a crude 10 painted on the cowl, Wilkinson vanquished everything he went against. He won the class B event for cars in his class, the free-for-all and the pursuit event. The pursuit race was the most interesting of all events. The cars were placed at measured intervals around the track and all started on signal. Every time a car was passed, that entry had to drop out of the race. By the tenth lap, all were gone except two Chandlers driven by Wilkinson and Masters. Wilkinson soon passed Masters to claim the event. Owner Marrone and driver Wilkinson carried home three beautiful trophies for their efforts.[4]

Drivers in Australia and New Zealand also loved the performance of the Chandler. There were dealers located in all but one state of Australia and Chandler was actively seeking a dealer for that territory (West Australia). They were represented in

New Zealand with a dealer in Auckland and also had a dealer on the Australian island of Tasmania.

On Tuesday, August 12, 1919, a convoy of fourteen Tourings, Roadsters and six unbodied chassis left Sydney, headed for Brisbane, 850 miles to the north. Marcus Clark & Company, Ltd., the Chandler Distributor in Sydney, had contracted to deliver the twenty autos to Bradley & Holland, their dealer in Brisbane, but a maritime strike had prevented them making delivery. Many Bradley & Holland customers had been promised their cars by the start of the Brisbane cattle sales on August 18. In order to keep faith with those customers both firms decided it would be best to drive the cars overland rather than not make delivery. The trek would be over 850 miles of roads that were fair at best and downright horrible at worst. The convoy left Sydney at 3:30 p.m. and journeyed to Kotoomba before stopping for the night with the only casualty being a bent axle caused by striking a culvert.

Early Wednesday morning they set off for Mudgee which was reached without mishap and only two punctured tires. Along the way a demonstration of the automobiles was given at Lithgow. Leaving Mudgee Thursday morning, the drivers found good roads all the way to Tamworth and made excellent time. Of course, opportunities for publicity were in abundance and company officials were accompanied by a host of photographers and press agents.

They reached Tamworth where they lodged for the night without further incident. Leaving Tamworth Friday morning they headed for Glen Innes. Herds of sheep on the way slowed their progress. The chief mechanic took advantage of the situation by chasing a hare for three miles before he caught it. They reached their destination without further incident.

On Saturday the goal was to reach Warwick by nightfall. During the journey they picked up a worker headed for the cane fields at Brisbane and he accompanied them for the rest of the trip. Hill climbing and stream fording presented the photographers with many great opportunities for publicity shots. Past the border of Queensland the roads became close to impassable but the convoy reached Warwick without major difficulty.

The group left Warwick Sunday morning and made a short run to Ipswich without any trouble and could have made their destination at Brisbane easily, but plans had been made for a reception at Albert Square the next morning and a large crowd of spectators was expected. Arriving on time at 9:30 a.m., they were greeted by a

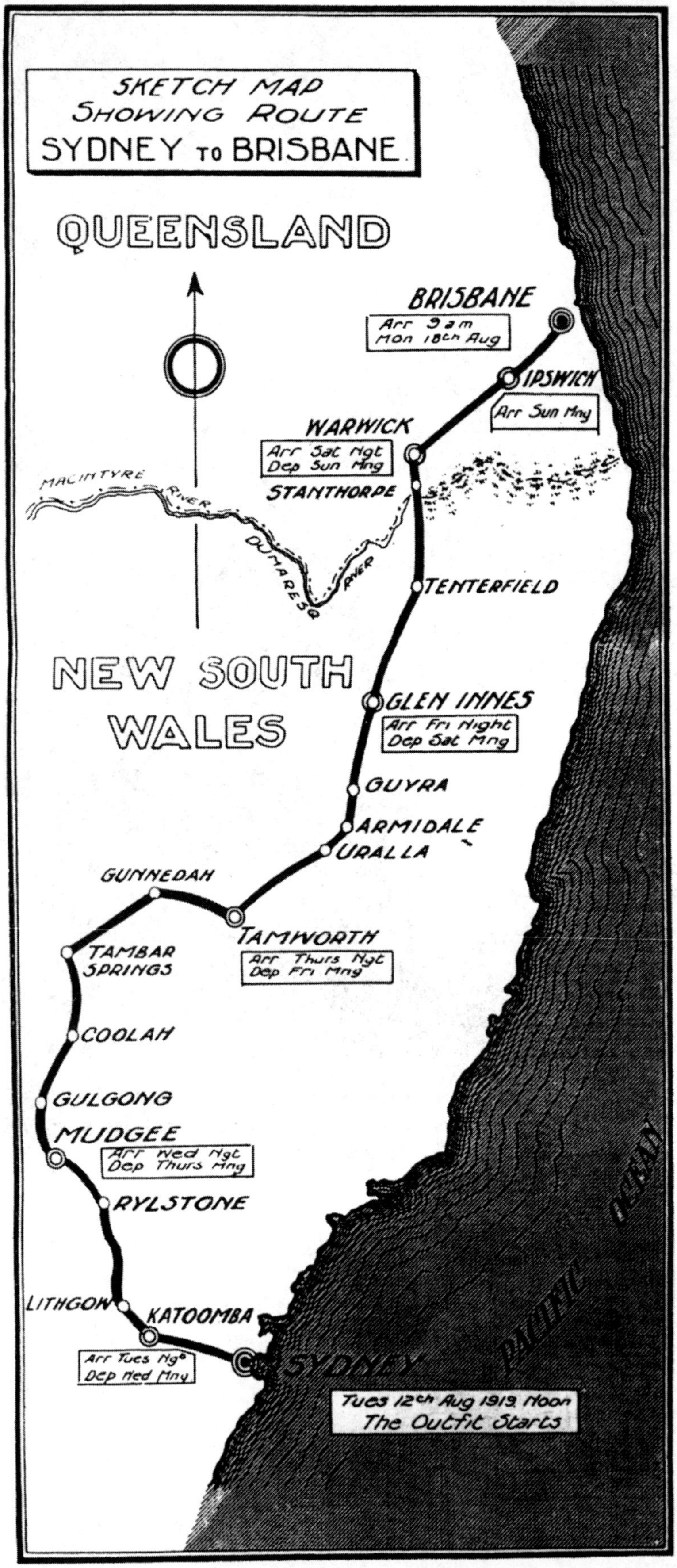

Marcus Clark & Company, Ltd., caravan route.

throng of people. After the festivities of the day the drivers made a run to the Military Hospital at Enoggera Camp where they gave rides to about 50 wounded veterans and the nurses who cared for them. Even though the six day trip was made out of necessity, it was also used as a publicity affair for Chandler and the Dunlop Rubber Company, whose tires were used on all the automobiles.[5]

On Saturday, October 25, 1919, Bradley and Holland, Chandler agents for Queensland, staged a speed event on the Toll Bar Range ascending into Toowoomba. A Chandler fitted with a race body but otherwise stock and with the transmission sealed in high gear made the climb in one minute forty-five seconds (00:01:45) and shattered a record in doing so. The previous record was two minutes forty-two seconds (00:02:42) using all gears. George Ferris drove the Chandler, accompanied by J. Lilly as mechanic. The event was certified by a committee of seven prominent businessmen of Toowoomba. The tuner and tester (mechanic) who prepared and maintained the car was presented with a silver cup and the driver received an inscribed gold medal.[6]

Cup Week in Australia, the week of the Melbourne Cup horse race, is a major national event. The Howitzer Battery

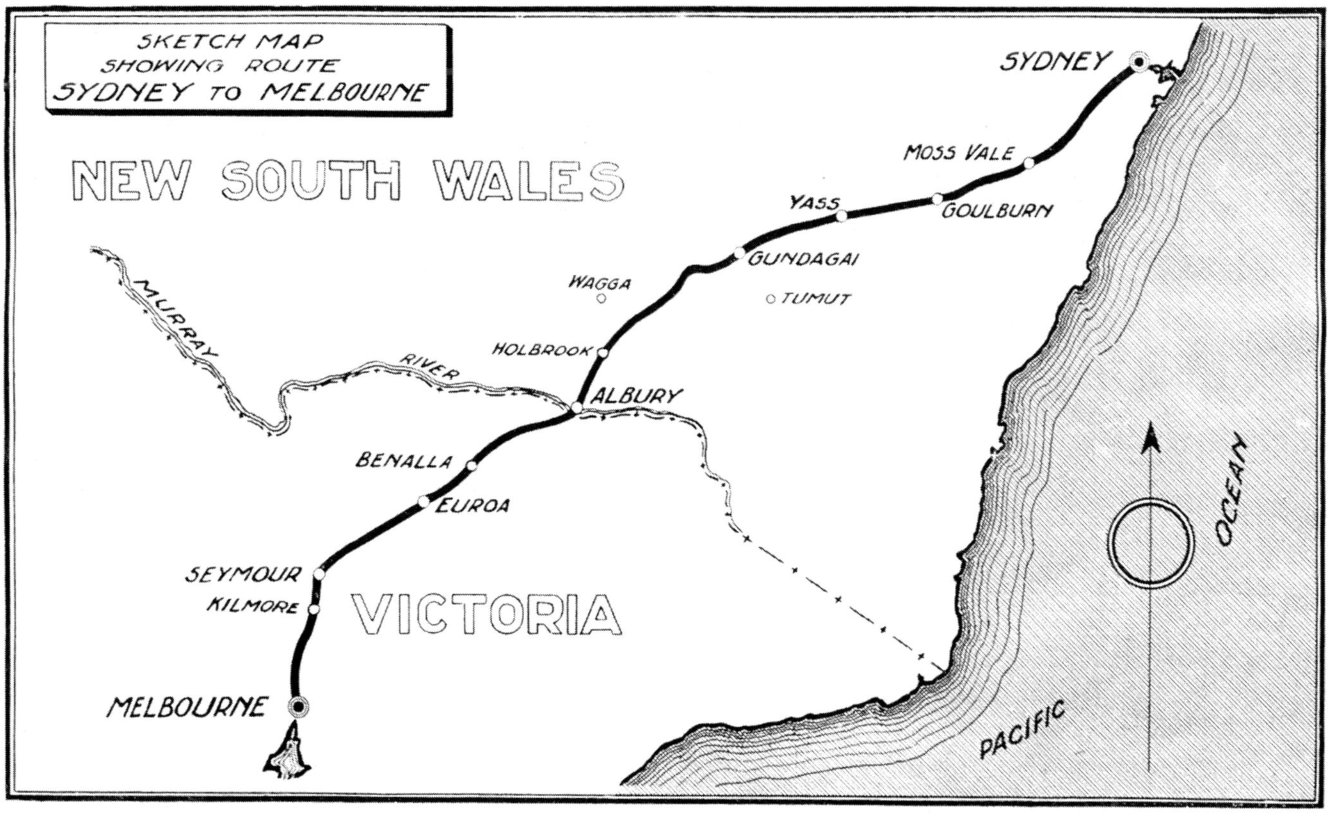

Top: Hill climbing on the Toll Bar Range. Bottom: Howitzer Battery Company, Sydney to Melbourne caravan route.

Company, Chandler dealers in Melbourne and Hobart, Tasmania, had purchased seven automobiles from Marcus-Clark, Chandler distributor in Sydney, and had promised delivery before Cup Week. All trains and boat transports were so heavily booked that delivery was impossible by the promised time unless the cars were driven overland.

The 600 plus miles was considerable shorter than the trek from Sydney to Brisbane but far more demanding. To complicate matters the trip had to be completed in 50 hours. At 6:30 a.m. on Saturday, October 25, the caravan headed south. A severe thunderstorm on Friday night had cast some doubt as to whether they would get started on time but they managed to do so. The first day's journey saw them lodging for the night at Yass, 189.5 miles into the trip. At 6 a.m. the next morning they departed and for the next 27.5 hours they drove continuously. This segment saw them encountering bad roads, questionable road signs and vast herds of sheep looking for pasture as a severe drought was gripping the country. Several miles of unnecessary travel was caused by inaccurate road signs, but the drivers kept a steady pace day and night. Many forms of wildlife were encountered, especially rabbits by the thousands.

By nightfall on Sunday evening, they had about 200 miles to go and one car suffered a battery failure. It was placed between two others that had headlights and the journey continued. One of the cars got hung up on a bridge which necessitated some strenuous work to free it. The group reached Seymour by 7 a.m. Monday and lost an hour hunting for gasoline. With only 90 minutes left to cover 68 miles, they beat the deadline with five minutes to spare, arriving at the *Melbourne Herald* at 9:25 a.m. After 27 hours without sleep it was a welcome relief to have the trip completed. The Howitzer Battery Company had fulfilled a promise to their customers and Cup Week would be celebrated by the happy new Chandler owners.[7]

The Black's Spur road in Victoria is one of Australia's more infamous climbs. Many a motorist has paid the price for mistakes on the mountain. When the Howitzer Battery Company and the Dunlop Rubber Company decided to stage a publicity stunt sometime in 1919–20, the Spur was the first choice. A Chandler, stripped of its body, windshield and rear fenders, was prepared for the event. The start of the run was at the kiosk that marks the beginning of the Spur. A Chandler Touring car had been driven ahead to clear the road of wagons and excursionists. Then the stripped-down car, driven by W.J. Tighe and accompanied by a passenger, was off in a cloud of dust at the word "Go." In a flash he had reached the "devil's elbow" and disappeared from sight. In seven minutes and twenty seconds (00:07:20) the Chandler completed the three and one-half mile climb while sealed in high gear. The feat was appropriately celebrated and the Howitzer Battery Company invited the car world to equal or better the effort.[8]

The Moncrieff Engineering Company of Adelaide, South Australia, was in need of cars in the spring of 1920. Five Tourings they had ordered from the Marcus Clark Company of Sydney were ready for delivery. Whether overland delivery was a necessity or a publicity stunt is not known but on Saturday, February 28, 1920, Mr. T.E.L. Moncrieff, owner of the dealership, along with his wife, driver, newspaper reporters and Chandler officials, started the 1,000 mile journey from Sydney to Adelaide. At 9 a.m. they were off and made their way to Goulburn where they stopped for lunch before continuing to Yass for the night. To this point the roads were passable with some being good. A severe drought was gripping the country and water was scarce. This meant no baths with just one-half cup of water for the men to shave. Leaving Yass at 9:15 Sunday morning they had lunch at Temora and headed for Barellan, where water had to be shipped in by train. They arrived without incident and pushed on to Leeton, rolling in at 11:40 p.m. tired and hungry. Being behind schedule they hired two guides to pilot them to Hay and decided to travel all night. The guides proved to know as little about the country as the travelers and after driving all night they wound up back at Leeton. They finally arrived at Hay in time for a late breakfast. The country between Hay and Leeton was total desolation with not a blade of grass or drop of water and hardly any living thing except flocks of sheep just waiting to perish. The only vegetation seen was at Leeton where an irrigation system furnished the needed water. The caravan refueled at Hay and headed for Wentworth with a tea stop at Ballranald at 7 p.m. Traveling all night they arrived at Wentworth at 4 a.m. The roads between Leeton, Hay and Wentworth were unmarked with nothing but desert as far as the eye could see. Many extra miles were traveled due to the party's unfamiliarity with the land.

The cars were serviced at Wentworth and the group decided to alter their plan, targeting arrival at Adelaide on Wednesday, March 3, at 5:30 p.m. instead of Tuesday. Leaving Wentworth at 2:45 p.m., they headed for Renmark. A lack of defined roads and many needless excursions caused delays leading to the schedule change. They arrived at Renmark, on schedule, Tuesday evening and decided to stay the night. Renmark, a thoroughly modern town, had all the amenities that travelers would want. A comfortable hotel provided hot baths, good beds and a welcome night of rest. A garage was available for any repairs that needed to be made.

The caravan left Renmark at 9:30 Wednesday morning, headed for Adelaide and home. That part of the journey was enjoyable as they saw beautiful vineyards and orchards where everything was green in contrast to the last few days. They arrived at Morgan at 12:20 where wheat fields stretched as far as the eye could see, and headed on to Eudunda, over bad roads in the hills, on through Kapunda and Gawler, to Adelaide at 5:45 p.m. Wednesday, March 3.

After five days and what turned out to be closer to 2,000

miles than the expected 1,000 because of unmarked roads, the Chandlers had reached their destination and customers were waiting for them. With no mechanical breakdowns and only two punctured tires, they had proved that the Chandlers were worthy of the slogan "Chandler Keeps Faith."[9]

On February 13, 1920, in Auckland, New Zealand, a Chandler touring car was making history. W.S. Miller of Khyber Pass piloted the Chandler from Auckland to Wellington in 14 hours and 6 minutes (14:06:00), covering a distance of 471 miles. The previous record of 22 hours and 6 minutes (22:06:00) running time had been made over a period of three days. Miller made his run nonstop and beat the train time by 4 hours and 50 minutes. He was accompanied by George Campbell of Campbell Motor Company, Chandler dealer in Auckland, and George Smith.

Colonel Stanley's 1913 Chandler, Car #4 (photograph courtesy Roger Anderson).

The Tuesday following the event, February 17, Miller drove the same car from Picton to Bluff, a distance of 704 miles, in 17 hours and 40 minutes (17:40:00) running time, also nonstop. The feat was certified by the Auckland Automobile Association. On this run Miller was again accompanied by George Smith and Tom Butt as a guide from Picton to Christchurch.

The *Wellington Evening Star* correspondent, although complimenting Mr. Miller, nonetheless was not enthusiastic about the feat and wished it would not be repeated. He objected to the excessive speed and feared someone would try a similar feat and be injured or killed.[10]

Back in the United States Chandler held two records on Mt. Diablo, California. In May 1923 a Chandler traveled farther up the mountain, in high gear, than any previous attempt and won both the *Oakland Tribune* Cup and the H.O. Alexander Trophy. Chandler won the Alexander Cup for exceeding by 109 feet the best mark previously made by a six cylinder car and the Tribune Trophy for exceeding by 35 feet the best mark previously made by a twelve cylinder car. To reach the summit of 4,000 feet, one must traverse eleven miles of steep, twisting, dangerous road. Chandler was the only car ever to hold both trophies.[11]

Colonel King Stanley, Indian scout, explorer and trail blazer, was fond of cross country trips in his 1913 Chandler Touring car. The Colonel had racked up 279,000 miles on the fourth Chandler built and it was still going strong with its original engine. He had completed 33 round trips (coast to coast) across the United States when he and Grace C. Stanley got married at radio station W.O.R. in Newark, New Jersey, on June 21, 1923, and headed out on their honeymoon trip. This, supposedly, was the first wedding ever performed on live radio. Spending some time traveling in the east, they soon headed west. Mrs. Stanley kept a daily log of their activities and reported them to Chandler for inclusion in the *Chandler Bulletin*. It is not known if Chandler sponsored any of these activities, but there must have been some connections as the Stanleys later did the same in a Cleveland. King Stanley was reputed to be a great horseman by Frank Hopkins, a great horseman himself. The movie *Hidalgo* was based on Hopkins' supposed exploits.[12]

In July 1923 a Chandler broke a record by ascending the 5,984 foot Western Continental Divide in a time of 13½ minutes (00:13:30). Bert Campbell of the *Helena Independent* was the official observer.[13]

In Argentina, Señor Ermanno Blanchiardi was a successful driver of a Chandler, winning the 1922 and 1923 LaPlata Grand Automobile Race. In the 1923 event he defeated 16 entries, including many expensive American cars, in winning the 410 kilometer event. However, Blanchiardi was supposedly driving a machine fitted with a Curtiss OX-5 airplane engine and other modifications while winning the 1922–23 events. He did campaign a Chandler with the original engine earlier in his career. More research would be needed to confirm whether he ran with the original Chandler engine or the Curtiss OX-5 in 1922 and 1923.[14]

On September 10, 1923, Ralph Mulford drove a stock Chandler Touring car to a world's record on Mt. Washington, New Hampshire. The mountain was the highest accessible peak east of the Rocky Mountains at the time and the event was known as the "Climb to the Clouds." Mulford made the eight mile run in 17 minutes flat (00:17:00), four minutes faster than any previous attempt. The summit is at an elevation of 6,293

Top: **Señor Blanchiardi in his Chandler race car (Argentina).** ***Bottom:*** **Señor Blanchiardi's Curtiss-powered Chandler in its present configuration (courtesy R M Sotheby's).**

feet with some grades as steep as 16 percent.

In a trial run on the day before, Mulford had actually broken the record by two minutes, but it was not official and he wanted the run to be legitimate. Official records date the run as September 10 but Chandler records say September 9 was the date. Regardless, it was a great achievement.[15]

Chandlers also competed successfully in Cuba. In the 1923 annual race from Havana to Guanajay and back, a 1918 Chandler won first place. Driving a stock Chandler, Herminio Mascort of Havana won a double victory in the 1924 Noche-Guayabal-Noche race. Racing against 12 contestants, all driving specially prepared cars, Mascort bested them all to win first place overall and was also awarded a sporting cup for the best performance of a stock car. Two trophies—not bad for a day's work.[16]

During the summer of 1925 Emiliano Solorzano of Havana, Cuba, won several events in his Chandler race car. Racing at Havana, he not only won his class but picked up several other trophies. He had the fastest first lap in first class, fastest first lap in second class, fastest lap in all races and fastest overall speed for all races. He finished second in the open event, where cars of all classes participated. He might have won except for a broken distributor cable which was not detected before the race and caused a ten minute delay for repairs during the race. With all his difficulties he still managed to finish second. The car was sponsored by J. Ulloa & Company, Chandler dealers in Havana, and the event was held under the auspices of *La Noche*, the Havana newspaper.[17]

On February 4, 1925, Ralph Mulford, famous for his driving ability, drove a Chandler to a world record on the board track at Culver City, California. Running wide open, stopping for oil and gas only, he covered the distance of 1,000 miles in 689 minutes at an average speed of 86.96 mph—the fastest 1,000 miles ever covered by an automobile to that date. The Roadster had been stripped of its fenders, running boards and top and fitted with a smaller, less wind resistant windshield. The rear end gears had been changed to a high speed setup but all else was stock. The race was sanctioned by AAA.

Mulford's time was quite an accomplishment for a stock or semi-stock car considering that an airplane hauling the U.S. mail could only average slightly more than 78 mph from coast to coast.

Race cars were recording higher speeds, though; the Indianapolis 500 would be won that year by Peter DePaolo, driving a Duesenberg, at an average speed of 101.3 mph.[18]

The mountains between Salt Lake City and Brighton, Utah, proved for many years to be too steep to negotiate in high gear—that is, until a Chandler made the attempt. The elevation is 4,800 feet higher at Brighton than at Salt Lake, a tortuous mountain road of 26 miles and 63 sharp curves in between. A stock Chandler, locked in high gear and with the shift lever removed, conquered the mountain with relative ease in the summer of 1925.

The feat was observed by three Salt Lake City newspaper representatives and certified by John Helverson, Salt Lake City sealer of weights and measures. The car was also inspected by Gordon Croft, president of the Croft Cylinder Grinding Company, as being stock in every respect.[19]

Top: **Ralph Mulford racing to a record on Mount Washington, Gorham, New Hampshire, September 9, 1925.** ***Bottom:*** **Ralph Mulford, at the wheel, is greeted by well wishers after his record-breaking "Climb to the Clouds" run up Mount Washington (factory photograph, author's collection).**

Chandler had perfected the Pikes Peak engine on the Colorado mountain from whence its name arose. In 1925 they were back to try their luck in the famous hill climb, having always fallen short of victory before. This year they had two of the top drivers of racing fame in Ralph Mulford and Charlie "Chuck" Myers. Mulford had been a fixture of the event since the beginning in 1916 and Myers had won in class three the previous year. Myers had shown in practice, the day before, that he was fast. In fact, it was reported that one of his practice runs had broken the record set by Mulford in a Hudson during the 1916 race.[20]

A rule change for 1925 directed that the Penrose Trophy would go to the winner based on time alone and piston displacement would not be a factor.

Race day, September 7, came and drivers started at 10 minute intervals. Thirteen cars were registered but apparently only ten started. They were racing against time and the mountain, not each other. Myers was the last to start; his teammate Mulford had already blown his engine at mile seven and was finished. Myers got off to a lightning start and those who witnessed it knew he would win, provided he did not wreck or have mechanical difficulty.

With bulldog determination he kept the accelerator to the

floor, slamming the Chandler into the curves and hoping nothing would break. Nothing did and 17 minutes, $48\frac{2}{8}$ seconds later (00:17:48.25) he crossed the finish line a winner, having also broken Mulford's nine-year-old record. The Penrose Trophy now belonged to Chandler and Myers. Fred Chandler, Jr., was there, along with a host of Chandler officials and friends, to welcome and congratulate Myers on his amazing performance. Of course the Chandler engine had been modified with a supercharger and other innovations, but all other entrants had done likewise. A Stutz was second and a Marmon third. The Pikes Peak engine had now fully justified its name!

Chuck Myers was a young Colorado Springs mechanic who was engaged to be married at the time. His bride-to-be had objected to his race driving and he supposedly had promised her that this would be his last race. She must have dropped her objections as he was back winning races a few years later. Myers made his record-setting Pikes Peak run with only five days of preparation.[21]

The following year, on August 2, 1926, a Chandler 20th Century Sedan smashed all previous time marks for the torturous Mt. Hood loop, low gear run. The car was sealed in low gear and the clutch pedal removed to prevent coasting on the downhill runs. For 7 hours and 45 minutes (07:45:00) the Chandler wound around the mountains at an average speed of 24.28 mph for the 172 mile run. When it was over, Chandler had beaten the previous record by 1 hour and 47 minutes (01:47:00). An extra gas tank was mounted above the trunk rack at the rear, enabling the test to be run without stopping to refuel. It was a grueling test of Chandler durability, under extreme conditions, but the car passed with flying colors.[22]

Top, left to right: **Eliot Libby (one of the Mount Washington Auto Road owners), driver Ralph Mulford and James T. Sullivan of the *Boston Globe* swap stories about the record-breaking run (factory photograph, author's collection). *Bottom:* Emiliano Salorzano, the winning driver at Havana, Cuba, summer 1925.**

In September 1926 a Chandler Big Six Metropolitan Sedan, sealed in second gear with gear shift disconnected and clutch pedal removed, made a record breaking 235 mile test run from Butte to Bozeman, Montana, and returned. The car averaged a speed of 24.75 mph for the entire 8 hour, 28 minute (08:28:00) trip, in second gear with throttle wide open. No oil or water was added during the run as both the radiator and oil intake had been sealed before departure. Of necessity, fuel was taken at Bozeman for the return run. As this and the previous month's event proved, Chandlers were built to withstand such hardships.[23]

Chandlers also made inroads in the Brazilian racing scene. Joas Bosco de Rezende of Motto and Rezende, Chandler distributors in Rio de Janeiro, was a race driver of notable fame. Sometime in 1926, driving a Chandler, he won the famous Tijuca Hill climb at Rio de Janeiro, defeating 19 other cars in the climb known as "The Course of Death." He made the climb in 12 minutes and 5 seconds (00:12:05) over an 18 kilometer course. In 1927, he piloted a Chandler to victory in the race held at Belo Horizonte, Brazil. Rezende covered the 13 miles of dirt track in 9 minutes and 16 seconds (00:09:16) for an average speed of 84.18 mph.[24]

On May 5, 1928, at São Paulo, Brazil, Rezende took the first place trophy for the Touring Class, starting from a dead stop, and also the Touring Class, starting from a rolling start. Two days later on May 7, he repeated the same feats, this time driving a specially prepared racing car. All four winning times were Brazilian records. Four trophies in three days was not a small achievement. All races were sponsored by the *São Paulo Journal*.[25]

Top: **Charlie Myers pilots the Chandler to a record up Pikes Peak, Colorado, September 7, 1925.** ***Bottom:*** **Charlie Myers, winner of the Pikes Peak race.**

Chandler claimed at least one victory in Chile. In 1927 a Chandler won the 385 kilometer race between Santiago and Panimavida, averaging 69 kilometers per hour and covered the entire distance in 5 hours, 34 and 2⁄10 minutes (05:34:12). The race was run under harsh conditions, there being no bridges over rivers and streams. Of the eleven cars entered only five finished.[26]

Uruguay proved to be another hotbed of Chandler performance feats. In the summer of 1927 a Chandler Special Six was driven over a course of five miles of dirt roads for a total of 508 miles without stopping. The race course, near Montevideo, was designed with sharp curves, two steep grades and lots of rough roads. The run was supervised by the Automobile Mechanics Club of Uruguay. Rigorously inspecting the Chandler after the event, the club found it to be in perfect order.[27]

There were many other records such as a run from San Francisco to Portland, Oregon, in the fastest time ever recorded in a closed car. Various records were set in India and Australia as well. In India Chandler won the Trophy Cup and was the only car to complete a perfect score of 200 in the Bombay-Poona reliability run. At the annual flexibility contest in Sydney, Australia, Chandler was triumphant over 22 other cars in all-around performance.[28]

Mt. St. Helena in California was conquered by a Chandler in a test to see if the mountain could be crossed in high gear. The Chandler not only succeeded but did so while carrying four passengers. It was driven by Roy Woolford, a Chandler factory representative.[29]

At Muroc, Dry Lake, California, a Big Six Chandler Roadster set a record of 115 mph over a measured mile course by covering the distance in 31.1 seconds (00:00:31.1).[30]

By 1926 Chandler held a total of 18 official records for racing, hill climbing and endurance.[31]

There probably was not a hill of any major proportions that Chandler did not conquer during its lifespan. These are but a few of the many examples of Chandler exploits.

***Top, left:* Charlie "Chuck" Myers being congratulated by Fred Chandler, Jr., after winning the Pikes Peak Race on September 7, 1925 (*Chandler Bulletin*, Saturday, September 12, 1925). *Top, right:* The Penrose Trophy awarded to Pikes Peak winner Charlie Myers. *Middle, left:* Chandler race car from Argentina, possibly Blanchiardi's (courtesy Roger Anderson). *Middle, right:* A Chandler race car (courtesy Roger Anderson). *Bottom:* 1925 Chandler race car owned by Lindley Bothwell, wearing a 1940 or earlier paint scheme (courtesy Roger Anderson).**

• **Twelve** •

Chandler Specifications[1]

Prototype
Serial # 1–550

Weight—2,985 pounds, fully equipped with top, wind shield, battery, lamps, starter, speedometer, extra tire and rim, water, oil, gasoline, and tools ready for the road.

Left Side Drive—Center Control.

Wheel Base—120 inches.

Wheels—Artillery type 34 × 4 inches, fitted with Firestone Demountable Rims, and mounted on ball bearings.

Motor—35 H.P. 3⅜ × 5 inches. "L" head type. Cylinders cast in two blocks. Valves enclosed. Imported silent chains driving cam shaft, pump and magneto and enclosed in oil tight case. Cam shaft and cams cut from solid forging. Heavy crank shaft. Liberal sized bearings of white bronze.

Oiling—Oiling by positive gear pump in oil base, forcing oil into reservoirs over all principal bearings, cam and pump-driving chain case and into individual constant level troughs under each connecting rod and piston. Accessible filling tube for oil reservoir. Oil gauge on motor base. Oil pump and strainer accessible for inspection and cleaning. All exterior oil pipes eliminated.

Ignition—Bosch High Tension Magneto.

Carburetor—Stromberg "Little Six." Hot air and dash priming attachments.

Self Starter—Westinghouse Electric Starter built into motor. All moving parts enclosed.

Cooling—Centrifugal pump. Square tube radiator.

Electric Lighting—Westinghouse Electric Lighting Generator with large storage battery, single wire system and automatic switches. Solar electric head lights throughout. Electric Side lamps built into windshield, and tail lamp in combination with illuminated license bracket.

Clutch—Multiple disc, ball bearing clutch. Discs of Raybestos and steel in oil tight case with motor.

Transmission—Three speeds and reverse. Nickel steel gears and shafts mounted on imported annular ball bearings, enclosed in case with motor and clutch, forming unit power plant.

Center Control—Gear shift and brake levers directly connected to transmission case, giving center control.

Rear Axle—Floating type. Annular ball bearings in wheels, shafts and differential. Drive shafts removable. Differential and main drive bevel gears adjustable and easily removable.

Brakes—14" Double, internal. Faced with heat proof friction material.

Propeller Shaft—Double Hartford Universal Joints.

Torsion Rod—Pressed steel, triangle section, forward end fitted with double spring buffers.

Steering Gear—Irreversible and adjustable for wear. Ebonized steering wheel.

Steering Radius—38 foot circle.

Gasoline System—Gasoline tank of twenty gallons capacity suspended in rear. Gasoline gauge showing quantity in tank. Air pressure generated by metal plunger pump on one valve lifter.

Body—Five passenger coach type. Stream line design.

Upholstering—10 and 12 inch cushions. High grade tufted leather. High grade springs. Rear seat 47 inches in width. High backs on front and rear seats.

Wind Shield—Built in without rods or braces. Adjustable for rain vision or ventilation.

Top—Mohair top. Patent locking Bair top holders. Dust covers.

Curtains—Side curtains, "Jiffy" quick attachable, patent type.

Horn—Electric motor horn mounted on motor base under bonnet.

Dash Fittings—Jones speedometer. Air pressure gauge, clock, all electrically illuminated.

Central Board—Button, switches, etc., mounted on control board in easy reach of operator.

Color and Finish—Bodies, wheels, frame and running gear finished in Victoria blue with silver stripe. Fenders, hood and cowl black. All hardware, lamps and fittings nickeled.

Price Complete—$1785. Chassis only, $1585

Other Models—Deliveries of Runabout, Coupe and Limousine models will be made in September. Full details will be announced later.

Model 14

Serial # 2–550

Weight—2,985 pounds or less, fully equipped with top, wind shield, battery, lamps, starter, speedometer, tools, and extra rim.

Left Side Drive—Center Control. Entrance to front seats from either side.

Wheel Base—120 inches. 10½ inches road clearance.

Turning Radius—37 foot circle.

Wheels—Artillery type, ball bearing—34 × 4 inches fitted with Firestone Straight Side or Clincher Demountable and Detachable Rims.

Motor—35 H.P. 3⅜ × 5 inches. "L" head type. Cylinders cast in two blocks. Valves enclosed. Imported silent chains driving cam shaft, pump and magneto and enclosed in oil tight case. Cam shaft and cams cut from solid forging. Heavy crank shaft. Liberal sized bearings of white bronze.

Oiling—Oiling by positive gear pump in oil base, forcing oil into reservoirs over all principal bearings, cam and pump-driving chain case and into individual constant level troughs under each connecting rod and piston. Accessible filling tube for oil reservoir. Oil gauge on motor base. Oil pump and strainer accessible for inspection and cleaning. All exterior oil pipes eliminated.

Ignition—Bosch High Tension Magneto.

Carburetor—Stromberg "Little Six." Hot air and dash priming attachments.

Self Starter—Westinghouse Electric Starter built into motor. All moving parts enclosed.

Cooling—Centrifugal pump. Mayo genuine. Mercedes type honeycomb radiator.

Electric Lighting—Westinghouse Electric Lighting Generator with large storage battery, single wire system and automatic switches. Solar electric lights throughout. Tail lamp in combination with illuminated license bracket.

Clutch—Multiple disc, ball bearing clutch. Discs of Raybestos and steel in oil tight case with motor.

Transmission—Three speeds and reverse. Nickel steel gears and shafts mounted on F. & S. imported annular ball bearings, enclosed in case with motor and clutch, forming unit power plant.

Center Control—Gear shift and brake levers directly connected to transmission case, giving center control.

Rear Axle—Floating type. F. & S. imported annular ball bearings in wheels, shafts and differential. Drive shafts removable. Differential and main drive bevel gears adjustable and easily removable.

Brakes—14" Double, internal. Faced with heat proof friction material.

Propeller Shaft—Double Hartford Universal Joints.

Torsion Rod—Pressed steel, triangle section, forward end fitted with double spring buffers.

Steering Gear—Irreversible and adjustable for wear. Ebonized steering wheel.

Gasoline System—Gasoline tank of twenty gallons capacity suspended in rear. Gasoline gauge showing quantity in tank. Air pressure generated by metal plunger pump on one valve lifter.

Body—Five passenger coach type. Stream line design.

Upholstering—10 and 12 inch cushions. High grade tufted leather. High grade springs. Rear seat 47 inches in width. High backs on front and rear seats.

Wind Shield—Built in without rods or braces. Adjustable for rain vision or ventilation. Folds down for clear vision.

Top—Mohair top. Patent locking Bair top holders. Dust covers.

Curtains—Side curtains, "Jiffy" quick adjustable.

Horn—Electric motor horn mounted on motor base under bonnet. Button for knee or hand.

Dash Fittings—Jones speedometer. Air pressure gauge, New Haven eight-day clock, all electrically illuminated.

Central Board—Button, switches, etc., mounted on control board in easy reach of operator.

Color and Finish—Bodies, wheels, frame and running gear finished in dark Victoria blue with silver stripe. Fenders black. All hardware, lamps and fittings nickeled and black.

Price Complete—F.O.B. Cleveland $1785. Chassis only, $1585

Other Models—Information regarding Runabout, Coupe and Limousine and Sedan models on request.

Model 15

Serial # 551–2500

Weight—2,985 pounds or less, fully equipped with top, wind shield, battery, lamps, starter, speedometer, tools, and extra rim.

Left Side Drive—Center Control. Entrance to front seats from either side.

Wheel Base—120 inches. 10½ inches road clearance.

Turning Radius—37 foot circle.

Wheels—Artillery type, ball bearing—34 × 4 inches fitted with Firestone Straight Side or Clincher Demountable and Detachable Rims.

Motor—35 H.P. 3⅜ × 5 inches. "L" head type. Cylinders cast in two blocks. Valves enclosed. Imported silent chains driving cam shaft, pump and magneto and enclosed in oil tight case. Cam shaft and cams cut from solid forging. Heavy crank shaft. Liberal sized bearings of white bronze.

Oiling—Oiling by positive gear pump in oil base, forcing oil into reservoirs over all principal bearings, cam and pump-driving chain case and into individual constant level troughs under each connecting rod and piston. Accessible filling tube for oil reservoir. Oil gauge on motor base. Oil pump and strainer accessible for inspection and cleaning. All exterior oil pipes eliminated.

Ignition—Bosch High Tension Magneto.

Carburetor—Stromberg "Little Six." Hot air and dash priming attachments.

Self Starter—Westinghouse Electric Starter built into motor. All moving parts enclosed.

Cooling—Centrifugal pump Mayo genuine. Mercedes type honeycomb radiator.

Electric Lighting—Westinghouse Electric Lighting Generator with large storage battery, single wire system and automatic switches. Solar electric lights throughout. Double globes in front lights for either city or country use. Tail lamp in combination with illuminated license bracket.

Clutch—Multiple disc, ball bearing clutch. Discs of Raybestos and steel in oil tight case with motor.

Transmission—Three speeds and reverse. Nickel steel gears and shafts mounted on F. & S. imported annular ball bearings, enclosed in case with motor and clutch, forming unit power plant.

Center Control—Gear shift and brake levers directly connected to transmission case, giving center control.

Rear Axle—Floating type. F. & S. imported annular ball bearings in wheels, shafts and differential. Drive shafts removable. Differential and main drive bevel gears adjustable and easily removable.

Brakes—14" Double, internal. Faced with heat proof friction material.

Propeller Shaft—Double Hartford Universal Joints.

Torsion Rod—Pressed steel, triangle section, forward end fitted with double spring buffers.

Steering Gear—Irreversible and adjustable for wear. Ebonized steering wheel.

Gasoline System—Gasoline tank of twenty gallons capacity suspended in rear. Gasoline gauge showing quantity in tank. Air pressure generated by metal plunger pump on one valve lifter.

Body—Five passenger coach type. Stream line design. Crowned fenders.

Upholstering—10 and 12 inch cushions. High grade tufted leather. High grade springs. Rear seat 47 inches in width. High backs on front and rear seats.

Wind Shield—Built in without rods or braces. Adjustable for rain vision or ventilation. Folds down for clear vision.

Top—Mohair top. Patent locking Bair top holders. Dust covers.

Curtains—Side curtains, "Jiffy" quick adjustable.

Horn—Electric motor horn mounted on motor base under bonnet. Button for knee or hand.

Dash Fittings—Jones speedometer. Air pressure gauge, New Haven eight-day clock, all electrically illuminated.

Central Board—Button, switches, etc., mounted on control board in easy reach of operator.

Color and Finish—Bodies, wheels, frame and running gear finished in dark Victoria blue with silver stripe. Fenders black. All hardware, lamps and fittings nickeled and black.

Price Complete—F.O.B. Cleveland $1785. Chassis only, $1585.

Other Models—Information regarding, Coupe, Limousine and Sedan models on request.

Model 15B

Serial # 2501–3999

Weight—2,885 pounds fully equipped with top, wind shield, battery, lamps, starter, speedometer, tools, and extra rim.

Left Side Drive—Center Control. Entrance to front seats from either side.

Wheel Base—120 inches. 10½ inches road clearance.

Turning Radius—37-foot circle.

Wheels—Artillery type—ball bearing—34 × 4 inches fitted with Firestone Straight Side or Clincher Demountable and Detachable Rims.

Motor—35 H.P. 3⅜ × 5 inches. "L" head type. Cylinders cast in two blocks. Valves enclosed. Imported silent chains driving cam shaft, pump and magneto and enclosed in oil tight case. Cam shaft and cams cut from solid forging. Heavy crank shaft. Liberal sized bearings of white bronze.

Oiling—Oiling by positive gear pump in oil base, forcing oil into reservoirs over all principal bearings, cam and pump-driving chain case and into individual constant level troughs under each connecting rod and piston. Accessible filling tube for oil reservoir. Oil gauge on motor base. Oil pump and strainer accessible for inspection and cleaning. All exterior oil pipes eliminated.

Ignition—Bosch High Tension Magneto.

Carburetor—Automatic, double jet. Hot air, and hot water jacket dash regulating attachments.

Self Starter—Separate Electric Starter built into motor. All moving parts enclosed.

Cooling—Centrifugal pump. Mayo genuine Mercedes type honeycomb radiator.

Electric Lighting—Separate Electric Lighting Generator with large storage battery, single wire system and automatic switches. Solar electric lights throughout. Double globes in front lights for either city or country use. Tail lamp in combination with illuminated license bracket.

Clutch—Multiple disc, ball bearing clutch. Discs of Raybestos and steel in oil tight case with motor.

Transmission—Three speeds and reverse. Nickel steel gears and shafts mounted on F. & S. imported annular ball bearings, enclosed in case with motor and clutch, forming unit power plant.

Center Control—Gear shift and brake levers directly connected to transmission case, giving center control.

Rear Axle—Floating type. F. & S. imported annular ball bearings in wheels, shafts and differential. Drive shafts removable. Differential and main drive bevel gears adjustable and easily removable.

Brakes—14" Double, internal. Faced with heat proof friction material.

Propeller Shaft—Double Hartford Universal Joints.

Torsion Rod—Pressed steel, triangle section, forward end fitted with double spring buffers and ball and socket joint.

Steering Gear—Irreversible and adjustable for wear. Polished Walnut steering wheel.

Gasoline System—Gasoline tank of twenty gallons capacity suspended in rear. Gasoline gauge showing quantity in tank. Air pressure generated by metal plunger pump on one valve lifter.

Body—Five passenger coach type. Streamline design. Crowned Fenders.

Upholstering—10 and 12-inch cushions. High grade tufted leather. High grade springs. Rear seat 47 inches in width. High backs on front and rear seats.

Wind Shield—Built in without rods or braces. Adjustable for rain vision or ventilation. Folds down for clear vision.

Top—Mohair top. Patent locking Bair top holders. Dust covers.

Curtains—Side curtains, "Jiffy" quick adjustable.

Horn—Electric motor horn mounted on motor base under bonnet. Button for knee or hand.

Dash Fittings—Jones speedometer. Air pressure gauge. New Haven eight-day clock, all electrically illuminated.

Central Board—Button, switches, etc., mounted on control board in easy reach of operator.

Color and Finish—Bodies, wheels, frame and running gear finished in dark Victoria blue with silver stripe. Fenders black. All hardware, lamps and fittings nickeled and black.

Price Complete—F.O.B. Cleveland $1595. Chassis only, $1395.

Other Models—Information regarding, Coupe, Limousine and Sedan models on request.

Model 16

Serial # 4,000–15,000

Weight—2,890 pounds fully equipped with top, wind shield, battery, lamps, starter, speedometer, tools, and extra rim.

Wheel Base—122 inches. 10½ inches road clearance.

Turning Radius—38-foot circle.

Wheels—Artillery type—34 × 4 inches—fitted with Firestone Straight Side Demountable and Detachable Rims.

Motor—35 H.P. 3⅜ × 5 inches. "L" head type. Cylinders cast in two blocks. Valves enclosed. Silent chains driving cam, pump and magneto shafts and enclosed in oil tight case. Liberal sized bearings of white bronze.

Oiling—Oiling by positive pump on motor base, forcing oil into reservoirs over all principal bearings, cam and pump-driving chain case and into individual constant level troughs under each connecting rod and piston. Accessible filling tube for oil reservoir. Oil gauge on motor base. Oil pump accessible for inspection and cleaning.

Ignition—Bosch High Tension Magneto. Bosch spark plugs.

Carburetor—Rayfield G 3 Automatic, double jet. Hot air, and hot water jacket. Dash regulating attachments.

Self Starter—Gray & Davis Separate Electric Starter built into motor. All moving parts enclosed.

Cooling—Centrifugal pump. Mayo genuine Mercedes-type honeycomb radiator. Belt driven self-oiling fan.

Electric Lighting—Separate Gray & Davis Electric Lighting Generator with large Willard storage battery, single wire system and automatic switches. Electric lights throughout. Double bulbs in front lights for either city or country use. Tail lamp in combination illuminated license bracket.

Clutch—Multiple disc, imported ball bearing clutch. 13 discs of Raybestos and steel in oil tight case with motor.

Transmission—Three speeds and reverse. Nickel steel gears and shafts mounted on imported annular ball bearings, enclosed in aluminum case with motor and clutch, forming unit power plant.

Center Control—Left side drive. Center control. Gear shift and brake levers directly connected to transmission case. Entrance to front seats from either side.

Rear Axle—Full floating type. Worm bevel gears, imported annular ball bearings in wheels, shafts and differential. Drive shafts removable. Differential and main drive bevel gears adjustable and easily removable.

Brakes—14" double, internal. Faced with heat proof friction material.

Propeller Shaft—Fitted with double Hartford Universal Joints.

Torsion Rod—Pressed steel, triangle section, forward end fitted with double spring, buffers and ball and socket joints.

Steering Gear—Irreversible and adjustable for wear. Polished Walnut steering wheel. Steering post rigidly anchored to body.

Gasoline System—Gasoline tank suspended in rear. Gasoline gauge showing quantity in tank. Gasoline forced to carburetor by Stewart Vacuum System.

Body—Roomy seven-passenger type. Streamline design. Crowned Fenders.

Upholstering—10 and 12-inch cushions. High grade hand buffed tufted leather. High grade springs. Rear seat 47 inches in width. High backs on front and rear seats.

Wind Shield—Built in without rods or braces. Adjustable for rain vision or ventilation.

Top—Golde Patent one man crowned top, covered with high finish "Neverleek." Patent locking Bair top holders. Dust covers completely covering bows.

Curtains—Side curtains, "Jiffy" quick adjustable.

Horn—Electric motor horn mounted on motor base under bonnet. Button for knee or hand.

Control Board Fittings—Stewart-Warner Magnetic speedometer, carburetor adjustor, switches etc., mounted on control board in easy reach of operator. All electrically illuminated.

Color and Finish—Bodies, wheels, frame and running gear finished in dark Chandler blue. Fenders black. All hardware, lamps and fittings nickeled and black.

Price Complete—F.O.B. Cleveland

Touring Car, 7 passengers	$1295
Roadster, 2 passengers	$1295
Cabriolet, 3 passengers	$1650
Coupe, 4 passengers	$1900
Sedan, 5 passengers	$2450
Limousine, 7 passengers	$2450
Chassis only	$1095

Model 17

Serial # 15,001–35,000

"New and greater." The Model 17 serial numbers would be carried through the 1918 Model, Service Series 25.

Weight—2,985 pounds, equipped.

Wheel Base—123 inches. 10½ inches road clearance.

Wheels—Artillery type—34 × 4 inches—fitted with Firestone Straight Side Demountable and Detachable Rims.

Tires—34 × 4. Non-skid on rear.

Motor—3⅜ × 5 inches. "L" head type. Cylinders cast in two blocks. Valves enclosed. Silent chains driving cam, pump and magneto shafts and enclosed in oil tight case. Large bearings.

Oiling—Positive feed.

Ignition—Bosch High Tension Magneto.

Cooling—Centrifugal pump.

Self Starter—Gray & Davis Separate Electric Starter.

Electric Lighting—Separate Gray & Davis Electric Lighting Generator with large Willard storage battery, single wire system and automatic switches. Electric lights throughout. Double bulbs in front lights for either city or country use. Tail lamp in combination with illuminated license bracket.

Clutch—Multiple disc.

Transmission—Three speeds and reverse. Nickel steel gears and shafts mounted on annular ball bearings.

Control—Left side drive. Center control.

Rear Axle—Full floating type, spiral bevel gears, annular ball bearings throughout.

Brakes—14" double, internal and external.

Propeller Shaft—Fitted with double universal Joints.

Torsion Rod—Pressed steel.

Steering Gear— Irreversible and adjustable for wear.

Gasoline System—Large gasoline tank suspended in rear. Stewart Vacuum System.

Body—Roomy seven-passenger type. Streamline design.

Fenders—Full crowned fenders.

Upholstering—10 and 12-inch cushions. Long-grain, semi-glazed high grade leather.

Wind Shield—Adjustable for rain vision, clear vision, or ventilation.

Top—One man type. Dust covers completely covering bows.

Curtains—Side curtains, quick adjustable.

Horn—Electric motor horn.

Control Board Fittings—Stewart-Warner Magnetic speedometer, carburetor adjustor, switches etc., mounted on control board in easy reach of operator. All electrically illuminated.

Color and Finish—Chandler Blue. Fenders, wheels, and motor hood black. All hardware, lamps and fittings nickeled and black.

Price Complete—F.O.B. Cleveland

Touring Car, 7 passengers	$1295
Roadster, 2 passengers	$1295
Cabriolet, 3 passengers	$1650
Convertible Sedan, 7 passengers	$1795
Coupe, 4 passengers	$1950
Sedan, 5 passengers	$2250
Limousine, 7 passengers	$2450
Chassis only	$1095

New Series: Model 18

Serial # 35,001–65,000, Service Series 25

Weight—Touring car or roadster, 2,985 pounds, equipped.

Wheel Base—123 inches. 10½ inches road clearance.

Wheels—Artillery type—34 × 4 inches—fitted with Firestone Straight Side Demountable and Detachable Rims.

Tires—34 × 4. Non-skid on rear.

Motor—Bore 3½ inches. Stroke, 5 inches. "L" head type. Cylinders cast in two blocks. Valves enclosed. Silent chain drive for cam, pump and magneto shafts. Chains are enclosed in oil tight case and run in constant shower or oil. Extra large bearings throughout.

Oiling—Oil pump is driven by cam shaft and can be quickly removed for inspection or cleaning. Oil pumped directly to the main bearings and through leads to every working part. Individual oil trough under each connecting rod, into which the rod dips at every revolution, automatically maintains constant oil level, insuring proper lubrication.

Ignition—High Tension Magneto.

Cooling—By centrifugal pump, cellular radiator and adjustable belt-driven self-oiling fan.

Self Starter—Separate Electric Starter.

Electric Lighting—Separate Electric Generator with large Willard Storage Battery, single wire system and automatic switches. Double bulbs in front lights. Tail lamp in combination with license bracket.

Clutch—The clutch is of the multiple disc type. The center control lever and foot control pedal are mounted in unit with the transmission and clutch case.

Transmission—Three speeds and reverse. Nickel steel gears and shafts mounted on ball bearings.

Control—Left side drive, center control. Control levels most conveniently arranged for driver.

Propeller Shaft—Fitted with double universal Joints.

Torsion Rod—Of triangular pressed steel construction fitted with spring buffer and ball and socket joint on the forward end.

Rear Axle—Full floating type, spiral bevel gears, ball bearings throughout.

Brakes—Internal expanding and external contracting brakes, faced with special heat proof friction material, fitted with equalizers and very simple in adjustment.

Springs—Semi-elliptic rear; Semi-elliptic front. All bearings fitted with bronze bushings and compression grease cups.

Steering Gear—Worm and sector steering gear fitted with 18-inch polished walnut wheel. Steering post rigidly anchored to body. Splendid provision for adjustment for wear and for lubrication of all steering gear parts.

Gasoline System—Large gasoline tank suspended in rear. Stewart Vacuum System.

Fenders—Full crowned fenders.

Upholstering—10 and 12-inch cushions, long-grain, semi-glazed, high grade leather, hand buffed leather.

Windshield—Adjustable for rain vision, clear vision, or ventilation.

Top—Golde patent one man type covered with genuine Pantasote, with neat-fitting top boot completely covering the bows. Bair patent top holders and bow separators. Storm curtains of the quick adjustable patent type.

Horn—Electric motor horn.

Control Board Fittings—Stewart-Warner Magnetic Speedometer, carburetor adjuster, switches, fuse box. etc., all mounted on control board in easy reach of operator and all electrically illuminated.

Finish—All bodies are finished in special Chandler Blue: fenders, wheels, and motor hood black; except roadster wheels, which are cream. All hardware and fittings nickeled or black.

Body Types and Prices—

Touring Car, 7 passengers	$1595
Roadster, 4 passengers	$1595
Convertible Sedan, 7 passengers	$2295
Convertible Coupe, 4 passengers	$2195
Limousine, seating five in the enclosed compartment	$2895
Chassis only	$1395

All prices F.O.B. Cleveland, Ohio

1919

Serial # 65,001–82,000, Service Series 27

Note: There is a discrepancy of 200 cars in serial numbers of service series 27 using this listing compared to another official Chandler source.

Weight—Touring car or roadster, 2,985 pounds, equipped.

Wheel Base—123 inches. 10½ inches road clearance.

Wheels—Artillery type—34 × 4 inches—fitted with Firestone Straight Side Demountable Rims.

Tires—34 × 4. Non-skid on rear.

Motor—Bore, 3½; Stroke, 5 inches. "L" head type. Cylinders cast in two blocks. Valves enclosed. Silent chain drive for cam, pump and magneto shafts. Chains are enclosed in oil tight case and run in constant shower or oil. Extra large bearings throughout.

Oiling—Oil pump is driven by cam shaft and can be quickly removed for inspection or cleaning. Oil pumped directly to the main bearings and through leads to every working part. Individual oil trough under each connecting rod, into which the rod dips at every revolution, automatically maintains constant oil level, insuring proper lubrication.

Ignition—Bosch High-Tension Magneto.

Cooling—By centrifugal pump, cellular radiator and adjustable belt-driven self-oiling fan.

Self Starter—Separate Electric Starter.

Electric Lighting—Separate Electric Generator with large Willard Storage Battery, single wire system and automatic switches. Double bulbs in front lights. Tail lamp in combination with license bracket.

Clutch—The clutch is of the multiple disc type. The center control lever and foot control pedal are mounted in unit with the transmission and clutch case.

Transmission—Three speeds and reverse. Nickel steel gears and shafts mounted on ball bearings.

Control—Left side drive, center control. Control levels most conveniently arranged for driver.

Propeller Shaft—Fitted with double universal Joints.

Torque Arm—Of triangular pressed steel construction fitted with spring buffer and ball and socket joint on the forward end.

Rear Axle—Full floating type, spiral bevel gears, ball bearings throughout.

Brakes—Internal expanding and external contracting brakes, faced with special heat proof friction material, fitted with equalizers and very simple in adjustment.

Springs—Semi-elliptic rear; semi-elliptic front. All bearings fitted with bronze bushings and compression grease cups.

Steering Gear—Worm and sector steering gear fitted with 18-inch polished walnut wheel. Steering post rigidly anchored to body. Splendid provision for adjustment for wear and for lubrication of all steering gear parts.

Gasoline System—Large gasoline tank suspended in rear. Stewart Vacuum System.

Fenders—Full crowned fenders.

Upholstering—10 and 12-inch cushions, long-grain, semi-glazed, high grade, hand-buffed leather.

Windshield—Adjustable for rain vision, clear vision, or ventilation.

Top—Golde patent one man type, covered with genuine Pantasote, with neat-fitting top boot completely covering the bows. Bair patent top holders and bow separators. Storm curtains of the quick adjustable patent type.

Horn—Electric motor horn.

Control Board Fittings—Stewart-Warner Magnetic Speedometer, carburetor adjuster, switches, fuse box. etc., all mounted on control board in easy reach of operator and all electrically illuminated.

Finish—All bodies except Dispatch Car, are finished in special Chandler Blue: fenders, wheels, and motor hood black; except roadster wheels, which are cream. All hardware and fittings nickeled or black.

Body Types and Prices—

Touring Car, seven passengers	$1795
Roadster, four passengers	$1795
Dispatch Car, four passengers	$1875
Convertible Sedan, seven passengers	$2495
Convertible Coupe, four passengers	$2395
Limousine, seating five in the enclosed compartment	$3095
Chassis only	$1595

All prices F.O.B. Cleveland, Ohio

The prices as stated on succeeding pages of this catalogue are this date revised as follows:

Touring Car	$2095
Roadster	$2095
Dispatch Car	$2175
Sedan	$2795
Coupe	$2695
Limousine	$3395
Chassis	$1895

1920

Serial # 82,001–106,000, Service Series 27

Weight—Touring car or Roadster, 2,985 pounds, equipped.

Wheel Base—123 inches. 10 inches road clearance.

Wheels—Artillery type—33 x 4 inches—fitted with Firestone Straight Side Demountable Rims.

Tires—33 x 4 on Touring car, Roadster and Dispatch. 34 x 4½ on Sedan, Coupe, and Limousine. Non-skid on rear.

Motor—Bore, 3½ inches; Stroke, 5 inches. "L" head type. Cylinders cast in two blocks. Valves enclosed. Combination intake and exhaust manifold. Silent chain drive for cam, pump and magneto shafts. Chains are enclosed in oil tight case and run in constant shower or oil. Extra large bearings throughout. S.A.E. rating. 29.4 horsepower.

Oiling—Oil pump is driven by cam shaft and can be quickly removed for inspection or cleaning. Oil pumped directly to the main bearings and through leads to every working part. Individual oil trough under each connecting rod, into which the rod dips at every revolution, automatically maintains constant oil level, insuring proper lubrication.

Ignition—Bosch High-Tension Magneto.

Cooling—By centrifugal pump, cellular radiator and adjustable belt-driven self-oiling fan.

Self Starter—Separate Electric Starter.

Electric Lighting—Separate Electric Generator with large Prestolite Storage Battery, single wire system and automatic switches. Double bulbs in front lights. Tail lamp in combination with license bracket.

Clutch—The clutch is of the multiple disc type. The center control lever and foot control pedal are mounted in unit with the transmission and clutch case.

Transmission—Three speeds and reverse. Nickel steel gears and shafts mounted on ball bearings.

Control—Left side drive, center control. Control levels most conveniently arranged for driver.

Propeller Shaft—Fitted with double universal Joints.

Torque Arm—Of triangular pressed steel construction fitted with spring buffer and ball and socket joint on the forward end.

Rear Axle—Full floating type, spiral bevel gears, ball bearings throughout.

Brakes—Internal expanding and external contracting brakes, faced with special heat proof friction material, fitted with equalizers and very simple in adjustment.

Springs—Semi-elliptic rear; semi-elliptic front. All eyes fitted with bronze bushings and oil cups.

Steering Gear—Worm and sector steering gear fitted with 18-inch polished walnut wheel. Steering post rigidly anchored to body. Splendid provision for adjustment for wear and for lubrication of all steering gear parts.

Gasoline System—Large gasoline tank suspended in rear. Stewart Vacuum System.

Fenders—Full crowned fenders.

Upholstering—10 and 12-inch cushions, long-grain, semi-glazed, high grade, hand-buffed leather.

Windshield–Adjustable for rain vision, clear vision, or ventilation.

Top—Covered with genuine Neverleek, with neat-fitting top boot completely covering the bows. Bair patent top holders and bow separators. Clear vision storm curtains opening with the doors, and detachable rear quarter–bow curtains on Touring and Dispatch..

Horn—Electric motor horn.

Control Board Fittings—Stewart-Warner Magnetic Speedometer, carburetor adjuster, switches, fuse box, dash lamps, etc., all mounted on control board in easy reach of operator and all electrically illuminated.

Finish—All bodies (except Dispatch Car, which is Chandler rainbow blue) are finished in standard Chandler Blue; fenders, motor hood and running gear black; all wheels are standard blue except roadster wheels, which are cream. All hardware and fittings nickeled or black.

Body Types and Prices—

Touring Car, seven passengers	$1895
Roadster, four passengers	$1895
Dispatch Car, four passengers	$1975
Sedan. seven passengers	$2895
Coupe, four passengers	$2795
Limousine, seating five in the enclosed compartment	$3395
Chassis only	$1695

All prices F.O.B. Cleveland, Ohio
Prices listed above become effective January 1st, 1920

1921

Serial # 106,001–115,000, Service Series 27

There are three sets of specifications for 1921, dated September 27, 1920, January 1, 1921, and February 15, 1921. Only body styles and prices are different.

Weight—Touring car 2,985 pounds, equipped.

Wheel Base—123 inches. 10 inches road clearance.

Wheels—Artillery type—33 × 4 inches—fitted with Firestone Straight Side Demountable Rims.

Tires—33 × 4 on Touring car, Roadster and Dispatch. 34 × 4½ on Sedan, Coupe, and Limousine. Non-skid on rear.

Motor—Bore, 3½ inches; Stroke, 5 inches. "L" head type. Cylinders cast in two blocks. Valves enclosed. Combination intake and exhaust manifold. Silent chain drive for cam, pump and magneto shafts. Chains are enclosed in oil tight case and run in constant shower or oil. Extra large bearings throughout. S.A.E. rating. 29.4 horsepower.

Oiling—Oil pump is driven by cam shaft and can be quickly removed for inspection or cleaning. Oil pumped directly to the main bearings and through leads to every working part. Individual oil trough under each connecting rod, into which the rod dips at every revolution, automatically maintains constant oil level, insuring proper lubrication.

Ignition—Bosch High-Tension Magneto.

Cooling—By centrifugal pump, cellular radiator and adjustable belt-driven self-oiling fan.

Self Starter—Separate Electric Starter.

Lighting—Separate Electric Generator with large Prestolite Storage Battery, single wire system and automatic switches. Double bulbs in front lights. Tail lamp in combination with license bracket.

Clutch—The clutch is of the disc type. The center control lever and foot control pedal are mounted in unit with the transmission and clutch case.

Transmission—Three speeds and reverse. Nickel steel gears and shafts mounted on ball bearings.

Control—Left side drive, center control. Control levels most conveniently arranged for driver.

Propeller Shaft—Fitted with double universal Joints.

Torque Arm— Of triangular pressed steel construction fitted with spring buffer and ball and socket joint on the forward end.

Rear Axle—Floating type, spiral bevel gears, ball bearings throughout.

Brakes—Internal expanding and external contracting brakes, faced with special heat proof friction material, fitted with equalizers and very simple in adjustment.

Springs—Semi-elliptic rear; semi-elliptic front. All eyes fitted with bronze bushings and oil cups.

Steering Gear—Worm and sector steering gear fitted with 18-inch polished walnut wheel. Steering post rigidly anchored to body. Splendid provision for adjustment for wear and for lubrication of all steering gear parts.

Gasoline System—Large gasoline tank suspended in rear. Stewart Vacuum System.

Fenders—Full crowned fenders.

Upholstering—Long-grain, semi-glazed, high grade, hand-buffed leather in open models and driver's seat of Limousine. Silk velour in Sedan and Coupe and fine cloth in passenger compartment of Limousine.

Windshield—Adjustable for rain vision, clear vision, or ventilation.

Top—Covered with genuine Neverleek. Clear vision storm curtains opening with the doors, and permanent rear quarter bow curtains on all open models. Closed bodies all metal.

Horn—Electric motor horn.

Control Board Fittings—Stewart-Warner Magnetic Speedometer, carburetor adjuster, switches, fuse box, dash lamps, etc., all mounted on control board in easy reach of operator and all electrically illuminated.

Finish—All bodies (except bodies and hood of the Dispatch Car, which are Chandler rainbow blue, and two-passenger Roadster, which are battleship grey) are finished in standard Chandler Blue; fenders, motor hoods and running gear, black; all wheels are standard blue except four-passenger Roadster wheels, which are cream, and two-passenger Roadster wheels, which are black. All hardware and fittings nickeled or black on all open models and a dull silver finish on the enclosed models.

Body Types and Prices as of Sept. 27, 1920—

Touring Car, seven passenger	$2095
Roadster, four passenger	$2095
Dispatch Car, four passenger	$2175
Sedan, seven passenger	$3195
Coupe, four passenger	$3095
Limousine, seating five in the enclosed compartment	$3595
Chassis only	$1895

Body Types and Prices as of January 1, 1921—

Touring Car, seven passenger	$1895
Roadster, four passenger	$1895
Roadster, two passenger	$1895
Dispatch Car, four passenger	$1975
Sedan, seven passenger	$2995
Coupe, four passenger	$2895
Limousine, seating five in the enclosed compartment	$3495
Chassis only	$1695

Body Types and Prices as of February 15, 1921—

Touring Car, seven passengers	$1930
Roadster, four passengers	$1930
Roadster, two-passenger	$1930
Dispatch Car, four passengers	$2010
Sedan, seven passengers	$3030
Coupe, four passengers	$2930
Limousine, seating five in enclosed compartment	$3530
Chassis only	$1730

Cord Tires Standard Equipment
All prices F.O.B. Cleveland, Ohio
Wire wheels, spare tires and tire covers, extra equipment.

1922

Serial # 115,001–126,000 Service Series 29

Weight—Touring car 2,985 pounds.

Wheel Base—123 inches.

Wheels—Artillery type—Fitted with Firestone Straight Side Demountable Rims.

Tires—Cord tires standard equipment. 33 × 4 on open models; 34 × 4½ on closed models. Non-skid all around.

Motor—Bore, 3½ inches; Stroke, 5 inches. "L" head type. Cylinders cast in two blocks. Valves enclosed. Combination intake and exhaust manifold. Silent chain drive for cam, pump and magneto shafts. Chains are enclosed in oil tight case and run in constant shower or oil. Extra large bearings throughout. S.A.E. rating. 29. 4 H.P.

Oiling—Oil pump is driven by cam shaft and can be quickly removed for inspection or cleaning. Oil pumped directly through leads to the main bearings. Individual oil troughs under each connecting rod, into which the rod dips at every revolution, automatically maintains constant oil level, insuring proper lubrication.

Ignition—High-Tension Magneto, water-proof type.

Cooling—By centrifugal pump, cellular radiator and adjustable belt-driven self-oiling fan. All radiator shells nickel plated. Motometer standard equipment on all models.

Starter—Separate Electric Starter.

Lighting—Separate Electric Generator with automatic switches. Large storage Battery. Single wire system. Double bulbs in head lamps, which are of barrel type. Miniature head lamps on cowl. Tonneau lamps in Dispatch and Touring cars. Tail lamp in combination with license bracket.

Clutch—The clutch is of the disc type. The center control lever and foot control pedal are mounted in unit with the transmission and clutch case.

Transmission—Three speeds and reverse. Nickel steel gears and shafts mounted on ball bearings. Speedometer drive located inside transmission housing and totally enclosed in oil.

Control—Left side drive, center control. Control levels most conveniently arranged for driver.

Propeller Shaft—Fitted with flexible disc universal joints.

Rear Axle—Floating type, spiral bevel nickel steel gears, roller bearings in differential and ball bearings in rear wheels.

Brakes—External contracting. Service brake on rear wheels, fitted with equalizers and very simple in adjustment. Emergency brake on transmission. All brakes faced with special heat-proof friction material.

Springs—Semi-elliptic, specially heat treated. All eyes fitted with bronze bushings and oil cups. Rear springs underslung.

Steering Gear—Worm and gear type, fitted with 18-inch polished walnut wheel. Steering post rigidly anchored to body.

Splendid provision for adjustment for wear and for lubrication of all steering gear parts.

Gasoline System—Vacuum. Tank suspended in rear, with gauge and filler being located at opposite ends. The filler cap is of bayonet type, operated by a simple half turn.

Fenders—Full crown, with a special raised design, front fenders fitted with splasher flaps.

Steps—Highly polished aluminum, fitted with moulded rubber treads. Running boards optional.

Upholstering—Long-grain, high grade, hand-buffed leather. In open models and driver's seat of Limousine. Mohair velvet throughout in Sedan and Coupe, and a rich cloth in passenger compartment of Limousine.

Windshield—Adjustable for rain vision, clear vision, or ventilation. Stanchions on Dispatch and Touring cars and Limousine are of rectangular design. Roadster stanchions are round. Stanchions on all open models are highly nickel plated. Pivoting of the upper glass is controlled by wingbolts. Windshield wipers standard on all models.

Top—Open models covered with a high quality material. Lined with grey whipcord. Permanent rear quarter–bow curtains. Side curtains open with the doors.

Horn—Electric, mounted on left side of motor on rear cylinder block.

Control Board Fittings—Speedometer, cowl ventilator, control, carburetor adjuster, switches, fuse box, dash lamps, etc., all mounted on control board in easy reach of operator and all electrically illuminated.

Standard Body Finish—Touring cars and 4-passenger Roadster, Chandler green; Dispatch car and 2-passenger Roadster, Chandler maroon; Sedan, Coupe and Limousine, Chandler blue.

Optional Body Finish—Touring cars, Chandler blue; 4-passenger Roadster, Maroon; Dispatch car and 2-passenger Roadster, Chandler twilight grey. Sedan, Coupe and Limousine, Chandler green.

Body Types—

Touring Car, five passenger
Touring car, seven passenger
Roadster, four passengers
Roadster, two-passenger
Dispatch Car, four passenger
Sedan, seven passengers
Coupe, four passengers
Limousine, seating five in the enclosed compartment

1923

Serial # 126,001–140,000
Service Series 32—Pikes Peak Motor

Wheel Base—123 inches.

Wheels—Artillery type fitted with straight-sided demountable rims. Royal Dispatch and four-passenger Roadster equipped with disc-steel wheels.

Tires—Non-skid cord on all models. All closed models and Royal Dispatch equipped with oversize 33 × 4½—all other models 32 × 4.

Motor—Bore, 3½ inches by 5 inch stroke. "L" head type. Cylinders cast in one block with separate crank case and detachable head. Crank-shaft extra heavy and carried on four main bearings.

Pistons—Special Chandler, designed to minimize formation of carbon.

Roller Valve Lifters—Designed for quiet operation and long-life.

Crank Case—Aluminum four-point suspension.

Oiling—Gear pump driven from camshaft providing pressure feed to crank shaft, camshaft, accessory shaft and Morse single timing chain. Connecting rods, wrist pins and cylinder walls lubricated by splash.

Carburetor—Stromberg Model 32, automatic type, no valves or springs to get out of adjustment. Quick starting and economical.

Ignition—High tension from generator and storage battery. Combination automatic and hand control. All wires contained in enameled metal tube, giving unusual protection from moisture, oil and dirt. Bosch magneto optional at extra charge.

Cooling—Centrifugal pump, cellular radiator and adjustable belt-driven self-oiling six-bladed fan.

Motometer—Standard equipment on all models.

Starter—Electrical, separate unit. Ample reserve power for cold weather.

Frame—Extra heavy pressed steel, channel section, rigidly reenforced with five cross members.

Lighting—Separate unit electric generator with automatic switches. Large storage Battery. Single wire system. Double bulbs in barrel-type head lamps. Miniature head-lamps on cowl. Tonneau lamps in Dispatch and Touring cars. Tail lamp in combination with license bracket.

Clutch—Disc type. Very easy to operate. Central control lever and foot control pedal are mounted in unit with the transmission and clutch case.

Transmission—Three speeds and reverse. Nickel steel gears and shafts mounted on ball bearings. Speedometer drive located inside transmission housing and totally enclosed in oil.

Control—Left side drive center control. All levels most conveniently arranged for driver. Steering wheel of black rubber-like composition handsomely finished and fitted to the hand.

Propeller Shaft—Fitted with large size flexible disc universal joints.

Rear Axle—Floating type, spiral bevel nickel steel gears, roller bearings in differential and ball bearings in rear wheels.

Front Axle—Drop forged I-beam section with steering spindle supported on taper roller bearings.

Brakes—External contracting service brake on rear wheels, fitted with equalizers and very simple in adjustment. Emergency brake on transmission skid reducing. All brakes faced with special heat-proof friction material and effective anti-rattlers.

Springs—Semi-elliptic, specially heat treated. All eyes fitted with bronze bushings and oil cups. Rear springs under-slung.

Steering Gear—Worm and gear type. Steering post rigidly anchored to body. Splendid provision for adjustment for wear and for lubrication of all steering gear parts.

Gasoline System—Vacuum feed from 20 gal. tank suspended in rear with gauge and filler on opposite ends of tank. Filler cap is of bayonet type, operated by a simple half turn.

Fenders—Full crown, with a special raised design, front fenders fitted with splasher flaps.

Steps—Highly polished aluminum fitted with moulded rubber treads are standard on all models except five-passenger Touring and Chummy Sedan, which are equipped with running boards.

Running Boards—Running boards of handsome design are standard equipment on five-passenger Touring and Chummy Sedan and are optional equipment on all other models except Royal Dispatch.

Upholstering—Long-grain, high grade, hand-buffed leather in open models and driver's seat of Limousine. Mohair velvet throughout in Metropolitan and seven-passenger Sedans. Plush velour in Chummy Sedan. Rich cloth in passenger compartment of Limousine. Royal Dispatch and four-passenger Roadster are upholstered in unpleated Spanish leather.

Windshield—Adjustable for rain vision, clear vision, or ventilation. Royal Dispatch has special one-piece windshield. Windshield wipers standard on all models.

Tops—Open models covered with a high quality material lined with grey whipcord. Permanent rear quarter bow curtains. Side curtains open with the doors. Khaki tops standard on four-passenger Roadster and Royal Dispatch and optional on all open models.

Horn—Large size electric mounted under engine hood.

Control Board Fittings—Speedometer, cowl ventilator control, carburetor adjuster, switches, fuse box, dash lamps, etc., all mounted on control board in easy reach of operator and all electrically illuminated.

Standard Body Finish—Five-passenger Touring, blue; seven-passenger Touring, blue; four-passenger Roadster, green; Royal Dispatch, special green; all closed models, blue.

Optional Body Finish—Seven-passenger Touring, green; four-passenger Roadster, maroon; Royal Dispatch, maroon; Limousine, green.

Body Types—Touring Car, five passenger; Touring car, seven passenger; Royal Dispatch, four passenger; Roadster, four passengers; Chummy Sedan, five passenger; Metropolitan Sedan, five-passenger; Sedan, seven passengers; Limousine, seating five in the enclosed compartment.

1924

Serial # 140,001–147,000 Service Series 32 A

Wheel Base—123 inches.

Wheels—Artillery type, straight-side demountable rims. Royal Dispatch, Comrade and four-passenger Roadster equipped with disc-steel wheels.

Tires—Non-skid cord. All closed models, also Royal Dispatch and Comrade, oversize 33 × 4½—others 32 × 4.

Motor—Bore, 3½ inches by 5 inch stroke. L-head. Cylinders cast in one block with separate crank case, detachable head. Four-bearing crank shaft.

Pistons—Special Chandler, minimize formation of carbon.

Valve Lifters—Quiet roller type.

Crank Case—Aluminum four-point suspension.

Oiling—Gear pump driven from camshaft providing pressure feed to crank shaft, connecting rods, camshaft, accessory shaft and silent timing chain. Wrist pins and cylinder walls lubricated by spray.

Carburetor—Stromberg Model OE2 automatic.

Ignition—High tension from generator and storage battery. Combination automatic and hand control. All wires contained in enameled metal tube. Bosch magneto optional at extra charge.

Cooling—Centrifugal pump, cellular radiator, thermostatic control, belt-driven self-oiling six-bladed fan; Motometer.

Starter—Electrical, separate unit. Ample reserve power.

Frame—Extra heavy pressed steel, channel section, rigidly reenforced with five cross members and two motor supports.

Lighting—Separate unit electric generator with large storage Battery. Single wire system. Double bulbs in barrel-type head lamps. Miniature head-lamps on cowl. Tonneau lamps in Dispatch and Touring cars.

Clutch—Disc type.

Transmission—Traffic transmission. Campbell patents, three speeds and reverse. Main shafts mounted on ball bearings. Speedometer drive enclosed.

Propeller Shaft—Large flexible disc universal joints.

Rear Axle—Floating, spiral bevel nickel steel gears, roller bearings in differential and ball bearings in rear wheels.

Front Axle—Drop forged I-beam section; roller bearing steering spindles.

Brakes—External contracting service brake on rear wheels, fitted with equalizers. Emergency brake on transmission. Anti-rattlers on brakes.

Springs—Semi-elliptic, specially heat treated, with bronze bushings and oil cups. Rear springs under-slung.

Steering Gear—Worm and gear type. Steering post rigidly anchored. Large steering wheel of composition, molded to fit the hands.

Gasoline System—Vacuum feed from 20 gal. tank in rear.

Fenders—Full crown, with a special raised design, front fenders with splasher flaps.

Steps and Running Boards—Highly polished aluminum steps, fitted with moulded rubber treads, are standard on Metropolitan Sedan and Royal Dispatch; running boards with polished guard plates on all other models.

Upholstering—Hand-buffed leather in Touring models and driver's seat of Limousine. Unpleated Spanish leather in Royal Dispatch, four-passenger Roadster and Comrade Roadster. Plush in all closed cars except Limousine (broadcloth) and Metropolitan Sedan (Mohair).

Windshield—Adjustable for rain vision, clear vision, or ventilation. Royal Dispatch and Comrade have special one-piece windshield. Windshield wiper on all models.

Tops—High grade material backed with grey whipcord. Permanent rear quarter bow curtains. Khaki standard on four-passenger Roadster and green Royal Dispatch; on other models at extra cost.

Control Board Fittings—Speedometer, cowl ventilator control, carburetor adjuster, switches, fuse box, dash lamp, etc.

Models	*Capacity*	*Color*	*Optional*
Comrade	2–3	Light Brown	Light Blue
Royal Dispatch	4	Light Green	Maroon, Light Blue
Roadster	4	Dark Green	Maroon
Touring	5	Dark Blue	
Touring	7	Dark Blue	Maroon
Chummy Sedan	5	Dark Blue	
Chummy Sedan Special*	5	Light Blue	
Four Door Sedan	5	Dark Blue	
Four Door Sedan Special*	5	Light Blue	
Metropolitan Sedan	5	Dark Blue	Light Blue
Sedan	7	Dark Blue	
Limousine	7	Dark Blue	Green

**Special paint work; equipped with rear vision mirror, nickel radiator shell, De Luxe trunk rack and bars, and front bumper—$100 extra.*

1925

Serial # 147,001–148,000, Service Series 33

Wheel Base—123 inches.

Wheels—Artillery type, straight-side demountable rims. Royal Dispatch, Comrade and four-passenger Roadster have disc-steel wheels.

Tires—Genuine supersize Balloon Tires—6.20/21—on all models.

Motor—Bore 3½ inches by 5 inch stroke. L-head. Cylinders cast in one block with separate crank case, detachable head. Four-bearing crank shaft.

Pistons—New type, cast iron.

Valve Lifters—Quiet roller type, lubricated by spray.

Crank Case—Aluminum four-point suspension.

Oiling—Gear pump driven from camshaft providing pressure feed to crank shaft, connecting rods, camshaft, accessory shaft and silent timing chain. Wrist pins and cylinder walls lubricated by spray.

Carburetor—Designed especially for the Pikes Peak Motor to give smooth acceleration at all speeds.

Ignition—High tension from distributor and storage battery. Combination automatic and hand control. All wires contained in enameled metal tube. Bosch magneto optional at extra charge.

Cooling—Centrifugal pump, cellular radiator, thermostatic control, belt-driven self-oiling six-bladed fan; monometer; standard on all models.

Starter—Electrical, separate unit. Ample reserve power.

Frame—Extra heavy pressed steel, channel section, rigidly re-enforced with five cross members and two motor supports.

Lighting—Separate unit electric generator with large storage Battery. Single wire system. Barrel-type head lamps. Miniature head-lamps on cowl. Tonneau lamps in Dispatch and Touring cars. Tail lamp in combination with license bracket.

Clutch—Dry plate, disc type; requires no lubrication.

Transmission—Traffic transmission. Campbell patents, three speeds and reverse. Main shaft mounted on ball bearings. Speedometer drive enclosed.

Propeller Shaft—Large flexible disc universal joints.

Rear Axle—Floating; spiral bevel nickel steel gears, roller bearings in differential and ball bearings in rear wheels.

Front Axle—Drop forged I-beam section.

Brakes—External contracting service brake on rear wheels, fitted with equalizers. Emergency brake on transmission. Mechanically operated front wheel brakes optional at extra cost. Anti-rattlers on brakes.

Springs—Semi-elliptic, specially heat treated, with bronze bushings. Rear springs under-slung.

Steering Gear—Worm and gear type. Steering post rigidly anchored. Large steering wheel of composition, molded to fit the hands. Increased ratio assures ease of steering.

Gasoline System—Vacuum feed from 20 gal. tank in rear.

Fenders—Full crown, with a raised design, front fenders with splasher flaps.

Steps and Running Boards—Highly polished aluminum steps, fitted with molded rubber treads, are standard on Royal

Dispatch; running boards with polished guard plates on all other models.

Upholstering—All open models, genuine hand-buffed leather. Limousine, leather in driving compartment, fine quality cloth in tonneau. All other closed models, high-grade fabrics.

Windshield—Adjustable for rain vision, clear vision, or ventilation. Royal Dispatch and Comrade have special one-piece windshield. Windshield wiper on all models.

Tops—High grade black material backed with grey whipcord. Khaki standard on four-passenger Roadster and green Royal Dispatch; on other models at extra cost.

Control Board Fittings—Speedometer, carburetor adjuster, switches, fuse, dash lamp, etc.

Models	*Capacity*	*Color*	*Optional*
Comrade	2–3	Light Brown	Light Blue
Royal Dispatch	4	Light Green	Maroon, Light Blue
Roadster	4	Dark Green	Maroon
Touring	5	Dark Blue	
Touring	7	Dark Blue	Maroon
Chummy Sedan	5	Dark Blue	
Four-Door Sedan	5	Dark Blue	
Sedan	7	Dark Blue	
Limousine	7	Dark Blue	Green

1925

Serial # 148,001–159,624, Service Series 33 A

Wheel Base—123 inches.

Wheels—Artillery type, straight-side demountable rims. Royal Dispatch, Comrade and four-passenger Roadster have disc-steel wheels.

Tires—Genuine supersize Balloon Tires—33 × 6—on all models.

Motor—Bore 3½ inches by 5 inch stroke. L-head. Cylinders cast in one block with separate crank case, detachable head. Four- bearing crank shaft.

Pistons—New type, cast iron.

Valve Lifters—Quiet roller type, lubricated by spray.

Crank Case—Aluminum four-point suspension.

Oiling—Gear pump driven from camshaft providing pressure feed to crank shaft, connecting rods, camshaft, accessory shaft and silent timing chain. Wrist pins and cylinder walls lubricated by spray.

Carburetor—Designed especially for the Pikes Peak Motor to give smooth acceleration at all speeds.

Ignition—High tension from distributor and storage battery. Combination automatic and hand control. All wires contained in enameled metal tube. Bosch magneto optional at extra charge.

Cooling—Centrifugal pump, cellular radiator, thermostatic control, belt-driven self-oiling six-bladed fan; Motometer standard on all models.

Starter—Electrical, separate unit. Ample reserve power.

Frame—Extra heavy pressed steel, channel section, rigidly reenforced with five cross members and two motor supports.

Lighting—Separate unit electric generator with large storage Battery. Single wire system. Barrel-type head lamps. Miniature head-lamps on cowl. Tonneau lamps in Dispatch and Touring cars. Tail lamp in combination with license bracket.

Clutch—Dry plate, disc type; requires no lubrication.

Transmission—Traffic transmission. Campbell patents, three speeds and reverse. Main shaft mounted on ball bearings.

Propeller Shaft—Tubular; flexible disc universal joints.

Rear Axle—Floating; spiral bevel nickel steel gears, roller bearings in differential and ball bearings in rear wheels.

Front Axle—Drop forged I-beam section.

Brakes—External contracting service brake on rear wheels, fitted with equalizers. Emergency brake on transmission. Mechanically operated front wheel brakes optional at extra cost. Anti-rattlers on brakes.

Springs—Semi-elliptic, specially heat treated, with bronze bushings. Rear springs under-slung.

Steering Gear—Worm and gear type. Steering post rigidly anchored. Large steering wheel of composition molded to fit the hands. Increased ratio assures ease of steering.

Gasoline System—Vacuum feed from 20 gallon tank in rear.

Fenders—Full crown, with a raised design.

Steps and Running Boards—Highly polished aluminum steps, fitted with molded rubber treads, are standard on Royal Dispatch; running boards with polished guard plates on all other models.

Upholstering—All open models, genuine hand-buffed leather. Limousine, leather in driving compartment, fine quality cloth in tonneau. All other closed models, high-grade fabrics.

Windshield—Adjustable for rain vision, clear vision, or ventilation. Royal Dispatch, Sport Touring and Comrade have special one-piece windshield. V.V. type in Metropolitan, Chummy and Coach Imperial.

Tops—High grade black material backed with grey whipcord. Khaki standard on four-passenger Roadster and green Royal Dispatch; on other models at extra cost.

(D denotes Duco; V denotes Varnish)

Models	*Pass.*	*Standard Color*	*Optional*
Comrade	*2	D—Two-tone Gray-Green	None
Royal Dispatch	4	V—Light Green	V—Maroon, Light Blue
Roadster	4	V—Dark Green	V—Maroon
Touring	5	D—Two-tone Gray-Green	D—Luxor Blue
Touring	7	D—Sagebrush Green	V—Dark Blue

Models	*Pass.*	*Standard Color*	*Optional*
Coach Imperial	5	D—Luxor Blue	None
Chummy Sedan	5	D—Sagebrush Green	V—Luxor Blue
Four-Door	5	V—Dark Blue	D—Sagebrush Green
Metropolitan	5	D—Two-tone Brown	D—Sagebrush Green
Sedan	7	D—Sagebrush Green	V—Dark Blue
Limousine	7	V—Dark Blue	V—Green

**Two extra in rumble seat.*

1926 Early

Serial # 159,625–165,000, Series 35—Traffic Transmission

Wheel Base—123 inches.

Wheels—Artillery type, straight-side demountable rims.

Tires—Genuine supersize 33 × 6 Balloon Tires on all models.

Motor—L-head. Bore 3½ inches by 5 inch stroke. Cylinders cast in one block with separate crank case, detachable head. Large four-bearing crank shaft.

Pistons—New improved type, cast iron.

Valve Lifters—Quiet roller type, lubricated by spray.

Crank Case—Aluminum four-point suspension.

Oiling—Gear pump driven from camshaft providing pressure feed to crank shaft, connecting rods, camshaft, accessory shaft and silent timing chain. Wrist pins and cylinder walls lubricated by spray.

Carburetor—Special Schebler, designed especially for the Pikes Peak Motor to give smooth acceleration at all speeds.

Ignition—High tension from distributor and storage battery. Combination automatic and hand control. All wires contained in enameled metal tube.

Cooling—Centrifugal pump, cellular radiator, belt-driven self-oiling six-bladed fan; Motometer standard on all models.

Starter—Electrical, separate unit. Ample reserve power.

Frame—Extra heavy pressed steel, channel section, rigidly reenforced with five cross members and two motor supports.

Lighting—Separate unit electric generator with large storage Battery. Single wire system. Barrel-type head lamps. Miniature head-lamps on cowl. Tonneau lamps in Touring cars. Tail lamp in combination with license bracket.

Clutch—Dry plate, disc type; needs no lubrication.

Transmission—Traffic transmission. Campbell patents, three speeds and reverse. Main shaft mounted on ball bearings.

Propeller Shaft—Tubular; flexible disc universal joints.

Rear Axle—Floating; spiral bevel steel gears, roller bearings in differential and ball bearings in rear wheels.

Front Axle—Drop forged I-beam section.

Brakes—External contracting service brake on rear wheels, fitted with equalizers. Emergency brake on transmission. Mechanically operated front wheel brakes optional at slight extra cost. Anti-rattlers on brakes.

Springs—Semi-elliptic, specially heat treated, with bronze bushings. Rear springs under-slung. Patented anti-rattlers on shackles.

Steering Gear—Worm and gear type. Patented flexible coupling between gear housing and steering shaft. Increased ratio assures ease of steering. Steering wheel, large size, walnut serrated.

Gasoline System—Vacuum feed from 20 gallon tank in rear. Gas gauge on instrument board.

1926 Late

Serial # 165,001–174,000, Service Series 35—Traffic Transmission dropped

Wheel Base—124 inches.

Pikes Peak Motor—Completely Chandler built. Bore 3½ inches, Stroke 5 inch. Cylinders are of fluxed grey-iron cast in one block and are honed. Detachable head of special design to control temperature in firing chambers.

Crankshaft—Carried on four heavy bronze-backed bearings mounted in heavily-webbed bearing bridges, cast integral in one piece aluminum base. Construction permits full oil pressure to bearings.

Crank Case—Aluminum four-point suspension in frame.

Pistons—Special design, of light fluxed grey-iron, with extra large piston pins in bronze bushings. Exhaustive tests fail to show the slightest tendency to become irregular and slap. Special rings and large drain-holes keep excess oil from reaching firing chamber.

Valve Lifters—Quiet roller type, extra large. Lubricated by spray.

Oiling—Specially designed pump with cut steel gears located outside crankcase and driven from camshaft, providing pressure feed to crankshaft, connecting rods, camshaft, accessory shaft and silent timing chain. Piston pins and cylinder walls lubricated by spray. A handy oil draining valve at the left side of the motor makes it simple and easy to drain the crankcase.

Carburetor—Schebler, specially designed for the Pikes Peak Motor's new, quick-vaporizing manifold.

Manifold—Exclusively Chandler. The unique design of the intake manifold insures perfect distribution of gas to all six cylinders at all speeds, and entirely eliminates any tendency of raw fuel to "puddle" and flow into any one or two cylinders improperly, in excess amounts. A novel feature of the exhaust manifold is the exclusive common center hot-spot chamber with three distinct passages from two cylinders each. This feature does away with all back pressure reaction of any one exhaust on the other, and contributes a notable smoothness to the motor.

Gasoline System—Vacuum feed from large tank in rear. Constant reading gasoline gauge on instrument board.

Ignition—Bosch, from distributor and battery. Combination automatic and hand control. Cables protected enameled metal conduit. Bosch generator and separate starting motor.

Timing—Morse patent single-chain with serrated nut adjustment on outside of crankcase.

Cooling—Centrifugal pump on accessory shaft with extra large stuffing nuts to overcome leakage. Six blade fan, self oiling with V-type belt and aluminum alloy pulleys. Extra-large cellular radiator and large water line around cylinders and valve seals.

Transmission—Selective sliding, three speeds forward and reverse. Main shaft mounted on ball bearings. Gear ratios and teeth designed to give extra ease in shifting.

Clutch—Dry plate, disc type; requires no lubrication.

Propeller Shaft—Light tubular construction provided with three flexible fabric discs at each end, requiring no lubrication. This construction eliminates any possibility of back lash.

Rear Axle—Specially designed, horizontally-welded heavy pressed-steel housing, reinforced with internal steel sleeve. A heavy malleable casting is riveted over-all to carry brake disc and drive through spring. The axle drive-shaft is accurately centered to drive wheels through hub flange. Floating type. The shaft is 1⅜ inches in diameter with eight splines in differential member.

Differential—Spiral bevel nickel-steel gears, accurately machined and heat treated. Extra heavy pinion carriers with no spacers to wear and allow pinion to work forward. Large Timken bearings on pinion-shaft and differential.

Brakes—External contracting service brake on rear wheels, fitted with equalizers. Emergency brake on transmission. Mechanically operated front wheel brakes optional at extra cost.

Front Axle—Drop forged, sturdy I-beam section.

Chassis—Designed for exceptionally strenuous service. Frame is of heavy gauge steel with five separate, hot-riveted cross members, and two motor base supports. Front wheel brakes are mounted on specially-designed sturdy I-beam (not on frame), thus eliminating all unnecessary wear from spring deflection.

Steering Gear—Special Chandler design worm and sector type. Steering post rigidly anchored. Increased ratio makes Chandler the easiest of all cars to steer and park. Flexible disc coupling in steering post removes all internal strains and stresses.

Drive—Improved Hotchkiss, eliminating radius rods and torque arms.

Springs—Extremely long, easy-riding springs. Front 40¾ inches, rear 59¼ inches. Shackle bolts equipped with patented enclosed anti-rattling device which keeps uniform tension on shackles at all times, retains lubricant, and prevents annoying sideway, slaps and rattles.

Lubrication—All moving parts of the entire chassis are thoroughly lubricated by the "One Shot" system of automatic chassis lubrication.

Lighting—Separate unit electric generator with large storage battery. Single wire system. Barrel-type head lamps. Miniature head-lamps on cowl. Tonneau lamps in Touring cars. Tail lamp in combination with license bracket.

Wheels—Artillery type, demountable rims.

Tires: Genuine super-size 33 × 6 inch antiskid. Balloon tires on all models.

Chandler 1926 Models

Twentieth Century Sedan	5 Passenger
Brougham	5 Passenger
Metropolitan Sedan De Luxe	5 Passenger
Chandler Sedan	7 Passenger
Comrade Roadster	2 Passenger
(Two extra in rumble seat)	
Sport Touring	5 Passenger
Touring Car	7 Passenger
Chandler Limousine	7 Passenger

1927

Serial # 174,001–180,000, Service Series 35—Chandler Big Six

Motor—Complete Chandler built. L-head type. Bore 3½ inches by 5 inch stroke. Cylinders are cast in one block and are honed. Detachable head.

Crankshaft—Drop forging, statically and dynamically balanced. It is carried on four heavy bronze backed bearings. Construction permits full pressure lubrication to all bearings. Front and rear end flywheels are featured.

Crank Case—Aluminum, four point suspension in frame.

Pistons—Special design, of light fluxed gray iron, with extra-large piston pins in bronze bushings.

Lubrication—Full pressure to all main connecting rod and camshaft bearings. All parts float constantly on a film of oil. A handy oil drain at the left of the motor makes it easy to drain the oil from the crankcase.

Oil Filter—To insure clean oil in the motor at all times, an oil filter is used; it eliminates all dirt and foreign particles from the oil, which if left it would act as an abrasive on the bearings; also does away with frequent oil changes.

Carburetor—Schebler, specially designed for quick starting and the Special Chandler rapid vaporizing manifold.

Air Cleaner—An integral part of the carburetor is an air cleaner, which rejects any dirt from entering the motor through the carburetor.

Manifold—Exclusive Chandler design. It perfectly vaporizes present-day low grade fuels and promotes the highest efficiency with motor.

Gasoline System—Vacuum feed from large tank in rear. Constant reading gauge on instrument board.

Ignition—Distributor, high tension coil, and battery. Combination automatic and hand spark control.

Timing—Morse patented silent chain with serrated nut adjustment on outside of crankcase.

Cooling—Centrifugal pump in accessory line. Fan is self oiling. Extra large cellular radiator. Water flows around combustion chambers, cylinder walls and valve seats.

Thermostat—Even temperature throughout the cooling system in all seasons and climates is assured through the use of an automatic thermostat.

Clutch—Dry plate, disc type, needs no lubrication.

Propeller Shaft—Light tubular construction with fabric discs requiring no lubrication.

Rear Axle—Specially designed, horizontally welded heavy pressed steel housing, reinforced with internal steel sleeve. It is a floating type.

Differential—Spiral bevel, nickel steel gears, machined and heat treated. Large Timken bearings on pinion shaft and differential.

Four Wheel Brakes—Mechanically operated, external contracting four wheel brakes, standard on all models.

Front Axle—Drop forged, sturdy I beam section.

Steering Gear—Specially designed, worm and sector type.

Chassis—Strong, substantially constructed with six cross members. Front wheel brakes and controls are mounted on specially designed sturdy supports (not on frame) thus eliminating all unnecessary wear from spring deflection.

Springs—Semi-elliptic type. Front 40¾ inches, rear 59¼ inches. Shackle bolts feature patented anti-rattling devise.

Lubrication—all moving parts of the chassis are lubricated by the One Shot automatic oiling system. One step on a plunger oils the entire car.

Tires—Genuine super size 33 × 6 inches Balloon tires standard equipment.

Body Finish—Beautiful colors with all models.

Upholstery—Blue-gray mohair with Metropolitan Sedan, Metropolitan De Luxe Sedan, Seven-Passenger Sedan De Luxe and Coupe. Broadcloth with the Twentieth Century Sedan. Black leather with the Five and Seven Passenger Tourings. Spanish leather optional with Seven Passenger Touring. Roadster is upholstered in Spanish leather.

Standard Equipment—Newly designed nickeled radiator shell, emblem, one piece ventilating type windshield, speedometer, non-glare reflectors, barrel type head and cowl lamps, motor driven horn, electric light on instrument board, windshield cleaner. Closed cars feature smoking set, Circassian finished instrument board, Circassian finished door panels with special inlay garnish window mouldings and gasoline gauge, rear view mirror and automatic windshield cleaner. Toggle grips with Metropolitan Sedan, Metropolitan Sedan De Luxe, Seven-Passenger Sedan De Luxe and Coupe. Gasoline gauge and thermometer with Metropolitan Sedan, Metropolitan Sedan De Luxe, Coupe, Seven- Passenger Sedan De Luxe and Roadster. Trunk rack and aluminum bars with Metropolitan Sedan, Twentieth Century Sedan, Metropolitan Sedan De Luxe. Arm rests featured with Metropolitan Sedan, Seven-Passenger Sedan De Luxe, Metropolitan Sedan De Luxe and Coupe. Vanity case with Metropolitan Sedan De Luxe and Seven-Passenger Sedan De Luxe. Windshield wings with Roadster and Five-Passenger Touring. Transmission lock with all models.

Special Equipment—Bumpers, bumperetts, combination tail and stop light and shock absorbers can be secured at the combination price of $38.00.

All Prices F.O.B. Factory

Metropolitan Sedan	$1595.00
Metropolitan Sedan De Luxe	$1695.00
20th Century Sedan	$1495.00
7 Pass. Sedan De Luxe	$1895.00
4 Passenger Coupe	$1675.00
5 Passenger Touring	$1545.00
7 Passenger Touring	$1645.00
Comrade Roadster	$1695.00

1927—Model 31

Serial # C 15, 598–C 30,000, Standard Six Series

These specifications are a combination of two issued about one month apart.

Motor—New and specially designed "L" head type designed to Pikes Peak Motor principle. Built complete in Chandler plants. Clean and compact. Detachable cylinder head.

Cylinders—Six cast en bloc integral with the crankcase. Bore 3 inches. Stroke 4¼ inches.

Pistons—Cast iron. Three rings to a piston. One oil wiping ring, two plain.

Connecting Rods—Drop forged steel, I-beam section, light in weight yet sturdy in design. All rods perfectly balanced.

Crankshaft—Drop forging of heavy design; statically and dynamically balanced. Front and rear flywheels minimize vibration.

Camshaft—Drop forging, carbonized and hardened; mounted on three large bearings.

Lubrication—Motor—Full pressure system to all crankshaft, connecting rod and camshaft bearings. Positively driven by gear type oil pump. All motor parts function constantly on a film of lubricant.

Oil Filter—The addition of an oil filter in connection with the oiling system of the motor purifies the lubricant, thus eliminating foreign particles from getting into the oil and acting as an abrasive on various bearing surfaces. Frequent oil changes are unnecessary.

Carburetor—Schebler with special features which promote exceptional mileage and rapid pick-up.

Air Cleaner—To eliminate any possibility of dirt entering the motor through the carburetor an air cleaner is used. This not only increases motor efficiency but naturally adds to the life of the motor.

Ignition—Delco Remy distributor and high tension coil. Combination automatic and hand controlled spark advance.

Manifold—Specially designed to properly preheat various grades of gasoline. Easy starting is promoted.

Cooling System—Water circulated by pump, driven through a flexible disc coupling on the accessory shaft. Valves and plugs are generously water jacketed.

Thermostat—An automatic thermostat is an integral part of the cooling system and keeps the water at the right operating temperature both summer and winter and in all climates.

Clutch—Borg and Beck single plate, heavy duty type.

Lubrication—Chassis—One Shot automatic lubrication system oils chassis parts.

Propeller Shaft—Flexible fabric discs are used. No lubrication is required, yet long service is assured.

Rear Axle—Floating type, housing of pressed steel. Spiral bevel, nickel steel gears. Chrome nickel steel drive shafts. Adjustable Timken roller bearings.

Front Axle—Semi-elliptical type, front and rear; bronze—bushed eyes, rear springs under slung.

Four Wheel Brakes—External contracting 12⅜ inches standard equipment.

Emergency Brake—Located on the rear of transmission.

Tires—30 × 5.00 Balloon standard equipment.

Finish—Lacquer with all models. Duotone colors with various models.

Colors—Standard Sedan—Lotus Blue, upper structure black with black bead and stripe. Optional color—Cleveland Blue with raised bead. Standard De Luxe Sedan—Black upper structure—sage brush green lower with Brewster green between beads. Wheels—Brewster green. Optional color. Beaver brown with black upper structure. Standard Coupe—Upper structure black; body blue and buff. Optional color—Blue devil blue. De Luxe Coupe—Two-tone green with raised bead. Roadster—Beige brown above upper bead and Nevada gray below upper bead. Standard Touring—Two-tone beige brown with raised black bead. Standard Touring De Luxe—Two-tone sage brush green with raised bead. Natural wood wheels.

Upholstery—Blue-gray mohair with De Luxe Sedan. Broadcloth with regular Sedan. De Luxe Coupe is upholstered in mohair. Black leather upholstery with the regular Coupe and Touring. Corduroy is optional with Coupe. Smart Spanish leather is standard with Roadster and Touring De Luxe.

Equipment—Adjustable windshield and cowl ventilator with Touring car. New ventilating type windshield, speedometer, barrel type head lamp, non-glare reflectors, cowl lights, motor driven horn, electric light on instrument board, tools, windshield cleaner, nickel radiator shell, cap and emblem with all models. Dome light, robe rail, foot rest and sun visor with Sedan and De Luxe Sedan. Rear view mirror and automatic windshield cleaner with all closed models. Roadster and Touring De Luxe features wind shield wings. Trunk and trunk rack with De Luxe Touring. Circassian finished instrument board, door panels with special inlay and garnish mouldings with De Luxe Sedan and De Luxe Coupe.

All Prices F.O.B. Factory

Five Passenger Sedan	$995.00
Five Passenger De Luxe Sedan	$1095.00
Coupe	$1035.00
De Luxe Coupe	$1125.00
Touring	$945.00
De Luxe Touring	$1005.00
Roadster	$1135.00

1927—Model 43

Serial # 77,526–90,000, Chandler Special Six

Motor—New and specially designed "L" head type built entirely in Chandler plants. Six cylinder design.

Cylinders—Six cast en bloc separate from the crankcase. Bore 3⅛ inches. Stroke 4¾ inches.

Pistons—Cast iron. 3 piston rings to a piston. One oil wiping ring, two plain.

Connecting Rods—I-beam section, Drop forged steel, light in weight yet substantial at points where greatest stress comes.

Crankshaft—Drop forging; design of generous proportion with front end flywheel and perfectly balanced, eliminates any vibration period. Three substantial bronze backed bearings hold crankshaft in perfect alignment.

Lubrication—Motor—Full pressure to all crankshaft, connecting rod and camshaft bearings. Oil pump is gear type located in the bottom of the oil pan, driven by spiral gears from the camshaft. The pressure oiling system allows working parts of the motor to float constantly on a film of oil.

Oil Filter—An Innovation is the new oil filter which purifies the oiling system through the motor; All foreign particles which might act as an abrasive on the bearing surfaces are eliminated.

Carburetor—Schebler Model S-1

Air Cleaner—Attached to the carburetor is an air cleaner, which eliminates all dirt and foreign particles from entering the motor.

Manifold—To ensure easy starting and the most power from each drop of gasoline, a specially designed external heat applicator is used.

Ignition—Distributor and high tension coil. Combination automatic and hand controlled spark advance is feature.

Starting and Lighting—Two unit system.

Cooling System—Water circulated by pump, driven through a flexible disc coupling on the accessory shaft. The thickness of the radiator core and frontal area insures ideal cooling in all climates.

Thermostat—To keep the cooling system at the most satisfactory temperature in all seasons and climates, an automatic thermostat is used.

Clutch—Borg & Beck 10 inch shifting single plate type; no lubrication necessary. Design of mounting insures perfect alignment.

Lubrication—Chassis—One Shot automatic lubrication system (covered by Bowen Products Corp.) oils every moving chassis part.

Transmission—Unit power plant construction with center control.

Propeller Shaft—Fitted with flexible fabric discs instead of the mechanical type. No lubrication necessary.

Rear Axle—Floating type. Pressed steel housing, spiral bevel, nickel steel gears. Chrome nickel steel drive shafts. Adjustable Timken roller bearings.

Front Axle—Drop forged I-beam. Chrome nickel steel spindles and steering arms. Ball type tie rods provides automatic take-up for wear. Timken roller bearings in wheels. Ball bearings in steering mechanism.

Springs—Semi-elliptical type, front and rear, bronze bushed eyes, rear springs underslung. Leaves are alloy steel.

Four-Wheel Brakes—14 inch external contracting mechanical four wheel brakes.

Emergency Brake—Located on the rear of transmission. Operates on the propeller shaft, and then through the rear axle differential. Equalization in braking effort is assured.

Balloon Tires—31 × 5.25 standard.

Finish—Lacquer with all models.

Colors—Special Sedan—Body in two-tone sage brush green with black bead and special striping. Wheels are light sage brush green. Coupe—Upper structure black, body blue and buff.

Optional color—Blue devil blue. De Luxe Coupe—Two-tone green with raised bead. Sport Touring—Two-tone sage brush green with dark green raised bead. Disc wheels match the body. Touring—Two-tone brown with raised bead in black.

Upholstery—Blue gray mohair with Sedan and De Luxe Coupe. Genuine leather with Touring and Coupe. Corduroy is optional with Coupe. Spanish leather with Sport Touring.

Equipment—Nickeled radiator shell, cap and emblem, adjustable ventilating type windshield, speedometer, barrel type head and cowl lamps, non-glare reflectors, windshield cleaner, motor driven horn, electric light on instrument board, tools and spare rim. Rear view mirror and automatic windshield cleaner with closed cars. Circassian finished instrument board, door panels with special inlay and garnish mouldings with Sedan and De Luxe Coupe. Robe rail, and foot rest with Sedan. Windshield wings, trunk and rack, and disc wheels with Sport Touring.

All Prices F.O.B. Factory

Five Passenger Sedan	$1295.00
Coupe	$1195.00
Touring	$1145.00
Sport Touring	$1295.00
De Luxe Coupe	$1285.00

These prices were taken from Automobile Topics, *August 7, 1926.*

1927—Model 37 Early

Serial # E100,001–E100, 200, Royal Eight (first 200 cars)

Eight Motor—Completely Chandler built. "L" head type, bore, 3³⁄16 × 4¾" stroke. Unusual power, smoothness and flexibility are notable features. Advanced design manifold.

Cylinders—Eight in line, providing clean external appearance and accessibility.

Counterbalanced Crankshaft—Drop forging, with special balance weights at every main bearing throw. Front and rear flywheels are used; vibration is reduced to the vanishing point. Five main bearings, all of substantial size.

Lubrication—Full pressure to crankshaft bearings and valve lifters. Oiling system allows all working parts to float constantly on a film of oil. Level indicator and oil filter located on left side of motor.

Oil Purifier—To make frequent oil changes unnecessary and to keep the oil clean, an oil purifier is used with the oiling system.

Carburetor—Schebler special type; features remarkable economy and idling qualities.

Air Cleaner—To eliminate all foreign particles of dirt and dust from entering the cylinders through the carburetor and thus acting as an abrasive, the air cleaner is used on the carburetor.

Cooling—A special water jacket on left side of motor provides distribution of water for cooling each cylinder equally with the others.

Thermostat—An automatic thermostatic safeguards the cooling system and insures uniform temperature in all seasons.

Transmission—Selective sliding. Main shaft mounted on ball bearings. Easy shifting a notable advantage.

Clutch—Dry plate, disc type, needs no lubrication.

Propeller Shaft—Sturdy tubular construction provided with flexible fabric discs at each end, requiring no lubrication. This construction eliminates any possibility of backlash.

Rear Axle—Specially designed and Chandler built, horizontally-welded, heavy pressed steel housing, reinforced with internal steel sleeve. A heavy malleable casting is riveted over-all to carry brake disc and drive through springs. The axle drive-shaft is accurately centered to drive wheels through hub flange. Floating type.

Chassis—Designed for exceptionally strenuous service. Frame is of heavy gauge steel with five separate, hot-riveted cross-members, a large tubular cross-member, and in addition sturdy motor base supports. Front wheel brakes and controls are mounted on specially designed sturdy I-beam (not on frame), thus eliminating all unnecessary wear from spring deflection.

Steering Gear—Special Chandler design worm-and-sector type. Steering post rigidly anchored. Liberal ratio makes Chandler easy to steer and park.

Springs—Extra long, easy riding, semi-elliptical type front and rear. Bronze bushed eyes. Rear springs underslung.

Rear Axle—Floating, spiral bevel nickel steel gears, roller bearings in differential.

Chassis Lubrication—All moving parts of the chassis are thoroughly lubricated by the One Shot system of chassis lubrication.

Brakes—Four wheel brakes mechanically operated, external contracting type standard with all models.

Tires—Genuine super-size, 33 × 6 balloon tires, 6 ply.

Body Finish—Beautiful colors with all eight models.

Upholstery—Exquisite super-fine silver gray mohair upholstery or De Luxe broadcloth optional with Royal Eight Sedan.

Royal Eight Five Passenger Sedan Equipment—Beautiful nickel plated three bar radiator with emblem, ventilating type, one piece windshield, smoking set, vanity case, one piece Circassian finished window mouldings with door panels in same finish with special inlay, Circassian finished instrument board with instruments grouped in bronze panel, gasoline gauge, thermometer, speedometer, oil indicator, electric clock, indirect lighting with instruments, combination cigar lighter and emergency lamp, rear view mirror, automatic windshield cleaner, toggle grips, arm rests with rear seats, foot dimmer headlight switch, statuary bronze finished hardware, heater, shaded reading lights, silk shades on rear windows, nickel plated head and cowl lamps, non-glare reflectors, tools and spare rim.

Royal Eight Sedan	$2195	Royal Eight Coupe	$2195
Royal Eight Seven-Passenger Sedan	$2295	Royal Eight Roadster	$2195

These prices were taken from Automobile Topics, *January 22, 1927.*

1927—Model 37A

Serial # E100,201–E103,000, Royal Eight

Eight Motor—Chandler built throughout. Incorporates Pikes Peak motor principles. "L" head type, bore, 3¼ × 4¾" stroke. Unusual power, smoothness and flexibility are notable features. Advanced design manifold.

Cylinders—Eight in line, providing clean external appearance and accessibility.

Counterbalanced Crankshaft—Drop forging, with special balance weights at every main bearing throw. In addition, a rotating balancer is used; vibration is reduced to the vanishing point. Five main bearings, all of substantial size.

Lubrication—Full pressure to all crankshaft, connecting rod, camshaft bearings and valve lifters. Oiling system allows all working parts to float constantly on a film of oil.

Oil Purifier—To make frequent oil changes unnecessary and to keep the oil clean, an oil purifier is used with the oiling system.

Carburetor—Schebler special type; features remarkable economy and acceleration qualities.

Air Cleaner—To eliminate all foreign particles of dirt and dust from entering the cylinders through the carburetor and thus acting as an abrasive, the air cleaner is used on the carburetor.

Starting and Lighting—Delco-Remy.

Thermostat—An automatic thermostat safeguards the cooling system and insures uniform temperature in all seasons.

Clutch—Dry plate, disc type, needs no lubrication.

Rear Axle—Specially designed and Chandler built, horizontally-welded, heavy pressed steel housing, reinforced with internal steel sleeve. A heavy malleable casting is riveted over-all to carry brake disc and drive through springs. The axle drive-shaft is accurately entered to drive wheels through hub flange. Floating type.

Chassis—Designed for exceptionally strenuous service. Frame is of heavy gauge steel with four separate, hot-riveted cross-members, two large tubular cross-members, and in addition, sturdy motor base supports. Front wheel brakes and controls are mounted on specially designed sturdy I-beam (not on frame), thus eliminating all unnecessary wear from spring deflection.

Steering Gear—Special Chandler design worm and sector

type. Steering post rigidly anchored. Liberal ratio makes Chandler easy to steer and park.

Chassis Lubrication—All moving parts of the chassis requiring oil are thoroughly lubricated by the One Shot system of chassis lubrication.

Brakes—Four wheel brakes mechanically operated, external contracting type, standard with all models.

Tires—Genuine super-size, 32 × 6.00 balloon tires; 6 ply.

Body Finish—Beautiful duotone colors with all eight models.

Upholstery—Exquisite super-fine silver-gray mohair upholstery with Royal Eight Sedan, Seven Passenger Sedan, Coupe and Country Club Coupe. De Luxe broadcloth optional at $100 additional cost. Spanish leather with Roadster and Touring Car.

Equipment with Closed Car—Beautiful new Chandler nickel plated three bar radiator with new emblem, one piece, ventilating type windshield; smoking set; vanity case; one piece Circassian-finished window mouldings; Circassian-finished door panels; instrument board finished in Circassian, with instruments grouped in bronze panel, electro lock, light control from steering wheel, gasoline gauge, thermostat, speedometer, oil indicator, electric clock, indirect lighting with instruments, combination cigar lighter and emergency lamp, rear view mirror, automatic windshield cleaner, toggle grips, arm rests with rear seats, statuary bronze finished hardware, heater, shaded reading lights, silk shades on rear windows, nickel plated head and cowl lamps, twin beam lights, tools and spare rim.

Equipment with Roadster and Touring Car—Beautiful new Chandler nickel plated radiator with new emblem, one piece windshield, Circassian instrument board with instruments grouped in bronze panel, electro lock, light control from steering wheel, gasoline gauge, thermostat, speedometer, oil indicator, electric clock, indirect lighting with instruments, combination cigar lighter and emergency lamp, rear view mirror, automatic windshield cleaner, statuary bronze finished hardware, nickel head and cowl lamps, twin beam lights, tools and spare rim. Windshield wings are standard with Roadster. Detachable top with Roadster.

Special Equipment—Combination tail and stop light, bumpers, bumperetts, and shock absorbers special equipment with all models, at the combination price.

Five Passenger Sedan	$1995	Seven Passenger Sedan	$2195
Five Passenger De Luxe Sedan	$2195	Seven Passenger Touring	$1995
Four Passenger Cabriolet	$2095	Three Passenger Country Club Coupe	$1995
Four Passenger Coupe	$1995		

1928 (Early) Big Six Series

Serial # 180,001–182,500, Service Series 35 A

Motor—Completely Chandler built. Pike's Peak motor. "L" head type. Bore 3½" × 5" stroke. Cylinders are cast en block and are honed. Detachable head.

Crankshaft—Drop forging, statically and dynamically balanced. It is carried on four heavy bronze backed bearings. Construction permits full pressure lubrication to all bearings. Front and rear end flywheels are featured.

Crank case—Aluminum, four point suspension in frame.

Pistons—Special design, of light fluxed gray iron, with extra large piston pins in bronze bushings.

Lubrication—Full pressure on all main, connecting rod, and camshaft bearings. All parts float constantly on a film of oil. A handy oil drain at the left of motor makes it easy to drain the oil from the crankcase.

Oil Filter—To insure clean oil in the motor at all times, an oil filter is used; it eliminates all dirt and foreign particles from the oil, which if left behind it would act as an abrasive on the bearings—also does away with frequent oil changes.

Carburetor—Schebler, specially designed for quick starting in conjunction with the exclusive Chandler rapid vaporizing manifold.

Air Cleaner—An integral part of the carburetor is an air cleaner, which rejects all dirt from entering the motor through the carburetor.

Starting and Lighting—Delco-Remy.

Manifold—Exclusive Chandler design. It perfectly vaporizes present-day low-grade fuels and promotes the highest efficiency with motor.

Gasoline System—Vacuum feed from large tank in rear. Constant reading gauge on instrument board.

Ignition—Distributor, high tension coil, and battery. Combination automatic and adjustable spark control.

Timing—Morse patented silent chain with serrated nut adjustment on outside of crankcase.

Cooling—Centrifugal pump in accessory line. Fan is self-oiling. Extra large cellular radiator. Water flows around combustion chambers, cylinder walls and valve seats.

Thermostat—Even temperature throughout the cooling system in all seasons and climates is assured through the use of an automatic thermostat.

Clutch—Dry plate, disc type, needs no lubrication.

Propeller Shaft—Large tubular construction with fabric discs requiring no lubrication.

Rear Axle—Specially designed, horizontally welded, heavy pressed steel housing, reinforced with internal steel sleeve. It is a floating type.

Differential—Spiral bevel, nickel-steel gears, accurately machined and heat treated. Large Timken bearings on pinion shaft and differential.

Four-wheel Brakes—Mechanically operated, external contracting four-wheel brakes, standard with all models.

Front Axle—Drop forged, sturdy I-beam section.

Steering Gear—Specially designed, worm and sector type.

Chassis—Strong, substantially constructed with six cross members. Front wheel brakes and controls are mounted on specially designed sturdy supports (not on frame), thus eliminating all unnecessary wear from spring deflection.

Springs—Semi-elliptical type. Front 40¾", rear 59¼". Shackle bolts feature patented anti-rattling device.

Lubrication—All moving parts of the chassis are lubricated by the One Shot automatic oiling system. One push on a plunger oils the entire car.

Tires—Genuine super-size, 33 × 6.00 Balloon tires, standard equipment.

Body Finish—Sparkling two-tone colors with various models. There are also optional body colors.

Upholstery—Blue-gray mohair with Metropolitan Sedan, Metropolitan De Luxe Sedan, Seven Passenger De Luxe Sedan, Coupe and Country Club Coupe. Spanish leather with Seven Passenger Touring and Roadster.

Standard Equipment—Smartly designed nickeled radiator shell with newly designed Chandler insignia, one piece ventilating type windshield, transmission lock, speedometer, non-glare reflectors, barrel type head and cowl lamps, motor driven horn, electric light on instrument board, windshield cleaner. Closed cars feature smoking set, Circassian-finished instrument board, Circassian-finished door panels with special inlay garnish window mouldings, rear view mirror and automatic windshield cleaner. Toggle grips with Metropolitan Sedan, Metropolitan Sedan De Luxe, Seven Passenger Sedan De Luxe, and Coupe. Gasoline gauge and thermometer with all models. Trunk rack and rack, and aluminum bars. Arm rests featured with Metropolitan Sedan, Seven Passenger Sedan De Luxe, Metropolitan Sedan De Luxe, and Coupe. Vanity case with Metropolitan Sedan De Luxe, Seven Passenger Sedan De Luxe. Windshield wings with Roadster and Seven Passenger Touring. Detachable top with Comrade Roadster.

Special Equipment—Bumpers, bumperetts, combination tail and stop light and shock absorbers can be secured at the combination price of $46.00.

Metropolitan Sedan	$1495	Metropolitan Sedan De Luxe	$1595
Seven Passenger Sedan De Luxe	$1795	Four Passenger Coupe	$1675
Three Passenger Country Club Coupe	$1675	Seven Passenger Touring	$1695
Four Passenger Comrade Roadster	$1695		

All prices F.O.B. Factory

1928 Early Model 35 A Royal Six Sedan

Serial # 180,001–182,500 (Royal Six was numbered in the Big Six Series)

Motor—Completely Chandler built. "L" head type. Bore 3½" × 5" stroke. Cylinders are cast en block and are honed. Detachable head.

Crankshaft—Drop forging, statically and dynamically balanced. It is carried on four heavy bronze backed bearings. Construction permits full pressure lubrication to all bearings. Front and rear end flywheels are features.

Crankcase—Aluminum, four point suspension in frame.

Pistons—Special design, of light fluxed gray iron, with extra large piston pins in bronze bushings.

Lubrication—Full pressure to all main, connecting rod and camshaft bearings. All parts float constantly on a film of oil. A handy oil drain at the left of motor makes it easy to drain the oil from the crankcase.

Oil Filter—To insure clean oil in the motor at all times, an oil filter is used, it eliminates all dirt and foreign particles from the oil, which if left in would act as an abrasive on the bearings; also does away with frequent oil changes.

Carburetor—Schebler, specially designed for quick starting in conjunction with the exclusive Chandler rapid vaporizing manifold.

Air Cleaner—An integral part of the carburetor is an air cleaner, which rejects all dirt from entering the motor through the carburetor.

Manifold—Exclusive Chandler design. It perfectly vaporizes present-day low-grade fuels and promotes the highest efficiency with motor.

Gasoline System—Vacuum feed from large tank in rear. Constant reading gauge on instrument board.

Ignition—Distributor, high tension coil, and battery. Combination automatic and hand spark control.

Starting and Lighting—Delco-Remy.

Timing—Morse Patented silent chain with serrated nut adjustment on outside of crankcase.

Cooling—Centrifugal pump in accessory line. Fan is self-oiling. Extra large cellular radiator. Water flows around combustion chambers, cylinder walls and valve seats.

Thermostat—Even temperature throughout the cooling system in all seasons and climates is assured through the use of an automatic thermostat.

Clutch—Dry plate, disc type, needs no lubrication.

Propeller Shaft—Light tubular construction with fabric discs requiring no lubrication.

Rear Axle—Specially desiginternal steel sleeve. It is a floating type.

Differential—Spiral bevel, nickel-steel gears, accurately machined and heat treated. Large Timken bearings on pinion shaft and differential.

Four Wheel Brakes—Mechanically operated, external contracting four-wheel brakes, standard with all models.

Front Axle—Drop-forged, sturdy I-beam section.

Steering Gear—Specially designed, worm and sector type.

Chassis—Strong, substantially constructed with six cross members. Front wheel brakes and controls are mounted on specially designed sturdy supports (not on frame) thus eliminating all unnecessary wear from spring deflection.

Springs—Semi-elliptical type. Front 40¾", rear 59¼". Shackle bolts feature patented anti-rattling device.

Lubrication—All moving parts of the chassis are lubricated by the One Shot automatic system. One push of a plunger oils the entire car.

Tires—Genuine super size, 33 × 6 Balloon tires, standard equipment.

Body Finish—Two optional two-tone body colors with Royal Six Sedan.

Upholstery—Exquisite silver-gray mohair.

Equipment with Royal Six Sedan—Beautiful Chandler nickel plated three-bar radiator with distinctive new insignia, one piece, ventilating type windshield; smoking set; vanity case; one piece Circassian-finished window mouldings; Circassian-finished door panels; Instrument board finished in Circassian, with instruments grouped in bronze panel; gasoline gauge, thermostat, speedometer, oil indicator, electric clock, indirect lighting with instruments, combination cigar lighter and emergency lamp, rear view mirror, automatic windshield cleaner, toggle grips, arm rests with rear seats, foot dimmer headlight switch, statuary bronze finished hardware, shaded reading lights, silk shades on rear windows, nickel plated head and cowl lamps, transmission locks, flat-lite reflectors, tools and spare rim.

Special Equipment—Combination tail and stop light, bumpers, bumperettes, and shock absorbers, special equipment with Royal Six Sedan at the Combination Prices.

Price F.O.B. Factory—Royal Six Sedan $1795

Price taken from *Motor Age*, October 13, 1927

1928 Model 37 A Royal Eight Series

Serial # G 103,001–106,000

Eight Motor—Chandler built throughout. Incorporates Pikes Peak motor principles. "L" head type, bore 3¼" × 4¾" stroke. Unusual power, smoothness and flexibility are notable features. Advanced design manifold.

Cylinders—Eight in line, providing clean external appearance and accessibility.

Counter-Balanced Crankshaft—Drop forging, with special balance weights. In addition, a rotating balancer is used; vibration is reduced to the vanishing point. Five main bearings, all of substantial size.

Lubrication—Full pressure to all crankshaft, connecting rod, camshaft bearings and valve lifters. Oiling system allows all working parts to float constantly on a film of oil.

Oil Purifier—To make frequent oil changes unnecessary and to keep the oil clean, an oil purifier is used with the oiling system.

Carburetor—Schebler special type; features remarkable economy and acceleration qualities.

Starting and Lighting—Delco-Remy.

Thermostat—An automatic thermostat safeguards the cooling system and insures uniform temperature in all seasons.

Clutch—Dry plate, disc type, needs no lubrication.

Rear Axle—Specially designed and Chandler-built, horizontally-welded, heavy pressed steel housing, reinforced with internal steel sleeve. A heavy malleable casting is riveted on each end to carry brake disc and drive through springs. The axle driveshaft is accurately centered to drive wheels through hub flange. Floating type.

Chassis—Designed for exceptionally strenuous service. Frame is of heavy gauge steel with four separate pressed steel cross-members, two large tubular cross-members, and in addition, sturdy motor base supports. Front wheel brakes and controls are mounted on specially designed I-beam (not on frame) thus eliminating all unnecessary wear from spring deflection.

Steering Gear—Special Chandler design worm and sector type. Steering post rigidly anchored. Liberal ratio makes Chandler easy to steer and park.

Chassis Lubrication—All moving parts of the chassis requiring oil are thoroughly lubricated by the One Shot system of chassis lubrication.

Brakes—Westinghouse Four Wheel vacuum brakes, invented and developed by the Westinghouse Air Brake Company standard equipment on all models.

Tires—Genuine super-size, 32 × 6.00 balloon tires; 6-ply.

Body Finish—Beautiful duotone colors with all eight models.

Upholstery—Exquisite super-fine silver-gray mohair upholstery with Royal Eight Sedan, Seven Passenger Sedan, Coupe and Country Club Coupe. De Luxe broadcloth is optional at additional cost. Spanish leather with Cabriolet and Touring car.

Equipment with Closed Cars—Beautiful new Chandler nickel-plated three-bar radiator; one-piece, ventilating type windshield; smoking set; vanity case; one-piece Circassian walnut finish window mouldings; Circassian walnut finish door panels; with special Decalcomania design; instrument board finished in two-tone Circassian walnut, with instruments grouped in bronze panel; electro lock, light control from steering wheel; foot dimmer headlight switch; gasoline gauge; thermometer, speedometer; oil indicator, electric clock; indirect lighting with instruments; combination cigar lighter and emergency lamp; rear view mirror; automatic windshield cleaner; toggle grips; arm rests with rear seats; statuary bronze finished hardware; heater; shaded reading lights; silk shades on rear windows; nickel-plated bullet type head and cowl lamps; twin beam lights; tools and spare rim. Rumble seat with Cabriolet.

Equipment with Touring Car—Beautiful new Chandler nickel-plated radiator; one-piece windshield; Circassian instrument board with instruments grouped in bronze panel; electro lock; light control from steering wheel; foot dimmer headlight switch; gasoline gauge; thermometer; speedometer; oil indicator; electric clock, indirect lighting with instruments, combination cigar lighter and emergency lamp; rear view mirror, automatic windshield cleaner; nickel-plated finished hardware; nickel-plated bullet type head and cowl lamps; twin beam light; tools and spare rims.

Special Equipment—Combination tail and stop light; bumpers, bumperettes; and shock absorbers, special equipment with all models; at an extra cost of $56.00. Six wire wheels, two mounted on sides, with trunk rack and trunk included as special equipment at extra cost with any Royal Eight model.

All Prices F.O.B. Factory

Five-Passenger Sedan	$1995	Seven-Passenger Sedan	$2195
Five-passenger De Luxe Sedan	$2195	Seven-Passenger Touring	$1995
Four-Passenger Cabriolet	$2095	Four-Passenger Coupe	$1995
Three-Passenger Country Club Coupe	$1995		

1928 Late

Model 137 Royal 8, Serial # E 106,001–108,000
Model 135 Big Six, Serial # 182,501–188,000
Model 131 Invincible Six, Serial # 40,001–45,000

Motors—Completely Chandler built. Royal Eight motor bore 3⅜" × 4¾" stroke. Big Six motor bore 3¾ × 5 stroke. Special Six Invincible motor bore 3⅛" × 4¾" stroke. All motors incorporate the notable Pikes Peak high compression power principle.

Lubrication—Full pressure to all crankshaft, connecting rod, and camshaft bearings. Oiling system allows all working parts to float constantly on a film of oil.

Starting and Lighting—Delco-Remy

Thermostat—An automatic thermostat safeguards the cooling system and insures uniform temperature in all seasons or climates.

Chassis Lubrication—All moving parts of the chassis requiring oil are thoroughly lubricated by the One Shot system of chassis lubrication.

Brakes—Four-wheel Westinghouse Vacuum Brakes standard equipment with all models.

Tires—Genuine super-size 32 × 6.00. 6 ply balloon with Royal Eight and Big Six models. 30 × 5.00 balloon with all Special Six models.

Body Colors—Beautiful duotones colors with all Royal Eight, Big Six and Special Six models.

Upholstery—Mohair with all Royal Eight and Big Six Sedans and Coupes and Special Invincible De Luxe Sedan, with exception of Special Invincible and regular Special Sedan, which are upholstered in rich figured wool plush. Royal Eight and Big Six Cabriolets are upholstered in genuine champagne leather. Special Cabriolet, Special Sportster, Royal Eight Touring and Big Touring are all upholstered in hand buffed Spanish leather. Special Invincible Touring, regular Special Touring and Special Coupes are upholstered in hand buffed leather.

Equipment with Royal Eight Closed Cars: Beautiful new Chandler nickel-plated three bar radiator; one piece, ventilating type windshield; smoking set; vanity case; one-piece Circassian walnut finished window mouldings; Circassian walnut finished door panels; with special Decalcomania design; instrument board finished in two-tone Circassian walnut, with instruments grouped in bronze panel; electro lock; light control from steering wheel; foot dimmer headlight switch; gasoline gauge; thermometer, speedometer; oil indicator; electric clock, indirect lighting with instruments; combination cigar lighter and emergency lamp; rear view mirror; automatic windshield cleaner; toggle grips; arm rests with rear seats, statuary bronze finished hardware; heater, shaded reading lights; silk shades on rear, and quarter windows; nickel-plated bullet type head and cowl lamps; twin beam lights; tools and spare rim. Rumble seat with Cabriolet.

Equipment with Royal Eight and Touring Car: Beautiful new Chandler nickel-plated three bar radiator; one piece windshield; Circassian instrument board with instruments grouped in bronze panel; electro lock; light control from steering wheel; foot dimmer headlight switch; gasoline gauge; thermometer, speedometer; oil indicator; electric clock, indirect lighting with instruments; combination cigar lighter and emergency lamp; rear view mirror; automatic windshield cleaner; nickel-plated finished hardware; nickel-plated bullet type head and cowl lamps; twin beam lights; tools and spare rim.

Big Six Standard Equipment: Beautiful new Chandler nickel-plated radiator shell; one-piece ventilating type windshield; electro lock; speedometer; bullet type head and cowl lamps, instrument board indirectly lighted, windshield cleaner. Closed cars feature Circassian finished instrument board; Circassian finished door panels. Toggle grips with Royal Six Sedan, Seven Passenger Sedan, Coupes and Country Club Coupe. Circassian finished instrument board with Touring Car. Gasoline gauge and thermometer with all models. Smoking set and vanity case with Royal Six Sedan and Seven Passenger Sedan and Metropolitan Sedan. Windshield wings and side tire carriers with Seven Passenger Touring. Foot dimmer switch with Royal Six Sedan. Heater with Royal Six and Big Six Seven Sedans.

Special Equipment: can be secured at an extra cost. Six wire wheels, two wheels mounted on side, trunk rack and trunk with any Royal Eight or Big Six model, at extra cost.

Special Six Equipment: Beautiful new Chandler nickel-plated radiator shell, adjustable ventilating type windshield, speedometer, windshield cleaner, bullet type head and cowl lamps, twin beam head lights, gasoline gauge on dash, Circassian finished instrument board with instruments grouped under glass and indirectly lighted, electro ignition lock, light control from steering wheel, dome light, robe rail and foot rest with sedan. Cadet visor with Special Invincible Sedan and Special Invincible De Luxe Sedan and Cabriolet. Sun visor integral with roof on all other closed models. Rear view mirror on all models. Landaulet arms with rumble seat Coupe and Cabriolet. Arm rests with rear seat of Invincible De Luxe Sedan. Circassian-finished door panels with Cabriolet, Coupe, Sedan and Rumble Seat Coupe, Invincible Sedan and Invincible De Luxe Sedan. Sportster has windshield wings, tonneau cowl and windshield.

Special Equipment: Bumper, bumperettes, combination tail and stop light and shock absorbers can be secured at an extra cost. Six wire wheels, two wheels mounted on side, trunk rack and trunk can be secured with any Special Six Model at extra cost.

All Prices F.O.B. Factory

Royal Eight Series		***Big Six Series***	
Five Passenger Sedan	$1995	Metropolitan Sedan	$1525
Five Passenger De Luxe Sedan	$2195	Royal Six Sedan	$1725
Seven Passenger Sedan	$2195	Seven Passenger Sedan	$1925
Four Passenger Cabriolet	$2095	Coupe	$1725
Four Passenger Coupe	$1995	Country Club Coupe	$1725
Three Passenger Country Club Coupe	$1995	Cabriolet	$1825
Seven Passenger Touring	$1995	Seven Passenger Touring	$1725

Special Six Series

Five Passenger Special Sedan	$995
Five Passenger Special Touring	$995
Five Passenger Special Invincible Sedan	$1085
Five Passenger Special Invincible De Luxe Sedan	$1155
Four Passenger Special Cabriolet (Rumble Seat)	$1215
Four Passenger Special Roadster (Rumble Seat)	$1155
Three Passenger Special Coupe	$1055
Four Passenger Special Rumble Seat Coupe	$1155
Five Passenger Special Invincible Touring	$1085
Five Passenger Special Sportster	$1165

Note: Whether carrying the title of Invincible or not, all Special Six models except the Five Passenger Special Sedan and Five Passenger Special Touring probably had the larger engine. This is consistent with all trade publications of the day.

1928 Model 31 A Special Six Series
Serial # C 30,000–C 40,000

Motor—Especially designed "L" head type designed to Pikes Peak motor principle, built complete in Chandler plants. Clean and compact. Detachable cylinder head.

Cylinder—Six cast en bloc integral with the crankcase. Bore 3", stroke 4¼".

Pistons—Cast iron. Three rings to a piston. One oil wiping ring, two plain.

Connecting Rods—Drop-forged steel, I-beam section, light in weight yet sturdy in design. All rods perfectly balanced.

Crankshaft—Drop forging of heavy design—statically and dynamically balanced. Front and rear flywheels minimize vibration.

Camshaft—Drop forging, carbonized and hardened; mounted on three large bearings.

Lubrication—Motor—Full pressure system to all crankshaft, connecting rod and camshaft bearings. Positively driven by gear type oil pump. All motor parts function constantly on a film of lubricant.

Oil Filter—The addition of an oil filter in connection with the oiling system of the motor purifies the lubricant, thus eliminating foreign particles from getting into the oil and acting as an abrasive on various bearing surfaces. Frequent oil changes are unnecessary.

Carburetor—Schebler, with special features which promote exceptional mileage and rapid pick-up.

Air Cleaner—To eliminate any possibility of dirt entering the motor through the carburetor an air cleaner is used. This not only increases motor efficiency but naturally adds to the life of the motor.

Ignition—Delco-Remy distributor and high tension coil. Combination automatic and hand controlled spark advance.

Manifold—Specially designed to properly pre-heat various grades of gasoline. Easy starting is promoted.

Cooling System—Water circulated by pump, driven through a flexible disc coupling on the accessory shaft. Valves and plugs are generously water-jacketed.

Thermostat—An automatic thermostat is an integral part of the cooling system and keeps the water at the right operating temperature both summer and winter and in all climates.

Clutch—Borg and Beck single plate, heavy duty type.

Lubrication—Chassis—One Shot automatic system oils various chassis parts.

Propeller Shaft—Flexible fabric discs are used. No lubrication is required, yet long service is assured.

Rear Axle—Floating type, housing of pressed steel. Spiral bevel, nickel steel gears. Chrome nickel steel drive shafts. Adjustable Timken roller bearings.

Springs—Semi-elliptical type, front and rear; bronze-bushed eyes; rear springs underslung with special self-adjusting shackles.

Four-Wheel Brakes—External contracting 12⅜ standard equipment.

Emergency Brake—Located on rear of transmission.

Tires—30 × 5.00 Balloon standard equipment.

Finish—Duotone colors with various models.

Upholstery—Blue-gray mohair with special De Luxe Sedan and De Luxe Coupe and De Luxe (Rumble Seat) Coupe. Rich figured wool plush with Special Sedan. Black leather with Touring and Coupe. Smart Spanish leather with Roadster, Sportster, Touring De Luxe and Coupe (Rumble Seat).

Equipment—Beautiful new radiator with new design cap and insignia, adjustable ventilating type windshield, speedometer, windshield cleaner, barrel type head and cowl lamps, twin beam lights. Circassian-finished instrument board with instruments grouped under glass, motor driven horn, electro lock ignition, light control from steering wheel. Electric light on instrument board and tools, with all models. Dome light, robe rail and foot rest with sedans. Sun visor integral with roof, rear view mirror and automatic windshield cleaner with all closed models. Landaulet arms with Rumble Seat Coupe. Button seats and arm rests on both sides of rear seat of De Luxe Sedan. Circassian-finished door panels with special inlay with De Luxe Sedan and De Luxe Coupes. Roadster, Touring De Luxe and Sportster, have windshield wings, rear view mirror and automatic wind shield cleaner. All De Luxe models feature nickeled head and cowl lamps. Sportster has tonneau cowl and windshield.

Special Equipment—Bumpers, bumperetts, combination tail and stop light and shock absorbers can be secured at the combination price of $44.00.

All Prices F.O.B.

Five Passenger De Luxe Sedan	$1135	Four Passenger De Luxe Coupe (Rumble Seat)	$1235
Five Passenger Sedan	$995	Three Passenger De Luxe Coupe	$1125
Four Passenger Coupe (Rumble Seat)	$1135	Five Passenger Touring	$945
Three Passenger Coupe	$1035	Five Passenger De Luxe Touring	$1005
Four Passenger Roadster (Rumble Seat)	$1135	Five Passenger Sportster	$1145

1929 Royal 85

Serial # E 108,001–E 110,000

1929 Model 135 Big Six

Serial # 188,001–199,000

Motors—Completely Chandler built. Royal "85" power plant. Bore 3 ⅜, stroke 4¾; cylinders eight in line. Big Six motor bore 3¾ × 5" stroke. All motors incorporate the notable Pikes Peak high compression power principle.

Connecting Rods—Drop forged steel, I-beam section, light in weight yet sturdy in design. All rods perfectly balanced.

Crankshaft—Drop forging of heavy design; statically and dynamically balanced.

Camshaft—Drop forging, carburized and hardened.

Manifold—New and specially designed to properly pre-heat various grades of gasoline, which insures easy starting.

Thermostat—An automatic thermostat safeguards the cooling system and insures uniform temperatures in all occasions.

Clutch—Dry plate, disc type, needs no lubrication.

Lubrication—Motor—Full pressure to all crankshaft, connecting rod and camshaft bearings. Positively driven by gear type oil pump. All motor parts function constantly on a film of oil.

One Shot System—All moving parts of the chassis requiring oil are thoroughly lubricated by the One Shot system of chassis lubrication.

Rear Axle—Specially designed, horizontally welded, heavy pressed steel housing, reinforced with internal steel sleeve. Floating type.

Steering Gear—Specially designed Ross steering gear. Steering post rigidly anchored. Liberal ratio makes Chandler easy to steer and park.

Brakes—Four wheel Westinghouse Vacuum Brakes, invented and developed by the Westinghouse Air Brake Company.

Springs—Semi-elliptical type, front and rear; rear springs underslung with special self-adjusting shackles.

Chromium Finish—All external parts that ordinarily require nickeling are chromium plated, which insures more beautiful finish and will not tarnish or discolor.

Tires—Genuine super-size, 32 × 6.00 balloon tires.

Body Colors—Striking duotone colors with all models.

Upholstery—Mohair with all Royal Eight and Big Six Sedans and Coupes. Broadcloth optional with the De Luxe Sedan without extra cost. Royal "85" and Big Six Cabriolets are upholstered in genuine champagne leather. Royal "85" Touring and Big Six Touring are upholstered in hand buffed Spanish leather.

Equipment with Royal "85" Closed Cars—Beautiful new Chandler chromium plated three bar radiator with new emblem; one-piece, ventilating type windshield; smoking set; vanity case; one-piece Circassian walnut finished window mouldings, Circassian walnut finished door panels; with special Decalcomania design; Instrument board finished in two-tone Circassian walnut, with instruments grouped in two-tone Butler panel; electro lock, light control from steering wheel; dimmer headlight switch, gasoline gauge; thermometer, speedometer; oil indicator; indirect lighting with instruments; combination cigar lighter and emergency lamp; rear view mirror; automatic windshield cleaner; toggle grips; arm rests with rear seats; two-tone Butler finished hardware; heater; shaded reading lights; silk shades on rear, and quarter windows; chromium plated bullet type twin beam head lamps; bullet type chromium plated cowl lamps; tools and spare rim. Rumble seat with Cabriolet. Equipment on Royal "85" Touring is the same with exception of heater, smoking set and vanity case.

Big Six Equipment—Beautiful new Chandler chromium plated three bar radiator with new emblem; one piece ventilating type windshield; electro lock, speedometer, bullet type head and cowl lamps, instrument board indirectly lighted, windshield cleaner. Closed cars feature Circassian finished instrument board; Circassian finished door panels. Toggle grips with sedan models and Four Passenger Coupe; Circassian finished instrument board with Touring car. Gasoline gauge and thermometer with all models. Smoking set and vanity case with Metropolitan, Seven Passenger Sedan and Four Passenger Coupe; heater with Seven Passenger Sedan.

Special Equipment—Bumper, bumperettes, combination tail and stop light and shock absorbers can be secured at an extra cost of $56.00. Six wire wheels, two mounted on sides, with trunk rack and trunk included also as special equipment, with any model at an extra cost.

Important—The Chandler-Cleveland Motors Corporation, believing that the policy of making changes in models and list prices only at annual periods is not conducive to progress and to prompt adjustments in changing conditions, hereby reserves the right to make changes in the design, equipment and construction of its various models, and to add new models, and to change its list prices, without notice at any time.

All Prices F.O.B. Factory

Royal "85" Series

Royal "85" Sedan	$1795
Royal "85" De Luxe Sedan	$1995
Royal "85" Cabriolet (Rumble Seat)	$2095
Royal "85" Seven Passenger Sedan	$2195
Royal "85" Berline	$2295
Royal "85"Seven Passenger Touring	$1995
Royal "85" Four Passenger Coupe	$1925
Royal "85" Three Passenger Country Club Coupe	$1925

Big Six Series

Metropolitan Sedan	$1525
Seven Passenger Sedan	$1925
Berline	$2025
Coupe	$1725
Country Club Coupe	$1725
Cabriolet (Rumble Seat)	$1825
Seven Passenger Touring	$1725

1929 Series 65 (Model 132)

Serial # C 45,001–C 55,000

Motor—Chandler built throughout. Incorporated Pikes Peak motor principle. Bore 3⅛". Stroke 4¼".

Connecting Rods—Drop-forged steel, I-beam section, light in weight, yet sturdy in design. All rods properly balanced.

Crankshaft—Drop forging of heavy design; statically and dynamically balanced.

Camshaft—Drop forging, carbonized and hardened; mounted on large bearings.

Lubrication—Motor—Full pressure system to all crankshaft, connecting rod and camshaft bearings. Positive driven gear type oil pump. All moving parts function constantly on a film of oil.

Manifold—Specially designed to properly pre-heat various grades of gasoline, which insures easy starting.

Thermostat—An automatic thermostat safeguards the cooling system and insures uniform temperature in all seasons.

Clutch—Single plate, heavy duty type.

Lubrication—Chassis—Alemite Zerk.

Rear Axle—Floating type, housing of pressed steel. Spiral bevel nickel steel gears. Adjustable Timken roller bearings.

Brakes—Four–wheel mechanical, external contracting.

Tires—29 × 5.00 balloon.

Springs—Semi-elliptical type, front and rear; rear springs underslung with special self-adjusting shackles.

Chromium Finish—All metal parts that ordinarily require nickeling are chromium plated, which insures more beautiful finish and will not tarnish or discolor.

Body Colors—Striking duotone colors with all models.

Upholstery—Rich figured plush with regular sedan. Mohair with De Luxe Sedan and Coupe. Spanish leather with Cabriolet, Sportster and Touring car.

Equipment—Newly designed Chandler three-bar radiator with attractive, newly created Chandler emblem; one piece ventilating type windshield, rear view mirror, speedometer, windshield cleaner, bullet twin beam head lights, bullet cowl lamps, gasoline gauge on dash, attractive two-tone gray finished instrument board with instruments grouped under glass (Circassian finished instrument board with De Luxe Sedan, and Coupe). Electro ignition lock, light control from steering wheel, Dome light, robe rail and built-in foot rest with all Sedan models. Landaulet arms with Rumble Seat Coupe and Cabriolet. Arm rests with De Luxe Sedan. Circassian window mouldings and door panels with De Luxe Sedan. Sportster has windshield wings, tonneau cowl and rear windshield.

Special Equipment—Combination tail and stop light, bumpers, bumperettes and Lovejoy shock absorbers special equipment at an extra cost of $50.00. Westinghouse Vacuum Brakes—Those desiring Westinghouse brake equipment on a "65" model can secure it at an extra cost of $75.00.

One Shot Lubrication—This automatic system of lubrication is optional with any "65" model at an extra cost of $60.00.

All Prices F.O.B. Factory

"65" Series

Five Passenger Sedan	$895.00
Five Passenger De Luxe Sedan	$995.00
Three Passenger Coupe	$875.00
Four Passenger Rumble Seat Coupe	$955.00
Three Passenger Cabriolet	$1075.00
Five Passenger Touring Car	$895.00
Five Passenger Sportster	$995.00

1929 Royal "75" Eight Series

Serial # 1,001–10,000

Eight Motor—Designed and built complete by Chandler. Embodies individual Pikes Peak power principles. "L" head type with a bore of 3" × 4½" stroke.

Cylinders—Eight in line, providing clean external appearance and accessibility.

Crankshaft—One of sturdiest shafts ever put into an eight cylinder motor; statically and dynamically balanced.

Manifold—Character of design is such as to provide proper pre-heating of various grades of gasoline. Starting is also greatly facilitated in cold weather.

Thermostat—An automatic thermostat safeguards the cooling system and insures uniform temperatures in all seasons.

Clutch—Smooth acting, single plate, heavy duty type.

Lubrication—Motor—High pressure to all crankshaft, connecting rod and camshaft bearings. Positively driven by gear type oil pump. The different motor parts function constantly on a film of oil.

One Shot Oiling System—No need for an oil can or grease gun. All moving parts of the chassis requiring lubrication are thoroughly oiled by this system, by just pressing a plunger.

Rear Axle—Floating type. Spiral bevel nickel steel gears. Chrome-nickel steel drive shafts. Adjustable Timken roller bearings.

Brakes—Four wheel Westinghouse Vacuum Brakes, invented and developed by the Westinghouse Air Brake Company.

Springs—Semi-elliptical type, front and rear; rear springs underslung with special self-adjusting shackles.

Chromium Finish—All external metal parts that ordinarily require nickeling are chromium plated, which insures more beautiful finish and will not tarnish or discolor.

Body Colors—Attractive duotone colors with all models.

Upholstery—Distinctive blue-gray mohair with Sedan, Brougham and Coupe. Broadcloth or mohair optional with De Luxe Sedan. Smart leather is optional at extra cost with Coupe.

Equipment with Closed Car—Beautiful new Chandler Chromium plated three-bar radiator with new style emblem; one piece ventilating type windshield; smoking set and vanity case with Sedan and De Luxe Sedan; Circassian finished door panels and instrument board; instruments grouped in glass panel indirectly lighted; tow-tone Butler hardware; electro lock; light control from steering wheel; gasoline gauge; thermometer, speedometer; oil indicator; rear view mirror; Automatic windshield cleaner with all models; foot rest with Sedan and De Luxe Sedan. Special Equipment—Combination tail and stop light; bumpers; bumperettes and Lovejoy shock absorbers, special equipment with all models at an additional cost. Six wire wheel, two mounted on sides, with trunk rack and trunk included, also special equipment with any model, at an extra cost.

Important—The Chandler-Cleveland Motors Corporation, believing that the policy of making changes in models and in list price only at annual periods is not conducive to progress or to prompt adjustments to changing conditions, hereby reserves the right to make changes in the design, equipment and construction of its various models, and to add new models, and to change its list prices, without notice at any time.

Royal "75" Brougham	$1295
Royal "75" De Luxe Sedan	$1495
Royal "75" Sedan	$1395
Royal "75" Coupe	$1295
Royal "75" Rumble Seat Coupe	$1295

Chandler Identification Charts

To determine the year and model of a particular Chandler, see the following charts which contain all models and serial numbers.

"'UNIVERSAL PARTS LIST'"

As nearly as possible this book covers all important parts of each model we have produced.

For the convenience of our distributors and dealers we have endeavored to arrange these parts in groupings according to their uses and at the same time have endeavored to show the various parts which are common to all models.

You will note the quantities used have been grouped in six columns, as follows: Model 14, 15, 15-B, 16, 17 and N. S.

Model 14 comprises those cars numbered between 1 and 550.

Model 15 those cars numbered from 551 to 2500.

Model 15-B those cars numbered from 2501 to 3999.

Model 16 those cars numbered from 4000 to 14999.

Model 17 those cars numbered between 15000 and 35000.

N. S., which means New Series, refers to those cars following Model. 17--those cars numbered between 35000 and to the end of the present series.

While the part numbers listed under those various headings may be used as a general thing, particularly for stock orders, it is important wherever parts are ordered for use in any particular car, that the serial number of that car be mentioned, since in some cases various parts overlapped and were used in two series of cars.

Reference to the notes throughout the book will enable you to determine which parts are the ones affected and the various cars on which certain parts were used.

We believe the arrangement of this book in loose-leaf form will prove of great assistance, since additional sheets whenever necessary may be made up and forwarded for insertion as often as practical.

New sheets showing corrections or changes will be forwarded at intervals for installation in the book in place of the original sheet.

New sheets as they are received should be inserted promptly in their proper places.

Chandler identification chart #1.

***Opposite:* Chandler and Cleveland identification chart #2.**

HOW TO IDENTIFY YOUR CHANDLER OR CLEVELAND CAR

CHANDLER BIG SIX MODELS

4,000- 15,000	3⅜x5	1916	16
15,001- 35,000	3⅜x5	1917	17 (Series 25)
35,001- 65,000	3½x5	1918	18 (Series 25)
65,001- 82,000	3½x5	1919	Series 27
82,001-106,000	3½x5	1920	Series 27
106,001-115,000	3½x5	1921	Series 27
115,001-126,000	3½x5	1922	Series 29
126,001-140,000	3½x5	1923	32
140,001-147,000	3½x5	1924	32A
147,001-159,624	3½x5	1925	33, 33A
159,625-174,000	3½x5	1926	35
174,001-180,000	3½x5	1927	35
180,001-182,500	3½x5	1928	35A
182,501-188,000	3¾x5	1928	135
188,001-199,000	3¾x5	1929	135

On Chandler Big Six models, the serial number of all cars from 4,000 to 72,000 is stamped on a brass plate attached to the right motor arm. The serial number of cars manufactured after No. 72,000, is stamped on the right side of the frame just back of the front fender iron (opposite the rear of the front wheel, 28 inches from the front of the frame). The motor number of cars with serial numbers 72,001 to 126,001, is stamped on the right front motor leg. The motor number of cars with serial numbers after 126,000, is stamped on the left front motor leg.

CHANDLER ROYAL 8 MODELS

E100,001-E103,000	3¼x4¾	1927	37
E103,001-E106,000	3¼x4¾	1928	37A
E106,001-E108,000	3⅜x4¾	1928	137
E108,001-E110,000	3⅜x4¾	1929	85

On Chandler Royal 8 models, the car serial number will be found on a plate attached to the dash or else is stamped on the outside right front frame channel under the fender. The motor number is stamped on a plate attached to the dash or on the top of the water pump.

Car Serial Numbers	Bore and Stroke	Year	Model

CLEVELAND MODEL 43

60,000-70,299	3⅛x4¾	1925	43 Cleveland
70,300-77,525	3⅛x4¾	1926	43 Cleveland

On Cleveland Model 43, the car serial number and the motor number are the same. This number is stamped on a plate attached to the dash or to the right front frame member.

CHANDLER MODEL 43

77,526-90,000	3⅛x4¾	1927	43 Special Six

On Chandler Model 43, the car serial number and the motor number are the same. This number is stamped on a plate attached to the dash or to the right front frame member.

CLEVELAND MODEL 31

C2,001- C3,900	2⅞x4¼	1925	31 Cleveland
C3,901-C15,597	2⅞x4¼	1926	31 Cleveland

On Cleveland Model 31, the car serial number is stamped on the outside of the right front frame channel under the fender, and on a plate attached to the dash. The motor number is on the left side of the crankcase next to the front motor support plate, or on the left side of the timing chain case.

CHANDLER MODELS 31, 31A, 131 AND 132

C15,598-C30,000	3 x4¼	1927	31 Standard Six
C30,001-C40,000	3 x4¼	1928	31A Special Six
C40,001-C45,000	3⅛x4¼	1928	131 Invincible Six
C45,001-C55,000	3⅛x4¼	1929	132 Sixty-five

On Chandler Models 31, 31A, 131 and 132, the car serial number is stamped on the outside of the right front frame channel under the fender, and on a plate attached to the dash. The motor number is on the left side of the crankcase next to the front motor support plate, or on the left side of the timing chain case.

CHANDLER ROYAL 75 (SMALL 8)

1,001-10,000	3 x4¼	1929	Royal 75

On Chandler Royal 75 (Small 8), the car serial number is on a plate attached to the dash, or is on the outside of the right front frame channel under the fender. The motor number is on top of the water pump housing flange.

53

CHANDLER SERVICE DATA

*IDENTIFICATION CHART

Series		Year	Serial No.	Motor No.	†Features
25	Classified as one.	1917	15001 to 35000	12001 to 32000	"The Marvelous Motor"
25		1918	35001 to 65000	32001 to 62000	
27	Classified as one	1919	★ 65001 to 82200	62001 to 79200	"Improved Body"
27		1920	★ 82001 to 106200	79201 to 96000	
27		1921	106201 to 115000	96001 to 105000	
29		1922	115001 to 126000	105001 to 116000	"Hotchkiss Drive"
32		1923	126001 to 140000	116001 to 130000	"Pikes Peak Motor"
32A		1924	140001 to 147000	130001 to 137000	"Traffic Transmission"
33		1925	147001 to 148000	137001 to 138000	"Four Wheel Brakes"
33A		1925	148001 to 159624	138001 to 149000	"Push Type Clutch"
35		1926	159625 to	149001 to	"One Shot" System

*This "Key Chart" will be found a most valuable reference, however the information contained herein is merely approximate and should be used solely for classifying Chandler cars or parts thereof. Do not use for any other purpose nor specify "yearly models" as Chandler does not build them

†In the order introduced.

LOCATION OF NUMBERS

THE SERIAL NUMBER may be found on right side of frame channel opposite rear of front wheel. Numbers previous to 72000 were stamped on right front motor leg.

THE MOTOR NUMBER may be found on left front motor leg.

THE BODY NUMBER may be found on open bodies under the front seat on right side. Enclosed body numbers and job numbers may be found on right front door sill. Always specify complete numbers.

NOTE—When reference is made to "right" or "left," it is understood to mean from a seated position in the car.

★ **NOTE---There is a 200 car discrepancy in the 1919-1920 Serial Numbers for Service Series 27.**

Chandler identification chart #3.

COMPONENT PARTS OF ASSEMBLIES NOT SERVICED BY CHANDLER
(Subject to Exceptions for Export & Shortage Orders)

DESCRIPTION	MANUFACTURER	ADDRESS
Vacuum Tank	Stewart-Warner Products Corp	Chicago, Ill.
Carbureter	Wheeler-Schebler Carb.Co	Indianapolis, Ind.
Air Cleaner	A. C. Spark Plug Co	Flint, Mich.
Oil Filter	A. C. Spark Plug Co	Flint, Mich.
Battery	Prest-O-Lite Co	Indianapolis,Ind.
Distributor	Delco-Remy Corporation	Anderson, Ind.
Generator	Delco-Remy Corporation	Anderson, Ind.
Starter	Delco-Remy Corporation	Anderson, Ind.
Coil	Delco-Remy Corporation	Anderson, Ind.
Horn	Sparks-Withington Co	Jackson, Mich.
Electrolock	Mitchel Specialties Co	Philadelphia, Pa.
Emergency Lamp & Lighter	Cuno Manufacturing Corp	Meriden, Conn.
Gages	National Gage & Equipment Co	LaCrosse, Wis.
Speedometer	A. C. Spark Plug Company	Flint, Mich.
Radiator Core	Harrison Radiator Corp	Lockport, N. Y.
Timing Chain	Morse Chain Company	Ithaca, N. Y.
Thermostat	Bishop Babcock Company	Cleveland, Ohio.
Wood Wheels	Motor Wheel Corporation	Lansing, Mich.
Wire Wheels	Kelsey-Hayes Corporation	Detroit, Mich.
Windshield Cleaner	(Trico Manufacturing Company	Buffalo, N. Y.
	(Folberth Manufacturing Co	Cleveland, Ohio.
Vanity & Cigarette Cases	Grand Rapids Metal Craft Co	Grand Rapids,Mich.
Trunk (Steel)	Dustproof Metal Trunk Co	Detroit, Mich.
Trunk (Composite)	C. A. Taylor Trunk Works	Chicago, Ill.
Vacuum Brake	Westinghouse Air Brake Co	Wilmerding, Pa.
Windshield Wings	Standard Mirror Company	Buffalo, N. Y.
Disc Wheels	Budd Wheel Corporation	Detroit, Mich.
Lamp Bulbs	Miscellaneous	(Addresses on Request)
Glass	Miscellaneous	(Addresses on Request)
Spark Plugs	A. C. Spafk Plug Company	Flint, Mich.
Tires	(Goodrich & Goodyear	Akron, Ohio.
	(Kelly Springfield Tire Co	Cleveland, Ohio.
Motometers	Boyce Motometer Corporation	Long Island City,L.I.
Snubbers	Gabriel Snubber Mfg. Company	Cleveland, Ohio.
Shock Absorbers	Delco-Remy Corporation	Anderson, Ind.

CAR DESIGNATION

YEAR	MODEL	SERIAL		DATE	NO.
1925	Cleveland - Standard Six	C-2001	C-3900	Feb.'25	31
1926	Cleveland - Standard Six	C-3901	C-15597	Apr.'25	31
1927	Chandler - Standard Six	C-15598	C-23500	July'26	31
1927	Chandler - Standard Six	C-23501	C-30000	Apr.'27	31-A
1928	Chandler - Special Six	C-30001	C-40000	Aug.'27	31-A
1928	Chandler - Invincible Six	C-40001	C-45000	Jan.'28	131
1929	Chandler - "Sixty-Five"	C-45001		July'28	132

Chandler and Cleveland identification chart #4.

SERVICE (CLEVELAND SIX) BULLETIN

Vol. 1 April 1st, 1926 No. 14

Index

Introduction

In Service Bulletin, No. 9, Page 6, the necessary instructions for ordering service parts from the Fisher Body Corporation, Detroit, Mich., were given.

Do Not Blame Fisher Body for Poor Service —Maybe You Did Not Supply Complete Information

In spite of this, reports received from Fisher Body Corporation state that many orders from our Distributors and Dealers still cannot be filled or shipped because the Body and Job Number for which the respective parts are ordered, have been omitted on the order.

In order to facilitate our Distributors and Dealers when ordering body parts, a brief summary on servicing of all bodies is given on this page. of the bulletin. We kindly ask that you refer to this summary when ordering body parts, so that both the Fisher Body Corporation or our Service Stock Department can intelligently fill your orders and not have to guess what type of body the parts are being ordered for.

Summary on Servicing Body Parts

It is absolutely necessary when ordering body parts for Fisher Bodies that the job number and body number be given. These numbers can be found stamped on the right hand body sill adjacent to the right front door.

Give Body and Job Number

All touring bodies are serviced by the Cleveland Automobile Company as well as all closed bodies except those manufactured by Fisher. The body numbers on the touring bodies can be found under the front cushion stamped on the front seat riser. It is important when ordering body parts on bodies serviced by the factory to give the serial number of the car as well as the body number.

Give Body No. and Serial Number of Car

For your information, we are grouping under two headings the Body Job Numbers and corresponding approximate Serial Numbers, style of body, model and year manufactured. Under one, listing the Fisher Bodies serviced by the Fisher Body Corporation, and under the other, all bodies which are serviced by the Cleveland Automobile Company, and when ordering body parts, suggest that you make sure the necessary information, namely the Job Number and Body Number or Serial Number as the case may be, is given on your order, so that same can be filled correctly and without delay.

Cleveland identification chart #5A (see Part II for Cleveland history).

Bodies Serviced by Fisher Body Corporation

Important Note:—Give Job Number and Body Number when ordering Parts.

Compare the Body Job No. With This List When Ordering Parts from Fisher Body

Mod.	Year	Style of Body	Body Job No.	Approximate Serial No.
40	1919-20	Coupe—Sq. Cowl—3 pass.	3290	1001- 8000
40	1919-20	4 Dr. Sedan—Sq. Cowl	3280	1001- 8000
40	1920-21	4 Dr. Sedan—Sq. Cowl	4510	8000-25000
40	1920-21	Coupe—Sq. Cowl—3 pass.	4520	8000-30000
41	1922	4 Dr. Sedan—Sq. Cowl	4740	25000-40000
41-42	1923-24	2 Dr. Sedan—Sq. Cowl	4990	34500-60500
42	1923	4 Dr. Sedan—Sq. Cowl	4980	40000-56189
42-43	1924-25	4 Dr. Sedan—Rd. Cowl	5400	56190-72000
42-43	1924-25	2 Dr. Sedan—Rd. Cowl	5410	60500-65000
43	1925	4 Dr. De Luxe Sedan	5840	64000-
43	1925	Brougham	5850	64000-74000
43	1925	Coach	6090	66000-77000
43	1925	4 Dr. Sport Sedan	6170	67500-

Bodies Serviced by Cleveland Automobile Co.

Important Note:—Give Body Number and Serial Number when ordering Parts.

Compare Body No. and Serial No. of Car with This List When Ordering Body Parts from Factory

Mod.	Year	Style of Body	Body No.	Approximate Serial No.
40	1919-20	Touring	{ 1-6000	1001 -24999
			{ 1-11999	-
41	1922	Touring	12000-15000	25000-32000
42	1923-24	Touring	1-8000	32000-59999
43	1924-25-26	Touring	100-	60000-
42	1923-24	Bus. Mans Coupe, Sq. C.	O. B. 24000-	45000-59999
43	1924-25	Bus. Mans Coupe, Rd. C.		60000-72000
43	1926	Special Coupe	1-	73500-
43	1926	Special 4 Dr. Sedan	1-	73500-

Mod.	Year	Style of Body	Body No.	Interior Finish	Serial No.
31	1925	4 Dr. Sedan—1st style	1-2500	Gray Velour	C2000-6678
31	1925	4 Dr. Sedan—2nd style	2501-3000	Green Worsted	C6679-6999
31	1925-26	4 Dr. Sedan—3rd style	3001-6500	Corduroy	C7000-
31	1925-26	Coupe	1-	Corduroy or leather	C7200-
31	1925-26	Touring	2001-	—	C2000-

Cleveland identification chart #5B.

• THIRTEEN •

The Cleveland Model 40, 1919–1921

The Cleveland Automobile Company saw its beginning in February of 1919. Little fanfare accompanied the announcement of a new company formed to produce small, lightweight, six cylinder cars.[1]

The Cleveland name was not new to the automobile industry. No fewer than eight previous attempts to build a Cleveland car of some kind had fallen on hard times, beginning with the Cleveland Three-Wheeler built by the American Bicycle Company of Westfield, Massachusetts, in 1900. The new Cleveland Automobile Company, which produced cars from 1919 to 1926, was the most productive of the lot and the last Cleveland effort.

The Cleveland Three-Wheeler had been developed by the H.A. Lozier Company in their Toledo factory, but when the company was sold to the American Bicycle Company the design, tooling, any completed machines and everything associated with the project went to the new owners. Approximately 100 of the Three-Wheelers were sold by Lozier before the buyout. American immediately moved everything associated with the Three-Wheeler to the Westfield, Massachusetts, factory just purchased from Lozier.

Soon after came the Cleveland Electric by the Cleveland Machine Screw Company in 1900 and the Cleveland by the Hansen Automobile Company of Cleveland in 1902. This company became the General Automobile & Manufacturing Company in 1902. The Cleveland by the Cleveland Automobile Company of Cleveland was built in 1903–04; the Cleveland by the Cleveland Motor Car Company of Cleveland was built from 1905 to 1908 and in New York City from 1908 to 1909. The Cleveland Motor Carriage Company of Cleveland built a car from 1904 to 1909 with the Merchant & Evans Company of Philadelphia, Pennsylvania, helping out in the later years. This vehicle used a Garford chassis. The second Cleveland Electric was built by the Cleveland Electric Vehicle Company of Cleveland (formerly the Cuyahoga Motor Car Company) in 1909. The Cleveland Cyclecar was built by the Cleveland Cyclecar Company of Cleveland in 1914 but was discontinued in January 1915.

The previous Cleveland Automobile Company of 1903–1904 was not connected with the new company in any way.[2]

The Cleveland Automobile Company, though composed mostly of Chandler Motor Car Company officials, was formed not as a subsidiary of Chandler but as an entirely new venture. However, there was little doubt as to who was in control as the officers were all Chandler officials.[3]

The plan had been in the works since 1915, but with the entry of the United States into World War I and with Chandler heavily involved in making military equipment it was decided to postpone the beginning until hostilities had ended. Chandler could not dilute its engineering and production staff in a new endeavor until the war effort had ceased.[4] Now, with the prototype developed and rigorously tested, there would be no reason for further delay.

J.V. Whitbeck, who was chief engineer at Chandler, was elected president of the new company and designed the first vehicles to be offered by Cleveland.

Sidney Black, Chandler's assistant sales manager, was named vice president. Black, born at Saltsburg, Pennsylvania, on August 20, 1872, the son of Andrew and Anna Black, was married to Mattye Irene Ereseme and they were the parents of daughters Sydna and Rosalind. Black had joined the H.A. Lozier & Company as a young man. He was one of the best trick bicycle riders in the world, which set him in good standing with his employer. Lozier sent him to Paris in 1896 and from there he toured the world, performing before thousands reportedly including all the crowned heads of Europe. He left the bicycle business when the automobile started to become popular and became a dealer for several different manufacturers from his location in Cincinnati, Ohio. When the Chandler Motor Car Company was established in early 1913, Black sold his interest in Cincinnati and took a sales job with Chandler, being promoted to assistant sales manager by 1919. When the Cleveland Automobile Company was formed he was the logical choice to become vice president and general sales manager.

J.I. Krall, assistant treasurer and auditor at Chandler, became secretary-treasurer; Fred C. Chandler, president of

ANNOUNCEMENT OF THE CLEVELAND SIX

ITS makers are proud to present to the world the Cleveland Six, a product of engineering skill, devotion to ideals, and a desire to serve.

After three years of development in the engineering office and the shop and on the road, the Cleveland Six takes the center of the stage. And it will be in the spot light just so long as men buy automobiles.

It is not an eleventh-hour idea—the Cleveland Six—and it is not an uncertain quantity. It was ready almost three years ago. Experimental models had then been on the road for a year. Plans for production had been formulated. But our nation was at the brink of war, so the Cleveland waited.

These three years have been productive of much progress in design, and now the Cleveland comes to you a highly perfected car.

In a splendid new plant, the very last word in modern equipment and method, this car is built for a waiting public.

Managing this great plant, directing all its various departments, and guarding every operation, is a group of men whose sincerity of purpose is a guarantee of excellence in their car.

The men producing the Cleveland Six are men of broad and successful experience in the motor car industry. They are men of high standing in the industry, engineers and producers of the first rank. The Cleveland Six—their car—is the exponent of all that is best in six-cylinder light car construction. It is an achievement, an individual creation of distinctive merit.

OFFICERS

of the

Cleveland Automobile Company

J. V. WHITBECK, President
Chief Engineer, Chandler Motor Car Company

SID BLACK, Vice-President
Formerly Assistant Sales Manager, Chandler Motor Car Company

J. I. KRALL, Secretary-Treasurer
Formerly Assistant Treasurer, Chandler Motor Car Company

F. C. CHANDLER, Chairman of the Board of Directors
President, Chandler Motor Car Company

SAMUEL REGAR, Chairman of Finance Committee
Treasurer, Chandler Motor Car Company

Pages from the 1919 Cleveland catalog (courtesy Gary Smith).

Chandler Motor Car Company, would be chairman of the board of directors; and Samuel Regar, Chandler's present treasurer, was elected chairman of the Finance Committee. These five, along with J.A. Fayne, made up the Board of Directors.

R.C. Hodge was named purchasing agent and Edward Karlson, Chandler's production manager, was named the new factory superintendent.

Headquarters were temporarily established at the Hollenden Hotel while the new factory was being built at Euclid Avenue and London Road. A four-story concrete and brick structure, 600 × 80 feet with an attractive brick and cut stone frontage, would soon be constructed on a newly purchased 19 acre tract adjacent to the New York–Chicago and St. Louis (Nickel Plate) Railroad tracks. Ernest McGeorge, who had designed most of Chandler's buildings, designed the factory and John Gill and Son began construction in April.

John R. Hall, who for seven years had been Chandler's Chief of Production, was in charge of the design and layout of the facility. He was named production manager in March while retaining his position at Chandler as vice president of production.[5]

The factory was served by the Nickel Plate Railroad and had two sidetracks serving two loading docks of 600 and 800 feet. This was critical as Cleveland planned to ship as many as 3,000 cars per month while employing 1,200 to 1,400 workers.[6] If construction of the factory went as expected Cleveland planned to begin production on July 1.

Hornblower and Weeks, New York financiers, were chosen to handle the financial aspects of the new company. They had been heavily involved in Chandler's early finances and had been a major player in the startup of the Jordan Motor Car Company, Chandler and Cleveland's neighbor. Hornblower and Weeks were chosen because local banks balked at financing the new company. The Cleveland Automobile Company was incorporated at $2,800,000 under the laws of Delaware before the announcement of the new concern was made.[7]

Estimated to be priced at $1,000 to 1,200, the new car would be handled by those Chandler dealers who wished to do so and by new Cleveland dealers in territories where no Chandler dealers existed. In fact, Chandler stockholders were given first refusal of Cleveland stock before it was offered to the public.

The initial $1,400,000 of preferred was offered at $100 per share with a bonus of two shares of common for every 10

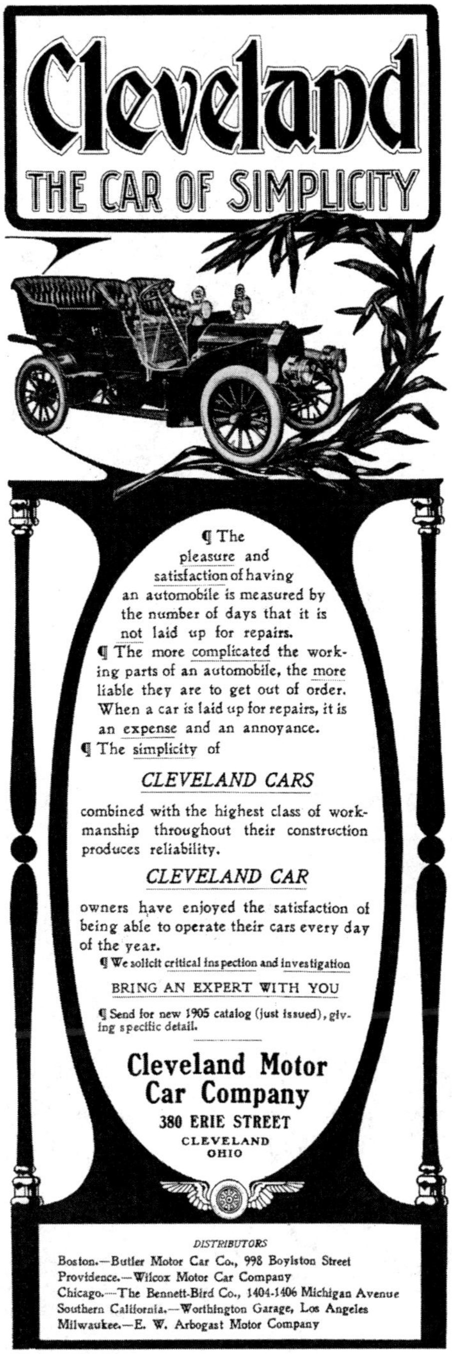

Left and above: **Two of the many Cleveland cars manufactured before the 1919 beginning of the Cleveland Automobile Company (left, *Motor*, May 1905; right, unknown trade magazine, courtesy Tom Baumann). *Below, left:* John Whitbeck (*The Journal of the Society of Automotive Engineers*, March 1919). *Below, right:* Sid Black (*Chandler Times*, July–August 1927).**

shares preferred held. Chandler stockholders could subscribe to one share of Cleveland for every five shares of Chandler held.

The prototype cars, having been developed and tested over an extended period of time, were shown to 125 Chandler distributors in late March. The distributors had been invited to Cleveland for a three-day conference to view the new offering and get acquainted with the company and its selling policies.[8]

The Cleveland rode on a 112-inch wheelbase frame made by Parish & Bingham of Cleveland and was powered by a six cylinder overhead valve engine with bore and stroke of 3 × 4½ of Cleveland's own design. There were valve covers to protect from dust, unlike some engines of the day. A Stromberg carburetor was fed by a Stewart vacuum tank. An oil cup filled with felt wicking protruded through the valve cover at the front and rear of the engine. This must be filled by the owner at intervals as it lubricated the valve lifters through grooves in the valve train lifter shaft. Ignition was by Bosch distributor and coil, but a Bosch Magneto could be substituted at a cost of $45.00. Gray & Davis

***Above:* The Cleveland factory in 1919. *Left, top and bottom:* Two views of the 1919 Cleveland Model 40 Touring.**

supplied the generator and starter with Borg & Beck supplying the clutch.

The engine and rear end were made by Cleveland, but Mechanics Machine Company built the transmission and final drive was of the Hotchkiss design. Artillery type wood wheels were standard but five wire wheels at an extra cost of $105 were available. Rims were straight side demountable by Firestone and tires were 32 × 4 Firestone Non Skid. Timken furnished all bearings.

Cooling was by a centrifugal water pump feeding a Mayo radiator, which was replaced with one supplied by Harrison before the model year ended. Suspension was semi elliptic entirely.

Body color was Cleveland Blue with hood, fenders, running gear, chassis and wheels painted black. Interiors were hand buffed, bright finish, long grain leather in the open cars only. Interiors of the closed models were "Of the finest quality, custom chosen materials."

Four body styles, designated the Model 40, would eventually be available but for the initial offering only the Five Passenger Touring could be purchased. It and the Three Passenger Roadster, available a short time later, were each priced at $1,385. The estimated price of $1,000 to $1,200 could not be met as the war had driven the cost of raw materials upward since the Model 40 was designed. All bodies were built by Fisher and neither of the open models had outside door handles. A unique feature of the Roadster was the absence of a trunk lid. To reach that area it was necessary to raise a lid just behind the seat.

Ernest Wooler resigned his position as engineer at Chandler shortly after the Cleveland was announced and was immediately named chief engineer at Cleveland. John V. Whitbeck had designed the original car but was too busy, as president of the company, to do any further engineering.[9]

Cleveland missed its target for starting production by only 30 days, launching by July 31. One of the first advertisements for the Cleveland appeared in a leading trade magazine on July

2. By the time production began there were orders for 30,000 automobiles in hand and by September most distributors had cars on hand, albeit only the Touring. The Roadster entered production by November.[10]

Automobile production had barely begun when Cleveland realized they needed more space and began an addition to the factory. A 200 × 80 foot building, with four floors, was designed by Ernest McGeorge and constructed by John Gill and Son beginning in October. A completion date of April 1920 was expected.[11]

By the end of 1919 Cleveland was producing about 15 cars per day. Prices had been raised slightly with the Touring and Roadster selling for $1,485. The Coupe and Sedan would go for $2,295 when they became available.

By the time of the New York show (January 3–10, 1920), the Coupe was in production but had not been previously shown. Although all four body styles were shown, the Sedan would not be available in quantity for a few months. By January, Cleveland had hit its stride and produced more that month than the total previous output to that date. In the spring, the new factory building which would give the company an output of 150 cars per day was completed. Cleveland stockholders received their first dividend on January 31, 1920. At that time it was announced that Cleveland was planning to increase its common stock from 14,000 to 300,000 of no par value which would give present holders 20 shares of the new stock for each one of the old now held and make the total outstanding common issue 280,000 shares.[12]

Cleveland's timing could have been better, as the new marque debuted with the economy in a steep decline from which it would need a couple of years to recover. But with three years of planning invested and a proven prototype ready to produce, the de-

Top: **1919 Cleveland Model 40 Roadster.** ***Middle:*** **1919 Cleveland Model 40 Roadster (*Motor Age*, November 13, 1919).** ***Bottom:*** **1920–21 Cleveland Model 40 Sedan.**

cision to go ahead with the venture was a foregone conclusion.

The success of the new company was due mainly to the fact that veteran automobile men were in control. With enough capital to see it through and the network of Chandler dealers, who would market the new cars, already well established, success was not an unreasonable expectation.

As soon as the new factory addition was completed, John Gill and Son began construction of a 200 × 80 foot machine shop. The new structure was designed to support two additional floors, had its own rail siding and was situated facing London Road. The building was parallel to the Cleveland plant, which was 264 feet to the west, and was designed by Ernest McGeorge. It was also designed to expand south along London Road.

Fifteen feet north of the machine shop stood an 82 foot square foundry building which was also designed to expand to the west toward the main factory. At the back of the site a 44 foot square boiler house was constructed by the Lundoff-Bicknell Company. It contained B&W Sterling boilers, Detroit stokers, Anderson air traps and Illinois stop and check valves. Next to the boiler house stood a 7½ × 175 foot smokestack.[13]

With the economy getting worse by the day, Cleveland agents were hard to find. Those dealers who also sold Chandlers would not be affected nearly as much as those who sold Cleveland only. The Cleveland had not been on the market long enough to establish a following. Potential dealers were reluctant to invest their money in such a poor business climate. By August 1920, 2,000 dealers were selling the Cleveland but there was still open territory for those wanting to become agents.

By the end of 1920 Cleveland had produced about 16,000 automobiles for the

***Top:* 1920–21 Cleveland Model 40 on assembly line with top being installed (factory photograph, author's collection). *Bottom:* 1920–21 Cleveland Model 40 Coupe.**

Above, left and right: **1919 Model 40.** ***Below, left:*** **1920–21 Cleveland Model 40 Touring (photograph courtesy Roger Anderson).** ***Below, right:*** **Cleveland ad, October 1919 (unknown trade magazine).**

calendar year and there had been very little change. The Touring and Roadster had acquired outside door handles and the spare tire carrier was changed slightly.

By August, prices for the Coupe and Sedan had been raised to $2,395 and $2,495, respectively, but the open cars remained at $1,485.

In December Cleveland announced that a Sport Roadster would be added to the line for 1921. Although it appeared at the New York (January 8–15, 1921) and Chicago (January 29–February 6) shows, the economy was so bad there was little interest in a new model. The Sport Roadster was not listed in the 1921 catalogue, and nothing more was heard until late in 1921 when a Special Roadster was listed as being available at $1,495.

With the start of 1921, prices were lowered with the Tour-

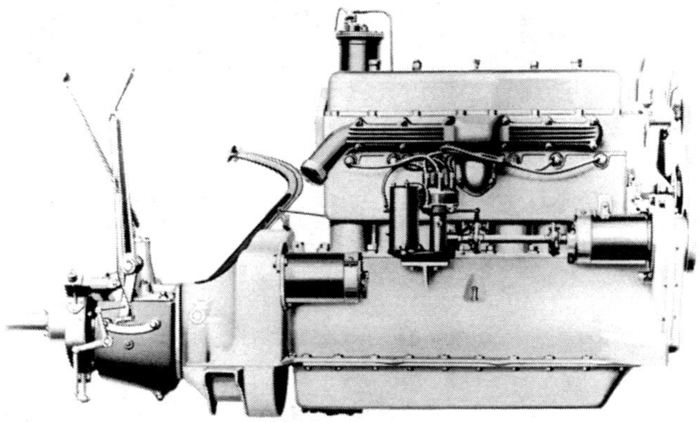

***Top:* 1920–21 Cleveland Model 40 Roadster (factory photograph, courtesy Roger Anderson). *Above, left and right:* 1920–21 Cleveland Model 40 engine.**

ing and Roadster selling at $1,435, the Coupe for $2,345 and the Sedan for $2,445.

In the terrible economy of 1921, production of automobiles would drop dramatically throughout the industry and Cleveland was no exception. Virtually all advertising in 1921 ceased and some dealers resorted to publishing their own catalogues.

By November prices had plunged dramatically with the Touring and Roadster selling for $1,295, the Coupe for $2,195 and the Sedan for $2,295. The Special Roadster was listed at $1,495. Cleveland produced only 12,200 automobiles during 1921.[14]

Very few changes had been made to the Cleveland since its introduction, other than outside door handles on the open models, but some good things were about to happen.

• Fourteen •

Models 41 and 42, 1922–1924

When the New York show opened on January 7, 1922, Cleveland showed new cars that were considerably improved over the previous Model 40. The new Cleveland Model 41 body featured several appointments that improved the appearance, backed up by mechanical revisions.

Up front, a nickel plated radiator shell had reworked corners and a Motometer at the top. Drum type headlights with nickel trim now flanked the new radiator, and miniatures of the headlights were mounted on the cowl. The instruments were slightly reconfigured. The Touring and Roadster now had nickeled windshield stanchions.

Taking a cue from Chandler, the new models came with aluminum step plates instead of running boards. (For traditionalists, running boards were still an option.) The top was reworked with a lower profile and no irons or bows visible at the rear of the Touring. The Roadster retained a small space behind the seat for storage but gained a locking deck lid for the convenience of those carrying larger items.

Cleveland Blue was the standard color on all body styles except the roadster, which came in Surrey Green with black fenders and cream colored wheels. If you preferred blue, it was available as an option. The Touring was available in Maroon as an option, but the Sedan and Coupe were available in Cleveland Blue only. The Coupe, like the Roadster, had a storage place behind the seat and the deck lids of both models were removable.[1]

The Sport Roadster which had been promised in January 1921 never materialized. Neither did it appear in the Cleveland catalogue for 1922—no mention whatsoever. Economic conditions were so bad that a new model was just not feasible.

Mechanicals were not neglected while all the body changes were being made. The cylinder bore was increased to 3¹⁄₁₆ inches but the stroke remained the same at 4½ inches. Roller type valve lifters replaced the mushroom style. Valve springs were now double with a smaller one placed inside a larger one. The oil filler tube was moved to the side of the engine for better accessibility and the oil could now be drained by turning a handle which extended from the oil pan upward beside the engine block. This eliminated the necessity of getting under the car while changing oil.[2]

Lighting, starter and ignition were now entirely Bosch. The Sedan and Coupe also received a new windshield cleaner.

Prices were adjusted downward with the closed cars taking a drastic cut. The Roadster now sold for $1,175 and the Touring for $1,195. The Coupe went for $1,550 while the Sedan was the most expensive at $1,595.[3]

To compete with others in the smaller car marketplace, Cleveland had to build a better looking, better performing, lower priced car and they did.

By August, Cleveland introduced a new Touring into its lineup. Commonly called the Chesterfield Special, it was a sporty version of a Touring. Equipped with wire wheels, windwings, two-piece nickel plated front bumper, khaki top, rear mounted trunk rack with aluminum guards and spare tire behind, it was quite appealing. Added to this was a rear view mirror, cowl ventilator and fancy leather interior to match the exterior finish of Beige Brown. The new creation sold for $1,295.[4]

On August 5, Cleveland again cut prices on all models with the Five Passenger Phaeton now selling for $1,095, the Chesterfield Phaeton for $1,260, the Two Passenger Roadster for $1,085, the Sedan for $1,585 and the Coupe for $1,495. Fisher Body was still building all Cleveland bodies as they had from the beginning.[5]

The 1923 models debuted in October with numerous changes, updates and additions. The Coupe was replaced by a Two-Door Sedan (which was called a Coupe at first but soon renamed), offering basic transportation for those who wanted a closed car for a family at an economical price. The front seats tilted forward for entry into the rear compartment, and there was a trunk space at the rear. Fitted with running boards and devoid of all nickel plating except the headlight trim, the Two-Door Sedan came in gray with no options and sold for $1,295.

A fancier version known as the Two-Door Special Sedan came with a number of refinements. The basic body form was the same, including the trunk space at the rear, but aluminum

***Top, left:* 1922 Cleveland Model 41 Touring. *Top, right:* 1922 Cleveland Model 41 Roadster (photograph courtesy Roger Anderson). *Bottom, left:* 1922 Cleveland Model 41 Roadster (photograph courtesy Cleveland State University Archives). *Bottom, right:* Interior view of the 1922 Roadster Model 41.**

step-plates and disc wheels graced this version, with wire wheels as an option. Topping a nickeled radiator shell was a Motometer with winged cap. An aluminum trunk rack and guards made this body style appealing at $1,395, but it was available only in Cleveland Blue.

The Four Door Sedan carried on as the basic offering for 1923, but a new deluxe model dubbed the Four-Door Special Sedan sported disc wheels with wire as an option, an aluminum trunk rack and guards, and a nickeled radiator shell, cap and Motometer. The interior was plush but the exterior color was still Cleveland Blue; it was priced at $1,595. Those needing a large sedan at an economical price could save $100 by opting for the standard Four-Door Sedan. There was no trunk at the rear, wheels were wood, step plates were replaced by running boards and there was no nickel plating except minor trim on the headlights. The radiator shell was painted body color and was topped by a flat cap. The interior was not as plush as the Special version.

On the 1923 Touring, the step plates were replaced by running boards, the nickeled radiator shell by one of body color and the Motometer and cap by a conventional cap. The body color was Cleveland Blue and the price is $995. The 1923 Touring was introduced with a two-piece windshield but that had been changed to a one- piece by the time of the New York Show and the printing of the 1923 showroom album and catalogue.

If you wanted a fancy touring car it was available as the Sport Model, replacing the Chesterfield Special. Disc wheels

Top, left: 1922 Cleveland Model 41 Coupe. *Top, right:* 1922 Cleveland Model 41 Coupe with special features. *Middle, left:* 1922 Cleveland Model 41 Chesterfield Special Touring (three factory photographs, courtesy Roger Anderson). *Middle, right:* Cleveland Model 41 Four Door Sedan (factory photograph, courtesy John W. Chandler). *Bottom, left:* 1923 Cleveland Model 41 Two Door Special Sedan. *Bottom, right:* 1923 Cleveland Model 41 Four Door Sedan (both factory photographs, courtesy Roger Anderson).

Top, left: **1923 Cleveland Model 41 Touring (late).** ***Top, right:*** **1923 Cleveland Model 41 Sport Model Touring (both factory photographs, courtesy Roger Anderson).** ***Above and right:*** **1923 Cleveland Model 41 Coupe, commonly called a Doctor's Coupe (above, factory photograph, courtesy Roger Anderson).**

were standard with wire as an option. A nickeled front bumper and nickeled radiator shell with fancy cap and Motometer graced the front while an aluminum trunk rack, trunk and guards adorned the rear. The only color was Beige-Brown. The windshield is one-piece with windwings and nickel plated stanchions. A rear view mirror, windshield wiper and Spanish leather interior made this model appealing at $1,260.

The Roadster, at $1,085, was unchanged and remained available in Surrey Green with Cleveland Blue as an option. All enclosed cars lost the loop type door handles in favor of a conventional type.

All Cleveland Sixes had an engine with a bore and stroke of 3⅟16 by 4½ and rode on a 112 inch wheelbase frame mated to wheels with 31 × 4 tires. Ignition was by a Bosch distributor and high tension coil with a magneto being an option. Stromberg furnished the carburetor and Bosch the generator.

The postwar recession having ended, Cleveland was prospering. By August 1922 they had earned in excess of $1 million net.[6]

***Top, left:* 1924 Cleveland Model 42 Special Touring (*Automobile Trade Journal*, October 1924). *Top, right:* 1924 Cleveland Model 42 Touring DeLuxe. *Bottom, left:* 1924 Cleveland Model 42 Special Four Door Sedan. *Bottom, right:* 1924 Cleveland Model 42 Three Passenger Coupe (three factory photographs, courtesy Roger Anderson).**

Cleveland took these models into 1923, but by May they returned the Coupe to the lineup in a slightly different version. It was a three window version (blind back) with the rear quarter and top being covered in fabric. Wood wheels, running boards and a painted radiator shell made this a favorite of salesmen and doctors who needed basic transportation at a reasonable price. Ample storage space behind the seat would accommodate a doctor's bag, and the large trunk afforded the salesman adequate space for his wares. This was a good, reasonably priced car at $1,195.

Cleveland had previously introduced models on a calendar year schedule, but they began to stray from that practice in August 1922 when they added the Chesterfield Special. During 1923 they added the Coupe in May and a Sport Touring by June. In September they introduced the entire 1924 line of eight body styles, collectively known as the Model 42.[7]

All 1924 bodies were the same as the previous year, but there was a newly designed radiator shell which came in painted form for the standard cars and nickel plated for the De Luxe and Special models. These models also had Motometers with dogbone caps added which gave the appearance of a much higher hood. One inch had already been added to the height of the radiator. The 1924 Clevelands were easy to recognize by the distinctive sway in the radiator shell, just under the Cleveland badge.

The De Luxe Touring and closed models carried a wide stripe of contrasting color edged in gold, which did wonders for their appearance. One other body change was the addition of a kick plate to the splash apron of all models having running boards. Another, barely mentioned change is the addition of an aluminum molding between the hood and the cowl. This molding, which would be more pronounced when the 1925 Model 43 arrived, is prominently shown on the examples in the 1924 catalogue, but only the Special Four Door Sedan is featured in the showroom album.

Cleveland's brochure for the 1924 Model 42 listed eight body styles but their press release contained nine. However, the Sport Touring was still shown as was the Special Four Door Sedan with the disc wheels and step plate option.[8]

The Sport Model had been replaced by a De Luxe Touring Model, priced at $1,145 and lacking the windwings, disc wheels and trunk. (The trunk rack and aluminum guard strips were still present, but the trunk became an option.) Step plates were still standard. The De Luxe Touring was still a nice looking car but not nearly as much so as the Sport Model.

Left: **1924 Cleveland Model 42 Special Coupe.** ***Above:*** **1924 Cleveland Model 42 Roadster.** ***Below:*** **Assembling Cleveland rear ends, 1923 (three factory photographs, courtesy Roger Anderson).**

The Four Door Sedan (now $1,395) and the Special Four Door Sedan ($1,495) continued but the Special no longer had disc wheels. Running boards with kick plates were standard but step plates were available as an option, as were disc wheels and balloon tires. Blue Devil Blue paint was an option to replace the standard Cleveland Blue.[9]

The Five Passenger Two Door Sedan, priced at $1,295, had proven to be Cleveland's best seller with seven out of ten orders for closed cars being for this model. It was practically identical to the 1923 model with only kick plates added to the splash aprons.

The Five Passenger Four Door Sedan ($1,395) and re-

Checking runout of 1923 Cleveland flywheel (factory photograph, courtesy Roger Anderson).

cently reinstated Three Passenger Coupe ($1,245) similarly carried over with only the kick plates added.

The Special Two Door Sedan continued with step plates, disc wheels, nickeled radiator shell with dogbone cap and Motometer, and trunk rack and aluminum guard strips. It was priced at $1,395. Although the brochure listed the Special Two Door as being available in Cleveland Coach Blue with an option of Blue Devil Blue, the press release also showed Beige Brown, Delft Blue, Simplex Green, Maroon and Red as color choices.

The Five Passenger Touring ($1,045) was the same as the previous year's model with the exception of the kick plates and a one-man top, distinguished by having no top irons visible at the rear.[10]

A Special Coupe, new to the line, differed from the standard version by having aluminum landau irons, step plates instead of running boards, nickeled radiator treatment and disc wheels. One significant difference from most Clevelands was the availability of eight body colors. Why so many is a mystery, but you could have Cleveland Coach Blue, Blue Devil Blue, Bavarian Blue, Delft Blue, Cleveland Carmine, Cleveland Maroon, Beige Brown and Simplex Green.[11]

Color had suddenly become a popular item on the Special models, but the palette remained limited for other models. Cleveland Blue was the sole color for the Standard Coupe, the Two Door and the Four Door Sedan, while a choice of Cleveland Coach Blue or Blue Devil Blue was available on the Touring, the De Luxe Touring, the Special Four Door Sedans and the Special Coupe.[12]

The Roadster was not listed or illustrated in Cleveland's 1924 brochure but was mentioned in the press release and was shown in the showroom album. This would account for the discrepancy between eight or nine models, but the fate of the Roadster is uncertain.

Mechanical changes were abundant on the 1924 Model 42.[13] A new automatic spark advance was added to the Bosch ignition system as well as a new Stromberg carburetor. The intake manifold was shrouded by the exhaust manifold, preheating the vaporized gasoline before it entered the combustion chamber. The valve train gained pressure lubrication and the fan was now self-lubricating. Steering was improved with the addition of ball bearings, and Timken roller bearings were now used throughout the new model.

Fisher Body still supplied all Cleveland bodies. Financially, Cleveland was doing well and vice president Sid Black expected a 60 to 70 percent gain in sales over the previous year if the present volume continued.[14]

At the New York show, which opened on January 5, 1924, at the Armory in the Bronx, Cleveland displayed five body styles and a stripped cutaway chassis finished in gray and white. These were the same cars Cleveland had been selling since September 1923, with nothing radically new.

Although the Roadster was being phased out, as had been apparent since it was not listed in all brochures for 1924 models, it was shown in the 1924 showroom album and was listed as being available in late January at a price of $1,085. Later, when the new Model 43 was introduced, it was announced that the Roadster had been dropped. Balloon tires as well as disc wheels were an option on all body styles with the wheels going for $30 extra and the tires for $70.

Cleveland was having trouble filling its orders by April and the factory was put on overtime with the personnel office hiring new workers on a regular basis. The Sedans had proved so popular that they now comprised nearly 50 percent of all body styles sold.

Prices were reduced considerably on four models. The Two Door Sedan was cut from $1,395 to $1,295, the Special Two Door Sedan from $1,495 to $1,395, the Four Door Sedan from $1,595 to $1,395 and the Special Four Door Sedan from $1,695 to $1,495.[15]

• FIFTEEN •

Models 43 and 31 and the "Mileage Motor," 1925–1926

In early June 1924, Cleveland unveiled its latest creations. More than 500 Cleveland dealers and distributors attended a two day conference at the Winton Hotel on June 2–3 where they viewed the new models, attended seminars, held discussions on selling the new models and enjoyed plenty of food and drink. What they had come to see was the Model 43. Cleveland had made drastic changes in both the body and the mechanical makeup of their car.[1]

A new "L" type flathead engine replaced the overhead valve version that Cleveland had used since its inception. Dubbed the Mileage Motor, it had a bore and stroke of 3⅛ × 4¾ and peak horsepower of 60 at 2,800 r.p.m., a nice increase over the former engine's 45 horsepower at 2,200 r.p.m. Crankshaft weight was increased from 50 to 67 pounds and lubrication was greatly improved. Main bearings were now bronze backed with the camshaft being placed on the right of the engine in order to improve lubrication, taking advantage of the oil being thrown by the crankshaft. The cylinder block was cast separately from the crankcase and contained large water passages to aid in cooling. Bosch electrics, Schebler S1 carburetor and Borg & Beck clutch were other features of the new model.[2]

Other mechanical changes accompanied the new engine, most notably including the wheelbase being lengthened to 115 inches. The Model 43 also adopted the Bowen "one shot" lubrication system. Balloon tires (31 × 5.25) were now standard equipment, but mechanical four wheel brakes were an option at $50.

The body grew in length and took on a higher, narrower radiator. Headlights were slightly different with only the bezel being nickel plated. A larger cowl added significantly to the appearance of the front end, which was lengthened by two inches. The fenders now had a double crown.

There were no more step plates on any body style as standard or optional equipment. The big news concerning bodies was that Cleveland was now building all their open bodies in their own factory. Although Fisher was still making the closed bodies, Clevelands would soon become entirely constructed at the factory.

Both the Touring and Touring De Luxe featured two-piece windshields and the one man top. The Touring De Luxe, Brougham, Sedan De Luxe and Special Coupe had nickeled radiator shells with a dogbone radiator cap with Motometer, and the Touring De Luxe was fitted with a front bumper. The Roadster was dropped.

The Special Coupe is not to be confused with the "Special" series which would come in 1926; rather, it was a special version of the regular Coupe.

Available body styles were the Four Door Sedan at $1,495; the Touring at $1,095; the Coupe at $1,295; the Five Passenger Two Door Sedan with trunk rack at $1,395; the Touring De Luxe with front bumper at $1,195 and the Special Coupe at $1,395.

All body styles were available in Cleveland Blue with the Touring De Luxe and Special Coupe also available in Blue Devil Blue. The array of colors that were available on the previous Model 42 had vanished.[3]

By July 1924, Cleveland employees were required to work overtime to keep up with demand, and production was increased by 50 percent.[4] The status quo didn't hold for long as Cleveland announced two new body styles in November: the Brougham, a wholly new body style, and the Four Door De Luxe, a refinement of an existing body. The Brougham was a two door, five window design similar to the Two Door Sedan. It featured a trunk rack and a nickeled radiator with dogbone cap and Motometer. Balloon tires were standard and four wheel brakes optional, although Cleveland emphasized their availability. A belt molding ran completely around the car from radiator to radiator. Blue Devil Blue paint below the belt and black above were separated by the belt molding in a contrasting color. Inside, the instrument board and windshield area were finished in Circassian walnut.

The Four Door De Luxe was a version of the standard Four Door with all the refinements and paint scheme of the

Top, left: **1925 Cleveland Model 43 Five Passenger Touring.** ***Top, right:*** **1925 Cleveland Model 43 Five Passenger Touring DeLuxe.** ***Middle, left:*** **1925 Cleveland Model 43 Three Passenger Coupe.** ***Middle, right:*** **1925 Cleveland Model 43 Five Passenger Sedan.** ***Bottom, left:*** **1925 Cleveland Model 43 Five Passenger Four Door Sedan.** ***Bottom, right:*** **1925 Cleveland Model 43 Five Passenger Brougham (all factory photographs, courtesy Roger Anderson).**

Brougham. Windshields of both models were one piece. Prices of the new body styles were not initially announced, but at the New York Show in January, they were displayed as $1,725.[5]

Shortly after announcing the Brougham and Four Door De Luxe, Cleveland unveiled another body style. The Coach Premier was a two door car with a 35-inch-wide door and smaller rear window, giving it the blind-back look with the body being four inches shorter than the longest Cleveland. Intended as an economy car, the Coach Premier came with a one piece windshield and no luxury appointments and a Bloomfield Green and Black Duco paint scheme. Interior appointments included an automatic windshield wiper, matte silver hardware, taupe green worsted upholstery, leather covered sun visor, and a foot rail. A trunk rack was standard. The price was $1,295, making it Cleveland's least expensive five passenger closed car.

Cleveland had the two door business well covered with the Two Door Sedan and the new Brougham which had just been announced. The Coach Premier was an improvement over the Two Door Sedan and the latter would soon fade away. In fact, all two door sedans would be gone when the 1926 models were announced.[6]

The New York show at the 258th Field Artillery Armory in the Bronx opened on Friday, January 2, 1925, and ran until Saturday, January 10. Cleveland was there, showing the Model 43 for the first time since its introduction in June 1924. They were pushing the Coach Premier and Brougham, those body styles having been introduced after the initial showing of the 43. Various other body styles were shown, but two newcomers drew considerable attention.[7]

The Model 31 was introduced with little fanfare with only

***Left, top:* 1925 Cleveland Model 43 Three Passenger Special Coupe (factory photograph, courtesy Roger Anderson). *Left, middle:* 1926 Cleveland Model 43 Sport Sedan (*Motor Age*, July 9, 1925). *Left, bottom:* 1926 Cleveland Model 43 Touring (factory photograph, courtesy Roger Anderson). *Right, top:* 1926 Cleveland Model 31 Touring (factory photograph, courtesy Roger Anderson). *Right, bottom:* 1926 Cleveland Model 43 Sport Touring.**

two body styles being shown, a Touring at $895 and a Sedan at $1,195. The new Model 31 was a smaller version of the 43 with a six cylinder "L" type flathead engine with bore and stroke of $2\frac{7}{8} \times 4\frac{1}{4}$. Horsepower was 25 percent less than the 43, peaking at 45 @ 2500 r.p.m.[8]

The chassis had a $108\frac{1}{2}$ inch wheelbase compared to the Model 43 at 115. A Stewart vacuum fuel tank fed a Johnson type H carburetor and American Bosch supplied the electrics. Like its counterpart it had a Borg & Beck clutch and "one shot" lubrication. The transmission very much resembled that of the 43, but the bell housing and case were one unit.

Brakes were two-wheel contracting with four-wheel available as an option, and 30 × 4.95 balloon tires are standard.

Only the Touring and Sedan were offered at first, but a Coupe and Touring Deluxe came later.[9] Other than size there was very little to distinguish the 31 from the 43. Running boards were plain on the 31 while the 43 still used kick plates. Both models featured belting which ran from the radiator to encompass the entire car. The Model 31 Sedan was fitted with a nickel plated radiator shell.

Paint was Duco Sagebrush Green with black belt accented with gold striping. The fenders and splash aprons were finished in black with the top of the Sedan also finished in black. The interior was leather for the Touring and taupe worsted for the Sedan. Fisher supplied the Sedan body and Cleveland built the Touring.

Although the 31 was shown in January, it would be late March when it arrived at dealerships.[10]

***Above:* 1926 Cleveland Model 31 Coupe. *Right:* The capacious trunk of the 1926 Model 31 Coupe (Standard).**

Cleveland was doing well when spring arrived: 2,000 cars were shipped in March, 3,000 were projected to be shipped in April and 1925 was expected to be the best year in Cleveland history. By June this optimism was holding true.[11]

The 1926 models appeared in August and immediately the Model 43 line gained a new body style. The Model 43 was now being called the "Special" series, and the fancy new Sport Sedan was a beauty. An adaptation of the Four Door sedan, it boasted several flourishes. At the front was a nickeled radiator shell with dogbone cap and Motometer, but farther back was something new. An oval window behind the rear door replaced the conventional window of the Sedan from which the new Sport Sedan saw its inception. Aluminum landau irons finished in black with polished fittings complemented the oval windows. An aluminum trunk rack and scuff bars adorned the rear.

Upholstery was a special shade of gray mohair. The seats were high backed and wide with the rear having armrests on both sides. The instrument panel was finished in Circassian walnut and silk curtains adorned the rear window. The Fisher-bodied Sport Sedan was priced at $1,725.

The Model 43 (Special) was available in four other body styles: the Four Door Sedan at $1,295, Coupe at $1,175, Touring at $1,095 and Sport Touring at $1,245.

The Sedan, Coupe and Touring came in Cleveland Blue Duco paint with belting in a contrasting color. The Sport Touring came in two-tone Sagebrush Green. Closed cars were still black above the belt. Standard upholstery was gray broadcloth for the Sedan and hand buffed leather with gray corduroy as an option for the Coupe. The Touring came with leather and the Sport Touring with Spanish leather.

The Model 43 (Special) Sport Touring was a fancy automobile. A nickeled radiator, cap and Motometer up front, a trunk at the rear, nickeled bumpers front and rear, disc wheels and wind wings made it quite deluxe. A one man top perfected the package.

The Coupe was a great improvement over the former style with rounded corners and larger doors. It replaced both the former Coupe and Special Coupe but did not retain the landau irons of the former Special Coupe. The Five Passenger Two Door Sedan (Coach) was also dropped.[12]

With the introduction of the 31 Series, Cleveland found it necessary to adjust their lineup of the 43 Series. They added the "Special" to that series and jockeyed their body styles somewhat, not wanting to compete with themselves in a marketplace as crowded as the automobile field was at that time. The 31 Series replicated the 43 to a great extent, offering smaller versions of existing body styles.

With the introduction of the 1926 models the Model 31 Coupe and Touring De Luxe became available to dealers. The visual differences between the two series were slight: the Model 31 lacked running board kick plates, the fenders were slightly different and the Touring did not have the one man top. The 31 also had a smaller trunk, the windwings were slightly different and an aluminum cowl band was added. The Coupe sold for $975, the Touring De Luxe for $1,025.

Both series still had the Bowen "one shot" lubrication system—just step on a plunger and your Cleveland was lubricated. Fisher still supplied all the closed car bodies. The engine, the Mileage Motor, was made entirely by Cleveland and all bodies were finished in Duco.

In September 1925, at the convention of Cleveland distributors and dealers, a price reduction was announced. Why a price reduction at this time? Cleveland was supposed to be as popular as ice water on a hot day.[13] They weren't alone as their neighbor Chandler announced drastic cuts at the same time. Cleveland was supposedly having the greatest year in its history in 1925. They were selling cars, but were they making money?[14]

The terms "Standard" and "Special" had now started to invade the Cleveland language in reference to the Model 31 and

Top, left: **1926 Cleveland Model 31 Touring DeLuxe.** ***Top, right:*** **1926 Cleveland DeLuxe Sedan.** ***Bottom, left:*** **1926 Cleveland Model 43 (Special) Mileage Motor cutaway illustration.** ***Bottom, right:*** **Mullins Body Corporation ad (*Automotive Industries*, April 2, 1925).**

43. In fact, Special had been an official name for the 43 since the Model 31 was introduced. This would later cause a great deal of confusion. This Special is not to be confused with the "Special" of the previous model, which only referred to a special version of that model.[15]

Someone still had faith in the Cleveland name as a large number of dealers were added to the network during the previous months.[16]

The strain of managing two automobile companies finally caught up with the officials of Cleveland and Chandler in December 1925, and the directors decided to merge the two companies. The papers were filed in the state of Delaware and the financial arrangements were being finalized with stockholders having until January 15, 1926, to exchange their stock.[17]Both companies would soldier on under their respective titles until the name officially became Chandler-Cleveland Motors Corporation in August 1926.

In January 1926 both the Model 43 and 31 underwent some engine updates. The crankshaft was beefed up and a flywheel was added at the front for better balance. Price increases ranging from $50 to $95 were announced for selected cars of both series.[18]

Cleveland continued to advertise and sell as aggressively as before the merger was announced. At this point it probably was unclear whether Cleveland would retain its identity or become a Chandler, or even whether the Chandler might become Cleveland. Bets were that Chandler would not become Cleveland as Fred C. Chandler would not want to lose his namesake.[19]

In March, the Cleveland Motor Sales Company of St. Louis took a standard 31 Coupe and turned it into a creation called the "Honeymoon Special." The car had about every amenity one could want for a camping trip. It had provisions for a bed, for cooking, for showering, if you could get by on fifteen gallons of water, and even for entertainment via an Atwater-

Top: **Building the 1925 Cleveland engine.** ***Bottom:*** **Testing the 1925 Cleveland engine (both factory photographs, courtesy Roger Anderson).**

Top: **Cutting gears for 1925 Cleveland rear axle.** ***Bottom:*** **Cleveland production line in 1925 (both factory photographs, courtesy Roger Anderson).**

Top: **Final inspection of 1925 Clevelands (factory photograph, courtesy Roger Anderson).** ***Bottom:*** **The Cleveland factory as it looked about 1922 (courtesy of U.S. Department of Interior, National Park Service).**

Kent radio. Other amenities too numerous to list were also available. It must have been one of a kind as nothing more was ever heard of the Honeymoon Special.[20]

A new sedan model joined the 31 series in April. Billed as the De Luxe Sedan, it was only a fancier version of the Four Door Sedan but it looked wonderful. Bumpers were added front and rear, the radiator shell was nickel with a nickeled dogbone cap and Motometer, and the paint was two-tone gray with a wide belt between the molding and the black top. The hood, above the molding, was finished in the belting color. The interior was broadcloth and the instrument panel was Circassian walnut. Balloon tires were standard. The display model was equipped with front wheel brakes although they probably were still an option.[21]

By June 1926 Cleveland was building all their bodies. An addition to the plant was large enough to build sedan and coupe bodies as well as the open cars which Cleveland had been building for some time with the help of suppliers like the Mullins Body Corporation of Salem, Ohio, who furnished sheet metal stamping for that purpose. Fisher had been supplying both Cleveland and Chandler with bodies for years, but the arrangement was coming to an end. For reasons unknown, Chandler severed their ties with Fisher in late 1925 and started buying bodies from seemingly anywhere they could find them. Since the two companies were so closely related, this probably affected Cleveland also, and now the ties with Fisher were completely broken.

This seemed like the right time for the combined companies to build all bodies for both Chandler and Cleveland, but they were forced to purchase bodies from several sources until the Cleveland facility was able to meet their needs.[22]

The Cleveland division of Chandler-Cleveland Motors was actively seeking dealers as late as July. Was this a smokescreen? Had they made the decision to drop Cleveland or was this a spur of the moment thing? Why would they sign a dealer in July and drop the name in August? These are questions that have never been answered and probably never will be. Another tantalizing question: Why drop Cleveland when it was doing better than Chandler?[23]

The Model 31 De Luxe Sedan was Cleveland's last hurrah. When the new models were introduced in August 1926 the Cleveland Automobile Company would be relegated to history. The Model 43 would go on as the Chandler Special and the 31 would do the same as the Chandler Standard.

Employees kept their jobs and officials returned to positions that, in many cases, they had previously held at Chandler. Some had held dual positions, and jobs were created for those who had not formerly been employed by Chandler or who had given up their positions when they went to Cleveland.

The question will always be asked—"Was the merger designed to save Cleveland or Chandler?"

It probably doesn't matter, as slightly more than two years down the road both would be history.

• **Sixteen** •

Racing, Hill Climbing, Distributors, Dealers and Advertising

Cleveland's lifespan was relatively short—only about seven years—but the marque did record some notable moments in history.

The Clark-Southwell-Hunter Company of Modesto, California, in midsummer of 1920 drove a Cleveland Six from Modesto to Yosemite National Park and returned with the fan belt removed and water pump inoperative to prove the efficiency of the cooling system. They supposedly towed a disabled vehicle several miles while performing this feat.

Later in 1920 a Cleveland Six was chosen as the pathfinder car for the *Dallas Times Herald* economy and durability run. Forty counties in Texas were chosen for this test and 1,185 miles were covered at an average speed of 20 miles per hour and an average of 15 miles per gallon of gasoline. The only problem encountered was a flat tire caused by a nail while crossing an old bridge.[1]

In 1922 a Cleveland was again chosen as a pathfinder car. The *Milwaukee Sentinel* sponsored an inspection tour of the new Highway 15 leading into Milwaukee. The Cleveland was driven 3,000 miles over a period of two months without a single failure.

In late summer 1924, Colonel King Stanley (also known as "Old Dead Shot"), the transcontinental traveler who had driven a Chandler from coast to coast several times, did the same thing in a "One Shot" Cleveland. Starting at Wellington, Colorado, the Colonel and his wife toured the Northwest and ended up in San Francisco where he led a caravan of fourteen Cleveland cars through the streets and received the key to the city from the mayor.

From San Francisco they were to travel to the Southwest before heading to Arizona and then eastward. Stanley reported that the Cleveland Six averaged about twenty miles per gallon of gasoline and never had any mechanical difficulties whatsoever.[2]

On Friday, November 3, 1924, Ralph Mulford drove a stock Cleveland Touring car to a record on Mount Diablo, California. Starting at the toll booth, he raced to the 4,000 foot summit over a distance of more than 11 miles in 0:22:36.6. The previous record was 0:25:00. This feat was accomplished at an average speed of 30 miles per hour and was officially observed by S. H. Halls, an Oakland newspaper representative.[3]

On Thursday, November 20, 1924, Ralph Mulford drove a Cleveland Six to a new record on Mount Wilson, California. He covered the nine and one-half mile climb of the treacherous mountain road in 0:24:47.4 and broke the former record of 0:25:48.5 held by Ralph DePalma.

W.P. Herbert Company, the Cleveland dealer in Los Angeles, sponsored the winning car and won the *Los Angeles Evening Express* permanent challenge trophy. The ascent was a total of 4,636 feet over a course with 144 sharp curves, no grade being less than 10 percent and none steeper than 16 percent. The car was strictly stock with the exception of the top and front fenders, which had been removed, and the addition of shocks for safety.[4]

On Wednesday night, December 3, 1924, at 9 p.m. starting at the Ferry building in San Francisco, a stock Cleveland Sedan driven by Charles Bowman, sales manager of the Chandler-Cleveland Motor Car Company of San Francisco, undertook a tortuous run to Portland, Oregon, and back. Bowman was assisted by Hart Brandon, service superintendent, and P.J. Newman, salesman for the San Francisco company. Blinding rain, snow storms and blizzards beset the team but 21 hours and 29 minutes later (21:29:00) they clocked in at the Western Union in Portland. The run was 4 hours and 4 minutes faster than the Shasta Limited, the fast Southern Pacific passenger train, on its scheduled run between the two cities.

Not resting on their record, the trio turned around and broke another record by arriving back in San Francisco 48 hours and 20 minutes (48:20:00) after leaving. The Cleveland had proven its ability to withstand mountains and foul weather by performing like the champion it was but the company was not satisfied with these results only. They wanted to know how it

Top, left: **1922 Cleveland Touring on one of many dependability runs (photograph courtesy Roger Anderson).** ***Top, right:*** **1923 Cleveland Touring chosen as official inspection car for Wisconsin Highway 15 opening.** ***Left, middle:*** **Colonel King Stanley on one of his transcontinental tours (photograph courtesy Roger Anderson).** ***Left, bottom:*** **The start of the record-breaking Mount Diablo Run (*Motor Age*, January 15, 1925).**

would stand up to rigorous speed tests and set out to pursue its ability on one of the famous tracks of that day.[5]

Sometime during December 1924 Ralph Mulford again drove the Cleveland Six to a record by piloting a stock Touring car to the end of the road in Icehouse Canyon, Mount Baldy, California, in 0:14:31.6, breaking the old record by 0:2:18.6. This feat was accomplished with the car in high gear and the gear shift lever sawed off. Cleveland was awarded the *Pomona Bulletin* permanent challenge trophy, given to the stock car making the best time, in high gear up the grueling ascent. This was the same car that set the Mt. Wilson record.[6]

Tuesday, December 16, 1924, saw a Cleveland Touring car on the famous 1¼ mile board track at Culver City, California. It had been stripped of its fenders and running boards and the windshield had been replaced with a small wind deflector. There, the Cleveland proved it could stand up to the speed trials as well. Ralph Mulford, who was doing most of Cleveland's competition driving and who could handle a race car under any conditions, drove the stripped-down racer 1,000 miles in 14:08:31.8 at an average speed of 70.6 miles per hour. The timing,

scoring and fluid replenishment were all supervised by Hal Weller of the American Automobile Association (AAA) and his assistant Joe Nikront. Another assistant, J.E. Bentz, observed the car while in the pits where only five quarts of water were added to the radiator during the run. They had no problems with tires as Firestone gum dipped tires were used. This was the car which Mulford had previously used in the Mt. Wilson and Mt. Baldy runs.[7]

The first run at the Culver Speedway did not satisfy Cleveland officials or Mulford, so he repeated the performance on Tuesday, January 27, 1925, by driving the Cleveland to an average speed of 80.6 miles per hour for the 1,000 miles in the time of 12:25:22.6

They had learned a few things on the first run which helped to make the second run successful. Larger headlights, mounted higher, a cowl mounted spot light and a reworked wind deflector were installed for the second run. Different tires were used and the running boards were reattached after having been removed on the first run. Just eight days later, on February 4, 1925, Mulford would pilot a Chandler around the same course at an average speed of 86.9 miles per hour for the 1,000 miles in a time of 11:29:54.[8]

During December 1924 a Cleveland Model 31 driven by C.H. Bigelow, a veteran Cleveland dealer from Los Angeles, covered the distance of 776 miles along the Arrowhead Trail between Los Angeles, California, and Salt Lake City, Utah in 20:02:0, averaging 38.76 miles per hour. The time beat the fastest Union Pacific train by 4:32:0 and the previous record by an automobile by 2:12:0. Of the 776 miles traveled,

***Top:* Ralph Mulford drives a Cleveland to a record on Mt. Wilson, California (*Automobile Topics*, January 31, 1925). *Middle:* Ralph Mulford receives the Los Angeles Evening Express Challenge Trophy for his record-breaking run on Mt. Wilson. *Bottom:* Ralph Mulford—just before the first run at Culver City, California, December 16, 1924 (factory photograph, courtesy Roger Anderson).**

188 were paved, 300 were dirt and 288 were over temporary routes and detours. The Cleveland Six left the Western Union Office at Salt Lake City at 4:30 a.m. on Sunday and arrived at the Western Union Office in Los Angeles at 11:32 p.m. the same day. The trip saw the Cleveland Six pass through Provo, Nephi, Beaver City, Cedar City, and St. George, Utah, then on to Las Vegas, Nevada, and through Barstow, Victorville and San Bernardino to Los Angeles.[9]

In late 1925 Cleveland staged a nationwide economy run. Eighty-six Cleveland cars were driven for 48 straight hours without having their engines stopped. These cars were driven all over the country and driving conditions varied greatly. While some had relatively straight concrete roads, others were subjected to dirt roads and hilly conditions. No two were exactly the same. Known as the National "One Shot" Non Stop Economy Run, this was a test to determine what the average car owner could achieve by driving a Cleveland. The Evans Motor Company of Akron, Ohio, won first and sixth place, having entered two cars.

The winner covered 2,236.1 miles at an average speed of 46.5 mph and averaged 28.3 miles per gallon of gasoline. The eight entries who achieved to best performance covered an average of 2,117.3 miles at an average speed of 44.1 mph and averaged 25.5 miles to the gallon of gasoline.

All 86 cars showed an average mileage of 1,565 for the 48 hours and an average speed of 32.6 mph with a gasoline consumption of 21.04 miles to the gallon. Each carried at least two passengers and an official observer was assigned to each vehicle for the 48 hours.[10]

During the summer of 1925 "Iron Man" Sargent Cole drove a Cleveland Six for 121¼ hours on the streets of Wilmington, Delaware, while handcuffed to the steering wheel. Cole was an aspiring actor and the publicity stunt probably was more for his own benefit than that of Cleveland. The engine was never stopped during the whole episode and the car traveled 1,565 miles with gasoline consumption averaging

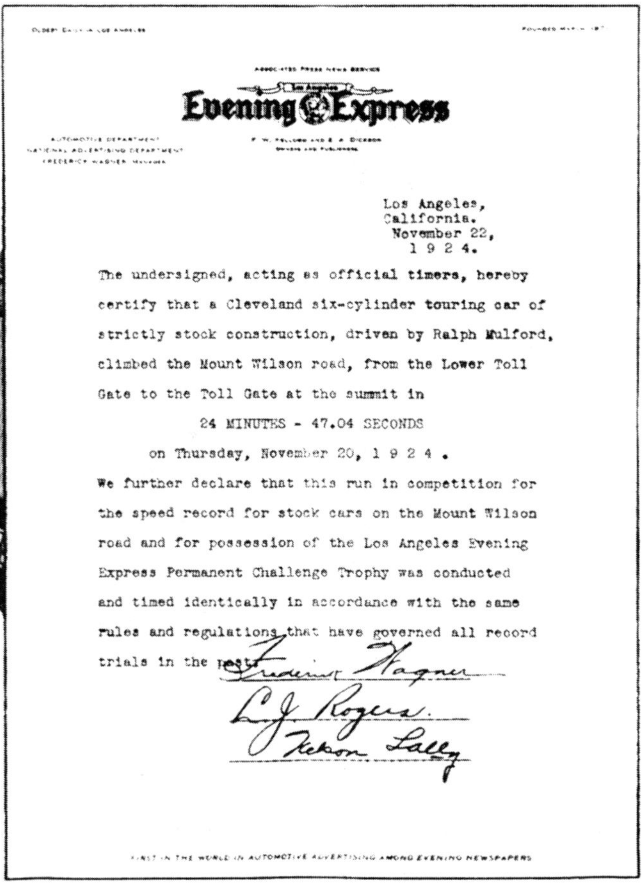

Evening Express

Los Angeles,
California.
November 22,
1 9 2 4.

The undersigned, acting as official timers, hereby certify that a Cleveland six-cylinder touring car of strictly stock construction, driven by Ralph Mulford, climbed the Mount Wilson road, from the Lower Toll Gate to the Toll Gate at the summit in

24 MINUTES - 47.04 SECONDS

on Thursday, November 20, 1 9 2 4.

We further declare that this run in competition for the speed record for stock cars on the Mount Wilson road and for possession of the Los Angeles Evening Express Permanent Challenge Trophy was conducted and timed identically in accordance with the same rules and regulations that have governed all record trials in the past.

Above: **The reward for Cleveland's record breaking run on Mt. Wilson.** ***Below:*** **Ralph Mulford pilots the Cleveland during the first record attempt at Culver City (factory photograph, author's collection).**

22 miles per gallon. Gasoline and oil were added while the car was in motion and Cole supposedly was given nourishment of light food and liquids. Nothing was said about a nature call while he was handcuffed to the wheel. The run ended at the *News Journal* building and the police chief sawed the handcuffs off while a large crowd cheered. This was pure dramatics as he could have just unlocked them.[11]

Some of the foregoing events were staged by the Cleveland Automobile Company, others by Cleveland dealers and still others by individuals. These are just a few of the many events in the life of the Cleveland. The Mount Diablo and Mount Wilson Hill climbs as well as both runs at the Culver City track were officially sanctioned events.[12]

Aftermath

After the merger of Chandler and Cleveland, the Cleveland continued to be built in the original factory for several months and bodies were also built there.

After Hupp bought Chandler-Cleveland they built bodies at the Cleveland plant until about 1934 but closed it down in October of that year. The Parker Appliance Co., later the Parker Hannefin Co., occupied the building in 1936. All machinery and equipment was removed and a few smaller manufacturers occupied the former machine shop.

Part of the factory still exists as a fairly modern building today. It has seen several tenants and was once occupied by the Cleveland Clinic but once again has been sold.[13]

Top: Celebrating the Culver City record, second run. *Middle:* The start of the National Economy Run—One Shot Non-Stop. *Bottom:* Participating in the National Economy Run—One Shot Non-Stop.

Distributors and Dealers

The Cleveland was designed and built to be a smaller, lower priced automobile than the Chandler for a number of reasons.

Initial cost and operating expenses were reason enough to own a Cleveland, but Chandler officials wanted a companion to the larger Chandler in order to keep their dealers from selling other brands. Most dealers sold two different lines of cars and some sold as many as three or more. If you could supply a medium priced car and one which would sell in the lower price bracket, it was less likely that the dealer would handle any other make. When the Model 31 was introduced, dealers had the advantage of having three distinct price ranges available and had less need to sell other brands.

Cleveland had the advantage of a built-in dealer network as most Chandler dealers took on the Cleveland line. However, there were many stand-alone Cleveland dealers.

The following is a short list of dealers who sold the Cleveland. No attempt has been made to determine which ones sold both lines.

Above: **Sargent Cole after completing his endurance run.** ***Below:*** **Block-Cleveland Company, Baltimore.**

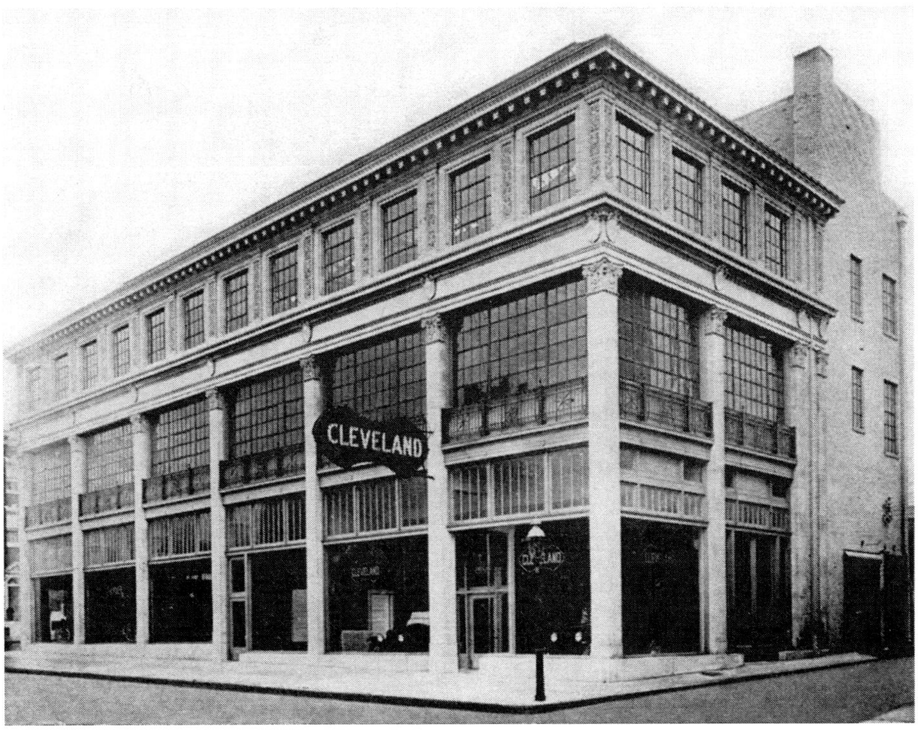

ABD Motor Company (Kansas City)
FWB Achen (Milwaukee)
B.A. Blenner (Richmond, Virginia)
Block-Cleveland Company (Baltimore)
C.C. Brown (Marion, Ohio)
Laverne C. Brown, Inc. (Brooklyn)
Buelte Motors Inc. (Rochester, New York)
Burmah Motor Sales Company (Rangoon, Burmah)
Campbell-Simpson Motor Company (Boise, Idaho)
Chandler-Cleveland Car Company (San Francisco)
Chandler-Cleveland Motor Car Company (Boston)
Clarke-Southwell-Hunter (Modesto, California)
L.S. Cobb (Fresno, California)
Dailey Automobile Company (Sioux Falls, South Dakota)
Euclid Motor Company (Cleveland)
Fitz Motor Car Company (Cambridge, Massachusetts)
J.E. French Company (San Francisco)
W.M. Harmon (Terre Haute, Indiana)
Mason B. Hatch (Buffalo, New York)
Thomas Hay & Son (Chicago)
W.P. Herbert (Los Angeles)
Herbert Brothers (Philadelphia)

Top: **Burmah Motor Works, Rangoon, Burma.** *Above:* **Peacock, Alexander & Hunter, Cleveland distributors for San Francisco.** *Right:* **A typical group of dealers supplied by one distributor (*Chan-Cleve Hub*, January 1921).**

Highland Motor Company (Denver)
Joseph C. Jones (Riverside, California)
Jones Chandler & Cleveland (Huntington, West Virginia)
Carl Jones Motor Company (Green Bay, Wisconsin)
Howard E. Kelly (Hamilton, Ohio)
Lawn Manor Motor Sales (Chicago)
C.H. Lines Motor Company (Fort Wayne, Indiana)
Main Garage (Conneaut, Ohio)
Malette Motor Company (Albuquerque)
McCarty-Greene Motor Company (Birmingham, Alabama)
McCord-Harris Company (Columbus, Ohio)
Millsap Motor Company (Cedar Rapids, Iowa)
(Continued on page 200)

CLEVELAND

Arctic, R. I., P. V. Auto Co.
Attleboro, Mass., Charles L. Rogers
Ayer, Mass., E. O. Proctor
Barton, Vt., Barton Auto Exchange
Bennington, Vt., G. Spencer Lee, 127 Branch Street
Berlin, N. H., Toohey Auto Co.
Bradford, Vt., Jacobs & Jacobs
Brattleboro, Vt., F. A. Betterley
Brockton, Mass., Bell-Gregory, Inc.
Central Falls, R. I., Wilford E. Lamarine
Centre Strafford, N. H., Lewis J. Brown
Claremont, N. H., J. H. Carroll
Concord, N. H., A. J. Boutwell & Son
East Greenwich, R. I., South End Garage
East Jaffrey, N. H., Louis F. Meyers
Fall River, Mass., Brainin Motor Co.
Foxboro, Mass., Clarence C. Fuller
Framingham, Mass., Framingham Motors Co.
Gardner, Mass., L. H. Parcher Co.
Georgiaville, R. I., Elmer W. Loomis
Gloucester, Mass., Gloucester Auto Sales Co.
Gt. Barrington, Mass., Berkshire Garage
Haverhill, Mass., George H. Smith
Henniker, N. H., Carl Rowe
Hingham, Mass., Wyman J. Curtis
Hudson, Mass., P. H. Lovett
Hyde Park, Mass., Albert Stonestreet
Keene, N. H., Burnell-Faulkner Co.
Laconia, N. H., J. S. Smith
Lawrence, Mass., Lawrence & Caswell, Inc.
Lebanon, N. H., E. A. French
Littleton, N. H., Moore's Garage
Lowell, Mass., C. A. Senter Auto Company
Lynn, Mass., Central Motors Co.
Malden, Mass., W. H. Pembrook
Manchester, N. H., Chandler & Cleveland Sales Co.
Manchester Centre, Vt., Gleason & Sykes
Nashua, N. H., Central Garage
Newburyport, Mass., Shattuck Motor Co.
Newport, R. I., Pelham Garage
North Adams, Mass., Barnard Bros.
Northampton, Mass., A. L. Gloyd
Norwood, Mass., O'Brien Bros.
Orange, Mass., Cleveland Sales Co.
Palmer, Mass., C. A. Smith
Pawtucket, R. I., Lewis E. O'Connor
Pittsfield, Mass., Berkshire Auto Co.
Plymouth, Mass., Old Colony Auto Sales Co.
Providence, R. I., Chandler Motors of Rhode Island
Rockland, Mass., Charles W. Briggs, 331 Market Street
Salem, Mass., Silsbury & Gamble Motors Co., 38 Leach Street
Shelburne, Mass., Bird Sales Co.
Springfield, Mass., Chandler Motors of Springfield, Inc.
Springfield, Vt., Adnabrown Garage
Stoneham, Mass., E. F. Bourgeau, 221 Main Street
Taunton, Mass., William McCarthy
Turners Falls, Mass., Turners Falls Garage
Waltham, Mass., MacGregory Garage, Inc.
Webster, Mass., City Garage
West Barnstable, Mass., Michelson & Atwood
Westerly, R. I., Frank G. Ahern
Westfield, Mass., Park Square Garage
Woburn, Mass., Salmon & Tobin
Woodstock, Vt., J. Martin & Moore
Woonsocket, R. I., Joseph E. Grenon
Worcester, Mass., Standard Motors, Inc.

Advertising the Cleveland (*The Literary Digest*, August 28, 1920).

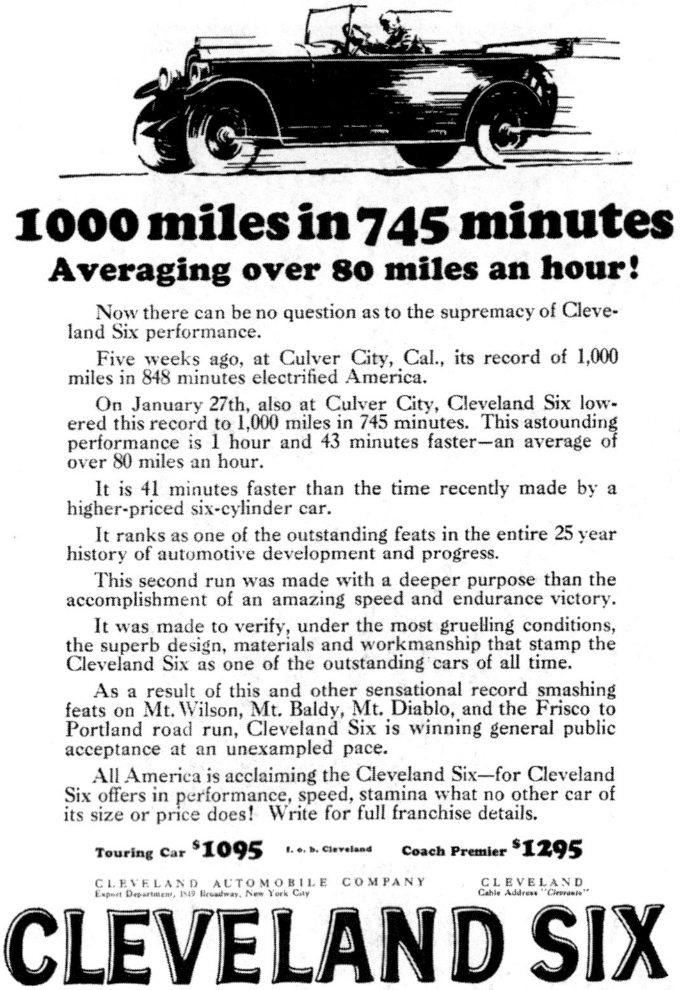

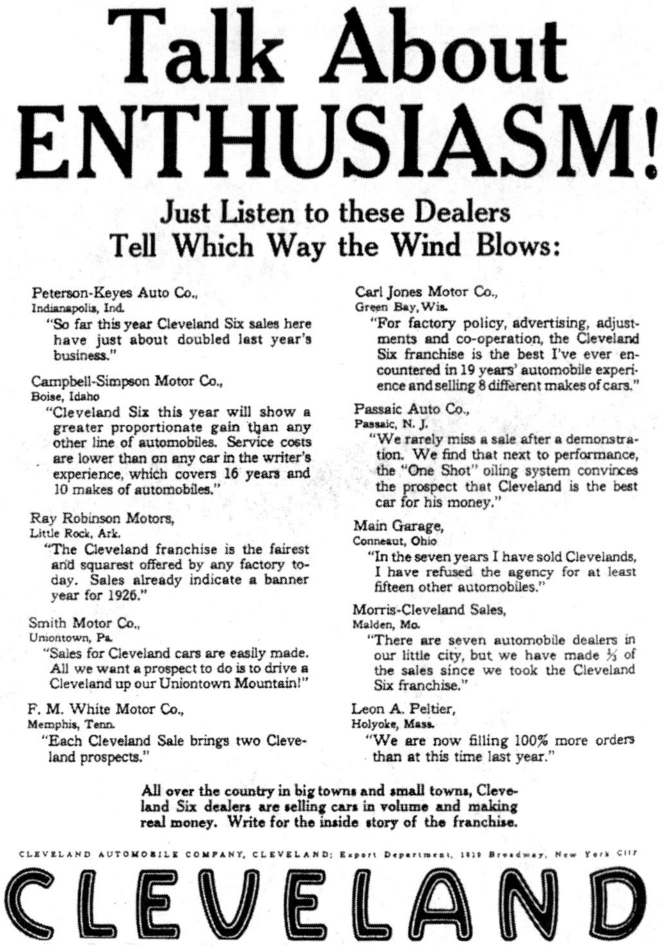

Top, left: **Selling speed (*Automotive Industries,* February 14, 1925). *Top, right:* Dealer testimonials (*Automobile Topics,* April 10, 1926). *Bottom:* 1921 Cleveland Five Passenger Sedan with special headlights and front bumper, posed with the Jimmy Hussey Theatrical Troupe.**

Top, left: **Al Wilson, barnstorming pilot, flew a "Jenny" and drove a Cleveland.** ***Top, right:*** **Cleveland ad (*The Literary Digest*, July 10, 1920).** ***Left, middle:*** **A portion of the Cleveland factory after Hupp ceased operations there (courtesy U.S. Department of Interior, National Park Service).** ***Left, bottom:*** **Main Cleveland factory after Hupp closed all operations there (courtesy U.S. Department of Interior, National Park Service).**

Cleveland main factory building after conversion to modern office space, circa 1970s (courtesy U.S. Department of Interior, National Park Service).

(Continued from page 196)
Monaca Motor Sales Company (Monaca, Pennsylvania)
Monmouth Auto & Tire Company (Newport, Kentucky)
Morris-Cleveland Sales (Malden, Missouri)
North Coast Automobile Company (Seattle)
E.R. Parker Automobile Company (Atlanta)
Passaic Auto Company (Passaic, New Jersey)
Peacock, Alexander & Hunter Company (San Francisco)
Leon A. Peletier (Holyoke, Massachusetts)
Peterson-Keyes Auto Company (Indianapolis)
Robertson & Malcolm (England)
Ray Robinson Motors (Little Rock, Arkansas)
Sherman-Duell (Jamestown, New York)
Smith Motor Company (Uniontown, Pennsylvania)
Stuber-Stone Sales Corp. (Detroit)
Stuyvesant Motor Company (Cleveland)
Vigilant Garage (W. Philadelphia, Pennsylvania)
Warren Auto Sales (Detroit)
Weamer Motor Company (Altoona, Pennsylvania)
Welbon Motor Car Company (Cincinnati)
F.M. White Motor Company (Memphis)
A.L. Zeckendorf Company (Cedar Rapids, Iowa)

Advertising

The Cleveland Automobile Company never advertised its product as extensively as the Chandler Motor Car Company did. Dealers were supplied with a steady stream of pamphlets and brochures, some quite colorful, and their annual catalogs were very descriptive.

Although Cleveland never used the better magazines of the day as extensively as Chandler, they did use those publications which were read by most citizens.

The trade publications were regularly used to get their message before the public as well.

• Seventeen •

Cleveland Specifications

1919 Model 40

Motor: Six cylinder, valve-in-head type, bore 3", stroke 4½", six cylinder cast en bloc separate from crank case; detachable cylinder head. Valve mechanism completely enclosed. Three bearing crank shaft of large diameter. Cam shaft and accessories driven by adjustable silent chain. Lubrication by gear pump positively driven by spiral gear from cam shaft.

Carburetor: Stromberg, fed by vacuum tank from 16 gallon tank at rear of chassis.

Ignition: Distributor and high tension coil. Bosch magneto optional at $45.00 extra cost.

Starting and Lighting: Gray & Davis two unit system.

Cooling: By centrifugal pump, cellular radiator and adjustable self-oiling, belt driven fan.

Transmission: Unit power plant construction with center control. Three speeds and reverse. Nickel steel gears and shafts. Main shaft mounted on annular ball bearings.

Clutch: Disc type.

Propeller Shaft: Fitted with double universal joints.

Rear Axle: Floating type. Pressed steel housing, spiral bevel gears. Timken bearings throughout. Chrome nickel steel drive shafts.

Front Axle: Drop forged I-beam. Chrome nickel steel spindles and gearing arms. Timken bearings in wheels.

Springs: Semi-elliptic front and rear; bronze and bushed eyes; rear springs underslung.

Steering Gear: Worm and sector type—irreversible—fitted with 18-inch walnut wheel.

Wheels: Wood—artillery type. Wire wheels (set of five) optional at $105.00 extra cost.

Rims: Firestone—Straight side—Demountable.

Tires: 32 × 4 non-skid.

Wheel Base: 112 inches.

Top: One-man type—fitted with door-opening curtains and bevel glass rear window.

Finish: Body—Cleveland blue upholstered in hand buffed, bright finished long grain leather. Hood, fenders and running board, black enamel. Wheels and chassis black.

Price

Touring Car (Five Passenger) $1385
Roadster (Three Passenger) $1385
Sedan (Five Passenger)
Coupe (Four Passenger)

1920 Model 40

Motor: Six cylinder, valve-in-head type—built complete in Cleveland Shops—bore 3" stroke 4½". Six cylinders cast en-bloc separate from crankcase; detachable cylinder head. Valve mechanism completely enclosed by covers. Three bearing crank shaft of large diameter, cam shaft and accessories driven by adjustable silent chain. Lubrication by gear pump positively driven by spiral gears from cam shaft.

Carburetor: Stromberg, fed by vacuum tank from 16 gallon tank at rear of chassis.

Ignition: Distributor and high tension coil. Bosch magneto optional at $46.50 extra cost.

Starting and Lighting: Bosch two unit system.

Cooling: By centrifugal pump, cellular radiator and adjustable self-oiling, belt-driven fan.

Transmission: Unit power plant construction with center control. Three speeds forward and reverse. Nickel steel gears and shafts. Main shaft mounted on annular ball bearings.

Clutch: Disc type.

Propeller Shaft: Fitted with double universal joints.

Rear axle: Floating type. Pressed steel housing, spiral bevel gears. Timken bearings throughout. Chrome nickel steel drive shafts.

Front Axle: Drop forged I-beam. Chrome nickel steel spindles and steering arms. Timken bearings in wheels.

Springs: Semi-elliptic, front and rear; bronze bushed eyes; rear springs underslung.

Steering Gear: Worm and sector type—irreversible—fitted with 18-inch walnut wheel.

Wheels: Wood—artillery type. Wire wheels (set of five) optional at $105.00 extra cost.

Rims: Firestone—straight side—demountable.

Tires: 32 × 4, non-skid on rear wheels.

Wheelbase: 112 inches.

Top: One-man type—fitted with door-opening curtains and bevel glass rear window.

Finish: Body—Cleveland blue upholstered in genuine hand-buffed leather. Hood, fenders and running board splasher—black enamel. Wheels and chassis black.

Prices

Touring Car (Five Passenger) $1465
Roadster (Three Passenger) $1465
Sedan (Five Passenger) $2475
Coupe (Four Passenger) $2375
Cord tires standard equipment with all models.

F.O.B. Factory

1921 Model 40

Motor: Six cylinder, valve-in-head type—built complete in Cleveland Shops—bore 3", stroke 4½", six cylinders cast en bloc separate from crankcase; detachable cylinder head. Valve mechanism completely enclosed by covers. Three bearing crank shaft of large diameter. Cam shaft and accessories driven by adjustable silent chain. Lubrication by gear pump positively driven by spiral gears from cam shaft.

Carburetor: Stromberg, fed by vacuum tank from 16 gallon tank at rear of chassis.

Ignition: Distributor and high tension coil. Bosch magneto optional at $45.00 extra cost.

Starting and Lighting: Gray & Davis two unit system.

Cooling: By centrifugal pump, cellular radiator and adjustable self-oiling, belt-driven fan.

Transmission: Unit power plant construction with center control. Three speeds and reverse. Nickel steel gears and shafts. Main shaft mounted on annular ball bearings.

Clutch: Borg and Beck.

Propeller Shaft: Fitted with double universal joints.

Rear Axle: Floating type. Pressed steel housing, spiral bevel gears. Timken bearings throughout. Chrome nickel steel drive shafts.

Front Axle: Drop forged I-beam. Chrome nickel steel spindles and steering arms. Timken bearings in wheels.

Springs: Semi-elliptic, front and rear; bronze bushed eyes; rear springs underslung.

Steering Gear: Worm and sector type—irreversible—fitted with an 18-inch walnut wheel.

Wheels: Wood—artillery type. Wire wheels (set of five) optional at $105.00 extra cost.

Rims: Firestone—straight side—demountable.

Tires: 32 × 4, non-skid on rear wheels.

Wheelbase: 112 inches.

Body: Fisher Body Corp.—outside door handles.

Top: One-man type—fitted with door-opening curtains and bevel glass rear window.

Finish: Body—Cleveland blue upholstered in genuine hand-buffed leather. Hood, fenders and running board, black enamel. Wheels and chassis black.

Prices

Touring Car (Five Passenger) $1685
Roadster $1685
Coupe (Four Passenger) $2690
Sedan (Five Passenger) $2795
Bosch Magneto Optional (extra on all models) $45

Above prices cover delivery in San Francisco and include freight and war tax. Prices taken from the San Francisco distributor catalog.

1922 Model 41

Motor: Specially designed six cylinder, built complete in Cleveland shops. Valve-in-head type, bore 3$\frac{1}{16}$" stroke 4½". Six cylinders cast en-bloc separate from crankcase. Combustion chambers are completely machined, thus ensuring uniform compression for each cylinder and reducing carbon accumulation to a minimum. Four point suspension. Valve mechanism completely enclosed. Three bearing crankshaft of large diameter eliminates engine vibration. Cam shaft and relative units are driven by adjustable silent chain. Lubrication by gear pump, positively driven by spiral gear from camshaft.

Carburetor: Stromberg, fed by vacuum feed system, from 16 gallon reservoir at rear of chassis.

Ignition: Distributor and high tension coil. Bosch magneto optional at slight extra cost.

Starting and Lighting: Bosch two unit system.

Cooling: By centrifugal pump, cellular radiator and adjustable self-oiling belt-driven fan.

Clutch: Disc type; friction disc of woven asbestos.

Transmission: Unit power plant construction with center control. Three speeds forward and reverse. Nickel steel gears and shafts; main shaft mounted on annular ball bearings.

Propeller Shaft: Fitted with double universal joints.

Drive: Hotchkiss type.

Front Axle: Drop forged I-beam. Chrome nickel steel spindles and steering arms. Timken bearings in wheels.

Rear axle: Floating type. Pressed steel housing, spiral bevel gears. Chrome nickel steel drive shafts. Timken bearings.

Springs: Semi-elliptic, front and rear; bronze bushed eyes and oil cups; rear springs underslung.

Steering Gear: Worm and sector type—irreversible—fitted with 18" walnut wheel.

Service Brakes: External contracting type, of ample size.

Emergency Brake: External contracting, mounted on rear of transmission; braking leverage takes place through the rear axle differential and is thereby equalized—no skidding in wet weather.

Frame: Channel—pressed steel of ample section—four cross members.

Wheels: Wood—artillery type.

Rims: Firestone—straight side—demountable.

Tires: Goodrich Silvertown or Goodyear Cord tires—32 × 4, standard equipment on all models.

Wheelbase: 112 inches.

Top: Clear vision, one-man type, covered with door-opening curtains and bevel glass rear window.

Colors: Touring, Cleveland blue; maroon is optional color. Roadster, surrey green with black fenders and cream colored wheels; Cleveland blue if desired. The Sedan and Coupe, Cleveland blue. Individual aluminum steps are standard equipment but running boards are optional with all models.

Equipment: Adjustable, ventilating type windshield; Cleveland winged nickel plated radiator cap; Motometer; speedometer; non-glare lenses; motor riven electric horn; foot rest in tonneau; electric tonneau light; robe rail; electric light on instrument board; tools and spare rim. A windshield cleaner is standard with the closed models.

Prices

Touring Car (Five Passenger) $1195
Roadster (Three Passenger) $1175
Sedan (Five Passenger) $1595
Coupe (Four Passenger) $1550

1923 Model 41

Motor—Specially designed, six cylinder, overhead valve type, built exclusively by Cleveland in its own shops. Bore 3$\frac{1}{16}$", stroke 4½"; motor develops over 45 h.p. Six cylinders cast en-bloc separate from crankcase. Crankshaft of generous proportions is held in alignment by three substantial bearings, thereby eliminating vibration. Adjustable silent chain drives cam shaft and relative units.

Lubrication: By gear pump positively driven by spiral gear from cam shaft. Saal oiling system throughout chassis.

Carburetor: Stromberg, fed by vacuum feed system from 16 gallon tank at rear of chassis.

Ignition: Bosch distributor and high tension coil. Bosch magneto optional at extra cost.

Starting and Lighting: Bosch two unit system.

Cooling: By centrifugal pump, cellular radiator and adjustable self-oiling, belt-driven fan.

Clutch: 10" disc type; friction discs of woven asbestos.

Transmission: Unit power plant construction with center control. Three speeds forward and reverse. Nickel steel gears and shafts. Main shaft mounted on Timken roller bearings.

Propeller Shaft: Fitted with double universal joints; oil lubricated.

Drive: Hotchkiss type.

Front Axle: Drop forged I-beam. Chrome nickel steel spindles and steering arms. Timken bearings in wheels.

Rear axle: Floating type. Pressed steel housing, spiral bevel gears, nickel steel gears. Chrome nickel steel drive shafts. Timken roller bearings.

Springs: Semi-elliptic, front and rear; bronze bushed eyes; rear springs underslung.

Steering Gear: Worm and sector type—irreversible—fitted with 18" serrated wheel.

Service Brakes: 14" external contracting type, lined with strong friction proof material.

Emergency Brake: External contracting, mounted on rear of transmission.

Frame: Channel—pressed steel of ample section—four cross members.

Wheels: Wood—artillery type, wire or disc optional at extra cost.

Tires: Goodyear or Oldfield 31 × 4 cord tires standard equipment with all models.

Top: Clear vision, one-man type covered with waterproof material, fitted with door-opening curtains and bevel glass rear window.

Colors: Touring, Cleveland blue; Roadster, surrey green with black fenders and cream colored wheels—Cleveland blue if desired. Four-Door and Two-Door Sedans both standard and special models, Cleveland blue. Sport model, beige brown.

Passenger Capacity: Five passenger Touring; three passenger Roadster; five passenger Four Door Sedan; five passenger Two-Door Sedan; five passenger Sport model.

Standard Equipment with Touring: Two-Door Sedan and Four-door Sedan; clear vision, windproof windshield, cowl ventilator, flat light reflectors, barrel type head lamps with cowl lights in duplicate, robe rail, speedometer, motor driven horn, dash light, tools and spare rim. Foot rest with Four-Door Sedan. Trunk rack featured with Two-Door Sedan. Sun visor with closed models.

Special Equipment furnished with Two-Door Special Sedans and Sport model. These types include all the standard equipment and the following which is special—windshield wiper, nickeled radiator, Motometer and winged cap, aluminum steps, disc wheels. Wire wheels at extra cost. Aluminum trunk rack and guards with Two-Door and Four-Door Special Sedans and Sport model but not with the Roadster. Rear vision mirror, trunk, front bumper, windshield wings and cleaner with Sport model.

All Prices F.O.B. Factory

Touring $995
Two-Door Sedan $1295
Four-Door Sedan $1495
Two-Door Special Sedan $1395
Four-Door Special Sedan $1595
Roadster $1085
Sport Model $1260

1924 Model 42

Motor: Six cylinder, specially designed, overhead valve type, built complete in Cleveland shops. Detachable head. Six cylinders cast en-bloc separate from crankcase. Crankshaft of generous proportions is held in alignment by three substantial bearings. Vibration is eliminated.

Carburetor: New type Stromberg, fed by vacuum feed system from 16 gallon tank at rear of chassis.

Ignition: Bosch distributor and high tension coil. Automatic spark advance. Electric generator and storage battery.

Starting and Lighting: Bosch two unit system.

Transmission: Unit power plant construction with center control. Three speeds forward and reverse. Nickel steel gears and shafts; main shaft mounted on Timken roller bearings.

Propeller Shaft: Fitted with double universal joints; lubricated by high pressure oiling system.

Drive: Hotchkiss type.

Front Axle: Drop forged I-beam. Chrome nickel steel spindles and steering arms. New ball type tie rod with automatic take up. Timken roller bearings in wheels and steering knuckle.

Rear Axle: Floating type. Pressed steel housing, spiral bevel, nickel steel gears. Chrome nickel steel drive shafts. Timken roller bearings throughout.

Springs: Semi-elliptic, front and rear; bronze bushed eyes; rear springs underslung.

Service Brakes: 14" positive acting, external contracting type, lined with substantial friction proof material.

Wheels: Wood—artillery type; wire or disc style optional at extra cost.

Tires: Goodyear or Firestone cord tires standard equipment. Balloon tires optional tires at extra cost.

Top: Clear vision type, covered with waterproof material, fitted with door-opening curtains and bevel glass rear window.

Colors: Touring, Cleveland blue. Touring De Luxe, Cleveland coach blue or blue devil blue. Standard Coupe and Two-Door and Four-Door Sedans, Cleveland blue. Special Coupe, Special Two-Door Sedan and Special Four-Door Sedan, Cleveland coach blue, optional finish blue devil blue.

Passenger Capacity: Five Passenger Touring; all Sedans accommodate five passengers; three passenger Coupe.

Standard Equipment with Touring, Coupe, Two-Door Sedan and Four-door Sedans: adjustable windshield; cowl ventilator; speedometer; barrel type head lamps; cowl lights in duplicate, flat light reflectors, motor driven horn, robe rail; electric light on instrument board, dome light in closed cars, tools and spare rim; foot rest with Four-Door Sedan; trunk rack featured with Two-Door Sedan.

Special Equipment: furnished with Two-Door and Four-Door Special Sedans, Special Coupe and Touring De Luxe. These types include all the standard equipment and the following which is special—nickeled radiator of new design; Motometer and winged cap and mirror; aluminum trunk rack, guards, and windshield cleaner. Steps, bumper and tonneau light with Touring De Luxe.

Two-Door Sedan $1295
Four-Door Sedan $1395
Coupe $1245
Special Two-Door Sedan $1395
Special Four- Door Sedan $1495
Special Coupe $1345
Touring Car $1045
Touring De Luxe $1145

All Prices F.O.B. Factory

1925 Model 43

Serial # 60,000–70,299

Motor: Entirely new "L" head type, specially designed by Cleveland engineers and built entirely in Cleveland shops. Water cooled six cylinder design. Developed H.P. 60. Suspension—rear of the motor is substantially bolted to arms running integral with flywheel housing. Front is securely bolted to frame cross member.

Cylinders: Six cast en bloc separate from the crankshaft. Detachable cylinder head. Bore 3⅛". Stroke 4¾".

Pistons: Cast iron, 4¼" long. Fitting clearance, .003".

Piston Rings: 3 to a piston. One oil wiping ring 3⁄16", two ⅛".

Connecting Rods: I-beam section. Drop forged steel; light in weight yet strong and substantial at points where greatest stress comes.

Valves: Six 1 5⁄16 clear diameter. Valves enclosed on right side. 30^0 seat 5⁄16" lift. Double valve springs eliminate periodic vibration and sticking valves at high motor speeds.

Crankshaft: Drop forging; design of generous proportion and perfectly balanced, eliminates any vibration period. Three substantial bronze backed Babbitt lined bearings hold crankshaft in perfect alignment.

Camshaft: Drop forging, carbonized and hardened; accurately mounted on three bearings. Designed to maximum area of valve opening and at the same time a gradual opening and closing to insure quiet operation.

Lubrication: Motor: full pressure system to all crankshaft connecting rod and cam shaft bearings. Oil pump is gear type, located in the bottom of the oil pan, driven from spiral gears from the crankshaft. This high pressure oiling system allows the interior working parts of the motor to float constantly on a film of oil—no metal contact. The thickness of the film being .003 on the connecting rod bearings and .0025 on the main bearings. Oil capacity 7 quarts. Chassis features "One Shot" automatic lubrication system.

Carburetor: Schebler Model S-1.

Ignition: Bosch distributor and high tension coil. Electric generator and storage battery. Automatic spark advance eliminates spark knock.

Starting and Lighting: Bosch two unit system.

Cooling System: Water capacity 4 gallons, circulated by pump driven through a flexible disc coupling on the accessory shaft and therefore has no radial load on its bearings. Water enters the cylinders in the center of the block and flows directly beneath the valve passages thus insuring equal cooling at both ends of the cylinder. Each cylinder barrel is completely surrounded by circulating water. The thickness of the radiator core and frontal areas insures ideal cooling in any climate.

Wheelbase: 115 inches.

Clutch: Borg & Beck 10" single plate type. Ease in shifting is a notable advantage. Design of mounting insures perfect alignment.

Transmission: Unit power plant construction with center control.

Propeller Shaft: Fitted with flexible fabric discs instead of mechanical type. No lubrication necessary. Rattle and back lash entirely eliminated.

Rear axle: Floating type. Pressed steel housing, spiral bevel, nickel steel gears. Chrome nickel steel drive shafts. Adjustable. Timken roller bearings are used. Special design permits positive adjustment.

Front Axle: Drop forged I-beam. Chrome nickel steel spindles and steering arms. Ball type tie rod with automatic take up for wear. Timken roller bearings in wheels. Ball bearings in steering mechanism.

Springs: Semi-elliptic type, front and rear; bronze bushed eyes; rear springs underslung. Leaves are chrome vanadium steel.

Service Brakes: 14" positive acting, external contracting type.

Four-Wheel Brakes: Specially designed 14" external contracting type optional at extra cost.

Wheels: Wood—artillery type; disc style optional at slight extra cost.

Balloon Tires: 31 × 5.25 Goodyear or Firestone.

Colors: Touring, Cleveland blue; Touring De Luxe, Cleveland blue or blue devil blue. Standard Coupe and Sedans, Cleveland blue; Special Coupe, Cleveland blue or blue devil blue.

Standard Equipment with Touring, Coupe, Five Passenger Sedan and Four-Door Sedan: adjustable windshield; cowl ventilator; speedometer; barrel type head lamps; cowl lights in duplicate, anti-glare reflectors; motor driven horn, robe rail; electric light on instrument board, dome light in Sedan models, tools and spare rim; foot rest with Four-Door Sedan and Touring De Luxe; trunk rack featured with Two-Door Sedan.

Special Equipment furnished with Touring De Luxe and Special Coupe. These types include all the equipment specified on the standard models and the following which is special: nickeled radiator of new design; Motometer and winged cap; aluminum trunk rack, guards, rear vision mirror and windshield cleaner. Front double spring bumper and tonneau light with Touring De Luxe model only. Aluminum top bows with Special Coupe.

Two-Door Sedan $1395
Four-Door Sedan $1495
Coupe $1295
Special Two-Door Sedan $1295
Special Four- Door Sedan $1725
Special Coupe $1395
Touring Car $1095
Touring De Luxe $1195

All Prices F.O.B. Factory

Prices taken from Automobile Trade Journal, July 1924, p. 59; Motor Age, January 1, 1925, p. 56; Automotive Industries, January 8, 1925, p. 56.

1926 Model 43

Serial # 70,300–77,525

Mileage Motor: Powerful "L" head type, specially designed by Cleveland Six engineers and built in its entirety in Cleveland Six shops.

Cylinders—Six cast en bloc separate from the crankshaft. Detachable cylinder head. Bore 3⅛". Stroke 4¾".

Pistons: Cast iron, 4¼" long. 3 piston rings to a piston. Fitting clearance, .003". One oil wiping ring 3⁄16", two plain ⅛".

Connecting Rods: I-beam section. Drop forged steel; light in weight yet substantial at points where greatest stress comes.

Valves: Six 1 5⁄16 clear diameter. Valves enclosed on right side. 30 degree seat 5⁄16" lift

Crankshaft: Drop forging; design of generous proportion and perfectly balanced, eliminates any vibration period. Three substantial bronze backed bearings hold crankshaft in perfect alignment.

Lubrication: Motor—full pressure system to all crankshaft connecting rod and cam shaft bearings. Oil pump is gear type, located in the bottom of the oil pan, driven from spiral gears from the crankshaft. This high pressure oiling system allows the interior working parts of the motor to float constantly on a film of oil—no metal contact. Oil capacity, 7 quarts.

Carburetor: Schebler Model S-1.

Ignition: Bosch distributor and high tension coil. Automatic spark advance eliminates spark knock.

Starting and Lighting: Bosch two unit system.

Cooling System: Water capacity 4 gallons, circulated by pump, driven through a flexible disc coupling on the accessory shaft. The thickness of the radiator core and frontal areas insures ideal cooling in any climate.

Wheelbase: 115 inches

Clutch: Borg & Beck 10" easy in shifting, single plate type. Design of mounting insures perfect alignment.

Lubrication: Chassis—One Shot automatic lubrication system (covered by Bowen Products Corp. patents) oils every moving chassis part.

Transmission: Unit power plant construction with center control.

Propeller Shaft: Fitted with flexible fabric discs instead of mechanical type. No lubrication necessary. No rattle and back lash.

Rear axle: Floating type. Pressed steel housing, spiral bevel, nickel steel gears. Chrome nickel steel drive shafts. Adjustable Timken roller bearings.

Front Axle: Drop forged I-beam. Chrome nickel steel spindles and steering arms. Ball type tie rod with automatic take up for wear. Timken roller bearings in wheels. Ball bearings in steering mechanism.

Springs: Semi-elliptic type, front and rear; bronze bushed eyes; rear springs underslung. Leaves are alloy steel.

Service Brakes: 4" positive acting, external contracting type.

Emergency Brake: Located on rear of transmission. Operates on the propeller shaft, and then through the rear axle differential. Equalization in braking effort is assured.

Four-Wheel Brakes: Specially designed 14" external contracting type optional at extra cost.

Balloon Tires: 31 × 5.25.

Finish: Duco finish, with all models.

Colors: Special Sedan, Coupe and Touring car, Cleveland blue with bead in contrasting color. Sport Touring is in two tone sage brush green.

Standard Equipment with closed cars, Special sedan and Coupe: adjustable one-piece, clear vision windshield; speedometer; barrel type head lamps; cowl lights in duplicate, antiglare reflectors; windshield cleaner; motor driven horn, electric light on instrument board, tools and spare rim. Foot rest and robe rail with Sedan.

Standard Equipment with open cars, Touring and Sport Touring: adjustable windshield, cowl ventilator, speedometer, barrel type head lamps; cowl lights in duplicate. Flat-lite reflectors, motor driven horn, electric light on instrument board, robe rail, tools, and spare rim. Tonneau light, windshield wings, front bumper, rear bumperetts, trunk rack and bars, trunk, disc wheels, rear vision mirror, windshield cleaner and foot rest with Sport Touring.

Special Sedan	$1295
Special Coupe	$1175
Coach Premier	$1295
De Luxe Sedan	$1595
Sport Sedan	$1625
Special Touring	$1095
Sport Touring	$1245

All Prices f.o.b. Factory. These prices taken from the Cleveland Six Messenger, Volume 5 # 9–10, September–October 1925, pp. 4–5.

1926 Model 31
Serial # 63,901–65,597

Engine: New and specially designed "L" head type Mileage Motor built complete in Cleveland Six plants. Clean and compact. Develops 45 H.P. Detachable cylinder head.

Cylinders: Six cast en bloc integral with the crankshaft. Bore 3" Stroke 4¼".

Pistons: Cast iron, 3²³⁄₃₂" long. 3 pistons rings to a piston. One oil wiping ring 3⁄16", two 1⁄8".

Connecting Rods: Drop forged steel I-beam section; light in weight, yet sturdy in design. All rods perfectly balanced.

Valves: Six 1¼", clear diameter. Valves enclosed on right side. 45 degree seat, 5⁄16" lift.

Crankshaft: Drop forging; carbonized and hardened; mounted on three large bearings.

Lubrication: Motor—full pressure system to all crankshaft, connecting rod and cam shaft bearings. Positively driven gear type oil pump. All motor parts work constantly on a film of lubricant.

Carburetor: Tillotson type.

Ignition: Bosch distributor and high tension coil. Automatic spark advance.

Manifold: Specially designed to properly preheat various grades of gasoline. Promotes easy starting.

Cooling System: Water capacity 2½ gallons, circulated by pump, driven through a flexible disc coupling on the accessory shaft. Water enters the cylinders in the rear of the block and flows around valves, plugs and combustion chambers. The thickness of the radiator core is ample for satisfying cooling.

Clutch: Borg & Beck single plate, heavy duty type.

Lubrication: Chassis—One Shot automatic lubrication system (covered by Bowen Products Corp. patents) oils every moving chassis parts.

Transmission: Unit power plant construction with center control.

Propeller Shaft: Flexible fabric discs are used. No lubrication is required, yet long service is assured without rattle and backlash.

Rear Axle: Floating type. Housing of pressed steel. Spiral bevel, nickel steel gears. Chrome nickel steel drive shafts. Adjustable Timken roller bearings.

Front Axle: Drop forged I-beam. Chrome nickel steel spindles. Timken roller bearings in wheels.

Springs: Semi-elliptic type, front and rear; bronze bushed eyes; rear springs underslung.

Service Brakes: 12⅜" external contracting type.

Emergency Brake: Located on rear of transmission. Operates on the propeller shaft, and then through the rear axle differential. Equalization in braking effort certain.

Four-Wheel Brakes: Specially designed 12⅜" external contracting type optional at extra cost.

Balloon Tires: Lee. Standard.

Colors and Finish: Duco with all models. sedan in two tone color; Coupe finished in Cleveland blue; Touring car in sage brush green; Touring De Luxe, two tone sage brush green. Raised bead in contrasting color with all models.

Equipment with Sedan, Coupe, Touring, and Touring De Luxe: Adjustable windshield and cowl ventilator with Touring and Touring De Luxe, new ventilating one-piece clear vision windshield with Sedan and Coupe. Speedometer, head lamps, Flat-lite reflectors, and cowl lights of barrel type design. Motor driven horn, electric light on instrument board, tools and spare rim with all models. Dome light, robe rail, foot rest, sun visor and windshield wiper with Sedan. Rear view mirror, windshield wiper, windshield wings, double bar front bumper, rear bumperetts, trunk rack, trunk and natural wood wheels with Touring De Luxe.

Touring Car	$895
Sedan	$995
Coupe	$975
Touring De Luxe	$1025

All Prices F.O.B. Factory. Prices taken from the Cleveland Six Messenger, Volume 5 # 9–10, September–October 1925, pp. 4–5.

Identification

To identify the year and model of a particular Cleveland, see identification charts at the end of Chapter Twelve.

Appendix A: Press Release of 1915 Nonstop Mexico to Canada Run

The following is the full text of a press release issued by Earl V. Armstrong, Inc., the Southern California Chandler distributor that sponsored a nonstop drive from Mexico to Canada in September–October 1915. A brief account of the event appears in Chapter Eleven.

Foreword

In one hundred and twenty hours of continuous travel, a Chandler Six touring car, "stock" in every detail save for two additional headlights and taped springs, traveled from Tia Juana, Mexico, to Blaine, Canada, without a single stop of either wheels or motor.

According to official observation, but one pint of water was added to the original capacity of the radiator during the entire trip. The gasoline consumption averaged sixteen miles to each gallon. The oil consumption averaged 200 miles to each quart.

The distance recorded on the speedometer was 1898.5 miles.

The Chandler had been run approximately 2000 miles before making this trip.

****

"Aw, my deah chap, but wasn't it awfully fatiguing?"

Thus spoke a true son of Britain in the refreshment room of the palatial Hotel Vancouver, in Vancouver, Canada. Dust covered, weary, un-bathed and unshaven for a hundred and twenty hours, five hardy Californians had just completed the most remarkable automobile trip in the annals of long distance motoring.

They had traveled, in a Chandler Six stock touring car, from Mexico to Canada—1898.5 long miles—WITHOUT A SINGLE STOP!

And the English comment was of physical feeling; there was no thought for the wonderful mechanical assemblage that had permitted traveling this great United States from end to end and without a halt of any sort, without a break in the rhythmic music emanating from under the hood, without a falter in the ever forward movement of the Goodyear shod wheels.

Never was a car called on to do more—and never did a car perform its part more like a thoroughbred. The Chandler was a veritable symphony of turned steel. On boulevard and city street, across desert sand and through rough mountain pass—under every condition of road of climate to be met in this country—it responded to each whim and mood of its drivers. "Wide open" or at snail's pace, the result was ever the same; there was no lull in the song of power and strength that hummed its way from one extreme boundary to the other, and established a record for reliability that will long endure.

****

But let us start with the five adventurers, and go straight through from beginning to end, from, Mexico, across 1898.5 miles of strenuous activity to the Canadian Customs House at Blaine, just outside of Vancouver. Let's even precede this with a few hours in Los Angeles, where the greatest no-stop run in history was conceived.

Al Waddell, full of "pep" and go, was looking around for a real automobile "stunt." He was tired of the prosaic. He wanted to do something that would make the whole country look up in attention, that would set the entire automobile contingent agog.

Al wandered down Hope Street, dispirited, obsessed with

the idea that there was nothing new under the sun in motordom. He halted in front of the salesroom of the Chandler Motor car Company of California. The door swung open, then shut—and the great test for man and machine was a'borning.

"Don," queried Al, "doesn't the Chandler want to stir up some excitement?"

"Surest thing you know, Al," replied Manager Don Smith, and straightway the Waddell idea was announced.

"What's the matter with a run from Mexico to Canada, without a stop of either WHEELS OR MOTOR?"

The suggestion was almost overpowering in its scope, in the bare suggestion of traversing the country from end to end without a single halt. A no-stop-of-the-motor run was big enough, but not to stop the wheels—WOW!

But the Chandler Sales Manager was nothing if not game. "Come right in and we'll see what Mr. Armstrong decides," and forthwith he and Al repaired to the sanctum of President Earl V. Armstrong.

The Armstrong verdict was quickly rendered.

"The Chandler can do it. Today is Thursday. Can you start Sunday?"

Waddell's "yes" was also snappy.

The Armstrong orders went forth. "Take that car that has run about two thousand miles. Equip it with swivel searchlights on each side, tape the springs, and change those fabric tires for Goodyear Cords"—and that was all the special attention the Chandler received on the eve of its greatest of all feats.

Mapping the route, arranging the details of supplies and the countless other necessities which man and motor must needs feel on a border-to-border tour seemed to be accomplished almost of themselves. One visit to Frank Jordan of the Automobile Club of Southern California, and within an hour each foot of the journey was visioned—the distance between towns, the condition of roads, where narrow mountain passes increased the hazard of being stopped by a blockade—each detail was in hand for study and discussion.

To make a long story short, at shortly after eight o'clock Sunday morning [September 26, 1915] the Chandler and its crew were at the starting line. From the foot of the international boundary monument grim, unfed Mexico stretched away to the South, the desolation broken only by the gaudy flags of Tia Juana fluttering in the lazy breeze.

The tarrying was brief. Lew Falk of the Panama-California exposition pasted seals on motor starting pedal and on the tires, the Universal Motion Picture operator turned his crank—and the great run made its entry into motoring history.

There was no excitement. Don Smith, at the wheel, followed an exact hundred yards behind his pilot. Up from the border and through somnolent San Diego the Chandler traveled as does the ordinary tourist. A few miles out and the pilot turned back—and the no-stop crew was left to its own resources and the prowess of the Chandler.

Fifty miles had been recorded on the speedometer, and the first cause for anxiety made itself manifest. A narrow stretch of temporary roadway, winding its ruddy span around some highway construction, loomed in awful nearness. "What if we meet another machine or a team, and are forced to stop or back up?" was the thought uppermost.

Right there began the use of a "system." Over the sides of the car scrambled three members of the crew. Up the roadway they raced, like a lot of renegade monkeys. There was no halt until the other end of the narrow place had been reached.

The energy was mis-spent. There was not a machine or team in sight, save one that was traveling in the same direction, far ahead and in no apparent danger of being stalled.

Almost to the minute, according to schedule, the Three Flags Traveler rolled into Los Angeles and came to a halt—ALMOST—in front of the Chandler sales room. Slowly the wheels revolved, and everybody seemed to move at once. It was the first test, for the car was due to take on gasoline and, if needed, oil and water.

The "patent" funnel was adjusted to the tank, and the fluid poured into the receptacle with scarcely the loss of a drop. There was plenty of oil, and water, too, but some overzealous aide had unscrewed the radiator cap and poured in a few drops of aqua pura before it was realized that not a bit was necessary.

Leaving Tijuana (note that the hood sides have been removed).

Claude Hunter took the wheel, and out of town the Chandler wended its way, the crew for the first time testing meals served truly "a la cart"; Mr. Armstrong had provided plentifully, and until far out San Fernando Road the travelers munched steak and potatoes, and traveled onward into pie and coffee.

Boquet Canyon provided the first REAL sample of strenuous activity. There seemed to be hundreds of machines coming toward the city. Ahead raced another Chandler, Lionel and Earl Armstrong waving like mad, literally pushing other cars aside in order to provide unobstructed passage. Once—a tense half minute—a machine was almost lifted from the pass, and the Chandler crawled by with not a second to lose before throttling down would have become an impossibility, and with very thin hairs spanning the distance between it and the stalled vehicle at the roadside.

Once through the canyon the no-stop crew was left to its own resources.

The Armstrong machine turned back, and Hunter relinquished the wheel to Andrew Kooler for the run over the Mojave Desert. The travelers began to adjust themselves for the long weary grind in front; the observers divided their "watches"; the order to "trim ship" found each man ready for his vigil.

At Mojave the car was slightly behind schedule, for the Boquet had cut into running time fearfully. Just the same, gasoline was taken on as a precaution; also, the depot lunch encounter received a slight play as a fortification against the run over Tehachapi.

The descent of White Wolf grade was easy, and the Chandler rolled into Bakersfield on time. Gasoline was again waiting, and with a full tank the easy run to Fresno was begun, with every prospect of being ahead of schedule.

It seems almost impossible to lose the way between Visalia and Fresno—but the Chandler's lookout accomplished it. Forty miles on the wrong highway were rolled off before the right trail was finally picked up.

And once the crew, now all wide awake, almost located "finis" for the no-stop feature of the trip. Hunter was at the wheel, and he piloted the car into a farmyard to ask the way. From the outside it looked like a big yard. Inside it was so pitifully small. A swerve toward the farm house—and all KNEW the trip was over. The next second the Chandler was plowing down perfectly good young orange trees—and was on its way with an unblemished record. Hunter had taken the only means of egress from the trap. Those two farmers who watched him cut down their potential profits in citrus fruit are probably standing there, wide-eyed, yet, wondering which asylum was shy five inmates.

Fresno gave the Travelers a royal reception. Ben Knoth, sent from Los Angeles, to act as relief driver from there on, took the wheel and piloted the Chandler up and down Eye Street, while the crew tried its best to create a shortage in the ham and egg market.

Fed and happy, the history makers were on their way at last, convoyed by George Murdock, "Hutch" and a host of other well wishers. All were anxious, for fifteen miles out of Fresno a new record was due to be established. In Chicago, last summer, poor old Harry Grant traveled five hundred and four miles without a stop. This was the only authentic instance of an automobile's traveling so far without a single halt being recorded. So when the speedometer registered 505 miles all felt that the Chandler had scored heavily. At least one world's record for consistency would not be denied.

From Fresno to Stockton (a tarrying for gasoline and food) and from Stockton to Sacramento (another supply station) all went as merrily as a wedding bell. A sharp spurt through a narrow river bed and one or two wordy brushes with "hoggish" teamsters served to enliven the run.

But beyond Sacramento began real "grief"; the boulevards were past, and not until well into Oregon would they be encountered again.

The wrong road—and much the poorer—was taken into Marysville. Ben Knoth and Joe Waddell took the driving and observing watches, and Al Waddell and Jack Griffin scouted for food. Hunter, tuckered out, lay on the edge of the sidewalk, wooing the sleep that would not come.

Out of Marysville, Griffin took a turn at the wheel; the

Taking on gasoline at Stockton, California, while the car is in motion.

road was good and fairly marked, and Chico and Red Bluff were reached without incident. At Chico the "night owls" had a chance to see the crew in action, for a new supply of gasoline was in order.

Knoth took the wheel at Red Bluff. A confusion of guiding signs—and at daylight the Chandler was far into the foothills, thirty miles off its rightful path. Redding, with its promise of breakfast, was reached many hours off schedule.

There was only one way to avoid a ferry—and a necessary stop of the forward movement of the Chandler's wheels. This was to traverse a narrow canyon and follow the Pitt River, via Fall River Mills, which consumed a good 10 hours extra time in making the detour.

A pilot was absolutely necessary, so one was engaged. Up hill and down dale, through narrow gorge and into heavily wooded mountain pass, the Chandler was led. Past Ingot, with its great deserted boarding houses, its piles of abandoned mining equipment, by Montgomery Creek, then the state salmon hatchery, to Fall River Mills, the car fought its way against obstacles in the shape of grades and narrow roads, well sprinkled with teams.

Not until McCloud was reached did good roads come again, and almost with their coming came grief. The road was lost again, Mount Shasta, stark and grim in the moonlight, was ever in sight. Its snow-clad sides served as a beacon, reminding each and every member of the crew that it was COLD.

At Hornbrook, on the Southern Pacific, it seems that the parade of freight trains is endless. But Al Waddell was cold—and mad! He was ready to battle the whole railroad system. Fortunately—both for Al and for the no-stop Chandler—a real human switchman was found. In a jiffy he had comprehended the great features of the trip. In another jiffy the long line of box cars had been divided, and half a dozen engines gave whistling cheer to the machine as it crossed the tracks to a free road. And that switchman did not stop there, for he acted as friend and guide while the car was taking on gasoline and finding the right highway beyond.

California was soon left behind, but the rise into Oregon almost spelled a finish for one member of the party. Joe Waddell in the observer's seat directed Hunter onto the wrong road. Then, in getting aright again, he was forced to open and close some gates in order to allow the machine to pass. Up the grade went the Chandler, but the guide was unable to follow. Ben Knoth and Al Waddell proved Good Samaritans, helping the exhausted pilot to a place where the car was running slowly again.

Medford and breakfast were reached in broad daylight. More gasoline, and all was ready for the run through Grants Pass, and on into the broad valley that would lead into Portland.

All would have been well—only the Chandler's crew harkened to the siren, the voice of a "short cut." Result: Roseburg was reached just before dark. Hazards innumerable had been overcome, for the narrow trail into Canyonville was liberally besprinkled with teams and other machines.

And then came more trouble. The highway was being improved. The Chandler was forced through virgin ground. In some places there were no other wheel marks to guide the pilot as he skirted around rocks and through dense clumps of trees. But the result was the same, for the wheels revolved over forward. What if Eugene was reached hours behind schedule?

Fifteen miles out of Eugene Al Waddell, in the observer's seat, awakened to the fact that the road to Albany and Portland, via Harrisburg, contained that dread bugaboo, a Ferry. A quick scanning of the Blue Book revealed the fact that the highway through Corvallis and then on to Albany was clear—the Willamette was spanned by a bridge!

It takes time and careful driving to find a turning place and a retracing of the road back to Junction City, but Al proved a valuable pilot. At last the right road was reached, but not until night watchmen had been disturbed and their slumbers broken. Salem was reached at daylight, and the entire Chandler crew was driven nearly into a frenzy. The gasoline tank was almost dry, and not a garage was open. Joe Waddell paced the streets like a loosened wildcat. He pounded on doors, ran here and there, and finally, just when it seemed that all the hard work

A jaunt around Portland, Oregon.

and ceaseless vigil to make a no-stop run must go for naught, he found a garage man. Oh! What a relief!

There are two or three first class roads leading into Portland from Oregon City, and that's why the Chandler missed a reception committee well worth while. Portland was on the lookout for the Chandler, for it was due to provide the greatest feature of the entire run from Mexico to Canada—the Chandler was to be allowed to cross the mighty Columbia on the railroad bridge. Save for the ferry, there is no other way to get from Portland to Vancouver, on the Washington side.

Entering the railroad bridge.

Never before had it been suggested that one lone automobile tie up five great transcontinental railroads, and acquire unto itself exclusive use of a great five million dollar structure. That's the reason why Superintendent A.H. Davidson and his assistant, Mr. Wegener, almost laughed at the Dulmage-Manley emissaries when the Portland agents for the Chandler suggested such a thing. But behind the Dulmage-Manley men came Douglas Shelor, and Shelor had with him Chester Mooers and a host of others. From scornful Mr. Davidson and Mr. Wagener became enthusiastic—and the great obstacle in the path of the no-stop travelers was removed.

No, not quite. Getting over the long span was no mean feat in itself, even if transcontinental trains were all sidetracked. There were scores of switches to be jumped; there were "frogs" galore; and there were more than three miles of rough ties to be ridden before the other end was reached.

Here again all Portland came to the rescue. Mr. Davidson himself was in charge of the laborers laying planks. Mr. Wegener ran here and there, forcing his gangs to top speed. And all the time the "draw" in the middle of the mighty Columbia was set, a bar against steamers large and small seeking a passage up or down the river.

The good offices of the Portlanders did not stop there. Their guests were fed and refreshed on the other side of the river, and a fleet of pilot cars led the way northward. For more than an hour the convoy pointed a clear way, and once again the Chandler and its crew were left to their own devices. And once again were these resources taxed to the utmost. Somewhere, near Toledo, the road was lost again. To make matters worse, a stranded autoist informed the no-stoppers that the bridge was being repaired—that the ferry must at last be utilized.

"If there's half a bridge up, we'll build the other half" was the grim response, and the Chandler picked its way toward the expected obstacle. By fallen trees, over heaps of brush, and at last onto the approach of the bridge—and the bridge was all there. It was clear sailing again!

Then came another test. Rain, the first of the trip, was falling, and it was nec-

Ready to cross the railroad bridge over the Columbia River.

essary to not only put up the top, but also to get skid chains onto the rear wheels—WHILE ON THE GO.

Hunter was at the wheel, Knoth and Al Waddell, on the side, accomplished their feat at the very first essay. Joe Waddell, and Griffin, on the other wheel, were less skillful. Time after time they were forced to try until finally both the inside and outside snaps were hooked, and the car was away again under full sail. The siren's allure was again followed out of Centralia—and the road was again lost. It was almost daylight before Tacoma was reached, and fully light before Seattle was left behind.

Then came a day of slippery grades and wet clothes. The highway was fine and good time was made. At Bellingham the reception committee was again on the job, with the glad tidings that the long weary grind was almost at an end. The border line and Canada was right at hand!

Perhaps the news didn't act as a tonic on the five tired travelers! It seemed like months since any member of the crew had slept. It was certain, as one look would prove, that none had shaved ever. Only the Chandler seemed to be oblivious of the nearness of the end. It purred its contented song even more cheerily than at starting. One or two little body "squeaks" were the only evidence that it had traveled more than 1800 miles without a falter.

***Top:* The finish at Blaine, Canada. *Bottom:* The boys who made it happen—five days without stopping car or engine over two thousand miles of travel.**

Then came Canada [Friday, October 1]—and the welcome end. First the United States Customs House, where the accommodating officials issued a passport on the run, even stretching a point by taking the serial numbers of the tires while the wheels revolved as the Chandler ran around in a short circle.

A few minutes later—and it was all over. A neat young Canadian Customs official came to the door of the little house. "Let me be the very first to congratulate you all" was his cheery salutation. "Here are your permits to enter Canada and good luck to you," and the greatest run in the history of automobiling had been accomplished.

Vancouver, a few miles beyond, hailed the no-stop pilgrims with shouts of acclaim. Everywhere they were given the right of way. Even the Englishman before mentioned—at the opening of this narrative—was glad to welcome the dirty, peaked motorists. Perhaps it was just thoughtlessness that caused him to neglect recognition of what Chandler Six had accomplished—or perhaps he really didn't know what wonders the car had performed.

The Chandler car was in charge of Claude H. Hunter, driver, assisted by Don Smith, Ben Knoth, and Andrew Kooler, relief drivers, A.L. Waddell and Jack Griffin, official observers, and Joe Waddell, Universal Motion Picture Corporation camera operator and assistant observer.

Thanks for aiding in the success of the no-stop run is due to Messrs. Lew Falk of the Panama-California Exposition, Douglas Shelor and Chester Mooers, of Portland, Messrs. Davidson and Wegener of the S.P. & S. Ry., the Dulmage-Manley Company, the Thompson–La Casse Company, and countless others who assisted materially at many points along the way.[1]

Appendix B: Chandler Dealer Contract, 1916

As of 1916, this is the contract dealers signed in order to sell Chandler automobiles. Terms were rather harsh toward the dealer, granting Chandler the right to determine what models and body styles it would ship, requiring full payment prior to shipment, compelling the dealer to accept an agreed-upon minimum number of cars per month, and leaving the dealer to collect from the shipper for any damage a car suffered in transit.

Agreement

Chandler Motor Car Co.

Cleveland, Ohio

AND

____

OF

____

1916-1917

THIS AGREEMENT made at Cleveland, Ohio, this.......day of..............191..,
between THE CHANDLER MOTOR CAR COMPANY of Cleveland, Ohio, hereinafter called the Manufacturer, and............................of............................,
hereinafter called the Dealer,

Witnesseth That

THE MANUFACTURER AGREES:

ONE: To grant, and it hereby does grant, to the Dealer, subject to the conditions and stipulations hereinafter expressed, the right from the............day of...................., 191..,
to the 30th day of November, 1917, but only during the continuance of this contract, to sell new Chandler Motor Cars to residents within the following described territory and not elsewhere:

....

....

....

....

....

That during the existence of this contract it will not knowingly sell or authorize any other person to sell its new Chandler cars to residents of said territory except for export to foreign countries. It is not to be held liable, however, for sales made to residents thereof by persons not specifically authorized by it so to do, and it expressly reserves the right to sell new Chandler Cars to persons, firms or corporations in said territory in exchange or in total or partial payment for advertising, supplies, materials or merchandise purchased or contracted for by it, and also to sell to anyone therein second-hand or shop-worn motor vehicles of any make whatsoever.

TWO: To ship for delivery to the Dealer, f. o. b. cars or boat at Cleveland, in the monthly allotments hereafter set forth................................(......) Chandler cars, of such current models as the Manufacturer may elect, at the net prices per car indicated on the attached schedule for said contracted number of cars—it being agreed that the Manufacturer reserves the right to change its standard car models and the list prices, net prices and rebates set forth in said schedule, or any one or more of them, at any time without notice, all such changes, whether of prices, rebates or models thereafter to govern this contract and to supersede those previously in force.

SCHEDULE OF MONTHLY ALLOTMENT OF CARS

	1916	1917											
During	Dec.	Jan.	Feb.	Mar.	Apr.	May	June	July	Aug.	Sept.	Oct.	Nov.	Total
No. of Cars													

After the Dealer has paid for the number of cars above contracted for, he shall be entitled to the rebate per car in force to him for such number at the time the respective cars were paid for by him; and on each car taken by him beyond said number, he shall be entitled to the net price, and rebate, if any, in force under this contract at the time such additional cars are respectively paid for.

THREE: To sell to the Dealer, Chandler automobile parts, except accessories, at a discount of....................per cent. (......%) from the list price for the same, current at the time of shipment.

FOUR: To replace defective parts returned under the guaranty herein given by the Manufacturer to the Dealer, provided that such part is returned to the Manufacturer by the Dealer, tagged with the number of the car from which the same was taken, the name and address of the owner, the date of sale of the car by the Dealer, and such other information as the Manufacturer may require, within forty-five (45) days after the replacing part was shipped by the Manufacturer and provided further that the Manufacturer, whose decision shall be final in this regard, shall deem such returned part defective within the meaning of the guaranty. All parts and accessories returned by the Dealer to the Manufacturer shall be accompanied by instructions for their disposition; if full instructions therefor have not been received by the Manufacturer within thirty (30) days after the receipt by it of such parts and accessories, the Manufacturer may make such disposition of the same as it may choose, and shall not be liable to the Dealer or any other person therefor. No credit shall be allowed except on the conditions above stipulated.

THE DEALER AGREES:

FIVE: To accept the automobiles mentioned in Clause TWO above, at the times, in the quantities and at the prices therein mentioned, and to pay for the same in cash or certified check, on or before delivery thereof to the carrier, or, at the election of the Manufacturer, upon presentation of draft therefor with exchange attached to the bill of lading. In case the Dealer fails to pay said draft on presentation—without this however constituting an excuse for his failure so to do—(a) he shall be chargeable with interest on such draft at six per cent. (6%) per annum from date of presentation together with all demurrage charges and all other expenses and losses necessarily incurred by reason of his failure to pay the same when presented, and (b) the Manufacturer at its option may recall said draft and ship and dispose of said cars elsewhere and charge the Dealer with all losses suffered through the Dealer's failure to pay for same including the original carrying charges, demurrage and all expenses and such part of the carrying charges and expenses incurred by the transfer, as the Manufacturer may deem equitable. All claims for errors, shortages, rebates and allowances other than for replacements the Dealer shall make within ten (10) days after the receipt of the goods. The drafts above mentioned, together with the bills of lading attached thereto, may be discounted, sold or transferred by the Manufacturer, and the transferee shall then have the same rights and the Dealer shall be under the same obligations with respect thereto, the cars represented by the bills of lading and the other matters specified in this clause, as are respectively given to the Manufacturer and imposed on the Dealer hereunder; and if the transferee offers to endorse and deliver the bills of lading to the Dealer or his order upon his paying the draft and making the other payments above stipulated, then the Manufacturer shall be regarded as having fulfilled its obligations hereunder with respect to the cars represented by said bills of lading.

SIX: To advertise vigorously and use his best efforts within the territory granted him to sell Chandler automobiles; to establish therein as soon as possible at all places where competing automobiles are sold, subdealers who, considering competition and other conditions in their localities, shall properly and to the satisfaction of the Manufacturer represent, display and push the sale of Chandler cars. To apprise the Manufacturer, before taking up the sale of any make or makes of automobiles other than those he is selling at the time of signing this contract, of his intention so to do. Not to sell directly or indirectly any Chandler Cars to residents outside of or for shipment outside of said territory without the written consent thereto of the Manufacturer and the Dealer in the territory where the purchaser resides; to report monthly to the Manufacturer or more often if called upon by it, all sales of Chandler cars, giving motor number, purchaser's name and address, and date of delivery, also the number of cars of each type in stock, the number of orders on hand for future delivery, the names and addresses of interested prospects and such other vital information as the Manufacturer may require.

SEVEN: To maintain a suitable sales room and service station satisfactory to the Manufacturer for the display and care of Chandler automobiles; to give at all times to Chandler users courteous and efficient repair and other service at reasonable prices; to keep on hand a stock of new Chandler automobile parts to the value, at current list prices, of not less than $.........., and to make no charge to owners of Chandler cars for such parts as the Manufacturer replaces or supplies gratis for use thereon; and to keep in stock, clean and in good order at all times, a complete line of Chandler cars of the current model.

EIGHT: To employ regularly and continuously as territorial traveling men or sales representatives not less than..........competent men whose duty it shall be to establish sub-dealerships and to be of general assistance to sub-dealers in the development of Chandler sales in their territories. To employ regularly for mechanical assistance to Chandler sub-dealers and owners of Chandler cars in sub-dealers' territories not less than..........skilled traveling mechanics or service men.

NINE: To pay to the Manufacturer in cash not later than the 15th of each month, for purchases of parts of the previous month; and not to make deductions from remittances for merchandise returned or for other claims until receipt of a credit memorandum therefor. For payments made within the time provided above the Dealer shall receive a discount of ten per cent. on his parts' account, but no discount shall be allowed on any parts' account unless paid in full as per statement rendered by the Manufacturer; and on failure of the Dealer to make payment as above, the Manufacturer may thereafter ship all parts and accessories to him C. O. D.

TEN: To pay to the Manufacturer at the date hereof in cash, the sum of............... ....Dollars ($...........). This sum shall, however, be returned to the Dealer on the expiration of this contract, or, if sooner canceled, as below provided, then at such cancellation or expiration, less only such sum as may be then due from the Dealer to the Manufacturer for current bills or upon other obligations, but the Dealer agrees first to return to his sub-dealers such portion of their deposits as they may, in the judgment of the Manufacturer, be entitled to.

ELEVEN: That the Dealer will not sell or offer for sale any new Chandler automobiles or parts at less than the Manufacturer's then current list prices therefor, except to regularly appointed sub-dealers of the Dealer, approved by the Manufacturer, and to them only on the condition that they likewise shall not sell them at less than the list prices current at the time of the sales by them; —all sub-dealers' contracts shall be executed in triplicate, and shall set forth clearly the discounts granted the sub-dealer on Chandler cars and parts and also the territory assigned to him. An exact signed copy of each sub-dealer's contract shall be deposited with the Manufacturer immediately on execution.

TWELVE: That the Manufacturer,—or, at its option, a Committee of three disinterested Chandler Dealers appointed by the Manufacturer,—shall be authorized to decide all disputes arising out of the alleged infringement, whether intentional or unintentional, by one Chandler Dealer of the territorial rights of any other Chandler Dealer, such decision to be final and binding on the Dealers. In no event, however, shall any claim lie against the Manufacturer by reason of such infringement.

THIRTEEN: That if the word "CHANDLER" is used in the name under which the Dealer's automobile business is conducted, he will, upon the cancellation or other termination of this contract or upon the request of the Manufacturer, discontinue the use of the same therein, and that he will thereafter neither directly nor indirectly use the same in connection with any automobile or motor vehicle business whatsoever in which he is interested or with which he is connected.

It is further agreed:

FOURTEEN: That the Manufacturer reserves the right to modify the Dealer's territory at any time during the life of this contract if, in the opinion of the Manufacturer, the Dealer is not properly promoting the sale of Chandler Cars in all or any part of the territory designated above.

FIFTEEN: That full performance by the Dealer at the times and in the manner stipulated is a condition precedent to performance by the Manufacturer hereunder, and that failure on the part of the Dealer to make any payments or perform any obligations required of him hereunder at the times and as herein stipulated and upon request by the Manufacturer, shall release the Manufacturer at its option from all further obligations hereunder.

SIXTEEN: That this is a personal contract and is not transferable by operation of law or otherwise in part or in whole without the Manufacturer's written consent, and that the insolvency or bankruptcy of the Dealer, the making of an assignment for creditors by him or the appointment of a receiver or trustee for him, shall be a termination of this contract without further action, and shall render the same void, but this shall not release the Dealer from the payment of any sum which he may then owe the Manufacturer. The Manufacturer shall have the right to cancel this contract at any time by giving to the Dealer notice to that effect either by registered letter, telegram or cable; and the Dealer shall have the right to cancel this contract at any time upon like notice to the Manufacturer provided that the Dealer has up to the time of such cancellation made all his payments and carried out all his obligations as required of him under this contract to said date.

SEVENTEEN: That all the agreements of the Manufacturer hereunder are made subject to strikes, lockouts, floods, fires, accidents, inability to get freight cars, delay or failure of contractors or manufacturers to deliver parts, material or equipment, and any other causes beyond the Manufacturer's control; and any failure or delay of the Manufacturer to deliver goods under this contract due to any of the above causes, shall not constitute a breach thereof or a failure of performance thereunder.

EIGHTEEN: That the Dealer hereby agrees to bear all loss, damage or injury to automobiles or goods shipped for delivery to him hereunder arising from theft, accident, or other cause after delivery thereof by the Manufacturer to the Common Carrier, and neither the Manufacturer nor his transferee shall be liable to the Dealer therefor. But this shall not constitute a passing of title to the cars or goods so shipped to the Dealer until fully paid for by him in cash.

NINETEEN: That the Manufacturer makes no warranties or representations as to goods shipped hereunder other than those contained in the guaranty published in the catalogue last issued by the Manufacturer prior to shipment of the goods in question.

TWENTY: That the Dealer is merely a purchaser hereunder and is not authorized or empowered to act as agent, accept service of process, transact business, incur obligations, make representations, warranties or promises, for or in the name of the Manufacturer, or to bind or obligate the Manufacturer in any way whatsoever.

TWENTY-ONE: That this instrument constitutes the entire agreement between the parties and that no variations thereof or additions thereto, shall be valid or binding on the Manufacturer except at its option unless they are made in writing and signed by the Manufacturer's President, Treasurer or Sales Manager, and a copy of them duly signed by the Dealer is deposited with the Manufacturer.

TWENTY-TWO: That the failure of the Manufacturer at any time to enforce any of the provisions of this contract or to exercise any option or right thereunder, or at any time to require performance by the Dealer of any provisions thereof, shall in no way be construed as a waiver of such provisions or rights, nor in any way affect the validity of this contract or any part thereof, or the right of the Manufacturer thereafter to enforce any of its provisions.

TWENTY-THREE: That this contract is to be governed by and construed according to the laws of the State of Ohio. It is understood, however, that this is a general form of Contract, designed for use in foreign countries as well as in the United States of America, wherever the Manufacturer may desire to sell automobiles, and that any provision herein which in any wise contravenes the laws of any country, state or jurisdiction, shall be deemed not to be a part of this contract therein, but this shall not in any way affect the validity of the balance of the contract therein.

TWENTY-FOUR: That the concellation or termination of this contract shall not release the Dealer, unless at the option of the Manufacturer, from the obligation to pay for goods shipped up to the time the Manufacturer receives or has notice of the cancellation or termination, nor from the payment of any other indebtedness to the Manufacturer. The Manufacturer shall not be obligated to ship any cars after such cancellation or termination and may recall any cars already shipped but not yet paid for by the Dealer. The Manufacturer shall, moreover, on the termination of this contract by expiration, cancellation or otherwise, have an option for thirty days from the date of termination to purchase from the Dealer at the then current net Dealers' prices, all or any part of his stock on hand of cars or other goods.

TWENTY-FIVE: This contract expires by limitation on November 30th, 1917.

THE CHANDLER MOTOR CAR COMPANY

By......................................

....

Chapter Notes

Chapter 1

1. Katz, John F., "Chandler: Built to Master a Mountain—and More," *Automobile Quarterly* 24: 4 (Fourth Quarter 1986), pp. 422–437; "New Men and Money at Lozier," *Motor*, September 1912, p. 102; "Leave Lozier for New Project," *Automobile Topics*, January 18, 1913, p. 703; Fisher, Tom (Historian), *Historic American Engineering Record,* Heritage Conservation and Recreation Services, U.S. Department of Interior, Washington, D.C., Document # HAER OH 11-G, p. 2; "Chandler Motor Car Company Its Name," *The Automobile*, February 6, 1913, p. 437.

2. "Trade Personals," *The Horseless Age*, July 2, 1913, p. 13; Kimes, Beverly Rae, "Lozier: The Big One That Got Away," *Automobile Quarterly* 7:4 (Spring 1969), pp. 348–365; Mulford, Ralph, "Racing with Lozier: A Memoir of Ralph Mulford," *Automobile Quarterly* 7:4 (Spring 1969), pp. 366–385; Goddard, Stephen B., *Colonel Albert Pope and His American Dream Machines*, Jefferson, NC: McFarland, 2000, p. 157; "New Organizations at Three Chandler Centers," *Chandler Bulletin* 6:8, August 1919, p. 3; "What the Industry Is Talking About," *Motor*, February 1926, p. 82; H.A. Lozier & Company envelope (1895) and Letterhead; "Lozier Admits Insolvency," *Motor Age*, December 10, 1914, p. 19; Philippi, Dick, "The Lozier," *The Horseless Carriage Gazette* 21:2, March–April 1959, p. 22.

3. *Ibid.*; Philippi, Dick, "The Lozier," *The Horseless Carriage Gazette* 21:2, March–April 1959, pp. 8–27; "Cases decided in the Superior Courts of Record of the state of New York," Volume 53, January 1, 1907.

4. Lyman, Olin, "A Famous Automobile Designer's Secret of Success," *Ambition* (publication of International Correspondence School) 17:2; *The Journal of the Society of Automotive Engineers*, March 1919, p. 149.

5. "Trade Personals," *The Horseless Age*, January 8, 1913, p. 97; "Lozier Men Resign to Make New Car," *The Horseless Age*, January 22, 1913, p. 175; "Leave Lozier for New Project," *Automobile Topics*, January 18, 1913, p. 703.

6. "Emise Organizes New Company," *Automobile Trade Journal*, February 1913, p. 108; "Emise Motor Car Company Formed," *The Automobile*, January 23, 1913, p. 277.

7. Chandler Sales Manual: "History of Company—1925," pp. 1–2; "Lozier Ex-Lieutenants Launch the Chandler Six," *Motor World*, February 6, 1913, p. 10.

8. "The Chandler Six," Chandler Motor Car Company brochure with temporary Detroit, Michigan, address, circa 1913; "Chandler Officials in Cleveland," *The Horseless Age*, March 19, 1913, p. 532.

9. Rose, William Ganson, "Cleveland—the Making of a City," Cleveland, OH: The World Publishing Company, 1950, p. 537; "Wheelman's Big Day—The C.W.C. Tournament Begins This Afternoon," *Cleveland Plain Dealer*, August 26, 1892, p. 5.

10. United States Federal Census for 1880–1930, various locations, U.S. Census Bureau, Washington, D.C., via Ancestry.com, 1/15/2013; U.S. passport applications, National Archives and Records Administration (NARA), Washington, D.C.; Cuyahoga County, Ohio, Marriage Records and Indexes, 1810–1873, via Ancestry.com, 1/15/2013; Beaumont Family Tree, via Ancestry.com, 1/15/2013.

11. United States Federal Census for 1900–1930, various locations, U.S. Census Bureau, Washington, D.C., via Ancestry.com, 1/15/2013; World War I registration cards, 1917–18, via Ancestry.com, 2/14/2012; Ohio Deaths, 1908–1953, https://family search.org/.pal, 2/14/2012; "Opens Factory Branch in City," *Cleveland Plain Dealer*, February 19, 1911, p. 55.

12. United States Federal Census for 1900–1930, various locations, U.S. Census Bureau, Washington, D.C., via Ancestry.com, 1/15/2013; New York Passenger Lists, 1820–1957, via Ancestry.com, 1/15/2013; Lyman, Olin, "Famous Automobile Designers Secret of Success," *Ambition* (publication of International Correspondence Schools), Scranton, Pennsylvania, 17:2, pp. 1–4; "Officers of the Society," *The Journal of the Society of Automotive Engineers*, March 1919, pp. 47–49.

13. United States Federal Census for 1900–1930, various locations, U.S. Census Bureau, Washington, D.C., via Ancestry.com, 1/15/2013; Earl, Philip I., *"This Was Nevada,"* Nevada Historical Society, June 14, 1998; "Death of Charles A. Emise, Chandler Vice-President, Marks Passing of a Real Pioneer of the Industry," *Chandler Bulletin* 8:10, October 1921, p. 3.

14. U.S. passport applications, 1795–1925, National Archives and Records Administration (N.A.R.A.), Washington, D.C., via Ancestry.com, 1/15/2013; United States Federal Census for 1890–1920, various locations, U.S. Census Bureau, Washington, D.C., via Ancestry.com, 1/15/2013; Ohio Deaths, 1908–1932, Ancestry.com, 1/15/2013; "Opens Coast Branch, Lozier Puts Sales System in Effect in San Francisco," *Cleveland Plain Dealer*, July 16, 1911, p. 5B; "Hall Goes to Detroit," *Automobile Topics*, November 11, 1911, p. 277; "Chandler Officers Ready to Greet Visitors," *Chandler Bulletin*, Convention Edition, January 23, 1923, p. 1; "Officers of Chandler Company Photographed at Factory," *Chandler Bulletin* 10:1, February 1923, p. 3.

15. United States Federal Census for 1900–1930, various locations, U.S. Census Bureau, Washington, D.C., via Ancestry.com, 1/15/2013; Lois Johnson's Family Tree, rootsweb.ancestry.com, 1/15/2013; U.S. Passport Applications, 1795–1925, National Archives and Records Administration (N.A.R.A.), Washington, D.C., via Ancestry.com,1/15/2013; New York Marriage Index, 1866–1937, Ancestry.com, 1/15/2013.

16. United States Federal Census for 1900–1920, various locations, U.S. Census Bureau, Washington, D.C., via Ancestry.com, 1/15/2013; Erlewine Family Tree, Ancestry.com, 1/15/2013; Michigan, Find a Grave Index, 1805–2011, Ancestry.com, 1/15/2013; "Prominent Men in Trade Who Assume New Duties," *Motor World*, February 20, 1913, p. 10.

17. United States Federal Census for 1890–1930, various locations, U.S. Census Bureau, Washington, D.C., via Ancestry.com, 1/15/2013; World War I Registration Cards, 1917–18, Ancestry.com, 1/15/2013; Ohio Deaths 1908–1932, Ancestry.com, 1/15/12.

18. "Chandler Locates in Cleveland," *Motor Age*, February 20, 1913, p. 17; "Chandler Factory in Cleveland," *The Horseless Age*, February 9, 1913, p. 86.

19. "Chandler Buys Factory Site," *The Automobile*, March 27, 1913, p. 713; "Chandler Orders New Plant," *Motor Age*, March 27, 1913; Fisher,

Tom (Historian), *Historic American Engineering Record,* Heritage Conservation and Recreation Services, U.S. Department of Interior, Washington, D.C., Document # HAER OH 11-G, p. 3.

20. *Green Book of Motor Stocks,* 5th Ed., New York: Dunham & Co., ca. 1919, pp. 20–21; Fisher, Tom (Historian), *Historic American Engineering Record,* Heritage Conservation and Recreation Services, U.S. Department of Interior, Washington, D.C., Document # HAER OH 11-G, p. 3.

21. "Chandler Motor Car Company Its Name," *The Automobile,* February 6, 1913, p. 437; Chandler Sales Manual: "History of Company—1925," pp. 1–2; Fisher, Tom (Historian), Historic American Engineering Record, Heritage Conservation and Recreation Services, U.S. Department of Interior, Washington, D.C., Document # HAER OH 11-G, p. 3.

22. "The New Chandler Six," *The Horseless Age,* March 5, 1913, p. 456; "Chandler Stock Good for Deposits," *Automobile Topics,* February 15, 1913, p. 27.

23. "Chandler Moving Into New Plant," *The Automobile,* August 7, 1913, p. 264; "Cleveland Car Makes Remarkable Run," *Cleveland Plain Dealer,* March 9, 1913, p. 22.

24. "First Chandler Six Still Useful," *Michigan Manufacturer and Financial Record,* June 2, 1913, pp. 8–9; Letter from Chandler Motor Car Company to C.S. Ransom, Albany, New York; Letter from C. S. Ransom to Amos Post, Catskill, New York, July 5, 1913; "First Chandler Cars Are Shipped," *Cleveland Plain Dealer,* August 3, 1913, p. 8., "Chandler 'Old No 3' Car Goes Merrily Along in Spite of Age," *Chandler Bulletin* 4:2, March 1917, p. 2.

25. "New Chandler Company Directors," *The Horseless Age,* August 20, 1913, p. 298; "New Incorporations," *The Horseless Age,* February 5, 1913, p. 307; "New Incorporations," *The Horseless Age,* January 19, 1915, p. 53.

26. "Not Only a Six You Can Afford to Buy—But a Six You Can Afford to Run," *The Saturday Evening Post,* Inside front cover, July 26, 1913; "Honest Comparisons to Convince Muddled Buyers," *The Saturday Evening Post,* November 15, 1913, p. 50.

27. "Chandler—Built by Men Who Know," Chandler Motor Car Company, owner's manual, circa July 1913.

28. "Design of a Car Body," U.S. Patent Office, Patent # 45,579; "Chandler Six of Light Construction," *The Automobile,* May 8, 1913, p. 994; Philippi, Dick, "The Lozier," *The Horseless Carriage Gazette* 21:2, March–April 1959, pp. 8–27.

29. "A True Lozier in Every Line and in Every Requirement of Service and Luxury," *The Automobile,* October 15, 1912, pp. 105–108; "Herein we present a complete table of the features the ideal Automobile should possess—We also present the CHANDLER—its features, late 1913 Chandler brochure distributed at January 1914 New York Auto Show.

30. "Chandler Parts and Prices," Chandler Motor Car Company Parts Book for Models 14, 15, 15 B, 16 and 17; "Characteristics of Chandler Lightweight Six Illustrated," *Motor Age,* December 11, 1913, p. 39; "A Briggs Body Plant," *The Automobile,* September 28, 1916, p. 543.

31. Schipper, J. Edward, "Two Buicks Win 500-Mile Reliability," *The Automobile,* December 11, 1913, pp. 1092–1097, 1121.

Chapter 2

1. "A Year's Service Has Not Suggested One Single Mechanical Improvement," *The Saturday Evening Post,* February 21, 1914, p. 67; "Chandler Made in Six Cylinders," *The Automobile,* January 1, 1914, p. 53.

2. "Choice of the Biggest, Strongest Distributors," *The Automobile,* February 26, 1914, pp. 96–97; "Herein we present a complete table of the features which the ideal Automobile should possess—We also present the CHANDLER—its features," late 1913 Chandler brochure distributed at January 1914 New York Auto Show.

3. "Chandler $1,785," *The Saturday Evening Post,* March 21, 1914, p. 71.

4. Chandler Motor Car Company, Owner's Manual, Model 15, circa January 1914; Chandler Motor Car Company, advertising booklet, Light Six at $1,785, circa 1914.

5. "Choice of the Biggest, Strongest Distributors," *The Automobile,* February 26, 1914, pp. 96–97.

6. "Which Light Weight Six Will You Buy?" *The Saturday Evening Post,* April 18, 1914, p. 60.

7. "Chandler Closed Cars for 1915," *The Literary Digest,* October 31, 1914, Chandler Motor Car Company advertising booklet, Light Six at $1,785, Model 15, circa 1914.

8. "Chandler Made in Six Cylinders," *The Automobile,* January 1, 1914, p. 53; "A Year's Service Has Not Suggested One Single Mechanical Improvement," *The Saturday Evening Post,* February 21, 1914, p. 67.

9. "Chandler," *The Horseless Age,* January 7, 1914, p. 15; Merksamer, Gregg D., *A History of the New York International Auto Show,* New York, New York: The Greater New York Automobile Dealer Association, 2000, pp. 42–43; "First Exhibit of Chandler Sixes," *Automobile Trade Journal,* February 1914, p. 166.

10. "Chandler Co. Declares a Dividend," *The Horseless Age,* February 11, 1914, p. 234; "Chandler Motor Declares Dividend and Re-elects Officers," *Automobile Topics,* February 14, 1914, p. 20; "Saxon and Chandler in C.A.C." *The Horseless Age,* March 25, 1914, p. 473; Fisher, Tom (Historian), *Historic American Engineering Record,* Heritage Conservation and Recreation Services, U.S. Department of Interior, Washington, D.C., Document #HAER OH 11-G, p. 3.

11. "Chandler Six Does 24.4 Miles a Gallon," *The Automobile,* May 7, 1914, p. 989; "Economy Test of Chandler Six," *The Horseless Age,* May 13, 1914, p. 744.

12. "Chandler Six Makes 23.7 Miles per Gallon," *The Automobile,* May 21, 1914, p. 1081; "A.C.A. Tests Chandler Fuel Miles," *Automobile Topics,* May 23, 1914, p. 117.

13. "How Much Should an Automobile Weigh?," *The Automobile,* May 28, 1914, pp. 112–113; "W.P. Herbert, President of the Philadelphia Automobile Trade Association," *The Horseless Age,* May 6, 1914, p. 712.

14. "$1,595, This New Profit-Sharing Price Astounds the Motoring Public," *The Saturday Evening Post,* July 11, 1914, inside front cover; "Chandler Price Reduced $190 and Power Added to Motor," *Motor Age,* July 2, 1914, pp. 34–35; *Chandler Parts Manual* for Model 15B, Chandler Motor Car Company, circa July 1914; Chandler advertising brochure for Model 15 & 15B, circa July 1914; "Special Body for Local Chandler Man's Car," unattributed newspaper article, circa 1914.

15. "Chandler Enters Run," *Cleveland Plain Dealer,* June 14, 1914, p. 17.

16. "Chandler Closed Cars for 1915," *The Literary Digest,* October 31, 1914; "Six Cylinder Pleasure Cars," *Automobile Trade Journal,* December 1914, pp. 156–157.

17. "Chandler Motor Car Company," *Automobile Trade Journal,* November 1914, p. 63; "Six Cylinder Pleasure Cars," *Automobile Trade Journal,* December 1914, pp. 156–157; Fisher, Tom (Historian), *Historic American Engineering Record,* Heritage Conservation and Recreation Services, U.S. Department of Interior, Washington, D.C., Document # HAER OH 11-G, p. 4–5.

18. "Chandler Springs Big Surprise by Reducing Price of Its Big Six," *Cleveland Plain Dealer,* January 24, 1915, p.13.

19. "Now with Seven-Passenger Body, Sweeps Aside All Competition," *Motor Age,* April 15, 1915, pp. 50–51; "Now with Seven-Passenger Body and Large Wheel Base, $1,295," *National Geographic,* March 1915; "The Pioneer Chandler Light Weight Six—A Full Seven Passenger Car $1,295," Chandler advertising booklet (Model 16) circa 1915.

20. "Cabriolet Body Wins Big Favors," *Cleveland Plain Dealer,* December 20, 1914, p. 14; "Six Cylinder Pleasure Cars," *Automobile Trade Journal,* December 1914, pp. 156–157.

21. "Now With Seven-Passenger Body, Sweeps Aside All Competition," *Motor Age,* April 15, 1915, pp. 50–51; "This Famous Light Six Leader Offers Still Greater Value," *The Saturday Evening Post,* April 17, 1915, p. 47; "New Seven Passenger Chandler," *The Automobile,* April 22, 1915.

22. "Chandler Shipping Record in May," *The Horseless Age,* June 23, 1915, p. 853; "Chandler Breaks All Sales Marks," *Cleveland Plain Dealer,* June 20, 1915, p. 17; "Chandler Factory Doubled in Size," *Cleveland Plain Dealer,* September 26, 1915, p. 14.

23. "A Touch of High Life at Cedar Point," *Chandler Bulletin* 2:2, August 1915, pp. 1, 3.

24. "Walker Co. Goes to Cleveland," *The Automobile,* November 18, 1915, p. 944; Fisher, Tom (Historian), *Historic American Engineering Record,* Heritage Conservation and Recreation Services, U.S. Department of Interior, Washington, D.C., Document # HAER OH 11-G, pp. 4–5.

25. "Chandler Motor Dividend $77.50," *Cleveland Plain Dealer,* July 1, 1915, p. 15; "Chandler Centers $10,000,000 Deal," *Cleveland Plain*

Dealer, November 2, 1915, p. 1; "Chandler Company Now a $10,000,000 Concern," *Chandler Bulletin* 2:5, November 1915, p. 1; Fisher, Tom (Historian), *Historic American Engineering Record*, Heritage Conservation and Recreation Services, U.S. Department of Interior, Washington, D.C., Document # HAER OH 11-G, p. 5.

26. "Chandler Autumn Offering of Beautiful Closed Cars," *The Literary Digest*, September 11, 1915, p. 545; "Chandler Leads in Service, Style and Price," *Cosmopolitan*, October 1916, p. 104; "Hundreds of Motor Car Purchasers Turning Now to These Models," *Cosmopolitan*, November 1916.

27. "Gobble! Gobble!," *Chandler Bulletin* 2:9, January 1916, p. 2.

28. "The New and Greater Chandler Six for $1,295," *The Saturday Evening Post*, January 22, 1916, pp. 42–43; "A Proven Mechanism," *Motor*, March 1916, pp. 16e–16f; "Thousands See the New Chandler and Praise Them at New York Auto Show," *Chandler Bulletin* 2:9, January 1916, pp. 1; "With Prices Unchanged at $1,295," *Motor*, January 1916, p. 146.

29. "New Bodies on Chandler," *Motor*, February 1916, pp. 77, 146; "Proven Mechanism," *Motor*, March 1916, pp. 16e–16f; "Distinguished Cars," *Life*, November 11, 1916, p. 773.

30. "The Month in Motordom," *Motor*, March 1916, p. 88; "Brady-Murray Gives Breakfast," *Chandler Bulletin* 2:9, January 1916, p. 4; "Emise Still Directs Chandler Sales," *Motor West*, October 15, 1917.

31. "Some Old Names Are Branded in New Theories This Year," *The Literary Digest*, May 13, 1916, p. 1403.

32. "Jordan Motor Car Co. Organized," *The Automobile*, January 27, 1916, p. 200.

33. "A Standard Auto Tread," *Ford Times* 9:6, January 1916, p. 283.

34. "Chandler 1916 Output to Be 20,000," *Automobile Trade Journal*, March 1916, p. 93; "Chandler Factory Letter to Frank Connor" (foreign sales representative for South America), April 24, 1916; "A Briggs Body Plant," *The Automobile*, September 28, 1916, p. 543; "Bird's-eye View of Chandler Factory, Reflecting What the Chandler Six Has Accomplished in Four Years," *Chandler Bulletin* 4:3, April 1917, pp. 4–5.

35. "Forty Chandlers in Drive Away," *Cleveland Plain Dealer*, May 21, 1916, p. 8.

36. "Chandler Ready with Winter Cars," *Motor Age*, September 21, 1916, p. 44.

37. "Chandler Boosts Production," "Walker Mfg. Company Shop," "A Briggs Body Plant," *The Automobile*, September 28, 1916, p. 543; Fisher, Tom (Historian), *Historic American Engineering Record*, Heritage Conservation and Recreation Services, U.S. Department of Interior, Washington, D.C., Document # HAER OH 11-G, pp. 5–6.

38. "W.S.M. Mead," *Automobile Trade Journal*, November 1916, p. 121a.

39. "Chandler Ready with Winter Cars," *Motor Age*, September 21, 1916, p. 44; "Two New Convertible Chandler Bodies," *The Automobile*, September 28, 1916, p. 537; "Chandler Leads in Service, Style and Price," *Cosmopolitan*, October 1916, p. 104; "Springfield Body Sues Fisher," *The Automobile*, November 23, 1916, p. 876; "Chandler Six $1595," *Harper's Magazine Advertiser*, August 1917; "Chandler Six," *The Literary Digest*, August 25, 1917, p. 82; "We Will Protect Your Rights and Ours," *Motor World*, November 29, 1916, p. 54.

40. Chandler Service Parts Price List—Service Series 25 through 35, Models 17 & 18.

Chapter 3

1. "Six Cylinder Chandler Features Are Retained," *Motor*, February 1917, pp. 96–97; "Why Chandler Leads," *The Literary Digest*, December 30, 1916, p. 1771; "This Great Car Leads All Sixes Because of Its Marvelous Motor," *The Saturday Evening Post*, January 20, 1917, pp. 58–59.

2. "This Great Car Leads All Sixes Because of Its Marvelous Motor," *The Saturday Evening Post*, January 20, 1917, pp. 58–59.

3. "Contracts Closed for $30,000,000 Worth of Chandler Automobiles," "10% Wage Increase and 10% Bonus to Employees," *Chandler Bulletin* 4:1, January 1917, p. 1.

4. "Cleveland Manufacturers Expanding," *The Automobile*, March 22, 1917, p. 603; Fisher, Tom (Historian), *Historic American Engineering Record*, Historic Conservation and Recreation Services, U.S. Department of Interior, Washington, D.C., Document # HAER OH 11-G, p. 6.

5. "Chandler Company Reelects Officers," *Chandler Bulletin* 4:2, March 1917, p. 1; "Factory Employees Buy $95,000 Bonds," *Chandler Bulletin* 4:5, June 1917, p. 8.

6. "Pleasure Car Exhibitors in Mechanics Building," *Automobile Trade Journal*, April 1917, pp. 142, 146.

7. "Extra—Record Day," *Chandler Bulletin* 4:3, April 1917, p. 1; "Surmounting Difficulties in the Traffic Department," *Chandler Bulletin* 4:3, April 1917, p. 2.

8. "32 Cars Damaged," *Chandler Bulletin* 4:2, March 1917, p.5.

9. "Chandler Price Must Advance $200 June 30," *Chandler Bulletin* 4:4, May 1917, p. 1; "Chandler Price Must Advance $200 June 30," *The Literary Digest*, June 9, 1917, p. 1830; *Great Events of the Twentieth Century*, Pleasantville, New York: 1977, Reader's Digest Association, p. 141.

10. "Employees Unfurl Stars and Stripes Over Chandler Factory Buildings," *Chandler Bulletin* 4:5, June 1917, pp. 1, 4–5.

11. "Leading Men Who Market the Chandler Gather in Convention," *Chandler Bulletin* 4:6, August 1917, pp. 1–3; "New Purchasing Agent," *Chandler Bulletin* 4:6, August 1917, p. 6.

12. "First Annual Outing Held at Cedar Point, O.," *Chandler Bulletin*, August 4, 1917, p. 5. (This was actually the second outing to be held.)

13. "Chandler 1917 Output 15,000 Cars," *Automotive Industries*, February 14, 1918, p. 385; "Chandler Shows Its Good Condition," *Automobile Topics*, November 17, 1917, p. 137; "Chandler Stock on 12 Per Cent Basis," *Automotive Industries*, February 28, 1918, p. 471; "Chandler Earns $2,328,403," *Motor Age*, February 28, 1918, p. 15; Fisher, Tom (Historian), *Historic American Engineering Record*, Historic Conservation and Recreation Services, U.S. Department of Interior, Washington, D.C., Document # HAER OH 11-G, p. 7.

14. "Kettering President of S.A.E.," *Automotive Industries*, January 10, 1918; "Interesting Body Types at the New York Show," *The Horseless Age*, January 1918, pp. 34, 40, 41, 43; "Four Passenger Cars," *Motor Age*, January 3, 1918, pp. 41, 45, 51, 53, 56, 65, 83; "Motor World—Before New York Show Issue," *Motor World*, December 16, 1917, pp. 29, 34, 37, 40, 66, 67; "Announcing the New Chandler Four Passenger Sport Model," *Chandler Bulletin* 5:1, January 1918, pp. 4–5.

15. "Entering Another Big Year," *Chandler Bulletin* 5:1, January 1918, p. 1.

16. "First Quality Has Put Chandler in First Place," *The Literary Digest*, May 11, 1918, p. 79; "Hundreds of Motor Car Purchasers Turning Now to These Models," *Cosmopolitan*, November 1916; "Chandler Motor Cars," Chandler advertising brochure, circa January 1918, pp. 4–6.

17. "Getting Cars In over the Road," *Motor World*, May 8, 1918, pp. 14–15; "Soldiers of Women's National Army Pilot Chandler Cars," *Chandler Bulletin* 5:4, June 1918, pp. 6–7.

18. "Detroit Shell Buys Springfield Body Plant," *Automotive Industries*, January 24, 1918, p. 251; "Cleveland as Tractor Hub," *Motor Age*, February 28, 1918, pp. 15–16; "Chandler to Make Tractors for Government," *Automotive Industries*, February 21, 1918, p. 425.

19. Fisher, Tom (Historian), *Historic American Engineering Record*, Historic Conservation and Recreation Services, U.S. Department of Interior, Washington, D.C., Document # HAER OH 11-G, p. 8; "Wave of Prosperity in Cleveland," *Automotive Industries*, March 21, 1918, p. 613; Katz, John F., "Chandler: Built to Master a Mountain—and More," *Automobile Quarterly* 24: 4 (Fourth Quarter 1986), pp. 422–437.

20. "Cleveland Shut Up Tight," *Automotive Industries*, January 24, 1918, p. 204; "Two New Tractor Plants to Rise on Chandler Group," *Cleveland Plain Dealer*, July 9, 1918, p. 20; "Chandler Reaches Quantity Production," *Motor Age*, December 26, 1918, p. 26.

21. "The Big Artillery Tractor That Chandler Built for the Fighting Men of Our Victorious Army," *Chandler Bulletin* 6:8, August 1919, pp. 4–5; Fisher, Tom (Historian), *Historic American Engineering Record*, Historic Conservation and Recreation Services, U.S. Department of Interior, Washington, D.C., Document # HAER OH 11-G, p. 7.

22. "Weeks Prices Change," *Motor Age*, May 30, 1918, p. 16; "One Organization for Ohio Factories," *Automotive Industries*, February 28, 1918, p. 470.

23. "Chandler Officials Help Employees Solve H-C-L," *Chandler Bulletin* 5:1, January 1918, p. 1.

24. "New York Motor Car Thieves Adopt New Methods," *Chandler Bulletin* 5:1, p. 2; "Automobile Activities, Nefarious and Otherwise," *Automobile Topics*, January 5, 1918, p. 942.

25. "Chandler Costs More," *Motor Age*, November 21, 1918, p. 11.

26. "Chandler Motor Cars," Chandler advertising brochure, November 4, 1918, p. 6; "Two New Tractor Plants to Rise on Chandler Group," *Cleveland Plain Dealer*, July 9, 1918, p. 20.

Chapter 4

1. Merksamer, Gregg D., *A History of the New York International Auto Show*, New York: The Greater New York Automobile Dealers Association, 2000, pp. 52–53; "Models Shown by the Car Dealers," *Automobile Trade Journal*, February 1919, pp. 156–157; "The Chicago Show," *Automobile Trade Journal*, February 1919, pp. 144–145, 310; "New Chandler April 10," *Motor Age*, April 10, 1919, p. 11; "Chandler New Model Announced," *Motor Age*, May 15, 1919, p. 29; "Three Closed Models Among New Chandler Offerings," *Motor Age*, October 9, 1919, p. 42; "Economy Without Sacrifice," *Literary Digest*, April 12, 1914, p. 143; "The New Chandler," *Motor*, May 1919, p. 88; "Chandler Body Design Changed in New Models," *Automobile Trade Journal*, May 1919, pp. 240–241.

2. Compton, Roy H., "Make Lookie Like Million," *Motor World*, January 22, 1919, pp. 12–15; "How Los Angeles Set Stage for Show," *Motor Age*, January 30, 1919, pp. 24–25.

3. "Oriental Effects Make Show Different," *Motor Age*, January 30, 1919, p. 25.

4. http://en.wikipedia.org/wiki/king_vidor, March 7, 2011; http://goldensilents.com/stars/florencevidor.html, March 7, 2011.

5. http://www.coachbilt.com/des/e/earl.htm, March 4, 2011.

6. Robertson, William, "New Automobile Concern to Build $400,000 Factory," *Cleveland Plain Dealer*, February 22, 1919, p. 18; "$14,000,000 in Orders Uncompleted," *Automotive Industries—The Automobile*, March 27, 1919, p. 723.

7. Untitled article, *The Journal of the Society of Automotive Engineers* IV:5, May 1919, p. 432.

8. "Chandler Hard Hit," *Motor World*, July 2, 1919, p. 44.

9. "Chandler Motor to Build," *Cleveland Plain Dealer*, July 8, 1919, p. 9; "Construction Has Started on 80% Increase to the Chandler Factory," *Chandler Bulletin* 6:11, October–November 1919, pp. 4–5; "Three Closed Models Among New Chandler Offerings," *Motor Age*, October 9, 1919, p. 42; Fisher, Tom (Historian), *Historic American Engineering Record*, Historic Conservation and Recreation Services, U.S. Department of Interior, Washington, D.C., Document # HAER OH 11-G, p. 8.

10. "Chandler Earns 2,800,000," *Automotive Industries—The Automobile*, August 28, 1919, p. 446; "Connor Promoted to Export Managership," *Chandler Bulletin* 6:8, August 1919, p. 2.

11. "Three Closed Models Among New Chandler Offerings," *Motor Age*, October 9, 1919, p. 42; "A Cozy Corner," *Motor World*, November 5, 1919, p. 2.

12. "Makers Victim of Trademark Pirate," *Automotive Industries—The Automobile*, January 8, 1920, p. 100.

13. "Miles Wins Promotion," "Familiar Faces at New Desks in the Purchasing Department," *Chandler Bulletin* 7:5, April–May 1920, p. 3.

14. "Chandler," *Motor Age*, January 29, 1920, p. 40; "See How Chandler Checks with High-Priced Cars," *The Literary Digest*, May 8, 1920, p. 149; "Why the Chandler Six Is a 'First Choice' Car," *Life*, July 22, 1920, p. 167; "80,000 Choose the Chandler Six for Its Known Superiority," *The Literary Digest*, September 25, 1920, p. 119; "Leadership Established by Superior Service," *The American Magazine*, October 1920, p. 193; "The Highest Degree of Comfort with Mechanical Excellence," *The Literary Digest*, October 23, 1920, p. 119; "Lower Prices of Cleveland Autos," *Cleveland Plain Dealer*, September 30, 1920, p. 16.

15. "Fisher Company to Build $500,000 Body Plant," *Automotive Industries*, February 19, 1920, p. 534; "Chevrolet North American Plants History," *Generator and Distributor*, Vintage Chevrolet Club of America Magazine, January 2011, pp. 16–17; "Fisher Body Plant Opens in Cleveland," *Automotive Industries—The Automobile*, December 1, 1921, p. 1091.

16. "The Highest Degree of Comfort with Mechanical Excellence," *The Literary Digest*, October 23, 1920, p. 119; "Cleveland Business Men to Build Homes," *Automotive Industries—The Automobile*, April 29, 1920, p. 1028; "Cleveland to Get Larger Coal Supply," *Automotive Industries—The Automobile*, October 14, 1920, p. 793.

17. "Real Restful Comfort and Pleasing Style," *The Literary Digest*, April 9, 1921, p. 83; "Announcing the Chandler Two-Passenger Roadster," Chandler advertising brochure (late 1920 specification section).

18. "Cleveland Reduces Number of Workers," *Automotive Industries—The Automobile*, December 4, 1920, p. 941.

19. "Men of the Industry," *Automotive Industries—The Automobile*, January 27, 1921, p. 199; Lyman, Olin, "A Famous Automobile Designer's Secret of Success," *Ambition* (Publication of International Correspondence School) Scranton, Pennsylvania, 17:2, pp. 1–4; "Chandler at $1,785, Back to 1913 Basis," *Automotive Industries—The Automobile*, June 16, 1921, p. 1348.

20. "Death of Charles A. Emise, Chandler Vice-President, Marks Passing of a Real Pioneer of the Industry," *Chandler Bulletin* 8:10, October 1921, p. 3; U.S. Passport Applications 1795–1925, National Archives and Records Administration (N.A.R.A.), Washington, D.C., Application of Gertrude Emise (widow of Charles A. Emise), August 13, 1922; "Chandler Directors Declare $1.50 Dividend," *Automotive Industries—The Automobile*, December 15, 1921, p. 1196.

21. "About the Bulletin," *Chandler Bulletin* 8:10, October 1921, p. 3; "A New Wave of Enthusiasm," *Chandler Bulletin*, Special "Carry On" Edition, # 4, January 9, 1922, pp. 1–12.

22. "New Chandler," *Motor World*, January 11, 1922, pp. 12–13; "Chandler Units Redesigned," *Automobile Trade Journal*, February 1922, p. 35; *"A New Wave of Enthusiasm," Chandler Bulletin*, Special "Carry On" Edition, # 4, January 9, 1922, pp. 1–12; "Chandler Makes Changes," *Automotive Industries—The Automobile*, January 12, 1923, p. 54.

23. "Chandler Prices Down," *Motor Age*, January 19, 1922, p. 29.

24. "A New Wave of Enthusiasm," *Chandler Bulletin*, Special "Carry On" Edition, # 4, January 9, 1922, pp. 1–12; "Chandler Factory Springs Surprises," *Cleveland Plain Dealer*, January 8, 1922, p. 8; "Chandler Dealers Get the News," *Automobile Topics*, January 21, 1922.

25. "Chandler Opens Touring Bureau," *Cleveland Plain Dealer*, March 26, 1922, p. 68.; "Four Million Miles by Thirty-one Cars," *Chandler Bulletin* 9:4, April 1922, p. 3.

26. "DuPont Inspects Fisher Body Plant," *Cleveland Plain Dealer*, May 3, 1922, p. 20; "General Motors to Take Over Fisher Body Corporation," *Autobody*, June 1926, p. 218.

27. "The Month in the Industry," *Motor*, June 1922, p. 72.

28. "Chandler Metropolitan Sedan, $2,395," *Motor World*, June 7, 1922, p. 38; "Chandler Metropolitan Sedan," *Motor Age*, June 22, 1922, p. 22; "New Chandler—Four Passenger Sport Model," *Motor*, July 1922, p. 26; "The Conspicuous Success of the Year," *The Saturday Evening Post*, August 19, 1922, p. 96; "Engineers to Drive Competitor Cars," *Automotive Industries*, October 26, 1922, p. 838.

29. "Four Cylinder, Small Displacement Models Feature London Show," *Motor Age*, November 16, 1922, p. 17.

Chapter 5

1. "Chandler Landslide for 1923 Has Started," *Chandler Bulletin* 10:1, February 1923, pp. 1–12.

2. "A Profit Opportunity," *Motor Age*, May 17, 1923, back cover; "Chandler Landslide for 1923 Has Started," *Chandler Bulletin* 10:1, February 1923, pp. 1–12.

3. Mulford, Ralph, "Racing with Lozier: A Memoir by Ralph Mulford," *Automobile Quarterly* 7:4 (Spring 1969) pp. 366–381; "Mulford Really a Gasoline Genius," *Cleveland Plain Dealer*, May 18, 1913, p. 8b.

4. "1923 Chandler Cars and the New Pikes Peak Motor," Chandler advertising brochure, January 1923; "Chandler Landslide for 1923 Has Started," *Chandler Bulletin* 10:1, February 1923, pp. 1–12; "Unmatched for Performance," *The Literary Digest*, February 24, 1923, p. 88.

5. "1923 Chandler Cars and the New Pikes Peak Motor," Chandler advertising brochure, January 1923; "Unmatched for Performance," *The Literary Digest*, February 24, 1923, p. 88.

6. "1923 Chandler Cars and the New Pikes Peak Motor," Chandler advertising brochure, January 1923; "San Francisco's Twin Peaks in High Is New Chandler's Feat," *Chandler Bulletin* 10:2, May 1, 1923, pp. 1–12; "Chandler Champion in Performance 1925," Chandler advertising brochure, circa late 1925;

"Chandler—This Is Progress," Chandler advertising brochure, circa 1926; "Casting Plant Burned," *Automotive Industries*, April 12, 1923, p. 846; "Executives Invited to Gothenburg Show," *Automotive Industries*, April 19, 1923.

7. "Bonus for Chandler Workers," *Motor Age*, August 2, 1923, p. 34; "Chandler Champion in Performance 1925," Chandler advertising brochure, circa 1925; "Financial Notes," *Automotive Industries*, April 12, 1923, p. 852.

8. "James M. Dunlap Dies/ Chandler Purchasing Agent Dies," *Chandler Bulletin* 10:3, October 1925, p. 5; "Familiar Faces at New Desks in Purchasing Department," *Chandler Bulletin* 7:5, April–May 1920, p. 3.

9. "Master Salesmen Entertained at Pike's Peak," *Chandler Bulletin* 10:3, October 1923, pp. 8–9.

10. "Chandler Convoys First Transcontinental Train," *Chandler Bulletin* 10:3, October 1923 p. 10.

11. "Announcing the Biggest Advance in Motor Car Design Since the Self-Starter!" *Motor Age*, October 4, 1923, four page advertising insert; "Performance," Chandler brochure announcing 1924 models, circa January 1924; "Two New Chandler Four Door Sedans," *Motor Age*, January 10, 1924, p. 21, "Chandler's New Four-Door Sedans at New Low Prices Are Center of Keen Interest at 1924 Automobile Shows," *Chandler Bulletin* 11:1, January 1924, pp. 1–2.

12. "Chandler Announces Single-Seat Roadster," *Motor Age*, December 6, 1923, p. 17; "Important Improvements Feature 1924 Chandler," *Chandler Bulletin* 10:3, October 1923, p. 2; "Two New Chandler Four Door Sedans," *Motor Age*, January 10, 1924, p. 21; "Chandler's New Four-Door Sedans at New Low Prices Are Center of Keen Interest at 1924 Automobile Shows," *Chandler Bulletin* 11:1, January 1924, pp. 1–2; "Performance," Chandler brochure announcing 1924 models, circa January 1924.

13. "Chandler's New Four-Door Sedans at New Low Prices Are Center of Keen Interest at 1924 Automobiles Shows," *Chandler Bulletin* 11:1, January 1924, pp. 1–5; "Traffic Transmission Ends Gear Clashing," *Chandler Bulletin* 10:3, October 1923, pp. 1–3.

14. "Traffic Transmission Wins Enthusiastic Comment," *Chandler Bulletin* 11:1, January 1924, p. 3.

15. "Open Territory," *Motor Age*, October 4, 1923, advertising insert.

16. "1925 Models—More to Talk About," *Motor Age*, August 7, 1924, back cover; "1925 Chandler Is Introduced," *Chandler Bulletin*, Special Edition, June 1924, pp. 2–4, 12.

Chapter 6

1. "Chandler Announces New Models for 1925," *Automobile Topics*, June 7, 1924, p. 332; "Announcing the 1925 Models," *Chandler Bulletin*, June 1924, pp. 1–3; "1925 Models—More to Talk About," *Motor Age*, August 7, 1924, back cover.

2. "Two Superb New Sedans," *Motor Age*, September 4, 1924, back cover; "Chandler Motor Car Company Announces 2 Improved Models," *Motor Age*, September 18, 1924, p. 41; "Two Chandlers and Two Clevelands," *Motor*, November 24, 1924, p. 48.

3. "Pikes Peak Race Won by Loesche," *Motor Age*, September 4, 1924, p. 34.

4. "Chandler Profits Increase," *Automobile Topics*, October 18, 1924, p. 859; "Chandler Pays Annual Bonus," *Automobile Trade Journal*, September 1, 1924, p. 70.

5. "Chandler and Rollin Add New Bodies," *Automotive Industries*, January 1, 1925, p. 28; "Chandler Offering Three New Models," *Automobile Topics*, January 3, 1925, pp. 676, 704, 729, 732, 768–769; "Some New Models for 1925," *Motor Age*, January 1, 1925, p. 23; "Chandler Pikes Peak–Traffic Transmission," Chandler advertising brochure, circa March 1925; "Auto Show Number," *Chandler Bulletin*, January 1925, pp. 1–8.

6. "Detroit Show Is Crowded Daily," *Automobile Topics*, January 24, 1925, p. 1055; "Descriptions of Car Exhibit at Chicago Show," *Motor Age*, January 29, 1925, p. 12; "Boston Show," *Automobile Topics*, March 14, 1925, p. 407.

7. "Chandler Off for Bermuda," *Automobile Topics*, March 3, 1925, p. 484.

8. "Chandler 1926 Models," Chandler advertising brochure, circa July 1925, pp. 1–16; "Chandler Adds Sedan Model Body," *Motor Age*, July 9, 1925, p. 21; "Chandler Has a Paneled Radiator," *Automobile Topics*, July 11, 1925, p. 815; "Novel Radiator Shell Features New Series Chandler," *Automobile Trade Journal*, August 1925, p. 71.

9. "Radio Controls Driverless Car," *Motor Age*, September 10, 1925, p. 22.

10. "Outlines Plans for Chandler Volume," *Chandler Bulletin*, Convention Edition, September 12, 1925, pp. 1–16.

11. "At the Body Plants," *Autobody*, November 1925, p. 202; Service Parts Price List, Chandler Flat Rate Section–Glass Specifications, circa 1926, p. 67: *Chandler Parts Book*, Special 6 Series (Edition of 1928–29), Body Section, pp. 129–303.

12. "Improvements Expected by Chandler-Cleveland," *Automobile Topics*, March 5, 1927, pp. 301, 305; "At the Body Plants," *Autobody*, November 1925, p. 202.

13. "Entertainment a Big Hit with Visitors," *Chandler Bulletin*, Convention Edition, September 12, 1925, pp. 13, 16.

14. "Chandler Sets Record for Pikes Peak Climb," *Automotive Industries*, September 10, 1925, p. 439; "Chandler Sets New Pikes Peak Record," *Chandler Bulletin*, Convention Edition, September 12, 1925, pp. 1, 15.

15. "Personals," *Autobody*, November 1925, p. 202.

16. "At the Body Plants," *Autobody*, November 1925, p. 202.

17. "Financial Notes," *Automotive Industries*, December 17, 1925, p. 1040.

18. "Chandler-Cleveland Merge," *Motor Age*, December 31, 1925, p. 32.

19. "Chandler Adapts to Bowen System," *Motor*, January 1926; "Higher Prices, Chassis Oiler on Chandler," *Automobile Trade Journal*, January 1926, p. 81; "Chandler Prices Up," *Motor Age*, January 7, 1926, p. 66.

20. "Chandler Announces Merger," *Motor Age*, February 4, 1926, p. 50; "Quality Not Only Sells, But Protects," *Motor Age*, August 5, 1926, back cover.

21. "Chandler Adds Berline," *Motor Age*, April 29, 1926, p. 32; "Announcing the Berline—The Ideal Car for Undertakers," Chandler advertising brochure, circa April 1926.

22. "Chandler Service Price Parts List," Flat Rate Supplement, Model 16 through Service Series 35, p. 10a.

Chapter 7

1. "For 1927—Astounding New Prices," *Automobile Topics*, August 14, 1926, p. 100; "Expansion Features Chandler's History," *Automobile Topics*, October 2, 1926, p. 708; "Chandler Completes New Royal Eight Line," *Automobile Topics*, March 12, 1927, p. 434; "Sidney Black at Buffalo Talks to Chandler Men," *Motor Age*, March 1, 1928, p. 12; "The New 1927 Chandler Big Six Series," Chandler advertising brochure, circa August 1926; "The New Chandler—A Development Unsurpassed," Chandler advertising brochure, circa August 1926; "The New 1927 Chandler Standard Series," Chandler advertising brochure, circa August 1926.

2. "Chandler Is Building a Magnificent Line of Motor Cars," Chandler advertising brochure, circa 1926; "Reduced Prices and Added Models in 1927 Line," *Automobile Trade Journal*, September 1926, pp. 60–61; "Chandler-Cleveland Has 19 Models in Line," *Automobile Topics*, August 8, 1926, pp. 1240–1241; "Chandler Extends Line to Include Thee Chassis Models," *Automotive Industries*, August 12, 1926, p. 259; "Chandler Line Now Includes Standard, Special and Big Six Models," *Motor Age*, August 12, 1926, pp. 22–23.

3. "Chandler Service Parts Price List," Flat Rate Supplement—Glass Specifications, p. 67; "For 1927—Astounding New Prices, Greater Beauty, Fine Quality," *Automobile Topics*, August 14, 1926, p. 100; "Reduced Prices and Added Models in 1927 Chandler Line," *Automobile Trade Journal*, September 1926, pp. 60–61.

4. "Announcing the New Special Six Series by Chandler," Chandler advertising brochure, circa August 1926.

5. "Chandler Service Parts Price List," Flat Rate Supplement—Glass Specifications, p. 67; "Body Details," *Motor* Specifications Book, 5th Ed., August 1926, pp. 116, 124, 127; "Chandler Is Building a Magnificent Line of Motor Cars," Chandler advertising brochure, circa fall 1926; "Chandler Special Six series parts book" (edition of 1928–29), p. 29; "Irving Florman Company" brochure, 1928.

6. *Ibid.*

7. "The New 1927 Chandler Standard Series," Chandler advertising brochure, August 1926; "Chandler Is Building a Magnificent Line of Motor Cars," Chandler advertising brochure, fall 1926; "Body Details," *Motor* Specifications Book, 5th Ed., August 1926, pp. 116, 124, 127; Service Bulletin to All Chandler Dealers from the Chandler-

Cleveland Motors Company, August 1926.

8. "Chandler Owners Loyal," *Automobile Topics*, September 25, 1926, pp. 614, 616; "Chandler Sales Increase 60 Percent During August," *Automobile Topics*, September 18, 1926, p. 507.

9. "Expansion Features Chandler's History," *Automobile Topics*, October 2, 1926, p. 708; "Chandler September Sales Gain Analyzed," *Automobile Topics*, October 23, 1926, p. 998; "Chandler Equipment Adds 26 Per Cent to Capacity," *Automotive Industries*, September 30, 1926, p. 590.

10. "Chandler Earns $381,512," *Automobile Topics*, November 13, 1926, p. 25; "Chandler Sales Gain in 12 Metropolitan Centers," *Automobile Topics*, November 27, 1926, p. 217; "Chandler's Latest Offering," *Automobile Topics*, December 4, 1926, p. 325.

11. "Outlines Plans for Chandler Volume" *Chandler Bulletin*, Convention Issue, September 12, 1925, p. 2; "Industry Starts New Year with Record Breaking Show," *Automobile Topics*, January 15, 1927, pp. 1030–1032; "New Royal Eight Gives Chandler a Line of 26 Types," *Automobile Topics*, January 22, 1927, pp. 1152–1153, 1166; Reed, Charles G., "New Chandler Royal Eight Makes Debut at Show," *Automobile Trade Journal*, February 2, 1927, pp. 47–48; "Chandler Completes New Royal Eight Line," *Automobile Topics*, March 12, 1927, p. 434; "New Chandler Motor Cars," Chandler advertising brochure, circa January 1927; "Foot Control Is Used to Dim Lights," *Cleveland Plain Dealer*, April 17, 1927, p. 45; "The New Royal Eight Series by Chandler," Chandler advertising brochure, March 1927; "The Magnificent New Royal Eight by Chandler," Chandler advertising brochure, January 1927; Chandler Royal 8 Parts Book, Edition of 1927–28.

12. "New Coupe for Three Is Chandler's Latest," *Automobile Topics*, April 23, 1927, p. 974; "Chandler Adds Coupes," *Automobile Trade Journal*, May 1927, p. 57; "Shipments Increase," *Motor Age*, July 21, 1927, p. 22; "Improvement Expected by Chandler-Cleveland," *Automobile Topics*, March 5, 1927, pp. 301–305.

13. "Chandler Adds 4 Men to Traveling Organization," *Automobile Topics*, February 26, 1927, p. 204.

14. "Chandler Adds Special Six," *Automobile Trade Journal*, June 1927, p. 52; "Chandler New Royal Eight and Sixes Win Enthusiastic Public Acceptance Wherever New Models Have Been Shown," *Chandler Bulletin* 5:1, February 1927, pp. 1, 3. (Note: *Chandler started renumbering their bulletins about this time. This number is a duplicate of an earlier one in January 1918.*)

Chapter 8

1. "Chandler Line-Up for 1928 Offers Wide Variety," *Automobile Topics*, July 30, 1927, p. 1076; "Now Is the Time to Buy a New Chandler," *Chandler Bulletin* 5:4, August–September 1927, pp. 1–3; "Well That's Certainly a Good Way to Buy a Motor Car," Chandler advertising brochure, circa January 1928.

2. "Chandler Line-Up for 1928 Offers Wide Variety," *Automobile Topics*, July 30, 1927, p. 1076; "The New Royal Eight Series by Chandler," Chandler advertising brochure, circa August 1927; "Prices, Weight and Equipment," *Motor Age*, October 13, 1927, p. 51.

3. "Now Is the Time to Buy a New Chandler," *Chandler Bulletin* 5:4, August–September 1927, pp. 1, 3; "Introducing the New Royal Six by Chandler," Chandler advertising brochure, circa August 1927.

4. "Announcing the New Special Six Series by Chandler," Chandler advertising brochure, circa August 1927; "Chandler Broadens Sales Possibility for Entire Selling Organization with New 1928 Line," *Chandler Times* 2:7–8, July–August 1927, pp. 2–5; "Now Is the Time to Buy a New Chandler," *Chandler Bulletin* 5:4, August–September 1927, pp. 1–3; "Special Six Sportster Added by Chandler," *Automobile Trade Journal*, October 1927, p. 66; Two Company Memorandums Issued by Sidney Black, Chandler Vice President, on July 14, 1927; "Chandler Has Sportster," *Motor Age*, September 15, 1927, p. 9; "Chandler's Line-Up for 1928 Offers Wide Variety," *Automobile Topics*, July 30, 1927, pp. 1076–1077.

5. "Chandler-Cleveland Reports Loss for 1927," *Automobile Topics*, March 17, 1928, p. 451.

6. "Westinghouse Vacuum Brakes on All New Chandlers," *Chandler Bulletin* 6:1, February 1928, pp. 1–3; Cleary, John, "Newness Dominates the Chicago Show," *Motor Age*, February 2, 1928, pp. 24–25; "And Now Westinghouse Vacuum Brakes on Chandler," Chandler advertising brochure, circa January 1928; "Well That's Certainly a Good Way to Buy a Motor Car," Chandler advertising brochure, circa January 1928; "High Powered Magnificence with New Ultra Smartness," Chandler advertising brochure, circa January 1928; "28 Finer Cars—First in America Equipped with Westinghouse Vacuum Brakes," *Motor Age*, January 5, 1928, pp. 98–99.

7. "Well That's Certainly a Good Way to Buy a Motor Car," Chandler advertising brochure, circa January 1928; "High Powered Magnificence with New Ultra Smartness," Chandler advertising brochure, circa January 1928; "Price Announcement and Changes," *Motor Age*, January 12, 1928, p. 18; "Prices, Weights and Equipment," *Motor Age*, March 3, 1928, p. 51; "28 Finer Cars—First in America Equipped with Westinghouse Vacuum Brakes," *Motor Age*, January 5, 1928, pp. 98–99; "Chandler Free from Shackle Noise," *Chandler Bulletin* 6:2, March–April 1928, p. 3.

8. "Luxury and Performance on a Basis of Equality," Chandler advertising brochure, circa January 1928; "Well That's Certainly a Good Way to Buy a Motor Car," Chandler advertising brochure, circa January 1928; "Westinghouse Vacuum Brakes on All New Chandlers," *Chandler Bulletin* 6:1, February 1928, pp. 1–3; "Prices, Weights and Equipment," *Motor Age*, March 3, 1928, p. 51; "Well That's Certainly a Good Way to Buy a Motor Car," Chandler advertising brochure, circa January 1928.

9. "Prices, Weight and Equipment," *Motor Age*, March 3, 1928, p. 51; "Well That's Certainly a Good Way to Buy a Motor Car," Chandler advertising brochure, circa January 1928; *Chandler Special Six Parts Book* (Edition of 1928–29), p. 18, Body Section, pp. 171–183; "33 Colors Used in Finishing Chandler," *Chandler Bulletin* 6:2, March–April 1928, p. 3; "Chandler Cars Are Being Shipped Daily to Far Corners of the Earth," *Chandler Bulletin* 6:2, March–April 1928, p. 4; "Chandler Canadian Business Grows," *Chandler Bulletin* 6:2, March–April 1928, p. 3.

10. "Sidney Black at Buffalo," *Motor Age*, March 1, 1928, p. 12.

Chapter 9

1. "Chandler-Cleveland Net," *Motor Age*, August 30, 1928, p. 11; "Crowds Flock to Chandler Showrooms to See New Sixes and Eights," *Chandler Bulletin* 6:4, August–September 1928, pp. 1–8.

2. "Prices, Weight, and Equipment," *Motor Age*, August 30, 1928, p. 43.

3. "Crowds Flock to Chandler Showrooms to See New Sixes and Eights," *Chandler Bulletin* 6:4, August–September 1928, pp. 4–5; "Chandler Shipments Up," *Motor Age*, August 30, 1928, p. 15.

4. *Ibid.*

5. "Mechanical Specifications," *Motor Age*, August 30, 1928, p. 46; "Crowds Flock to Chandler Showrooms to See New Sixes and Eights," *Chandler Bulletin* 6:4, August–September 1928, pp. 1–8; *Chandler Parts Book—Royal 8*, Edition No. 5 of 1927–28.

6. "Luxury Now Talks Prices," Chandler advertising brochure, circa August 1928; "The New Royal 75 by Chandler," Chandler advertising brochure, circa August 1928; "The New Royal 75 De Luxe Sedan by Chandler, Chandler advertising brochure, circa August 1928; "Mechanical Specifications," *Motor Age*, August 30, 1928, p. 46.

7. "Everything But Wings—The Last Word in Luxury," Chandler advertising brochure, circa August 1928.

8. "There's Something New Under the Sun," Chandler advertising brochure, circa August 1928; "Believe Me, I'm Glad I Looked at Chandler," Chandler advertising brochure, circa August 1928.

9. "Chandler-Cleveland Shows Loss," *Automotive Industries*, January 5, 1929, p. 37.

10. Fisher, Tom (Historian), *Historic American Engineering Record*, Historic Conservation and Recreation Services, U.S. Department of Interior, Washington, D.C., Document # HAER OH 11 G, p. 15; "Chandler President on Trip Abroad," *Cleveland Plain Dealer*, October 21, 1928, p. 78; "Report Hupp Has Acquired Chandler Stock," *The Cleveland Press* (undated newspaper article).

11. "Hupp-Chandler Deal Waits Final Word," *Automotive Industries*, December 1, 1928, p. 807; "Hupp Officers Take Chandler Positions," *Automotive Industries*, December 15, 1928, p. 881; "Hupp-Chandler Deal Consolidates," *Automotive Industries*, December 22, 1928, pp. 888–889; "Jordan to Increase Stock 100,000 Shares," *Automotive Industries*, December 1, 1928, p. 807; "Miles Wins Promotion," *Chandler*

Bulletin 7:5, April–May 1920, p. 3; "Hupp Purchases Chandler Firm," *The Cleveland Press*, November 23, 1928; "Chandler Car Completed in Home Factory," *The Cleveland Press* (undated newspaper article); "Report Hupp Has Acquired Chandler Stock," *The Cleveland Press* (undated newspaper article).

12. "Hupp-Chandler Deal Waits Final Word," *Automotive Industries*, December 1928, p. 807; Fisk, Ross, "The Chandler Motor Car Company," *The Hupp Herald* 24:2, Summer 1996.

13. Cuthbert, Bill, *The Hupmobile Story from Beginning to End*, Evansville, Indiana: M.T. Publishing Company, 2004, pp. 9–11; Godshall, Jeffrey I., "Hupmobile: Always a Good Car," *Automobile Quarterly* 16:1 (First Quarter 1978), pp. 62–87; "Hupmobile Plant Entirely Realigned and Completely Conveyorized," *Automotive Industries*, January 18, 1930, pp. 76–81.

14. Monnett, James G., Jr., "$250,000 Concern to Build Factory," *Cleveland Plain Dealer*, January 9, 1930, p. 14.

15. Monnett, James G., Jr., (no heading), *Cleveland Plain Dealer*, July 13, 1929, p. 10; "Engineers to Talk of Car Features," *Cleveland Plain Dealer*, Sunday, February 12, 1933.

Chapter 10

1. "This Month in Motordom," *Motor*, March 1916, p. 88.

2. "Changes in Executive Staff of Sales and Service," *Chandler Bulletin* 7:7, June–July 1920, p. 3.

3. "A New Wave of Real Enthusiasm," *Chandler Bulletin*, Carry on Edition, January 9, 1922, pp. 1–12.

4. "Sun Never Sets on Chandler," *Chandler Bulletin* 5:3, May–June 1927, p. 2.

5. "Entertainment a Big Hit with Visitors," *Chandler Bulletin*, Convention Edition, Saturday, September 12, 1925, p. 13; www.wikipedia.com, February 2, 2013.

6. "Two Pages of Beauty, Screen Stars and Chandler Comrade Roadsters," *Chandler Bulletin*, July 1925, p. 7; www.wikipedia.com, February 2, 2013.

7. *Ibid.*

8. *Ibid.*

9. *Ibid.*

10. "Hal Chase of Baseball Fame, Owns Chandler," *Chandler Bulletin* 4:3, April 1917, p. 7; www.wikipedia.com, February 2, 2013.

11. "Fame of Chandler Is World Wide," *Chandler Bulletin*, June 1924, p. 9; www.wikipedia.com, February 2, 2013.

12. "The Herbert-Cooke Company, Philadelphia," *Chandler Bulletin* 4:1, January 1917, p. 6; www.wikipedia.com, February 2, 2013.

13. "Daring Aviatrix Chooses Chandler, *Chandler Bulletin* 2:5, November 1915, p. 3; www.wikipedia.com, February 2, 2013.

14. "Well Known Actress Enjoys Her Chandler," *Chandler Bulletin* 5:1, January 1918, p. 2.

15. "Movie Actress Makes Folks Happy—On Screen and Off," *Chandler Bulletin* 6:11, November 1919, p. 7; www.wikipedia.com, February 2, 2013.

16. "Veteran Cyclist in His Chandler," *Chandler Bulletin* 4:2, March 1917, p. 5; www.wikipedia.com, January 14, 2015.

17. "More of Those Good Bouquet Letters," *Chandler Bulletin* 4:2, March 1917, p. 7; "El Paso Changes Their Viewpoint; Example of Eastern Idea of Us," *El Paso Herald*, Saturday, September 2, 1916.

18. "More of Those Good Bouquet Letters," *Chandler Bulletin* 4:2, March 1917, p. 7; www.wikipedia.com, February 2, 2013.

19. "Golf Champion Owns Chandler 'Special,'" *Chandler Bulletin* 4:6, p. 2; www.wikipedia.com, February 2, 2013.

20. "The 'So Long Letty' Girl and Her Chandler Convertible," *Chandler Bulletin* 2:9, January 1916, p. 2; www.wikipedia.com, February 2, 2013.

21. "Helen Keller and Her Chandler Coach," *Chandler Bulletin*, July 1925, p. 3; www.wikipedia.com, February 2, 2013.

22. "Two Popular Champions Meet," *Chandler Bulletin*, November and December 1926, p. 3; www.wikipedia.com, February 2, 2013.

23. "Irvin Cobb Likes Chandler," *Chandler Bulletin*, November–December 1916, p. 3; www.wikipedia.com, February 2, 2013.

24. "Royalty Buys a Chandler," *Chandler Bulletin* 6:3, May–June 1928, p. 8; www.wikipedia.com, February 2, 2013.

25. "Champion Rifle Shot Drives Chandler," *Chandler Bulletin* 2:2, August 1915, p. 1; National Rifle Association, National Firearms Museum, Washington, D.C.

26. "Chandler Favorite with Film Stars," *Chandler Bulletin* 5:4, June 1918, p. 5; www.wikipedia.com, January 14, 2015.

27. "Talented Singer Sees Atlanta in Chandler," *Chandler Bulletin* 4:4, May 1917, p. 5.

28. "Noted Psychologist Chooses a Chandler," *Chandler Bulletin* 5:5, October–November 1927, p. 4.

29. "Little Peggy Buys Chandler Eight," *Chandler Bulletin* 6:3, May–June 1928, p. 2.

30. "Doris Eaton—Actress, Dancer, Rancher," www.wikipedia.com, January 12, 2015.

31. "Sun Never Sets on Chandler," *Chandler Bulletin* 5:3, May–June 1927, p. 2.

Chapter 11

1. "Photographs from the Now Celebrated Mexico-to-Canada Non-Stop Run," *Chandler Bulletin* 2:5, November 1915, p. 4., "Chandler Six Completes Non-stop Run Across U.S.," from unknown trade magazine account. For the full press release recounting the event, see the Appendix in the present work.

2. "Chandler Car the Pathfinder on Master Drivers' Run," *Chandler Bulletin* 2:5, November 1915, p. 4.

3. "Chandler Wins Deerfield Races," *Chandler Bulletin* 2:5, November 1915, p. 3.

4. "Northward Bound," *Overlanding in Australasia* (publication of Marcus Clark & Company Ltd., Chandler distributor for Australia, Tasmania and New Zealand), pp. 3–5.

5. "On the Toll-Bar Range, Toowoomba, Q," *Overlanding in Australasia* (publication of Marcus Clark & Company Ltd., Chandler distributor for Australia, Tasmania and New Zealand), p. 13.

6. "Going South! Sydney to Melbourne—Racing the Clock," *Overlanding in Australasia* (publication of Marcus Clark & Company Ltd., Chandler distributor for Australia, Tasmania and New Zealand, pp. 6–8.

7. "Hill-Climbing—Ascending the Black's Spur at 30 miles an Hour," *Overlanding in Australasia* (publication of Marcus Clark & Company Ltd., Chandler distributor for Australia, Tasmania and New Zealand), p. 12.

8. "Westward Ho!" *Overlanding in Australasia* (publication of Marcus Clark & Company Ltd., Chandler distributor for Australia, Tasmania and New Zealand), pp. 9–11.

9. "New Zealand Records," *Overlanding in Australasia* (publication of Marcus Clark & Company Ltd., Chandler distributor for Australia, Tasmania and New Zealand), pp. 14–19; "Chandler Makes Roadtest Records in New Zealand," *Chandler Bulletin* 7:7, June–July 1920, p. 1, 7.

10. "Chandler Champion in Performance," Chandler Motor Car Company brochure, circa 1926; "Chandler Records Prove Performance Superiority," *Chandler Bulletin*, Convention Number, August 2 & 3, 1926, p. 2; "First Year's Record Shows Pikes Peak Motor Merits Name," *Chandler Bulletin* 11:1, January 1924, pp. 5–7.

11. "En Route from Here to There," *Chandler Bulletin*, June 1924, p. 5.

12. "Chandler Records Prove Performance Superiority," *Chandler Bulletin*, Convention Number, August 2 & 3, 1926, p. 2; "First Year's Record Shows Pikes Peak Motor Merits Name," *Chandler Bulletin* 11:4, January 1924, p. 5.

13. "Wins Speed Events in Cuba and Argentina," *Chandler Bulletin* 10:3, October 1923, p. 10; "Fame of Chandler Is World Wide," *Chandler Bulletin*, June 1924, pp. 8–10; "Two Winning Chandlers," *Chandler Bulletin*, July 1925, p. 4; "Chandler-Curtiss Racing Car—History," www.sportscardigest.com, 12-31-2013.

14. "Chandler Sets New Record Up Mt. Washington," *Chandler Bulletin* 10:3, October 1923, p. 12.

15. "Wins First Prize in Sweden," *Chandler Bulletin*, June 1924, p. 10.

16. "Chandler Wins Five First Prizes in Havana Races," *Chandler Bulletin*, July 1925, p. 4.

17. "Chandler Sets New 1000-Mile Mark," *Chandler Bulletin*, July 1925, p. 5; Bochroch, Albert R., *American Automobile Racing—An Illustrated History*, New York: Viking, 1974, p. 219.

18. "Famous Utah Climb Done in High Gear," *Chandler Bulletin*, July 1925, p. 12.

19. "Chandler Champion in Performance," Chandler Motor Car Company brochure, circa 1926; "Chandler Sets Record for Pike's Peak Run," *Automotive Industries*, September 10, 1925, p. 439; DeGeer, Stanley L., *Pikes Peak Is Unser Mountain*, Albuquerque: Pink Publishing Company, 1990, pp. 16–17.

20. Bochroch, Albert R., *American Automobile Racing—An Illustrated History*, New York: Viking, 1974, p. 219; "Chandler Sets New Pikes Peak Record," *Chandler Bulletin*, Convention Edition, Septem-

ber 12, 1925, pp. 15–16. "Chandler Sets Record for Pike's Peak Run," *Automotive Industries*, September 10, 1925, p. 439; "Chandler Champion in Performance," Chandler Motor Car Company brochure, circa 1926.

21. "Chandler Sedan Smashes All Low Gear Records," *Chandler Bulletin*, September–October 1926, p. 3.

22. "Chandler Sets New Second Gear Record," *Chandler Bulletin*, November–December 1926, p. 2.

23. "Chandler Wins Again in Brazil," *Chandler Bulletin* 5:5, October–November 1927, p. 7; "Chandler Wins Racing Classic," *Cleveland Plain Dealer*, April 17, 1927, p. 47.

24. "Chandler Is Victor in Brazilian Races," *Chandler Bulletin* 6:4, August–September 1928, p. 3.

25. "American Car Triumphs in Santiago–Panimavida Race," *Chandler Bulletin* 5:3, May–June 1927, p. 3.

26. "Chandler Makes Long Endurance Run," *Chandler Bulletin* 5:5, October–November 1927, p. 3.

27. "Chandler Champion in Performance," Chandler Motor Car Company brochure, circa 1927.

28. "First Year's Record Shows Pikes Peak Motor Merits Name," *Chandler Bulletin* 11:1, January 1924, p. 5.

29. "Chandler Champion in Performance," Chandler Motor Car Company brochure, circa 1927.

30. *Ibid.*

Chapter 12

1. All specifications are reproduced from Chandler literature. Any inconsistencies, errors or informational gaps are as they appear in the original sources.

Chapter 13

1. "Enter the Cleveland Car," *Motor Age*, February 20, 1919, p. 15.

2. *The American Car Since 1775*, New York: Automobile Quarterly Inc., 1971.

3. "Enter the Cleveland Car," *Motor Age*, February 20, 1919, p. 15; "New Cleveland Is in the $1,000 Field," *Automobile Topics*, February 22, 1919, p. 305.

4. "Cleveland Car Has Auspicious Start," *Automobile Topics*, March 22, 1919, p. 783; "New Cleveland Is in the $1,000 Field," *Automobile Topics*, February 22, 1919, p. 305; "Cleveland Motor Cars," Cleveland Automobile Company catalogue, 1919.

5. "Cleveland Car Has Auspicious Start," *Automobile Topics*, March 22, 1919, p. 783; "Men of the Industry," *Automotive Industries—The Automobile*, March 27, 1919, p. 718; Fisher, Tom (Historian), *Historic American Engineering Record*, Heritage Conservation and Recreation Services, U.S. Department of Interior, Washington, D.C., Document # HAER OH 11-G, p. 12; "Friendly Tips, About 'Big Ones,'" *Automobile Trade Journal*, April 1, 1922, p. 35.

6. "Contracts Let for New Cleveland Automobile Factory," *Automobile Trade Journal*, April 1919, p. 157.

7. "New Cleveland Is in the $1,000 Field," *Automobile Topics*, February 22, 1919, p. 305; Fisher, Tom (Historian), *Historic American Engineering Record*, Heritage Conservation and Recreation Services, U.S. Department of Interior, Washington, D.C., Document # HAER OH 11-G, p. 11.

8. "New Cleveland in Production July 1," *Automotive Industries—The Automobile*, March 27, 1919, p. 722; "Cleveland Car July 15," *Motor Age*, July 3, 1919, p. 13; "New Cleveland Is in the $1,000 Field," *Automobile Topics*, February 22, 1919, p. 305; "Dealers See New Cleveland Cars," *Automobile Topics*, March 29, 1919, p. 911.

9. "New Cleveland," *Motor World*, July 16, 1919, pp. 34–35; "Overhead Valve Engine in New Cleveland Six," *Automobile Trade Journal*, August 1919, pp. 207a–208a; (no heading), *The Journal of the Society of Automotive Engineers* IV:5, May 1919, p. 432; "New Cleveland Car Is Priced at $1365," *Automotive Industries—The Automobile*, July 17, 1919, p. 136.

10. "The Announcement of the Cleveland Six," *Motor World*, July 2, 1919, p. 83; "New Cleveland Has Orders for 30,000 Cars," *Automotive Industries—The Automobile*, September 4, 1919, p. 497; "Cleveland Roadster in Production," *Motor Age*, November 13, 1919, p. 22.

11. Fisher, Tom (Historian), *Historic American Engineering Record*, Heritage Conservation and Recreation Services, U.S. Department of Interior, Washington, D.C., Document # HAER OH 11-G, p. 12.

12. "New Cleveland Coupe Makes Its Bow," *Automobile Trade Journal*, February 1920, p. 267A; "Financial News," *Automotive Industries—The Automobile*, January 22, 1920, p. 339; "Cleveland Expansion," *Automotive Industries—The Automobile*, February 19, 1920, p. 538.

13. Fisher, Tom (Historian), *Historic American Engineering Record*, Conservation and Recreation Services, U.S. Department of Interior, Washington, D.C., Document # HAER OH 11-G, pp. 12–13.

14. "A Reasonable Limit of Speed," *The Literary Digest*, August 28, 1920, p. 97; "The Cleveland Will Meet You at the Shows," *Cleveland Six Messenger* 1:10, December 1920, p. 1; "Appeals to Dealers Who Measure Values," *Motor Age*, January 7, 1921, p. 248; "Passenger Car Manufacturers, Car Prices and Weights," *Automobile Trade Journal*, November 1921, p. 90.

Chapter 14

1. "Cleveland Six Motor Cars," *Cleveland Automobile Company Catalogue*, January 1922; "Cleveland Six Has Changes in Engine," *Motor Age*, January 26, 1922, p. 19; "Cleveland Six Has Many Refinements," *Motor World*, January 11, 1922, p. 14; "Cleveland Roadster and Coupe," *Motor*, July 1922, p. 44.

2. *Ibid.*

3. "Cleveland Six New and Extraordinary," *Motor World*, January 11, 1922, pp. 30, 74–75.

4. "Many Companies Reduce Prices," *Motor Age*, August 10, 1922, p. 28; "Cleveland Chesterfield Special Model," *Automobile Trade Journal*, September 1922, p. 60; "New Cleveland Sport Model Shows a Wealth of Attractive Equipment," *Motor*, September 1922, p. 39.

5. "Many Companies Reduce Prices," *Motor Age*, August 10, 1922, p. 28; "Cleveland Models Lower," *Motor Age*, October 26, 1922, p. 38.

6. "Cleveland Profits Over Million," *Automobile Topics*, September 16, 1922, p. 415; "Manufacturer Adding New Models to Line of Cars," *Automotive Industries*, October 26, 1922, p. 845; "Cleveland Models Lower," *Motor Age*, October 26, 1922, p. 38; "New Cleveland Models," *Automobile Trade Journal*, November 1922, p. 68; "A Brand New Cleveland," *Motor*, November 11, 1922, p. 28; "Another New Cleveland," *Motor*, November 11, 1922, p. 29; "Cleveland Six Motor Cars—A Complete Catalog Showing All Open and Closed 1923 Models," Cleveland Automobile Company catalogue, circa 1923; "Built for the Largest Market," *Motor Record*, March 1923, p. 20: "Value That Cannot Be Matched," *Saturday Evening Post*, March 10, 1923.

7. "Cleveland Adds a Coupe to Line," *Motor Age*, May 17, 1923, p. 12; "Cleveland Announces New Models," *Automobile Trade Journal*, June 1923, p. 82.

8. "Power—Cleveland Six," Cleveland Automobile Company catalogue for 1924, circa September 1923; "Improved Mechanical Units Feature New 1924 Cleveland Six Models," *Motor Age*, September 6, 1923, p. 18; "New Cleveland Has Body and Mechanical Changes," *Automotive Industries*, September 6, 1923, p. 503; "New Cleveland Models Feature Many Refinements," *Automobile Trade Journal*, October 1923, p. 68.

9. "Power—Cleveland Six," Cleveland Automobile Company catalogue for 1924, circa September 1923.

10. *Ibid.*; "Improved Mechanical Units Feature New 1924 Cleveland Six Models, *Motor Age*, September 6, 1923, p. 18.

11. "Cleveland Adds New Coupe to Its Line," *Motor Age*, December 6, 1923, p. 17.

12. "Power—Cleveland Six," Cleveland Automobile Company catalogue for 1924, circa September 1923.

13. "Cleveland," *Motor Age*, January 31, 1924, p. 21; "Cleveland Produces New Line of Models," *Motor World*, June 12, 1924, p. 42.

14. "Anticipate Record Year in Sales of Cleveland," *Automobile Topics*, September 8, 1923, p. 324; "New Cleveland Has Body and Mechanical Changes," *Automotive Industries*, September 6, 1923, p. 503; "Improved Mechanical Units Feature New 1924 Cleveland Six Models," *Motor Age*, September 6, 1923, p. 18; "Sport Model Dropped from Cleveland," *Motor Age*, January 10, 1924, p. 20.

15. "Cleveland Reduces Prices," *Motor Age*, January 10, 1924, p. 33; "Cleveland," *Motor Age*, January 31, 1924, p. 21; "Cleveland Produces New Line of Models," *Motor World*, June 12, 1924, p. 42; "Cleveland Factory at Capacity Pitch," *Automobile Topics*, April 12, 1924, p. 847.

Chapter 15

1. "Cleveland Produces a New Line of Models," *Motor Age*, June 12, 1924, p. 42.

2. "A Brand New Cleveland,"

Motor, July 1924, pp. 53, 102; "Cleveland Has Central Chassis Oiling System," *Motor World,* June 19, 1924, pp. 19–21; "Cleveland for 1925 Entirely New," *Automobile Trade Journal,* July 24, 1924, pp. 57–59; Cleveland Six sales manual for 1925 models.

3. "Cleveland Has Central Chassis Oiling System," *Motor World,* June 19, 1924, pp. 19–21; "Announcing the 1925 Cleveland," *Motor World,* June 19, 1924, pp. 62, 63; "Cleveland for 1925 Entirely New," *Automobile Trade Journal,* July 24, 1924, pp. 57–59.

4. "Overtime at Cleveland," *Motor Age,* July 10, 1924, p. 44.

5. "Two Chandlers and Two Clevelands," *Motor,* November 1924, p. 48.

6. "Announcing the Coach Premier," *Motor Age,* January 1, 1925, pp. 78–79; "Cleveland Company Offering Coach Premier at $1,295," *Motor Age,* January 1, 1925, p. 56.

7. "Some New Models for 1925," *Motor Age,* January 1, 1925, p. 22; "Coaches Play a Prominent Part at Shows," *Automobile Topics,* January 3, 1925, pp. 704, 729, 732, 768, 769.

8. "Six New Body Designs at the New York Show," *Automotive Industries,* January 8, 1925, pp. 55–56; "Cleveland Has Entirely New Chassis," *Motor Age,* January 8, 1925, p. 15.

9. "Descriptions of Car Exhibits at Chicago Show: Cleveland," *Motor Age,* January 29, 1925, p. 13; "Two Body Models Comprise New Cleveland Six Line," *Automotive Industries,* February 19, 1925, p. 296.

10. "New Cleveland Cars Shipped to Dealers," *Automobile Topics,* March 14, 1925, p. 394.

11. "Cleveland Increases Output," *Automotive Industries,* April 2, 1925, p. 641; "Record Shipments Made by Cleveland," *Automobile Topics,* April 18, 1925, p. 854; "Nationwide Approval and Increasing Sales," *Automobile Topics,* June 6, 1925, p. 392.

12. "Cleveland Has New Sport Sedan at $1,725," *Motor Age,* July 9, 1925, p. 36.

13. "Cleveland Six Motor Cars 1926 Series," Cleveland Automobile Company catalogue, circa August 1925; "Price Reductions, New Models in Chandler-Cleveland Line," *Automobile Trade Journal,* October 1925, p. 69.

14. "Briefing Automotive News," *Automobile Trade Journal,* October 1925, p. 82.

15. "Cleveland Six Motor Cars 1926 Series," Cleveland Automobile Company catalogue, circa August 1925; "Flat Rate Data," *Automobile Trade Journal,* July 1926, p. 77.

16. "New Cleveland Dealers," *Motor Age,* December 17, 1925, p. 37.

17. "Chandler-Cleveland Merge," *Motor Age,* December 31, 1925, p. 32; "Chandler-Cleveland Has 19 Models in Line," *Automobile Topics,* August 7, 1926; pp. 1246–1247; "Chandler Extends Line to Include Three Chassis Models," *Automotive Industries,* August 12, 1926, p. 259; "Chandler Line Now Includes Standard, Special and Big Six Models," *Motor Age,* August 12, 1926, pp. 22–23.

18. "Changes in Cleveland," *Automobile Trade Journal,* January 1926, p. 81.

19. "Dealers Today Are Wiser Than Yesterday," *Automobile Topics,* January 16, 1926, p. 1084; "There's Money in a Busy Showroom," *Automobile Topics,* January 30, 1926, p. 1298; "The Public's OK Means Dealers' Profits," *Automobile Topics,* February 13, 1926, p. 90; "Talk About Enthusiasm," *Automobile Topics,* April 10, 1926, p. 870.

20. "Honeymoon Special Coupe Built by St. Louis Concern," *Motor Age,* April 1, 1926, p. 19.

21. "Cleveland Announces New Sedan," *Motor Age,* April 22, 1926, p. 36.

22. "Cleveland Builds Bodies," *Motor Age,* June 24, 1926, p. 36; Fisher, Tom (Historian), *Historic American Engineering Record,* Historic Conservation and Recreation Services, U.S. Department of Interior, Washington, D.C., Document # HAER OH 11, p. 15.

23. "Garage Owners, Accessory Men, Good Salesmen, Etc.," *Automobile Digest,* July 1926.

Chapter 16

1. "Among the Hills, Minus Fan and Pump," *Cleveland Six Messenger* 1:10, December 1920, p. 2.

2. "Cleveland Six Chosen for Inspection Tour of New Highway," *Cleveland Six Messenger* 3:9, November–December 1920, p. 6; "Hobnobbing with Colonel King Stanley and His 'One Shot Cleveland Six,'" *Cleveland Six Messenger* 4:9–10, September–October 1924, pp. 3, 6.

3. "One-Shot Cleveland Six Holds Mount Diablo Record," *Evidence—5 Records in Eight Weeks* (booklet) Cleveland Automobile Company, circa 1925, pp. 7–10.

4. "Cleveland Six Establishes a New Mount Wilson Record," *Evidence—5 Records in Eight Weeks* (booklet), Cleveland Automobile Company, circa 1925, pp. 14–21; "Performance," *Cleveland Six Messenger* 5:12–1, December–January 1924–1925, pp. 1–3.

5. "Closed Car Record—San Francisco to Portland Oregon," *Evidence—5 Records in Eight Weeks* (booklet), Cleveland Automobile Company, circa 1925, pp. 22–24.

6. "Three More Records Broken by Cleveland," *Automobile Topics,* January 17, 1925, p. 967.

7. "Breaking Records on the Tracks and at the Shows," "Cleveland Shatters Records at the Shows," *Automobile Topics,* February 28, 1925, pp. 205, 272; "1,000 Miles in 848 Minutes," *Cleveland Six Messenger* 5:12–1, December–January 1924–1925, p. 8.

8. "1000 Miles in 745 Minutes," *Automobile Topics,* February 14, 1925, p. 96.

9. "Cleveland Six Lowers Salt Lake City, Utah–Los Angeles Record," *Evidence—5 Records in Eight Weeks* (booklet), Cleveland Automobile Company, circa 1925, pp. 11–13.

10. "A Nation Wide Economy Run," *Evidence—5 Records in Eight Weeks* (booklet), Cleveland Automobile Company, circa 1925, pp. 25–27; "Cleveland Six Economy and Durability Proven in Nationwide Demonstration," *Cleveland Six Messenger* 5:12–1, December–January 1924–1925, pp. 4–5.

11. "Sargent Cole, Endurance Driver Proves Cleveland's Stamina," *Cleveland Six Messenger* 5:9–10, September–October 1925, p. 1.

12. Bochrock, Albert R., *American Automobile Racing—An Illustrated History,* New York: Viking, 1974, p. 219.

13. Fisher, Tom (Historian), *Historic American Engineering Record,* Historic Conservation and Recreation Services, U.S. Department of Interior, Washington, D.C., Document # HAER OH 11 G, p. 16.

Appendix A

1. "Photographs from the Now Celebrated Mexico-to-Canada Non-Stop Run," *Chandler Bulletin* 2:5, November 1915, p. 4., "Chandler Six Completes Non-stop Run Across U.S.," from unknown trade magazine account.

Bibliography

Books

Bochroch, Albert R. *American Automobile Racing—An Illustrated History*. New York: Viking, 1974, p. 219.

Cuthbert, Bill. *The Hupmobile Story from Beginning to End*. Evansville, IN: M.T. Publishing Company Inc., 2004, pp. 9–11.

DeGeer, Stanley L. *Pikes Peak Is Unser Mountain*. Albuquerque: Pink Publishing Company, 1990, pp. 16–19.

Editors of Automobile Quarterly. *The American Car Since 1775*. New York: Automobile Quarterly, 1971.

Goddard, Stephen B. *Colonel Albert Pope and His American Dream Machines: The Life and Times of a Bicycle Tycoon Turned Automotive Pioneer*. Jefferson, NC: McFarland, 2000, p. 157.

Great Events of the Twentieth Century. Pleasantville, NY: The Readers Digest Association, 1977, p. 141.

Merksamer, Gregg D. *A History of the New York International Auto Show*. New York: Greater New York Automobile Dealers Association, 2000, pp. 42–43, 52–53.

Rose, William Ganson. *Cleveland: The Making of a City*. Cleveland, OH: The World Publishing Company, 1950, p. 537.

Wagner, Richard. *Golden Wheels*. Cleveland, OH: The Western Reserve Historical Society and The Cleveland Automobile Club, 1975, pp. 126–137.

Automotive Magazines

Antique Automobile

Clavel, E.S. "A Chandler from the Hinterlands." 27:3 (May–June 1963), pp. 159–161, back cover.

Gosden, W.E. "Coachwork by Willoughby of Utica, New York." 71:3 (May–June 2007), pp. 70–71.

Rothermel, Bill. "1930 Willys-Knight Great Six." 75:1 (January–February 2011), pp. 46–51.

Automobile Quarterly

Catlin, Ross. "Who Really Won the First Indy 500." 7:4 (Spring 1969), pp. 382–385.

Kimes, Beverly Rae. "Lozier: The Big One That Got Away." 7:4 (Spring 1969), pp. 348–365.

Mulford, Ralph. "Racing with Lozier: A Memoir." 7:4 (Spring 1969), pp. 366–381.

Godshall, Jeffrey I. "Hupmobile: Always a Good Car." 16:1 (First Quarter 1978), pp. 62–87.

Katz, John F. "Built to Master a Mountain—and More." 24:4 (Fourth Quarter 1986), pp. 422–437.

White, Roger B. "Body by Fisher." 29:4 (August 1991), pp. 46–63.

Cars & Parts

"The Cover Car." April 1979, pp. 1, 10–12.

Stevens, Bob. "1926 Chandler Comrade Roadster." May 2001, pp. 10–17.

Others

"Chevrolet North American Plants History # 24: Fisher Body Ohio Company." *Generator & Distributor* 50:1 (January 2011), pp. 16–17.

Cuthbert, Bill. "Chandler—Built by Men Who Know." *Horseless Carriage Gazette* 68:5 (September–October 2006), pp. 14–18, 50–53.

Fisk, Ross. "The Chandler Motor Company." *The Hupp Herald* 24: 2 (Summer 1996).

Ford Times 9:6, January 1916, p. 283.

McCourt, Mark. "Formal Performance." *Hemmings Classic Car* # 70 (July 2010), pp. 52–56.

Motor West, Oct. 15, 1917.

Thatcher, Sharon. "Chasing Chandler." *Old Cars Weekly* 39:14 (April 8, 2010), pp. 22–23.

Automotive Trade Journals

Autobody, Nov. 1925, p. 202; June 1926, p. 218; Nov. 1925, p. 202.

The Automobile, Oct. 15, 1912, pp. 105–108; Jan. 23, 1913, p. 277; Mar. 27, 1913, p.713; May 8, 1913, p. 994; Aug. 7, 1913, p. 264; Dec. 11, 1913, p. 1092; Jan. 1, 1914, p. 53; Feb. 26, 1914, pp. 96–97; May 7, 1914, p. 989; May 21, 1914, pp. 1080–1081; May 28, 1914, pp. 112–113; Jan. 7, 1915, p. 200; Nov. 18, 1915, p. 994; Sept. 28, 1916, pp. 537, 543; Nov. 23, 1916, p. 876; March 22, 1917, p. 603.

Automobile Topics, Nov. 11, 1911, p. 277; Jan. 18, 1913, p. 703; Feb. 15, 1913, p. 27; Feb. 14, 1914, p. 20; May 23, 1914, p. 117; Nov. 17, 1917, p. 137; Jan. 5, 1918, p. 942; Feb. 22, 1919, p. 305; March 22, 1919, p. 783; March 29, 1919, p. 911; Jan. 21, 1922; Sept.16, 1922, p. 415; Sept. 8, 1923, p. 324; June 7, 1924, p. 332; Oct. 18, 1924, p. 859; Jan 3, 1925, pp. 676, 704, 729, 732, 768–769; Jan. 17, 1925, p. 967; Jan. 24, 1925, p. 1055; Feb. 14, 1925, p. 96; Feb. 28, 1925, pp. 205, 272; March 14, 1925, pp. 394, 467; March 21, 1925, p. 484; April 18, 1925, p. 854; June 6, 1925, p. 392; July 11, 1925, p. 815; Jan. 16, 1926, p. 1084; Jan. 30, 1926, p. 1298; Feb. 13, 1926, p. 90; April 10, 1926, p. 870; Aug. 7, 1926, pp. 1240–1241; Aug. 14, 1926, p. 100; Sept. 18, 1926, p. 507; Sept. 25, 1926, p. 614–616; Oct. 2, 1926, p. 708; Oct. 23, 1926, p. 998; Nov. 13, 1926, p. 25; Nov. 27, 1926, p. 217; Dec. 4, 1926, p. 325; Jan. 15, 1927, pp. 1030–1032; Jan. 22, 1927, pp. 1151–1153, 1166; Feb. 26, 1927, p. 204; March 5, 1927, pp. 301–305; March 12, 1927, p. 434; April 23, 1927, p. 974; July 30, 1927, pp. 1076–1077; March 17, 1928, p. 451.

Automobile Trade Journal, Feb. 1913, p. 108; Feb. 1914, p. 166; Nov. 1914, p. 63; Dec. 1914, pp. 156–157; March 1916, p. 93; Nov. 1916, p. 121a; April 1917, p. 142, 146; Feb. 1919, pp. 144–145, 156–157; April 1919, p. 157; Feb. 1920, p. 267a; Nov. 1921, p. 90; Feb. 1922, p. 35; Sept. 1922, p. 60; Nov. 1922, p. 68; June 1923, p. 82; July 1924, pp. 57–59; Sept. 1924, p. 70; Aug. 1925, p. 71; Oct. 1925, pp. 69, 82; Jan. 1926, p. 81; Aug. 1926, p. 77; Sept. 1926, pp. 60–61.

Automotive Industries—The Automobile, Jan. 10, 1918, p. 1 (title page), 136; Jan. 24, 1918, pp. 204, 251; Feb. 14, 1918, p. 385; Feb. 21, 1918, p. 425; Feb. 28, 1918, pp. 470–471, 475; March 27, 1919, pp. 718, 722–723; July 17, 1919, p. 136; Aug. 28, 1919, p. 446; Sept. 4, 1919, p. 497; Jan. 8, 1920, p. 100; Jan. 22, 1920, p. 339; Feb. 19, 1920, pp. 534, 536; April 29, 1920, p. 1028; Oct. 14, 1920, p. 793; Nov. 4, 1920, p. 941; Jan. 27, 1921, p. 199; June 16, 1921, p. 1348; Dec. 1, 1921, p. 1091; Dec. 15,

1921, p. 1196; Oct. 26, 1922, pp. 838, 845; Jan. 22, 1923, p. 54; April 12, 1923, pp. 846, 852; April 19, 1923, p. 897; Sept. 6, 1923, p. 503; Jan. 1, 1925, p. 28; Jan. 8, 1925, pp. 55–56; Feb. 19, 1925, p. 296; April 2, 1925, p. 641; Sept. 10, 1925, p. 439; Dec. 17, 1925, p. 1040; Aug. 12, 1926, p. 259; Sept. 30, 1926, p. 590; Dec. 1, 1928, p. 807; Dec. 15, 1928, p. 881; Dec. 22, 1928, pp. 888–889; Jan. 5, 1929, p. 37; Jan. 18, 1930, pp. 76–81.

The Horseless Age, Jan. 8, 1913, p. 97; Jan. 22, 1913, p. 175; Feb. 9, 1913, p. 86; March 19, 1913, p. 532; July 2, 1913, p. 13; Aug. 20, 1913, pp. 298, 301; Feb. 11, 1914, p. 234; March 5, 1914, p. 456; March 25, 1914, p. 473 May 13, 1914, p. 744; Jan. 1, 1918, p. 43.

Motor, Sept. 1912, p. 102; Jan. 1916, p. 146; Feb. 1916, pp. 77, 146; March 1916, pp. 16e-16f, 88; Feb. 1917, pp. 96–97; Jan. 1922, p. 44; June 1922, p. 72; Nov. 1922, pp. 28–29; July 1924, pp. 53, 102; Nov. 1924, p. 48; Jan. 1926; Feb. 1926, p. 82; Aug. 1926, pp. 116, 124, 127.

Motor Age, Feb. 20, 1913, p. 17; March 27, 1913, p. 17; July 2, 1914, pp. 34–35; Dec. 10, 1914, p. 19; April 15, 1915, pp. 50–51; Sept. 21, 1916, p. 44; Jan. 3, 1918, pp. 41, 45, 53, 56, 65, 83; Feb. 28, 1918, pp. 15–16; May 30, 1918, p. 16; Nov. 21, 1918, p. 11; Dec. 26, 1918, p. 26; Jan. 30, 1919, pp. 24–25; Feb. 20, 1919, p. 15; April 10, 1919, p. 11; May 15, 1919, p. 29; July 3, 1919, p. 13; Oct. 9, 1919, p. 42; Nov. 13, 1919, p. 22; Jan. 29, 1920, p. 40; Jan. 27, 1921, p. 248; Jan. 19, 1922, p. 29: Jan. 26, 1922, p. 19; June 22, 1922, p. 22; Aug. 10, 1922, p. 28; Oct. 26, 1922, p. 838; Nov. 16, 1922, p. 17; May 17, 1923, back cover, p. 12; Aug. 2, 1923, p. 34; Sept. 26, 1923, p. 18; Oct. 4, 1923, 4 page adv.; Dec. 6, 1923, p. 17; Jan. 10, 1924, pp. 20–21; Jan. 31, 1924, p. 21; June 12, 1924, p. 42; July 10, 1924, p. 44; Aug. 7, 1924, back cover; Sept. 4, 1924, p. 4, back cover; Jan. 1, 1925, pp. 22–23, 78–79; Jan. 8, 1925, p. 15; Jan. 29, 1925, p. 13; July 9, 1925, p. 36; Sept. 10, 1925, p. 22; Dec. 17, 1925, p. 37; Dec. 31, 1925, p. 32; Jan. 7, 1926, p. 66; April 1, 1926, p. 19; April 22, 1926, p. 36; April 29, 1926, p. 32; June 24, 1926, p. 36; Aug. 12, 1926, pp. 22–23; July 21, 1927, p. 22; Jan. 5, 1928, pp. 98–99; Jan. 12, 1928, p. 18; March 1, 1928, pp. 12, 51; Aug. 30, 1928, pp. 11, 15, 43, 46.

Motor Record, March 1923, p. 20.

Motor World, Feb. 6, 1913, p. 10; Feb. 20, 1913, p. 500; Nov. 29, 1916, pp. 48, 54; Dec. 16, 1917, pp. 29, 34, 37, 40, 66–67; Jan. 22, 1919, pp. 12–15; July 2, 1919, pp. 44, 83–84; July 16, 1919, pp. 34–35; Nov. 5, 1919, p. 2; Jan. 11, 1922, pp. 12–14, 74–75; June 7, 1922, p. 38; June 12, 1924, p. 42; June 19, 1924, pp. 19–21, 62–63.

Chandler/Cleveland Company Publications

Chandler Bulletin 2:2, Aug. 1915, pp. 1, 3; 2:5, Nov. 1915, pp. 1, 3–4; 2:9, Jan. 1916, pp. 1–2, 4; 4:1, Jan. 1917, pp. 1–2, 5–7; 4:2, March 1917, pp. 1–2, 5–7; 4:3, April 1917, pp. 1–2, 4–5, 7–8; 4:4, May 1917, pp. 1–2, 5–7; 4:5, June 1917, pp. 1–2, 4–5, 8; 4:6, Aug. 1917, pp. 2, 4–5; 5:1, Jan. 1918, pp. 1–2, 7–8; 5:4, June 1918, pp. 2, 5–7; 6:8, Aug. 1919, pp. 3–5; 6:11, Nov. 1919, pp. 1–7; 7:5, April–May 1920, p. 3; 7:7, June–July 1920, pp. 1, 7; Carry On Edition, Jan. 9, 1922, pp. 1–12; 9:4, April 1922, pp. 1, 8; Convention Edition, Wednesday, Jan. 3, 1923, pp. 1–4; 10:1, Feb. 1923, pp. 1–12; 10:2, May 1923, pp. 1–12; 10:3, Oct. 1923, pp. 1–2, 8–10; 11:1, Jan. 1924, pp. 1–3, 5, 6–7, 10; June 1924, pp. 2–3, 5, 9; Auto Show Number 1925, pp. 1–8; July 1925, pp. 1, 3, 4–5, 6–7; Convention Edition, Saturday, Sept. 12, 1925, pp. 1–12; September and October 1926, pp. 3, 4–5; November and December 1926, pp. 2–3. ***New number sequence:*** 5:1, February 1927, pp. 1, 4–5; 5:3, May–June 1927, pp. 1, 3; 5:4, August–September 1927, pp. 1, 3, 7; 5:5, October–November 1927, pp. 4, 7; 6:1, February 1928, pp. 1, 3; 6:2, March–April 1928, pp. 3, 4; 6:3, May–June 1928, pp. 1–2, 8; 6:4, August–September 1928, pp. 1–8.

Chandler Times Special Convention Number, Aug. 2–3, 1926, pp. 1–8; 2:7–8, July–August 1927, pp. 2–5.

Cleveland Six Messenger 1:4, May 1920, pp. 1–3; 1:10, Dec. 1920, pp. 2–4, 6; 3:9, Nov./Dec. 1922, pp. 2–3, 6–8; 4:9–10, Sept./Oct. 1924, pp. 3, 5–6; 5:12–1, Dec./Jan. 1924–25, pp. 1–8; 5:9–10, Sept./Oct. 1925, pp. 1, 4–5.

Other Periodicals

The American Chauffeur, Jan. 1916, p. 23.

The American Magazine, Oct. 1920, p. 193.

Cosmopolitan, Oct. 1916, p. 104; Nov. 1916.

Harper's Magazine Advertiser, Aug. 1917.

Life, Nov. 11, 1916, p. 773.

The Literary Digest, Oct. 11, 1913, p. 641; Oct. 31, 1914; Sept. 11, 1915, p. 545; May 13, 1916, p. 1403; Dec. 30, 1916, p. 1773; Aug. 25, 1917, p. 82; May 11, 1918, p. 79; May 8, 1920, p. 149; Aug. 28, 1920, p. 97; Sept. 25, 1920, p. 119; Oct. 23, 1920, p. 119; Apr. 9, 1921, p. 83; Feb. 24, 1923, p. 88.

The National Geographic, March 1915.

The Saturday Evening Post, July 26, 1913, inside front cover; Nov. 15, 1913, p. 50; Feb. 21, 1914, p. 67; Mar. 21, 1914, p. 71; Apr. 18, 1914, p. 60; July 11, 1914, inside front cover; Apr. 17, 1915, p.47; Jan. 22, 1916, pp. 42–43; Jan. 20, 1917, pp. 58–59; Aug. 19, 1922, p. 96; Mar. 10, 1923, p. 176.

Newspapers

The Cleveland Plain Dealer Aug. 26, 1892, p. 5; Feb. 19, 1911, p. 55; July 16, 1911, p. 58; March 9, 1913, p. 22; Aug. 3, 1913, p. 8; May 18, 1913, p. 8b; June 14, 1914, pp. 17, 19; Dec. 20, 1914, p. 14; Jan. 24, 1915, p. 13; June 20, 1915, p. 17; July 1, 1915, p. 15; Sept. 26, 1915, p. 14; Nov. 2, 1915, p. 1; May 21, 1916, p. 8; July 9, 1918, p. 20; Feb. 22, 1919, p. 18; July 8, 1919, p. 9; Sept. 30, 1920, p. 16; Jan. 8, 1922, p. 8; March 26, 1922, p. 68; May 3, 1922, p. 20; April 17, 1927, p. 45; Oct. 21, 1928, p. 78.

The Cleveland Press, various undated press clippings from scrapbook in the Cleveland State University archives collection.

Historical and Genealogical Societies

Jewish Genealogy Society of Cleveland, Cleveland, Ohio

Nevada Historical Society, Reno, Nevada

Ohio Historical Society, Columbus, Ohio

Utah Historical Society, Salt Lake City, Utah

Libraries

Antique Automobile Club of America, Library & Research Center, Hershey, Pennsylvania

Automotive Hall of Fame Library & Archives, Dearborn, Michigan

Cleveland Public Library, Cleveland, Ohio

Durant Public Library, Durant, Iowa

Englewood Public Library, Englewood, New Jersey

Ida Rupp Library, Port Clinton, Ohio

Jackson District Library, Jackson, Michigan

Michael Schwartz Library & Archives, Cleveland State University, Cleveland, Ohio

National Automotive History Collection, Detroit Public Library, Detroit, Michigan

Sandusky Public Library, Sandusky, Ohio

Toledo Public Library, Toledo, Ohio

Western Reserve Library & Historical Society, Cleveland, Ohio

Other Sources

www.wikipedia.com

www.ancestry.com

http://goldensilents.com//florencevidor.html

http://wwwcoachbilt.com//des//e//earl.htm

Index

Numbers in ***bold italics*** indicate pages with photographs.